Long-term Research and Development in Science Education

Constructing Knowledge: Curriculum Studies in Action

VOLUME 21

The titles published in this series are listed at *brill.com/ckcs*

Long-term Research and Development in Science Education

What Have We Learned?

Edited by

Avi Hofstein, Abraham Arcavi, Bat-Sheva Eylon and Anat Yarden

BRILL

LEIDEN | BOSTON

Cover illustration: Icons representing the various research groups of the Department of Science Teaching, Weizmann Institute of Science, by Edna Rolnick, partly based on images from Shutterstock

All chapters in this book have undergone peer review.

The Library of Congress Cataloging-in-Publication Data is available online at https://catalog.loc.gov

Typeface for the Latin, Greek, and Cyrillic scripts: "Brill". See and download: brill.com/brill-typeface.

ISSN 2213-722X
ISBN 978-90-04-50360-1 (paperback)
ISBN 978-90-04-50361-8 (hardback)
ISBN 978-90-04-50362-5 (e-book)

This book is printed on acid-free paper and produced in a sustainable manner.

Contents

Preface

Mathematics and science education is a multi-faceted endeavor encompassing the creation of learning materials, preparation of teachers, and performing research on teaching and learning. At the Department of Science Teaching at the Weizmann Institute of Science, in Israel, the whole spectrum of these activities can be found under one roof. The Department was founded by the executive council of the Institute more than fifty years ago, as an acknowledgment of the great importance attributed by the Weizmann Institute to science education and in recognition that it is an academic discipline which will "enable young scientists interested in this activity to graduate doing their doctorate in science education" (de Shalit, 1968, p. 81).

Since its inception, the Department was involved in the development of innovative and up-to-date learning materials and pedagogical models and their implementation, teacher professional development and research on science teaching and learning as continuous, long-term activities that feed and guide each other through interactive spiral cycles. These activities are conceived, guided and tested with the highest academic standards, using and refining existing theoretical frames and methodologies or producing new ones when needed, with the ultimate goals of:

1 Advancing mathematics and science education as an academic discipline.
2 Enhancing the quality and effectiveness of mathematics and science education in schools.

The Department carries out research and development work in the teaching and learning of seven disciplines: Mathematics, Physics, Chemistry, Life Sciences, Earth and Environmental Sciences, Computer Science, Science and Technology in junior-high school. In addition, there are programs that focus on interdisciplinary work and Departmental programs that involve collaboration of faculty from several domains, such as the Rothschild-Weizmann graduate program for practicing science and mathematics teachers. Most of the work is geared towards science and mathematics education in grades 7–12. Recently, work in mathematics, and in science and technology education has been extended to grades K-6, as well as to introductory science and mathematics at the tertiary level.

This book offers reflections on the evolution of the Department, a description of a sample of the present projects, as well as a glimpse into the future. It is composed of two parts: Learning Science and Mathematics (9 chapters) and Professional Development of Science and Mathematics Teachers (7 chapters). The authors are faculty and staff members as well as current graduate students of the Department. Two renowned international scholars, Alan Schoenfeld (University of California, Berkeley) and Ilka Parchmann (Kiel University) offer their comments on the different chapters in the third part.

The book as a whole, as well as its individual chapters, are intended for a wide audience of curriculum developers, teacher educators, researchers on teaching and learning of science and mathematics and policy makers at the university level interested in advancing models of academic departments working under a common philosophy.

Throughout the book, readers will probably sense the passion, sense of mission and dedication of the faculty members as they present just parts of their work.

Reference

de Shalit, A. (1968). https://stwww1.weizmann.ac.il/en/wp-content/uploads/sites/26/2016/10/de-Shalit_creation_of_SciTeachDept.pdf

Acknowledgments

The editors and authors of this book acknowledge the help of Avi Tal and Edna Rolnick from the department's graphics unit. Without their dedication and diligence, we could have not finished this book. Also, many thanks to Shani Okavi-Partush for her help in the various stages of the book's development and production.

Figures and Tables

Figures

Tables

Notes on Contributors

Abraham Arcavi
is a professor in the Department of Science Teaching at the Weizmann Institute of Science. He works on the learning mathematics, the design of learning materials and teachers' professional development. He currently leads the VIDEO-LM Project for watching and discussing authentic videotaped lessons with an ad hoc framework and leads teacher communities who plan lessons together, try them out and then redesign them. He has served as the Secretary General of the International Commission on Mathematical Instruction and on several national and international committees. He has authored books and more than 80 papers and chapters in books. In 2019 he received the Award for Interdisciplinary Excellence in Mathematics Education from the Texas A&M University.

Michal Armoni
is an associate professor in the Department of Science Teaching at the Weizmann Institute of Science. She received her PhD degree from Tel Aviv University's School of Education, and her BA and MSc degrees in computer science from the Technion – Israel Institute of Technology. She has been engaged in computer science education for more than 25 years as an educator, a curriculum developer, and a researcher. She has co-authored several computer science textbooks for high school and middle school. Her research focuses on the processes of teaching and learning computer science, through the prism of fundamental computer science ideas.

Ron Blonder
is an associate professor in the Department of Science Teaching at the Weizmann Institute of Science. She is the head of the Chemistry Group and the head of the Rothschild–Weizmann Master's Program for Excellence in Mathematics and Science Teaching. Her research focuses on chemistry teachers' professional development in the context of contemporary science, using innovative technological tools and environments. She has published over 80 peer-reviewed and invited papers and book chapters in which she explores chemistry teachers' self-efficacy beliefs and knowledge development when they learn contemporary research in chemistry (mainly nanochemistry) and when they incorporate technological tools in their chemistry teaching. She has also investigated differentiated instruction in heterogeneous chemistry classes with and without the aid of technology to promote personalization in chemis-

try teaching. Dr. Blonder has applied the results of her educational research to chemistry teachers' professional development.

Miriam Carmeli
has been a member of the Department of Science Teaching at the Weizmann Institute of Science since 1986. She coordinated the Rothschild–Weizmann Program for Excellence in Mathematics and Science Teaching in 2008–2017 and participated in the team that designed the structure and contents of the program. Her main areas of activity include research, evaluation and implementation of innovative curricular projects in science education, and professional development frameworks for science teachers and leading teachers. She has been in charge of preparing reports on a wide range of departmental projects for a variety of stakeholders (e.g., the Jewish Agency, the Ministry of Education). Miriam is a graduate of the Hebrew University of Jerusalem in the fields of statistics and sociology.

Jason Cooper
is an associate staff scientist in the Department of Science Teaching at the Weizmann Institute of Science. His research concerns various aspects of teacher knowledge and professional development, with a particular focus on the relevance of advanced mathematics for teaching in primary and secondary schools. Much of his work seeks to understand the learning that takes place through interactions among different communities of mathematics education – teachers, mathematicians and education researchers, expansive learning that yields insights that are not available to any of these communities on their own.

Rachel Rosanne Eidelman
designed and developed COBLE (Chemistry Online Blended Learning Environment), a 3-year chemistry course for high-school students in collaboration with Dr. Yael Shwartz, and conducts research on the different aspects of online learning. She is currently serving as a senior pedagogical advisor and teacher for the COBLE project. Dr. Eidelman is an experienced high-school chemistry teacher, teaches in academia, develops online materials and courses, and owns a company that markets online pedagogical and technological knowledge.

Ruhama Even
is a professor (emerita) in the Department of Science Teaching at the Weizmann Institute of Science. Her long-term research and development work is structured around three main interrelated foci: the professional education and development of mathematics teachers, mathematics curriculum develop-

ment and analysis, and the interplay of factors involved in shaping students' opportunities to learn mathematics. She is the principal investigator of the Integrated Mathematics (Matematica Meshulevet) curriculum program, the MesiMatica formative assessment project, and the Thinking Far with Mathematics (Lahshov Rahok im Mathematica) mathematical literacy project. Ruhama serves as an editorial board member of JMTE, MERJ, and the Encyclopedia of Mathematics Education, for which she is also a section editor.

Bat-Sheva Eylon
is a professor (emerita) in the Department of Science Teaching at the Weizmann Institute of Science. She acted as head of the department in 2008–2015 and as pedagogical head of the Rothschild–Weizmann Master's Program for Excellence in Science Teaching. She is a Fellow of the AAAS and recipient of the Israeli EMET Prize in Education for 2015. She studies physics learning and teaching (grades 7–12), and professional development of teachers and teacher educators. She has headed research-based curriculum and teacher professional-development programs in science and technology. She has a BSc degree in physics and mathematics, an MSc degree in physics, and a PhD degree in science and mathematics education from the University of California at Berkeley.

Alex Friedlander
is a retired senior staff scientist, presently working as academic advisor in the Department of Science Teaching at the Weizmann Institute of Science. He is a curriculum designer, researcher, teacher and teacher educator. His interests lie in the domains of curriculum development, classroom practice, work with mathematically advanced students, learning and teaching of algebra, student assessment, mathematical literacy, and context-based learning. He also served as a member of the committee for the design of the national syllabus for teaching mathematics in elementary schools, the committee for the design of the national syllabus for teaching mathematics in teacher colleges, and the committee for the assessment of mathematical achievement at the elementary-school level.

Nurit Hadas
is a retired staff member, presently working as an academic advisor in the Department of Science Teaching at the Weizmann Institute of Science. She is a curriculum designer, teacher, teacher educator, and researcher. She led a curriculum project aimed at investigating the learning profile of math underachievers, and consequently designed the corresponding learning materials, aimed to ensure their success in the matriculation exams. She was also involved in the design of learning materials for students at the junior-high school level.

Her main research and design work is in the domain of teaching and learning geometry in general, and the use of dynamic geometry tools in particular.

Rina Hershkowitz

is a founding member of the Mathematics Group in the Department of Science Teaching at the Weizmann Institute of Science, and is presently an academic advisor in the department. Her activities focus on curriculum design, in-service teacher education and formative evaluation. She led some of the main curriculum projects of the Mathematics Group. She is also involved in math-education research. Her main interests lie in the domain of "the theoretical and practical views of learning and teaching geometry" and "knowledge shifts in the classroom." She was a member of the committee for the design of the national syllabus for teaching mathematics in high school, and served as president of the International Group for the Psychology of Mathematics Education.

Avi Hofstein

is a professor (emeritus) who has served for over 50 years as senior member of the Department of Science Teaching at the Weizmann Institute of Science, as head of the Chemistry Group and head of the department. Over the years, he has been involved in chemistry curriculum development, implementation (to include professional development of chemistry teachers) and research. His 150 publications cover, among others, effectiveness of the chemistry laboratory, science classroom learning environments, and the affective domain. In 2016, he received the ACS award for his achievements in understanding the field of learning in and from chemistry laboratories. In 2017, he was given the DCRA by the National Association for Research in Science Teaching (NARST).

Ronnie Karsenty

is a senior staff scientist in the Department of Science Teaching at the Weizmann Institute of Science. She specializes in professionalization processes of secondary mathematics teachers and professional development facilitators. She initiated, directed and researched several professional development projects, such as SHLAV and VIDEO-LM, and is currently co-head of the Math-VALUE project that conducts Lesson Study professional learning communities across Israel. Dr. Karsenty is the recipient of several awards, including the Maxine Singer Prize for Outstanding Scientists, awarded by the Scientific Council of the Weizmann Institute. She collaborates with international mathematics education experts from many countries in joint projects, working groups and research.

Boris Koichu
is an associate professor in the Department of Science Teaching at the Weizmann Institute of Science. His research is in the area of teaching and learning mathematics through problem solving and problem posing, from middle school to university. Part of his research is devoted to exploring the mechanisms of problem solving and problem posing in choice-affluent learning environments, such as dialogical mathematics classrooms or online problem-solving forums. Another part of his research focuses on exploring the potential of teacher–researcher partnerships for jointly investigating teaching and learning mathematics through problem solving.

Dorothy Langley
is on the academic staff of the Faculty of Instructional Technologies at the Holon Institute of Technology. Dr. Langley has been involved in physics education for many years, as a high-school physics teacher, and as a member of the Physics Group in the Department of Science Teaching at the Weizmann Institute of Science, where she also earned her MSc and PhD degrees for development and research of inquiry-oriented, computer-based learning materials. She was involved in the "Physics and Industry" program (2004–2015) and in the initial implementation of the Research Physics program and training of student research project mentors.

Ohad Levkovich
is the head of the National Center for High-school Biology Teachers in the Department of Science Teaching at the Weizmann Institute of Science, and serves as a high-school biotechnology teacher. Dr. Levkovich holds a BSc degree in biology (from Bar-Ilan University), an MSc degree in molecular genetics (from the Hebrew University of Jerusalem) and a PhD degree in science education (from the Weizmann Institute of Science). He has experience in high-school teaching, development of teaching and learning materials, and professional development of teachers. He studies learning using authentic scientific tools and bioinformatics.

Smadar Levy
explores the continuing professional development of physics teachers and teacher leaders. Since 2017, she has led the Israeli Network of Professional Learning Communities for Physics Teachers. Dr. Levy obtained an MSc degree in science education from Tel Aviv University (2000), and a PhD degree in science education from the Weizmann Institute of Science (2017). She was a high-school physics teacher for many years. She won the Orly Kaplan Award

for excellent doctoral thesis (2017), the Israeli Master Teacher Award (2014), and the Amos de-Shalit Prize for Excellence in the Teaching of Physics (2010).

Rachel Mamlok-Naaman
is from the Department of Science Teaching at the Weizmann Institute of Science, studied chemistry and chemistry education. Until September 2020, she was the head of the National Center for Chemistry Teachers, and until June 2016, served as the coordinator of the Chemistry Group in the Department of Science Teaching. She was the coordinator of chemistry teachers' programs in the framework of the Rothschild–Weizmann Master's Program for science teachers, and of projects in the framework of the European Union in Israel. In addition, Dr. Mamlok-Naaman is the chair of EuCheMS DivCED, an ACS titular member, and serves on editorial and advisory boards of science education journals and organizations. Her publications focus on topics related to student learning and to teachers' professional development.

Nir Orion
is a professor at the Weizmann Institute of Science and a pioneer in earth science education. His innovations range from kindergarten to high-school research projects. He and his research group have developed about 50 science programs, including hundreds of inquiry-based activities for the laboratory and outdoor learning environments. His curriculum materials promote the development of environmental insight through the earth systems approach, and his materials and methods are disseminated worldwide through workshops for science teachers in countries such as Argentina, Brazil, Chile, China, Ethiopia, Germany, India, Peru, Portugal, Spain, Uruguay and the United States. In 2012, he received the prestigious IUGS Science Excellence Award for his contribution for Earth science Education.

Ilka Parchmann
is a professor in Chemistry Education at Kiel University and Head of the Department of Chemistry Education at the Leibniz Institute for Science and Mathematics Education, IPN, in Kiel. She is currently the speaker of the IPN research line science communication and enrichment of learning.

Professor Parchmann has a teaching degree as a secondary-school teacher for chemistry and biology, and a PhD and further qualification in chemistry education. Her fields of research and development build on this expertise and combine design-based research approaches with investigations of interactions and effects in science outreach and learning environments. Exemplary programs creating interfaces between science and science education are *Chemie im Kontext* for school learning, the *Kieler Forschungswerkstatt* as a laboratory for students and (future) teachers, and the *Kiel Science Outreach Campus* as a framework and networking for co-design approaches.

Zahava Scherz
has been a senior research fellow of the Department of Science Teaching at the Weizmann Institute of Science. She has a BSc degree in chemistry, MSc degree in biophysics, and a doctorate in science education. Dr. Scherz has conducted research and development in the fields of artificial intelligence, learning skills in science, attitudes and perceptions about science, professional development of leading science teachers and professional learning communities. Her program LSS (Learning Skills for Science) has been adopted by thousands of schools in England and other countries. Dr. Scherz established and directed the Israel National Center for Science & Technology Teachers. She teaches graduate courses and has co-supervised 14 graduate students.

Alan Schoenfeld
is the Elizabeth and Edward Conner Professor of Education and Affiliated Professor of Mathematics at the University of California at Berkeley. A mathematician by training who studies issues of mathematical thinking, teaching, and learning, he has served as President of the American Educational Research Association and been awarded the Felix Klein Award for life-time achievement in mathematics education research by the International Commission on Mathematical Instruction. His research has focused on mathematical problem solving, models of the teaching process, and understanding aspects of learning environments, from the student perspective. His current research focus is the Teaching for Robust Understanding (TRU) Framework, which concerns the creation and support of learning environments from which students emerge being knowledgeable and flexible thinkers and problem solvers.

Yael Shwartz
is a senior staff scientist in the Department of Science Teaching at the Weizmann Institute of Science. She developed 'chemistry on line' – a 3-year chemistry course for high-school students, and has conducted research on different aspects of online learning, in collaboration with Dr. Rachel Rosanne Eidelman. Dr. Shwartz is the head of the National Center for Junior High School Science and Technology Teachers. As part of her role there, she is managing 20 professional learning communities of teachers. She is currently leading the development of the PeTeL (Personalized Teaching and Learning) online environment for middle-school science. Her research interests focus on science literacy for all, and professional development of teachers. She has been involved

in inquiry-based curriculum development, implementation and assessment, in both Israel and the United States.

Michal Tabach
is a professor in the School of Education at Tel Aviv University. Her main interests lie in the domain of integrating technology in mathematics education. As a young teacher, she taught mathematics with open digital tools on a regular basis, and became involved in research on student learning in a technological environment based on these tools. Consequently, she became involved in teacher education as a key factor in integrating technology into everyday school practices. She is currently leading two projects aimed at helping practicing teachers integrate technology into their practice, based on their pedagogical and mathematical needs.

Anat Yarden
is a professor, head of the Department of Science Teaching at the Weizmann Institute of Science, and head of the Biology Group in this department. She holds an undergraduate degree in Agricultural Sciences (from the Hebrew University of Jerusalem), an MSc and PhD degree in molecular biology (from the Weizmann Institute of Science), and carried out postdoctoral training in genetics (at Stanford University). The primary theme in all of her academic activities has been adapting practices employed by scientists to the processes by which students and teachers accumulate and advance their knowledge within the discipline of biology.

Edit Yerushalmi
is an associate professor and head of the Physics Education Research Group in the Department of Science Teaching at the Weizmann Institute of Science. The group is involved in research, curricular design and operation of nationwide professional development frameworks. Current projects include: the National Physics Teacher Center, "Gateway to Physics" – middle-school inquiry units; the National Network of Physics Professional Learning Communities; SEMEL – disciplinary internship workshops; "Interdisciplinary Computational Science" – advanced-level school subject; and the "Research Physics" training program for high-school teachers. She holds an MSc degree in physics from the Technion – Israel Institute of Technology, a PhD degree in science education from the Weizmann Institute of Science, and was a postdoctoral fellow in the Physics Department at the University of Minnesota.

PART 1

Learning Science and Mathematics

CHAPTER 1

The Laboratory in Chemistry Learning and Teaching

50 Years of Development, Implementation, and Research

Avi Hofstein and Rachel Mamlok-Naaman

Abstract

For over 60 years, learning and teaching in the chemistry laboratory have been extensively and comprehensively researched; hundreds of papers, reviews, and doctoral dissertations have been published worldwide with the goal of investigating the laboratory as a unique learning environment. This embracing of practical work, however, has been fraught with challenges and serious pedagogical questions about its educational effectiveness and benefits for teaching and learning chemistry. Since the early 1970s, the Chemistry Group in the Department of Science Teaching, Weizmann Institute of Science, has had ample opportunities to research different aspects of learning chemistry in the laboratory, in an attempt to answer the question: How are chemistry laboratories used? It is suggested that there is a call to rethink (and research) the goals for learning chemistry in the laboratory. This is especially true in an era when we are trying to promote the goal of teaching "chemistry for all students." For over 15 years, with our colleagues and students, we have researched the potential of an inquiry-type chemistry laboratory for the development of higher-order learning skills, namely, the skills required for future citizens.

Keywords

chemistry learning – learning in chemistry laboratory – chemistry experiments, laboratory learning environment – learning by inquiry – argumentation – metacognition – asking questions

1 General Introduction: Why Use Laboratories for Learning the Sciences?

This chapter presents a detailed description of studies related to research and development of the chemistry laboratory over the last half a century, in the

 | DOI: 10.1163/9789004503625_001

context of chemistry curriculum development and implementation professional development of chemistry teachers). Laboratory activities have been developed and researched. In this chapter, we shall describe research focusing on students and teachers' behavior in the chemistry laboratory during two time periods. Laboratory activities have long had a distinctive and central role in science curriculum as a means of making sense of the natural world. Since the nineteenth century, when schools began to teach science systematically, the laboratory has become a distinctive feature of science education (Edgeworth & Edgeworth, 1811 cited by Rosen, 1954). This is illustrated in a quote from Ira Remsen (1846–1927), the chemist who synthesized the sweetener saccharin in his laboratory and who was the 2nd president of Johns Hopkins University in the United States, recounting his memories as a child experiencing a chemical phenomenon:

> While reading a textbook of chemistry I came upon the statement, 'nitric acid acts upon copper'… and I [was] determined to see what this meant. [Having located some nitric acid] I had only to learn what the words 'acts upon' meant… In the interest of knowledge, I was even willing to sacrifice one of the few copper cents then in my possession. I put one of them on the table; opened the bottle marked 'nitric acid'; poured some of the liquid on the copper; and prepared to take an observation. But what was this wonderful thing I beheld? The cent was already changed, and it was no small change either. A greenish blue liquid foamed and fumed over the cent and over the table. The air… became colored dark red… How should I stop this? I tried to get rid of the objectionable mess by picking it up and throwing it out of the window… I learnt another fact – nitric acid… acts on fingers. The pain led to another unpremeditated experiment. I drew my fingers across my trousers and another fact was discovered. Nitric acid acts upon trousers… I tell it even now with interest. It was a revelation to me. Plainly, the only way to learn about it was to see its results, to experiment, to work in a laboratory.

After the First World War, and with the rapid increase in scientific knowledge, the laboratory was used mainly as a means for confirming and illustrating information previously learnt in a lecture or from textbooks. With the reform in science education in the1960s in many countries, the ideal became to engage students with investigations, discoveries, inquiry, and problem-solving activities. In other words, the laboratory became the core of the science learning process (Shulman & Tamir, 1973).

The National Science Education Standards (National Research Council, 1996, p. 23) define skills such as inquiry:

> the diverse ways in which scientists study the natural world and propose explanations based on the evidence derived from their work. Scientific inquiry also refers to the activities through which students develop knowledge and understanding of scientific ideas, as well as an understanding of how scientists study the natural world.

For many years, science educators have suggested the many benefits accrued from engaging students in science laboratory activities (Hofstein & Lunetta, 1982, 2004; Tobin, 1990). Tobin, for example, wrote that: "Laboratory activities appeal as a way of allowing students to learn with understanding and at the same time engage in the process of constructing knowledge by doing science" (Tobin, 1990, p. 403).

In curricular-type projects developed during the 1960s, the laboratory was intended to be a place for inquiring, developing, and testing theories, as well as for providing students with the opportunity to 'practice being a scientist.' Many research studies (summarized, for example, by Hofstein & Lunetta, 1982) were conducted with the goal of exploring the effectiveness of the laboratory in attaining the many objectives (both cognitive and affective) that had been suggested in the science education literature.

The traditional list of objectives includes:
- Understanding of scientific concepts
- Interest and motivation
- Attitude toward science
- Scientific practical skills and problem-solving abilities
- Scientific habits of mind
- Understanding the nature of science
- The opportunity to *do* science

Over the years, hundreds of papers and essays have been published exploring and investigating the uniqueness of the science laboratory in general and its educational effectiveness in particular. In addition, it is widely believed that the laboratory provides the only place in school where certain kinds of skills, abilities, and understanding might be developed. In other words, the laboratory provides a unique mode of instruction, learning, research, and assessment. Precisely what kind of objectives and aims will be attained in the laboratory depends on a wide range of factors. We suggest that, among others, these will include the teacher's goals, expectations, subject and pedagogical content knowledge, as well as the degree of relevance to the topic, the students' abilities and interests, and many other logistical and economic considerations related to the school setting and its facilities. The teacher should be in a position to judge whether the laboratory is the most effective learning environment for attaining a certain objective while teaching a certain topic. Teachers should be aware of the plethora of discussions and research studies on which goals are, in fact, better achieved through laboratory instruction than through other instructional (pedagogical) approaches (Hofstein & Lunetta, 1982, 2004). Criticism has centered on the tradition of conducting experiments with no clear purpose or goal. In addition, a significant mismatch was revealed between teachers' goals for learning in the science laboratory and those that were originally defined by curriculum developers and the science education milieu, the latter including both teachers and science education researchers.

1.1 *Some Historical Aspects of Practical Work in High-School Chemistry Laboratories*

During the major curriculum reforms in science education in the early 1960s and late 1970s, practical work in chemistry education was used to engage students in investigations, discoveries, inquiries, and problem-solving activities. In other words, the laboratory became (at least in the minds of science educators and curriculum developers) the center of science teaching and learning. For example, Professor George Pimental, editor and founder of the CHEM Study chemistry curriculum that was developed in the United States and later adopted and implemented in Israel by a group of scientists and chemistry teachers, claimed that the laboratory was designed to help students gain a better idea of the nature of science and scientific investigation by emphasizing the discovery approach. In addition, he suggested that it gives students an opportunity to observe chemical systems and to gather data that will be useful for the development of principles subsequently discussed in the textbook and in the chemistry classroom.

2 Assessment of and Research on the Chemistry Laboratory by the Chemistry Group in the Department of Science Teaching: The First Period

Since the 1960s, the Department of Science Teaching at the Weizmann Institute of Science has been involved in all facets of chemistry education, including the chemistry laboratory. During this span of over 50 years, two distinct periods of R&D related to the chemistry laboratory can be identified: the first from the late 1960s to the early 1990s, and the second from the early 1990s until today. The chemistry curricula that were developed and implemented provided an effective platform for researching the students' achievements and progress and the chemistry teachers' behavior in the laboratory classrooms. These studies focused on the following aspects:

- The chemistry laboratory: a unique mode of learning and instruction – assessment and research (Ben-Zvi et al., 1977); assessing students' performance and achievements using different modes of presentation in the chemistry laboratory (the filmed experiments) (Ben-Zvi et al., 1976; Hofstein, 1975).
- Students' attitudes toward and interest in school chemistry laboratory work (Hofstein, 2004).

2.1 *The Chemistry Laboratory: A Unique Mode of Learning and Instruction – Assessment and Research*

In their comprehensive review, Lazarowitz and Tamir (1994) suggested that the science laboratory offers a unique mode of teaching and learning, and that the abilities of students in the laboratory are only slightly correlated with their abilities in other non-practical learning experiences. A study on modes of learning and teaching in the context of chemistry was conducted by Ben-Zvi et al. (1977), with the main goal of identifying relationships between modes of learning in the chemistry laboratory and other modes of learning that prevail in high school chemistry. The study was undertaken in the context of a laboratory-centered program: *Chemistry for High School*, developed at the Weizmann Institute of Science in 1972. This program was developed and implemented in the Israeli educational system to replace the adopted version of the American CHEM Study program. To this end, a battery of tests was developed to cover at least the first three of the four phases of performance in the chemistry laboratory (Giddings et al., 1991): *planning and design* (formulating questions, predicting results, and formulating hypotheses to be tested by designing experimental procedures); *performance* in conducting an experiment (manipulating materials and equipment, making decisions about investigative techniques, observing and reporting findings); *analysis and interpretation* (processing data, explaining relationships, developing generalizations, examining the accuracy of data, outlining limitations, formulating new questions based on the conducted investigation); and *application* (making predictions about new situations, formulating hypotheses on the basis of investigative results, applying laboratory techniques to new experimental situations). These phases refer to both psychomotor skills (manipulation and observation) and cognitive abilities (investigating and processing a problem and its solution by practical means). The battery of tests included two practical tests using a scheme and criteria originally developed by Eglen and Kempa (1978), an observational test (Kempa & Ward, 1975), two paper and pencil achievement tests, and an attitude and interest questionnaire. Based on this research, it was found that practical abilities represent a different mode of learning than those cognitive abilities developed in a conceptual approach in which key chemistry concepts are taught (e.g., oxidation–reduction, acids–bases, equilibrium, and structure of matter).

2.2 *The Implementation of Filmed Experiments in the Chemistry Laboratory*

In a school's adaptation of the laboratory-based approach to chemical learning, there are instances when its implementation at the high-school level presents difficulties. For example, schools may lack equipment and materials due to economic constraints. In addition, there are occasional administrative problems related to lack of laboratory space. Recognizing these problems, the Chemistry Group at the Weizmann Institute (Ben-Zvi et al., 1976; Hofstein, 1975) conducted a research-based study to investigate the educational effectiveness of filmed experiments as an alternative to normal student-centered laboratory work. That study was conducted in the context of a new chemistry curriculum that was being developed and implemented. The curriculum was titled *Chemistry for high school* and it was aimed at grade 10–12 students. One of the main goals was to involve students in experimentation that included the abilities mentioned above. Filmed experiments (Ben-Zvi et al., 1976; Hofstein, 1975) were developed with the goal of enabling schools that suffer from lack of chemistry laboratory facilities to provide their students with filmed experiments. The use of the filmed experiments was accompanied by a pre–post experimental design (Figure 1.1).

In the research described above, the comparative effectiveness of filmed experiments and personalized chemical laboratory experiences was examined in relation to the following variables:

- Cognitive achievement (and understanding of chemistry concepts) measured by written paper and pencil tests
- Manipulative skills related to handling equipment and the use of apparatuses
- Observational attainment and problem-solving abilities in relation to laboratory situations.

In general, the performance of the two groups was remarkably similar on most variables. No significant differences were found for the cognitive variables

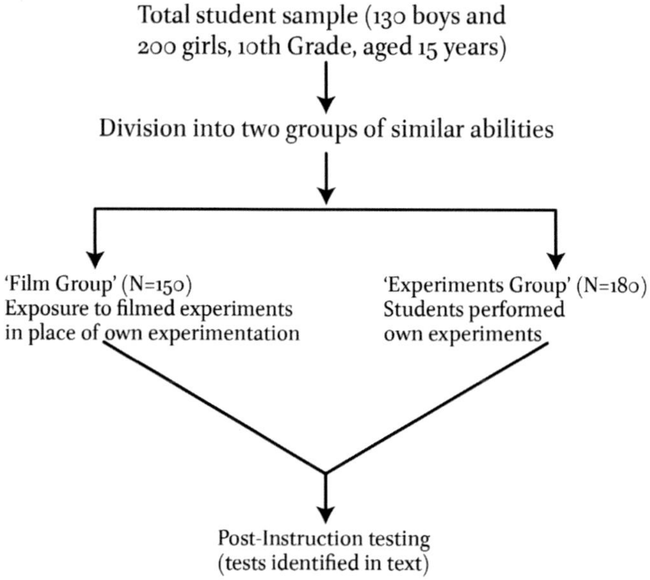

FIGURE 1.1 Research design of the comparative study (Ben-Zvi et al., 1976; Hofstein, 1975)

used. However, differences were found with respect to the practical abilities, where the experimental group outperformed the film group (differences were of a magnitude of 10%). Overall, it was found that vicarious methods could be used as an alternative for students' personal experimentation.

2.3 *Attitude toward and Interest in Chemistry Laboratories*

A review by Hofstein and Lunetta (1982) cites several studies indicating that students enjoy laboratory work in some courses, and that laboratory experiences result in positive and improved student attitudes and interest in science. Among the reviewed studies, Hofstein and Lunetta (1982) reported that students in Israel rated their personal involvement in the chemistry laboratory as the most effective instructional method for promoting their interest in chemistry when contrasted with teacher demonstrations, presentations, and classroom discussions. Other studies conducted in the 1970s and 1980s made similar claims. Ben-Zvi et al. (1976), for example, reported that chemistry students' personal involvement in chemistry laboratory investigations had been the most effective medium in their chemistry classes for promoting their interest in chemistry when contrasted with teachers' demonstrations, filmed experiments, classroom discussions, and teachers' lectures. In a study examining why students enrolled in optional advanced high-school chemistry courses, one of the key reasons offered was their experience with practical activities in the chemistry laboratory (Milner et al., 1987). Achievement in chemistry is therefore a combination of all of these various modes, and this needs to be taken into consideration when assessing students' abilities in chemistry. Although this study was conducted in the mid-1970s, it is still in alignment with more recent reforms in science, claiming that if we truly value the development of knowledge, skills, and attitudes that are unique to practical work in science laboratories, appropriate assessment of these outcomes must be developed and implemented continuously by teachers in their own laboratory classrooms.

2.3.1 Assessment of Students' Achievement and Progress in the Chemistry Laboratory

The first set of National Science Education Standards (National Research Council, 1996, for example, indicated that all of the students' learning experiences should be assessed, and that the assessment should be authentic. Attention to such *standards* however, promoted testing that did not generally incorporate the assessment of performance or inquiry, although there were a few noteworthy efforts to do so. Researchers, teachers, and testing jurisdictions, whose goal is to comprehensively assess the learning that takes place in school science in general, or in school laboratories in particular, should use appropriate assessment tools and methodologies to identify what the students are learning (conceptual as well as procedural). In the previous section, we presented the four phases that comprise practical work in the chemistry laboratory. Kempa (1986) suggested that these phases of experimental work provide a valid framework for the development and assessment of practical skills. To assess these phases, valid, reliable, and usable measures are required (see, for example, a review of the literature by Giddings et al., 1991). There are several distinct categories of assessment available to assess some or all of these phases: written evidence (either traditional laboratory reports or paper and pencil tests); one or more practical examinations; continuous assessment by the science teacher or researcher; and combined methods in which at least two of the assessment methods are employed.

3 Development of Inquiry-Type Chemistry Laboratories: New Goals and New Practice in the Chemistry Laboratory – The Second Period (1990 to Date)[1]

Toward the end of the 1990s, it was found (based on research in Israel and elsewhere; Hofstein & Kind, 2012) that practice in the laboratory had not changed as easily to the open-ended style of teaching as the curriculum projects suggested. Teachers rather preferred a safer 'cookbook' approach. Moreover, Johnstone and Wham (1982) in Scotland, in the context of chemistry teaching and learning, claimed that science educators were underestimating the high cognitive demand of practical work on the learner. In practical work, the student needs to handle a vast amount of information regarding names of equipment and materials, process instructions, data, and observations, overloading the student's working memory. This made laboratory learning complicated, rather than a simple and safe way toward learning. Based on the important publication related to science laboratories titled "*America's lab report*" published by the National Research Council (1996), it was suggested that:

> The science learning goals of laboratory experiences include enhancing mastery of science subject matter, developing scientific reasoning abilities, increasing understanding of the complexity and ambiguity of empirical work, developing practical skills, increasing understanding of the nature of science, cultivating interest in science and science learning, and improving teamwork abilities. The research suggests that laboratory experiences will be more likely to achieve these goals if they (1) are designed with clear learning outcomes in mind, (2) are thoughtfully sequenced into the flow of classroom science instruction, (3) integrate learning of science content and process, and (4) incorporate ongoing student reflection and discussion. (p. 13)

While the main goals and objectives of learning in the laboratory had focused in the past (first phase in this chapter) on practical abilities, this second period was now characterized by new goals and skills that every citizen should possess, namely higher-order learning and thinking skills. The concurrent era of curriculum in chemistry changed dramatically from focusing on the disciplinary approach to addressing a multidimensional approach, which was highly aligned with science education standards in the United States (National Research Council, 1996), United Kingdom (Campbell et al., 1994), and Israel (Hofstein & Mamlok, 2001). The new chemistry curricula were characterized by the slogan "learning by inquiry." It was suggested that the inquiry orientation could serve as a platform for the development of higher-order learning skills such as: planning and designing an investigation, conducting and recording observations, manipulating equipment, collecting data, analyzing and interpreting the collected data, hypothesizing, and finally, asking relevant questions. The key point to be made regarding the development of higher-order learning skills is that practical work is not a static issue but something that has evolved gradually over the years, and which is still developing. The development relates to: changing aims and goals for science (in the present case chemistry) education, developments in understanding science learning, changing views and understanding of science inquiry, and more recent developments in educational technologies. In reviewing the research literature in the last 50 years, it is clear that higher-order learning skills in the chemistry laboratory only emerged in the last 20 years or so. This, it is suggested, is based on the fact that our knowledge regarding students' learning in laboratories significantly changed the goals for learning chemistry in laboratories. The "new" goals are very often influenced by the movement from learning science (chemistry) for those who are planning to embark on a career in the sciences (chemists, engineers, and medical doctors) to teaching science (chemistry) "for all" students; in other words, a chemistry program for those students who will have to operate as literate citizens in their society. One of the key goals of contemporary science education is to provide students with the opportunity to develop scientific literacy in general, and chemical literacy in particular. Examples of chemical literacy components include understanding the particulate nature of matter, knowledge of chemical reactions between substances to create new ones, the ability to use laws and theories to explain various phenomena, the capacity to understand the application of chemistry knowledge to students' personal lives and to the society in which they live, and finally, the ability to implement higher-order learning (or thinking) skills in everyday manner. Thus, we are operating in an era in which chemistry is taught not only to those who will specialize in the sciences but also to those who are fondly called future citizens. They will be required to ask critical and relevant questions and seek answers, which will serve to make valid decisions. Thus, the development of students' abilities to ask questions, apply critical thinking awareness and control over the scientific procedures in which they are involved, and argue in an intellectual manner are seen, today, as important components of chemical literacy. In everyday life, science is often involved in public debate and used as evidence to support political views. Science frequently presents findings and information, which challenge existing norms and ethical standards in society. Citizens need to understand principles in scientific inquiry and how science operates at a social level. The natural question, of course, is to what degree and in what ways can the science laboratory help provide students with such understanding? Baird and White (1996) wrote that four conditions are necessary to induce the personal development entailed in directing purposeful inquiry: time, opportunity, guidance, and support. The science teacher should provide the students with experiences, opportunities, and the time to discuss their ideas about the problems that they have to solve during the learning activity. The teacher's role is to provide continuous guidance and support to ensure that the students develop control and awareness of their learning. This, it is suggested, can be accomplished by providing the students with more freedom to select the subject of their project, and manage their time and their actions in the problem-solving process. Moreover, Bybee (2000) reaffirmed the conviction that inquiry is central to the achievement of scientific literacy. He used the term inquiry in two ways: (a) inquiry as *content understanding* (in which students have opportunities to construct concepts, patterns and meaning about an idea to explain what they experience) and (b) inquiry as *abilities* (Bybee, 2000). Under the heading of abilities or skills, Bybee includes identifying questions, designing and conducting scientific investigations, formulating and revising scientific explanations, recognizing and analyzing alternative explanations, and communicating and defending scientific arguments. It is suggested that many of these abilities are aligned with those that characterize inquiry-type laboratories.

3.1 *The Chemistry Inquiry Laboratory Developed and Researched at the Weizmann Institute of Science*

The second period of R&D in the chemistry laboratory started at the Weizmann Institute (by the Chemistry Group) in the early 1990s in the context of reforming the way in which chemistry is taught and learned in Israel (Barnea et al., 2010) As part of this reform, changes were also made in the way chemistry is taught in the laboratory. A project related to learning chemistry by inquiry titled: *Learning in the chemistry laboratory by the inquiry approach* (Hofstein et al., 2004) was developed at the Weizmann's Department of Science Teaching. For this program, about 100 inquiry-type experiments were developed and implemented in 11th- and 12th-grade chemistry classes in Israel (for the nature and dynamics of these experiments, see Table 1.1.

A two-phase teaching process was used, including a guided pre-inquiry phase followed by a more open-ended inquiry phase. The inquiry chemistry laboratories were researched intensively and comprehensively in several studies conducted by the authors of this paper over a period of almost 20 years (Hofstein et al., 2019).

3.2 *The Classroom Laboratory Learning Environment*

To assess the students' perception of the classroom laboratory learning environment, a research study was conducted using the Science Laboratory Environment Inventory (SLEI) originally developed by Fraser et al. (1993) in Australia (see Table 1.2).

In the study conducted in Israel (Hofstein, 2006), a preferred and actual version of the SLEI (Science Laboratory Environment Inventory) were implemented to compare the students' perceptions of two types of chemistry laboratory: inquiry and confirmatory (Katchevitch et al., 2013).

TABLE 1.1 Inquiry-type chemistry laboratories (Hofstein et al., 2004)

Phase	Abilities and skills to be developed
Phase 1: Pre-inquiry	
– Describe in detail the apparatus in front of you.	
– Add drops of water to the small test tube, until the powder is wet. Seal the test tube immediately.	– Conducting an experiment
– Observe the test tube carefully, and record all of your observations in your notebook.	– Observing and recording observations
Phase 2: The inquiry phase of the experiment	
1. *Hypothesizing*	
– Ask relevant questions. Choose one question for further investigation.	– Asking questions and hypothesizing
– Formulate a hypothesis that is aligned with your chosen question.	
2. *Planning an experiment*	
– Plan an experiment to investigate the question.	– Planning an experiment
– Ask the teacher to provide you with the equipment and material needed to conduct the experiment.	
– Conduct the experiment that you proposed.	– Conducting the planned experiment
– Observe and clearly note your observations.	
– Discuss with your group whether your hypothesis was accepted, or you need to reject it.	– Analyzing results, asking further questions, and presenting the results

Regarding the students' perceptions of the laboratory learning environment, the gap between their actual and preferred learning environments for various scales was significantly smaller in the inquiry-experiment group than in the control group in in which confirmatory experiments were used. In addition, regarding the actual learning environment, the most predominant and statistically significant differences were observed for the Open-Endedness scale, with the inquiry group having a more favorable perception compared to the control group. These findings indicated a significant improvement in

TABLE 1.2 Scales and description of SLEI (from Fraser et al., 1993, reprinted with permission)

Scale name	Description
Student cohesiveness	Extent to which students know, help, and are supportive of one another
Open-endedness	Extent to which the laboratory activities emphasize an open-ended, divergent approach to experimentation
Integration	Extent to which laboratory activities are integrated with non-laboratory and theory classes
Rule clarity	Extent to which behavior in the laboratory is guided by formal rules
Material environment	Extent to which the laboratory equipment and materials are adequate

students' perceptions of the laboratory learning environment as a result of their laboratory experiences. It was noted that, regarding the preferred learning environment, there were only small differences between the two groups. This means that the expectations were similar, regardless of the type of laboratory to which the high-school chemistry students were exposed. We also found that the students in the inquiry group perceived that they were more involved in the learning process and found the procedures more open-ended compared to the control group in which confirmatory-type experiments were used. These findings are in alignment with recent trends to enhance the involvement of students in the learning process and in constructing their knowledge of scientific concepts and processes. A comparison of differences between actual and preferred laboratory learning environments revealed that integration of the laboratory experiences with other pedagogical interventions and classroom instructional techniques was associated with a significant reduction in the magnitude of those differences. In other words, the inquiry group found the actual learning environment to be significantly more aligned with their preferred environment than did the confirmatory group.

3.3 *Developing Higher-Order Learning Skills in the Chemistry Laboratory*

The inquiry laboratory provided an effective platform for researching students' behavior and development of higher-order skills. In this section, we discuss the development of three such skills – metacognitive skills, argumentation skills, and the ability to ask higher-order questions – resulting from inquiry-type chemistry laboratories.

3.3.1 Development of Metacognitive Skills

In addition to the cognitive and affective variables mentioned above, it is suggested that a properly designed inquiry laboratory can provide the students with opportunities to develop metacognitive learning skills. *Metacognition* refers to higher-order thinking skills that involve active control over (and awareness of) thinking processes in the context of learning. Activities such as planning how to approach a given learning task, monitoring comprehension, and evaluating progress toward the completion of a task are *metacognitive* in nature. White and Mitchell (1994) specified "good learning behaviors" for students who developed certain metacognitive skills. A large part of those behaviors (and skills) are actions that constitute an integral part of the inquiry laboratory activity, such as: asking questions, checking work against instructions, correcting errors and omissions, justifying opinions, seeking reasons for aspects of concurrent work, suggesting new activities and alternative procedures, and planning a general strategy before starting to work. Students participating in the inquiry laboratory activities are required to evaluate the experiment they have designed and monitor their thinking processes, thereby developing their metacognitive skills. Baird and White (1996), as well as Kuhn et al. (2000), argued that students who experience inquiry activity attain a desirable level of metacognition (see also Kipnis & Hofstein, 2008).

There is no single definition for metacognition, and its diverse meanings are represented in the literature that deals with thinking skills. Schraw (1998), for example, presents a model in which metacognition includes two main components: "knowledge of cognition" and "regulation of cognition." *Knowledge of cognition* refers to what individuals know about their own cognition or about cognition in general. It includes at least three different kinds of metacognitive knowledge: *declarative knowledge,* which includes knowledge about oneself as a learner and about factors that influence one's performance (knowing 'about' things); *procedural knowledge,* which refers to knowledge about doing things in terms of having heuristics and strategies (knowing 'how' to do things); *conditional knowledge,* which refers to knowing when and why to use declarative and procedural knowledge (knowing the 'why' and 'when' aspects of cognition). *Regulation of cognition* refers to a set of activities that help students control their learning. Although a number of regulatory skills have been described in the literature, three essential skills are included in all accounts: *planning,* which involves the selection of appropriate strategies and the allocation of resources that affect performance; *monitoring,* which refers to one's on going awareness of comprehension and task performance; and *evaluating,* which refers to appraising the products and efficiency of one's learning. When applied to science learning, metacognition is generally related to *meaningful learning* or learning with understanding, which includes being able to apply what has been learned in new contexts. Metacognition is also related to developing *independent learners* who are typically aware of their knowledge and of the options to expand it.

A two-phase teaching process was used, including a guided pre-inquiry phase followed by a more open-ended inquiry phase (see Table 1.1). Based on their research, Kipnis and Hofstein (2008) linked metacognitive skills (based on Schraw's, 1998 model) to various stages of the inquiry-oriented experiments: (a) while asking questions and choosing an inquiry question, the students reveal their thoughts about the questions that were suggested by their partners and about their own questions. At this stage, *metacognitive declarative knowledge* is being expressed; (b) while choosing the inquiry question, the students express their *metacognitive procedural knowledge* by choosing a question that leads to conclusions; (c) while performing their own experiment and planning changes and improvements, the students are demonstrating the *planning* component of *regulation of cognition*; (d) in the final stage of the inquiry activity, when the students write their report and must draw conclusions, they utilize *metacognitive conditional knowledge*; (e) during the whole activity, the students make use of the *monitoring* and *evaluating* components of *regulation of cognition*. In this way, they examine the results of their observations to decide whether they are logical. Knowledge-centered learning environments encourage students to reflect on their own learning progress (metacognition). Learning is facilitated when individuals identify, monitor, and regulate their own thinking and learning. To be effective problem-solvers and learners, students need to determine what they already know and what else they need to know in any given situation, including when things are not going as expected (Kipnis & Hofstein, 2008).

3.4 *Argumentation in the Chemistry Inquiry-Based Laboratory*

The second skill that was intensively researched in the inquiry laboratory was students' ability to argue about inquiry phenomena. Driver et al. (2000), in the United Kingdom, characterized argumentation as correcting the misinterpretation of the scientific method which has dominated much of science teaching in general and practical work in particular. Rather than focusing on the stepwise series of actions carried out by scientists in experiments, they claimed, focus should be directed toward the *epistemic practice* involved when developing and evaluating scientific knowledge. We sense two overlapping learning aims. First, that students should understand the scientific standards and their guiding epistemologies, and next, that they should be able to apply those standards in their own argumentation.

A way forward to understanding how practical work contributes to the development of students' epistemological understanding and argumentation skills might be to look more closely at the "teaching ecology" of the laboratory (Hofstein & Kind, 2012). It is strongly argued that bringing argumentation into science classrooms requires the enactment of contexts that transform them into knowledge-producing communities, encouraging dialogic discourse and various forms of cognitive, social, and cultural interactions among learners. The ecology that fosters this practice is created through the social and physical environment – the laboratory tasks, and the organization principles used by the teacher. A reconsideration of all of these factors is therefore needed for the science laboratory to contribute meaningfully and effectively to the new learning goal (Hofstein & Kind, 2012).

Beyond learning scientific concepts and acquiring higher-order learning skills, building an argument has significant social importance for students. While students are engaged in activities that provide them with the opportunity to develop argumentation skills, they are learning how to conduct a meaningful conversation with their peers. Needless to say, such skills are useful for overcoming life's challenges and are not used solely in the context of science learning.

A study on argumentation in the chemistry laboratory was conducted in Israel by Katchevitch et al. (2013) in the context of 12 years of R&D of inquiry-type chemistry laboratories in upper secondary school, grades 10–12 (for more details on the philosophy and rationale of the project, see Hofstein et al., 2004). The study focused on students' process of constructing arguments in the chemistry laboratory, while conducting different types of experiments. It was found that *inquiry-type* experiments could serve as an effective platform for formulating arguments, owing to the special features of this learning environment. The discourse was analyzed according to the following criteria – the components of the basic argument: claims, evidence, and scientific explanations. The analysis to identify the components of the argument was performed using Toulmin's model (Katchevitch et al., 2013). The discourse conducted during the *inquiry-type* experiments was found to be rich in arguments, whereas that during *confirmatory-type* experiments was found to be sparse in arguments.

In addition, it was found that the arguments developed during the discourse of an inquiry-type experiment were generated during the following stages of the inquiry process: hypothesis-building, analysis of the results, and drawing appropriate conclusions. On the other hand, the confirmatory-type experiment generated a small number of arguments. In addition, the characteristics

TABLE 1.3 Levels (ranked 1–4 with 4 being highest) of arguments in the inquiry chemistry laboratory (based on Erduran et al., 2004)

Components of the argument	Symbol	Level of the argument
Claim	C	1
Claim + Data, or Claim + scientific basis (Warrant)	CD/CW	2
Claim + Data + Warrant, or Claim + Data + Rebuttal, or Claim + Warrant + Rebuttal	CDW/CDR/ CWR	3
Claim + Data + Warrant + Backing	CDWB	4
Rebuttal that includes Claim + Data + Warrant	CDWR	5

of the arguments that were posed in the confirmatory-type experiments were at a low level (for the various levels of the arguments, see Table 1.3).

Based on the detailed analysis of the discourse that was conducted in the chemistry laboratory, the researchers in the Chemistry Group (Katchevitch et al., 2013) concluded that the open-ended inquiry experiments stimulate and encourage the construction of arguments, especially the stages of hypothesis definition, results analysis, and conclusion drawing. Some arguments were raised by individuals, and some by the group. Both types of arguments consisted of explanations and scientific evidence that linked the claims to the evidence. Therefore, it was suggested that the mentioned learning environments of open-ended inquiry experiments are an effective platform for raising chemistry-based arguments. Katchevitch et al. (2013) investigated the issue of complexity of the chemistry inquiry experiments and the posing of arguments. The criteria for complexity were obtained using content validation conducted by a few members of the Chemistry Group. The complexity of the inquiry experiments is presented in Table 1.4.

TABLE 1.4 Criteria for sorting complex/simple experiments (Katchevitch et al., 2013)

Type of experiment	Alignment with the concept or topic	Including concepts beyond the curriculum
Complex open-ended inquiry	No	Yes
Simple open-ended inquiry	Yes	No

Analysis of the discourse clearly showed that the more complex the experiment, the more arguments are posed by the groups of students. In addition, the more complex the experiments, the higher the level of the arguments produced.

3.4.1 Asking Questions in the Chemistry Laboratory

The third skill that we discuss in this chapter is the asking of relevant and higher-order questions. In an attempt to develop scientific literacy among students, teachers must create effective learning environments in which students are given opportunities to ask relevant and scientifically sound questions. The questions asked during a lesson are usually those initiated by the teacher and only rarely by the students, and the latter questions do not emerge spontaneously from the students; rather, they have to be encouraged. In addition, it was found by Hofstein et al. (2003) that when students do ask questions during the lessons, they are usually informative ones. The content of a question can indicate the level of thinking of the person who raises it. It should be noted that in general, the cognitive level of a certain question is determined by the type of answer that it requires. Several studies have noted the importance (and value) of questioning skills. Asking critical-type questions regarding a specific phenomenon to which the students are exposed through a certain experiment or an article can avoid the phenomenon of students asking factual-type questions). Zoller (1987) found that in science education, providing students with the opportunity to ask questions has the potential to enhance their creativity, as well as their higher-order thinking skills. More recently, Cuccio-Schirripa and Steiner (2000) suggested that "Questioning is one of the thinking processing skills which is structurally embedded in the thinking operation of critical thinking, creative thinking, and problem solving" (p. 210).

Hofstein et al. (2004) conducted a research study on the ability of high school (11th and 12th grade) chemistry students who are learning chemistry through the inquiry approach (see Table 1.1 in this chapter and in Hofstein et al., 2004) to ask meaningful and scientifically sound questions. Two aspects were investigated: (a) the students' ability to ask questions related to their observations and findings in an inquiry-type experiment (a practical test), and (b) the students' ability to ask questions after critically reading a scientific article. The student population consisted of two groups: an inquiry-laboratory group (experimental) and a traditional-laboratory group (control). Three common features were researched: (a) the number of questions that were asked by each of the students, (b) the cognitive level of the questions, and (c) the nature of the questions that were chosen by the students for further investigation. Importantly, it was found that students in the inquiry group who had experience in asking questions in the chemistry laboratory outperformed the control group in their ability to ask more and better questions. The activity of asking inquiry questions (which are, by definition, high-level questions) is one of the operations that the students are required to perform during every full inquiry experiment. In contrast, the students of the control group, who had learned the traditional-type program – which does not contain inquiry experiments – did not have any opportunity to practice the activity of asking questions and specifically, higher-level inquiry-type questions; therefore, their skills in asking questions, as indicated by the test, were lower than those of chemistry students who had been given the opportunity to ask questions in an inquiry-oriented chemistry laboratory.

4 Summary and Implications

This chapter presents several research studies that were conducted over a period of almost 50 years in the high-school chemistry laboratory. In this set of studies, a genuine attempt was made to provide chemistry students with opportunities to learn and assume responsibility for their own learning as a result of conducting experiments in the chemistry laboratory, and at a later stage, inquiry-type chemistry experiments. Over the years, the chemistry laboratory has fueled six PhD and MSc dissertations. Two periods were described in which the chemistry laboratory was one of the key pedagogies. We present clear evidence of students improving their ability to develop metacognitive skills, improving their argumentation abilities, and asking better (i.e., higher-level) and more relevant (i.e., related to the chemistry concept learned) questions. This occurred because the students were given the opportunity to be involved in these (and similar) skills. We chose the themes of metacognition, argumentation, and asking questions because we sincerely believe that these skills not only enhance effective chemistry learning, but will also serve in educating future literate citizens in their daily life activities, where the students who were involved in this project are very much aligned with the claim made by Tobin (1990):

> A crucial ingredient for meaningful learning in laboratory activities is to provide for each student opportunities to reflect on findings, clarify understanding and misunderstanding with peers, and consult a range of resources, which include other students, the teacher, and books and materials. (p. 415)

Achieving chemistry literacy for all students has become a central goal of education in many countries. Although admirable, this goal presents a challenge for both science curriculum developers and teachers who are working cooperatively toward this goal. The target population is not only those who will eventually embark on a career in the sciences, but also those who are often referred to as future citizens. As such, they will often find themselves in situations in which they will need to ask critical questions and seek answers, which will enable them to make valid decisions. Thus, the development of students' ability to ask questions should be seen as an important component of scientific literacy and should not be overlooked.

In recent years, there has been a substantial growth in understanding associated with teaching, learning and assessment in school chemistry laboratory work. At the beginning of the 21st century, when many are again seeking reform in science education, the knowledge that has been developed about learning based upon careful scholarship should be incorporated in that reform. The "less is more" slogan in "Benchmarks for Science Literacy" (American Association for the Advancement of Science, 1989, p. 320) has been articulated to guide curriculum development and teaching that is consistent with the contemporary reform. The intended message is that that formal teaching results in a greater understanding when students study a limited number of chemistry topics, in depth and with care, rather than a large number of topics much more superficially, as is the practice in many upper-secondary-school science classrooms. To make room for the inquiry laboratories in general and development of higher-order learning skills in particular, the syllabus (content) should be markedly reduced. Well-designed, inquiry-type laboratory activities can provide learning opportunities that will help students develop higher-order learning skills. They also provide important opportunities to help students learn to investigate (e.g., ask questions), construct scientific assertions, and justify those assertions in a classroom community of peer investigators in contact with a more expert scientific community. There is no doubt that such activities are time-consuming and thus, the education system must provide time and opportunities for teachers to interact with their students, as well as time for students to perform and reflect on such and similar complex inquiry and investigative tasks. Such experiences should be integrated with other science classroom learning experiences to enable the students to make connections between what is learned in the classroom and what is learned and investigated in the laboratory. This is based on the growing sense that learning is contextualized and that learners construct knowledge by solving genuine and meaningful problems. One of the most crucial problems regarding the implementation of inquiry-type laboratory experiments is the issue of assessing students' achievement and progress in such a unique learning environment. A large number of science teachers are not using authentic and practical assessments on a regular basis. To attain these important but demanding learning goals resulting from students' experiences in the laboratory, the education system must provide time, facilities, and opportunities for teachers to interact with their students, as well as time for students to perform and reflect on complex, investigative and inquiry-type skills, in both the science classroom and the science laboratory. In addition, the educational system must provide teachers with opportunities to enhance their professional skills in the science laboratory in general, and in inquiry laboratories in particular. Teaching the inquiry approach is challenging for both the teachers and their students (Krajcik et al., 2001). The teaching environment is highly student-centered, where the teachers are expected to encourage and challenge their students' learning and help them construct and understand the subject matter (Tobin, 1990). It is suggested that for teachers to provide their students with an environment that is suitable for learning by inquiry, they need to undergo an intensive process of professional development, so that they will have the appropriate skills, knowledge, and habits of thinking (Windschitl, 2002). In addition, teachers should change their teaching strategies or adopt new ones, such as: guiding instead of telling, supporting and encouraging students' interests, encouraging curiosity, accepting students' ideas, and responding to students' questions with new tactics, rather than giving them the immediate answers (Minstrell, 2000). In other words, teachers should gain unique pedagogical content knowledge so that they can be good facilitators and supporters for their students.

Building on what we know and on the scholarship of the past, there are important R&D opportunities toward enhancing the effectiveness of science education. Special opportunities identified in this chapter include developing and implementing teaching strategies, assessment tools, resources that are effective at helping teachers and students reach important learning goals, and that engage students (based on Hofstein et al., 2013):

- with different abilities, learning styles, motivational patterns, and cultural contexts;
- in using inquiry-empowering tools and strategies; and
- in justifying assertions on the basis of scientific evidence.

Appropriate professional development for teachers, informed by relevant scholarship, is important in helping teachers become more effective at teaching in student-centered inquiry-type science laboratories.

To sum up, based on the literature and findings from a series of research studies that we have conducted in Israel related to the educational effectiveness of the chemistry laboratory, we can assume that:

- school laboratory activities have unique potential as media for learning that can promote important science learning outcomes for students;
- teachers need knowledge, skills, and resources to teach effectively in practical learning environments;
- teachers need to enable students to interact *intellectually* as well as *physically*, involving both *hands-on* investigation and *minds-on* reflection;
- students' perceptions and behaviors in the science laboratory are greatly influenced by teachers' expectations and assessment practices, and by the orientation of the associated laboratory guide, worksheets, and electronic media;
- teachers need ways to find out what their students are thinking and learning in the science laboratory and classroom;
- teachers need to be provided with continuous professional development opportunities to collaborate with colleagues in the science education research community so as to understand, develop, and teach in ways that are consistent with contemporary professional standards.

5 Epilogue

In 1980, Pickering in the USA wrote that:

> The job of lab courses is to provide the experience of doing science. While the potential is rarely achieved, the obstacles are organizational and inherent in laboratory teaching itself. That is fortunate because reform is possible and reform is cheap. Massive amounts of money are not required to improve most programs; what is needed is more careful planning and precise thinking about educational objectives. By offering a genuine, unvarnished scientific experience, a lab course can make a student into a better observer, a more careful and precise thinker, and a more deliberative problem solver. And that is what education is all about.

Although this essay was written 40 years ago, we sincerely believe based on our 50 years of R & D experience in the chemistry laboratory practical work that it is still relevant today.

Note

1 Some of the information presented in this section is highly based (with permission) on Hofstein et al. (2019), published in the *Israeli Journal of Chemistry*.

References

American Association for the Advancement of Science (AAAS). (1989). *Project 2061: Science for all Americans*. AAAS.

Baird, J. R., & White, R. T. (1996). Metacognitive strategies in the classroom. In D. F. Treagust, R. Duit, & B. J. Fraser (Eds.), *Improving teaching and learning in science and mathematics* (pp. 190–200). Teachers College Press.

Barnea, N., Dori, J. Y., & Hofstein, A. (2010). Development and implementation of inquiry-based and computerized laboratories: Reforming high school chemistry in Israel. *Chemistry Education Research and Practice, 11*, 218–228. http://dx.doi.org/10.1039/c005471m

Ben-Zvi, R., Hofstein, A., Kempa, R. F., & Samuel, D. (1976). The effectiveness of filmed experiments in high school chemical education. *Journal of Chemical Education, 53*, 518–520. http://dx.doi.org/10.1021/ed053p518

Ben-Zvi, R., Hofstein, A., Samuel, D., & Kempa, R. (1977). Modes of instruction in high school chemistry. *Journal of Research in Science Teaching, 14*, 433–439. http://dx.doi.org/10.1002/tea.3660140507

Bybee, R. (2000). Teaching science as inquiry. In J. Minstrel & E. H. Van Zee (Eds.), *Inquiring into inquiry learning and teaching in science* (pp. 20–46). American Association for the Advancement of Science.

Campbell, B., Lazonby, J., Millar, R., Nicolson, P., Ramsden, J., & Waddington, D. (1994). Science: The Salters' approach – A case study of the process of large scale curriculum development. *Science Education, 78*, 415–447. http://dx.doi.org/10.1002/sce.3730780503

Cuccio-Schirripa, S., & Steiner, E. H. (2000). Enhancement and analysis of science question level for middle school students. *Journal of Research in Science Teaching, 37*, 210–224. http://dx.doi.org/10.1002/(sici)1098-2736(200002)37:2<210::aid-tea7>3.0.co;2-i

Driver, R., Newton, P., & Osborne, J. (2000). Establishing the norms of scientific argumentation in classrooms. *Science Education, 84*, 287–312. http://dx.doi.org/10.1002/(sici)1098-237x(200005)84:3<287::aid-sce1>3.0.co;2-a

Eglen, J. R., & Kempa, R. F. (1978). Assessing manipulative skills in practical chemistry. *School Science Review, 56*, 737–740.

Erduran, S., Simon, S., & Osborne, J. (2004). TAPping into argumentation: Developments in the application of Toulmin's argument pattern for studying science discourse. *Science Education, 88*, 915–933. http://dx.doi.org/10.1002/sce.20012

Fraser, B., McRobbie, C. J., & Giddings, G. J. (1993). Development and cross-national validation of a laboratory classroom instrument for senior high school students. *Science Education, 77*, 1–24. http://dx.doi.org/10.1002/sce.3730770102

Giddings, G., Hofstein, A., & Lunetta, V. N. (1991). Assessment and evaluation in the science laboratory. In B. E. Woolnough (Ed.), *Practical science* (pp. 167–178). Open University Press.

Hofstein, A. (1975). *The educational effectiveness of laboratory work in chemistry education* [Unpublished doctoral dissertation]. Weizmann Institute of Science.

Hofstein, A. (2004). The laboratory in chemistry education: Thirty years of experience with developments, implementation, and research. *Chemistry Education Research and Practice, 5*, 247–264. http://dx.doi.org/10.1039/b4rp90027h

Hofstein, A. (2006). Improving the classroom laboratory learning environment by using teachers' and students' perceptions. In D. Fisher & M. S. Kaine (Eds.), *Contemporary approaches to research on learning environments: Worldviews* (pp. 75–92). World Scientific. http://dx.doi.org/10.1142/9789812774651_0004

Hofstein, A., Dkeidek, A., Katchevitch, A., Levy Nahum, A., Kipnis, M., Navon, O., Shore, R., Taitelbaum, D., & Mamlok-Naaman, R. (2019). Research on and development of inquiry-type chemistry laboratories in Israel. *Israel Journal of Chemistry, 59*, 1–11. http://dx.doi.org/10.1002/ijch.201800056

Hofstein, A., & Kind, P. (2012). Learning in and from chemistry laboratories. In B. Fraser, K. Tobin, & C. McRobbie (Eds.), *Second international handbook of science education* (pp. 189–209). Springer. http://dx.doi.org/10.1007/978-1-4020-9041-7_15

Hofstein, A., Kipnis, M., & Abrahams, I. (2013). How to learn in and from the chemistry laboratory. In I. Eilks & A. Hofstein (Eds.), *Teaching chemistry – A study book* (pp. 153–182). Sense Publishers. http://dx.doi.org/10.1007/978-94-6209-140-5_6

Hofstein, A., & Lunetta, V. N. (1982). The role of the laboratory in science teaching: Neglected aspects of research. *Review of Educational Research, 52*, 201–217. http://dx.doi.org/10.3102/00346543052002201

Hofstein, A., & Lunetta, V. N. (2004). The laboratory in science education: Foundation for the 21st century. *Science Education, 88*, 28–54. http://dx.doi.org/10.1002/sce.10106

Hofstein, A., & Mamlok, R. (2001). From petroleum to tomatoes. *The Science Teacher, 68*, 46–48.

Hofstein, A., Navon, O., Kipnis, M., & Mamlok-Naaman, R. (2005). Developing students' ability to ask more and better questions resulting from inquiry-type chemistry laboratories. *Journal of Research in Science Teaching, 42*, 791–806. http://dx.doi.org/10.1002/tea.20072

Hofstein, A., Shore, R., & Kipnis, M. (2004). Providing high school chemistry students with opportunities to develop learning skills in an inquiry-type laboratory: A case study. *International Journal of Science Education, 26*, 47–62. http://dx.doi.org/10.1080/0950069032000070342

Johnstone, A. H., & Wham, A. J. B. (1982). The demands of practical work. *Education in Chemistry, 19*, 71–73.

Katchevitch, D., Hofstein, A., & Mamlok-Naaman, R. (2013). Argumentation in the chemistry laboratory: Inquiry and confirmatory experiments. *Research in Science Education, 43*, 317–345. http://dx.doi.org/10.1007/s11165-011-9267-9

Kempa, R. F. (1986). *Assessment in science*. Cambridge: Cambridge University Press.

Kempa, R. F., & Ward, J. F. (1975). The effect of different modes of task orientation on observational attainment in practical chemistry. *Journal of Research in Science Teaching, 12*, 69–76. http://dx.doi.org/10.1002/tea.3660120110

Kipnis, M., & Hofstein, A. (2008). The inquiry laboratory as a source for development of metacognitive skills. *International Journal of Science and Mathematics Education, 6*, 601–627.

Krajcik, J., Mamlok, R., & Hug, B. (2001). Modern content and the enterprise of science: Science education in the twentieth century. In L. Corno (Ed.), *Education across a century: The centennial volume* (pp. 205–238). National Society for the Study of Education.

Kuhn, D., Black, J., Keselman, A., & Kaplan, D. (2000). The development of cognitive skills to support inquiry learning. *Cognition and Instruction, 18*, 495–523. http://dx.doi.org/10.1207/s1532690xci1804_3

Lazarowitz, R., & Tamir, P. (1994). Research on using laboratory instruction in science. In D. L. Gabel (Ed.), *Handbook of research on science teaching and learning* (pp. 94–130). London: Macmillan.

Milner, N., Ben-Zvi, R., & Hofstein, A. (1987). Variables that affect students' enrolment in science courses. *Research in Science and Technological Education, 5*, 201–208. http://dx.doi.org/10.1080/0263514870050210

Minstrell, J. (2000). Implications for teaching and learning inquiry. In J. Minstrel & E. H. Van Zee (Eds.), *Inquiring into inquiry learning and teaching in science* (pp. 471–496). Washington, DC: American Association for the Advancement of Science.

National Research Council. (1996). *National science education standards*. Washington, DC: National Academy Press. http://dx.doi.org/10.17226/4962

Pickering, M. (1980). Are lab courses a waste of time? *Education Digest, 45*(9), 38.

Rosen, S. A. (1954). History of the physics laboratory in American public schools (to 1910). *American Journal of Physics, 22*, 194–204. http://dx.doi.org/10.1119/1.1933679

Schraw, G. (1998). Promoting general metacognitive awareness. *Instructional Sciences, 26*, 113–125.

Shulman, L. D., & Tamir, P. (1973). The role of the laboratory in science teaching. In R. M. W. Travers (Ed.), *Second handbook of research on teaching* (pp. 1098–1140). RandMcNally.

Tobin, K. G. (1990). Research on science laboratory activities: In pursuit of better questions and answers to improve learning. *School Science and Mathematics, 90*, 403–418. http://dx.doi.org/10.1111/j.1949-8594.1990.tb17229.x

White, R. T., & Mitchell, I. J. (1994). Metacognition and the quality of learning. *Studies in Science Education, 23*, 21–37. http://dx.doi.org/10.1080/03057269408560028

Windschitl, M. (2002). *An analysis of preservice science teachers' open inquiry experiences* [Paper presentation]. Annual American Educational Research Association Conference, New Orleans, LA, United States.

Zoller, U. (1987). The fostering of question asking capability: A meaningful problem-solving aspect of problem solving in chemistry. *Journal of Chemistry Education, 64*, 510–512. http://dx.doi.org/10.1021/ed064p510

CHAPTER 2

Introducing Contemporary Research Topics into School Science Programs

The Example of Nanotechnology

Ron Blonder

Abstract

Integrating contemporary research into science learning introduces students to the nature of science and the scientists behind the up-to-date research. In this way, students can learn about the open nature of scientific questions that await a research-based solution. However, core scientific concepts of contemporary research and recent R&D are usually not included in the school curriculum. Adapting modern science topics to the high-school level involves many challenges and concerns that have to be addressed. This chapter describes a 15-year journey of exploration toward adapting the emergent research field of nanotechnology to the high-school science level. It presents the different steps taken, components developed, and various considerations, as well as an analysis of the challenges that this process revealed and that had to be addressed. The discussion engages with the interconnections between scientific content, school science curriculum, teachers' knowledge and professional development, teaching materials, students' interest and motivation, and issues of communicating science. By generalizing the findings related to nanotechnology, it will become possible to include other contemporary research fields in school science.

Keywords

contemporary science – Delphi study – nanotechnology education – nature of science – science communication – professional development – high-school science – authenticity

1 Introduction

If we adults compare our children's science curriculum to what we studied three decades ago, we will usually find that the difference is small, even

 | DOI: 10.1163/9789004503625_002

nonexistent. Yet, scientific knowledge is constantly accumulating and new fields are reshaping scientific research. The educational system and learning programs react slowly to these changes. One might ask why we should change a science curriculum that covers the chosen basic concepts of science well. To answer this question, we must first examine the contribution of introducing modern science into the school. Once this approach proves valuable, we should design a methodology to invigorate the school science curriculum with new scientific developments. Contemporary research encompasses numerous fields and has developed in many different directions. My research group has chosen to focus on one case of contemporary scientific research – nanotechnology, also known as nanoscale science and technology (NST) (Jones et al., 2013).

In this chapter, I describe my 15-year research journey, with my students and colleagues, to develop methods and tools that will enable introducing NST into school science.

2 Why Should We Integrate Contemporary Research into High School?

I will start with the "why": Why is it beneficial to integrate contemporary research into science teaching? Do the envisaged benefits justify introducing cutting-edge scientific developments into high-school science lessons? The answer to this question has numerous aspects.

In 1902, John Dewey stated, "If we teach today's students as we taught yesterday's, we rob our children of tomorrow." Dewey's famous statement challenges science educators. One way to address this challenge is by adopting an approach that advocates science learning through contemporary research, offering students an opportunity to obtain up-to-date information on what science really is. In this way, students realize that the people involved in research are real, no different from them, and share the same concurrent norms. They also become acquainted with the open-ended nature of scientific issues that await research-based solutions (Blonder & Sakhnini, 2015). This approach obviously offers the students an opportunity to learn about developing research while it is still at the research laboratory stage (Blonder et al., 2010; Blonder & Sakhnini, 2016; Bryan & Giordano, 2015).

Learning topics such as nanotechnology seems to appeal to young students. Several studies have found that nanotechnology studies increased students' motivation to pursue science studies and scientific careers (Delgado et al., 2015; Hutchinson et al., 2011). Moreover, nanotechnology inspires both male and female students to pursue science careers, narrowing the gender gap (Srisawasdi, 2015). For example, a study that we conducted (Blonder & Dinur, 2011) focused on teaching the nanotechnology application of LEDs (light-emitting diodes). We found that the number of students who chose to enroll in an advanced chemistry class in school increased after they learned about LEDs. This result was supported by a second study (Blonder & Sakhnini, 2012) and by a longitudinal study that summarized the professional development of chemistry teachers. In the latter study, the teachers designed a teaching module in nanotechnology and evaluated it in their classes. Most of the teachers reported that the integration of nanotechnology increased the students' motivation to learn chemistry (Blonder & Mamlok-Naaman, 2016). The words of one junior-high-school student illustrate the students' enthusiasm: "We actually saw atoms with our own eyes!" (Margel et al., 2004). This enthusiasm made us realize that modern science has a motivational influence on students.

Incorporating modern scientific topics into the school curriculum offers an opportunity to expose students to unfamiliar aspects of science that are far from the image of a genius-scientist with whom they cannot identify (Stamer et al., 2019). This can be achieved by adapting primary literature to students' level (Yarden, 2009), encounters with scientists and hearing them describe their research, learning from teachers who keep track of and are familiar with ongoing research (Blonder & Mamlok-Naaman, 2016; Kapon et al., 2009), and inviting students to attend real scientific conferences (Blonder & Sakhnini, 2015).

Thus, there are many reasons for integrating contemporary science into school science studies. To achieve this, however, it is necessary to go through several stages, as I explain in the following.

3 What Should We Teach?

When dealing with contemporary scientific topics, there is no tradition to lean on in determining what the curriculum should include. Initially, sporadic teaching units are developed, representing the developers' knowledge and offering a partial view of a new field. In nanotechnology, units of this kind may include, for example, modern microscopic methods such as atomic force microscopy (Blonder, 2010; Blonder et al., 2010; Planinšič & Kovač, 2008); nano-ethical questions (Berne & Schummer, 2005; Schummer, 2007; Sweeney, 2006); a selected concept from the field of NST (Blonder & Sakhnini, 2012, 2015; Bryan et al., 2015); and nanotechnology applications (Blonder & Dinur, 2011; Hutchinson et al., 2011). Once the new field attracts the attention of the science-education community, systematic identification of the field's basic concepts to be included in the curriculum may begin (Blonder & Sakhnini, 2016).

Various studies have engaged with identifying the core concepts of NST at different educational levels. Spyrtou's research group (e.g., Manou et al., 2017) examined the possibility of adapting NST for preschool students. Huang et al. (2011) conducted a study to determine which core concepts of nanotechnology could be taught in elementary school. However, most of the research into identifying basic NST concepts has dealt with high-school science and tertiary education (Wansom et al., 2009).

Different research approaches have been used in identifying the NST concepts that should be included in the high-school science curriculum. In Germany, the Model of Educational Reconstruction (MER) was used (Parchmann & Komorek, 2008). MER takes into account teachers' perspectives and expert knowledge in developing a coherent educational program that combines scientific parameters with science education, derived through a dynamic exchange of opinions between the involved parties (Blonder et al., 2014; Langbeheim et al., 2020).

A different methodology was applied in the United States, where Stevens et al. (2009) developed the NST "Big Ideas" document following two workshops with scientists and science educators. "Big Ideas" are critical and fundamental core concepts that enable understanding the basics of nanoscience. Thirty-three scientists and science educators involved in NST research represented different scientific disciplines (e.g., chemistry, physics, and biology). The research aimed to reach consensus about the big ideas of NST and devise ways to introduce those ideas into the American science curriculum.

To validate our up-to-date international perspective, we began by mapping out essential NST concepts (Sakhnini & Blonder, 2015). We used a three-round Delphi methodology to reach a consensus on the essential concepts recommended for teaching NST in high-school science, and came up with eight essential NST concepts: (1) size-dependent properties, (2) innovations and applications of nanotechnology, (3) size and scale, (4) characterization methods, (5) functionality, (6) classification of nanomaterials, (7) approaches to the production of nanomaterials, and (8) the making of nanotechnology. Three of these concepts were new and had not been discussed in the earlier studies:

a. Functionality: a property attributed to a material or a specific area within it, granting it a distinct function or a bonding capacity.
b. Nanomaterial classification: categorizing nanomaterials according to their chemical composition, electrical conductivity, or source – natural nanomaterials, organic molecules, and synthetic nanomaterials, and their dimensionality – the number of dimensions in which a nanostructure expands beyond 100 nm (0D, 1D, 2D, and 3D).

c. The making of nanotechnology: how do scientists carry out nanoscience research and how are innovations transformed into applications?

An additional Delphi study followed, to find a nanotechnology application that would best suit the high-school level (Sakhnini & Blonder, 2016). It yielded five nanotechnology applications proposed by nanotechnology and education experts.

Reaching a consensus about the essential NST concepts to be taught in high-school science is a crucial stage in the process of introducing modern science into the school curriculum, since it provides the basic knowledge to understand the field of NST. The equally important next stage is determining who will teach these contemporary science contents in high school.

4 How to Bring NST to School Science?

Integrating contemporary R&D into a school science curriculum is challenging by definition. The experts developing contemporary knowledge and skills are not teachers, whereas professional teachers have never come across NST in their studies, as it had yet to emerge (Blonder, 2011; Drane et al., 2009). There are two possible solutions to this situation: (1) prepare the teachers for contemporary scientific research teaching in class; (2) train scientists in how to communicate the essentials of their research to school students.

4.1 *Professional Development of Teachers*

Several professional development courses in the field of nanotechnology have been developed for teachers (Blonder, 2011; Blonder et al., 2014; Bryan et al., 2012; Gardner & Jones, 2014; Gorghiu & Gorghiu, 2012; Lin et al., 2015; Tomasik et al., 2009). However, a number of challenges have emerged in preparing the teachers for this task: the content challenge, determining where it would be best to integrate NST concepts into the class curriculum, and the teachers' confidence in their ability to learn and later teach advanced modern science (self-efficacy beliefs).

In an advanced course on NST offered to the teachers in 2010 (Blonder, 2010, 2011), they did well in the knowledge test. Nevertheless, they felt that their understanding of nanotechnology was not sufficiently thorough to teaching the required content to their students. To bridge this gap, we developed and implemented a three-stage model to support teachers' learning of the new content and help them adapt it to their classroom (Mamlok-Naaman et al., 2010). According this model, the teachers attended (1) the scientific course lectures,

(2) a 'follow-up' tutoring lesson that was aimed at elaborating on the course lecture, and (3) a workshop, coordinated by a researcher from the chemistry teaching group, on applying the scientific knowledge to the educational field. Significantly, we found that the model created a better environment for the teachers to become acquainted with the content, and increased their self-efficacy beliefs concerning their ability to delve deeply into the content and adapt it to their classes.

Challenges notwithstanding, we found that the innovative content revived the teachers' enthusiasm about the subject that they were teaching (Blonder, 2011), and according to their reflective feedback, they managed to communicate that enthusiasm to their students. The primary purpose of teachers' participation in professional development courses is to expose them to the most recent research content. However, these courses are also an opportunity to teach new content using nontraditional teaching methods. We have found that teachers often implement nontraditional approaches in NST teaching. This makes sense, considering that teachers tend to adopt the methods they learned from their own teachers. As Putnam and Borko (2000) explained: "How a person learns a particular set of knowledge and skills, and the situation in which a person learns, become a fundamental part of what is learned" (p. 4). In this case, however, the teachers had no previous teaching model, and we found that they applied the teaching model that we used in the teachers' course to their own teaching. Moreover, we discovered that teachers went on to apply these various teaching approaches (such as using a teaching model, integrating videos, using a student-centered pedagogy, and having students create and present a poster exhibition) to other topics in the science curriculum. This habit was found to persist over 5 years (Blonder & Mamlok-Naaman, 2016).

4.2 *Scientists Communicating Scientific Content*

Another channel for introducing contemporary science into school is through the scientists, who are familiar with the new science and who have participated in its development. To better prepare scientists to communicate their current research, we designed a 1-hour intervention intended to familiarize them with the Junior High School (JHS) science curriculum. The intervention was designed to enhance the skills of physics experts in effectively reaching JHS students. Twelve physics NST researchers participated in the study. They were given two tasks: finding connections between NST concepts and physics concepts (force and energy) from the JHS curriculum (see below, "Where to integrate NST concepts into the science learning program?"), and describing their research verbally before and after looking for these connections. The experiment revealed that after looking for connections between the two sets of concepts, several scientists reworded their research description, replacing their previously difficult scientific jargon with concepts from the JHS physics curriculum. A qualitative examination of the results revealed that the session and the description task had differential effects on individual scientists. Although most of them succeeded in making the wording shift after the 1-hour intervention, we recommend exploring this approach further.

A different unique opportunity lies in direct meetings between scientists and students at a scientific conference. In this setting, students can see scientists "doing" authentic components of their scientific work and interact with them. This opportunity is connected to one essential concept of NST, "the making of nanotechnology" (Blonder & Sakhnini, 2015; Sakhnini & Blonder, 2015), defined as "revealing the mystery of nanotechnology, or in other words, how nanoscience research is performed and how innovations are transformed into applications" (Sakhnini & Blonder, 2015, p. 1711). This concept underscores the importance of exposing the students to an authentic environment and to activities that are well beyond mere scientific facts and experiment results. We have found that after attending a scientific nanotechnology conference and meeting scientists there, the students' perception of scientists changed. Students' participation in the conference influenced their emotional perspectives, their knowledge concerning nanotechnology, and their curiosity and interest in science. The conference also influenced the students' motivation and future plans (Blonder & Sakhnini, 2015).

If we wish to convey to students the nature of science and scientific work, we should provide them with an opportunity to receive a modern, realistic image of science. Today, scientists work in interdisciplinary groups and apply the tools and perspectives of other disciplines to solve current problems (Kähkönen et al., 2016). They use cutting-edge equipment (Blonder et al., 2008, 2010; Schwarzer et al., 2015), and attend prestigious conferences where they communicate their ideas (Blonder & Sakhnini, 2015; Laherto et al., 2018). Moreover, exposing students to modern science helps them understand that there is still much to discover, and that many questions remain open, reflecting the ever-developing nature of science. This insight is a call for school students to join the research and become the next scientists to explore new areas and find the answers to unsolved questions.

5 Where to Integrate NST Concepts in the Science Learning Program?

School students can be exposed to NST concepts through two main channels. These concepts can be connected to the formal school science curriculum or they can be accessible via informal outreach activities. These two channels are complementary (Bencze & Hodson, 1999) in their goals, intensities and required resources.

5.1 *Science School Curriculum*

Integrating modern science, such as NST, into the school science curriculum is challenging, as it requires determining the right points at which to insert its essential concepts. We conducted a series of studies to determine the best insertion points in the high-school chemistry curriculum (Blonder & Sakhnini, 2017), in the JHS science and technology curriculum (Sakhnini & Blonder, 2018), and in the JHS physics curriculum (Yonai & Blonder, 2020). All of the studies were designed to produce a rich set of connections between the field of NST and relevant topics from the school curriculum.

We based the first part of our research on the experience of high-school teachers who participated in the aforementioned nanotechnology course for teachers, and were therefore familiar with the eight essential concepts of NST (Blonder & Sakhnini, 2017). During the course, we asked the teachers to suggest insertion points for the essential NST concepts within the Israeli high-school chemistry curriculum, and to explain their choices. They submitted their suggestions to the course instructor, and these were discussed in the following session. After methodological analysis and validation of the proposed points, a network of connections emerged between all of the essential NST concepts and different points in the chemistry high-school curriculum topics. In all, 74 different optional insertion points were identified throughout the curriculum.

A similar methodology was used to identify insertion points for the eight essential NST concepts in the middle-school science and technology curriculum. Middle-school science and technology teachers who had taken the NST course and were familiar with the eight essential NST concepts (Sakhnini & Blonder, 2018) identified insertion points that reflected the relevance of the essential NST concepts from the perspective of pedagogical level. The search for connections yielded different results for the different curriculum components: whereas many insertion points were suggested in the chemistry, life sciences, and technology parts of the curriculum, the connections found in the physics–energy curriculum were few.

The need therefore arose to apply a different methodology to find the connections between the essential NST concepts and the physics part of the middle-school science curriculum.

To this end, we designed a guided session with physics NST scientists, intended to produce a map of connections between the two fields (Yonai & Blonder, 2020). During the session, the scientists received two sets of terms: the eight essential NST concepts and a list of the concepts from the physics curriculum, and were asked to identify all of the connections between each of the essential NST concepts and the physics curriculum. For example, the NST concept of characterization methods was connected to mechanical forces and was explained using the example of an atomic force microscope; the NST concept of size-dependent properties was connected to 7th-grade inquiry skills by explaining the size dependence of accuracy, errors, and defects. The connections suggested by the scientists and their corresponding context were validated by an experienced middle-school science teacher.

5.2 *Informal Science Education*

Another way to integrate NST concepts into school science is through informal science education. For our latest study, we have designed learning experiences that are based on a scanning electron microscope (SEM) that the Weizmann Institute of Science purchased for educational purposes. High-school classes arrive at the Institute and conduct laboratory experiments on the SEM in an authentic research environment.

The central purpose of the study, which is still ongoing, is to create a framework for developing and evaluating authentic outreach programs in research settings. The framework's initial development will explore the meaning that participating students, teachers, and research scientists assign to authenticity. Based on this framework, we plan to design authentic SEM activities and evaluate their outcomes from student and teacher perspectives, such as learning, motivation, interest, and attitudes.

6 Concluding Remarks

This chapter described the process of introducing the field of NST into high-school science. Through all of the stages, the combination of a deep understanding of NST content and science education research affected the resulting teaching practices. Initially, we identified essential NST concepts recommended for inclusion in the high-school science curriculum using the Delphi study methodology. Next, we identified insertion points for the essential NST concepts into science curricula. The need arose to use two different research methodologies to find the best insertion points, for smooth integration of NST concepts into the science curricula. The insertion points were first suggested by teachers who were familiar with the school science curricula, after they learned the NST concepts. However, to allocate the insertion points into the middle-school physics curriculum, a deeper knowledge of physics was required and only physics scientists who were exposed to the curriculum were able to suggest connections between the NST concepts and the physics curriculum.

Teachers' courses were developed, implemented, and studied, to determine how they affect the teachers' knowledge and their perceived self-efficacy beliefs with regard to teaching NST. We also studied how students experience the learning of specially developed NST units, and found that these topics increase their motivation to engage in further science studies. The last study mentioned is currently at the focus of our work, and involves an experiment in creating authentic learning environments where students are exposed to NST. These environments include participating in a scientific conference, or visiting the SEM laboratory. Further research is required to evaluate the cognitive and emotional influence of authentic learning environments on the students.

In this chapter, NST served as an example of the contemporary research that we would like to integrate into school science. All of the described steps are applicable to the integration of other emergent scientific fields into school science. The same research-based approach promises to be useful in constantly updating the school science curriculum and ensuring that it does not lag behind.

Acknowledgments

This chapter summarizes a 15-year journey. I did not travel alone: my research students made the journey unique. I would like to express my deep appreciation to Dr. Naama Benny, who showed me the beauty of differentiated instruction and the challenge of teaching gifted students; Dr. Shelley Rap, who made me an enthusiastic user of social networks and other advanced technologies, and joined me in creating the nano-festival; Dr. Sohair Sakhnini, who conducted the Delphi study of the essential NST concepts and initiated the study to adjust the essential NST concepts to school curricula; Dr. Ruth Waldman, who helped me improve my understanding of different dimensions of teachers' professional development; Yael Feldman-Maggor, who guided me through the novelty of online teaching, learning analytics, and fancy statistics; Enas Easa, whose heart and mind are dedicated to learning personalization, and who helped me understand how to reach each student through differentiated instruction; Ella Yonai, who joined me in exploring the way to connect the essential NST concepts with the physics curriculum and led me into the world of science authenticity with the SEM activity; Ehud Aviran, who studies the field of differentiated instruction in a technological environment; and Ayshi Sindiani-Bsoul, who connects the sustainable development goals to chemistry education.

Special thanks are owed to the hundreds of chemistry teachers who participated in my nano courses, developed novel teaching materials, and have revealed the beauty of the nano world to thousands of high-school chemistry students.

References

Bencze, L., & Hodson, D. (1999). Changing practice by changing practice: Toward more authentic science and science curriculum development. *Journal of Research in Science Teaching, 36*, 521–539. http://dx.doi.org/10.1002/(sici)1098-2736(199905)36:5<521::aid-tea2>3.0.co;2-6

Berne, R. W., & Schummer, J. (2005). Teaching societal and ethical implications of nanotechnology to engineering students through science fiction. *Bulletin of Science, Technology & Society, 25*, 459–468. http://dx.doi.org/10.1177/0270467605283048

Blonder, R. (2010). The influence of a teaching model in nanotechnology on chemistry teachers' knowledge and their teaching attitudes. *Journal of Nano Education, 2*, 67–75. http://dx.doi.org/10.1166/jne.2010.1004

Blonder, R. (2011). The story of nanomaterials in modern technology: An advanced course for chemistry teachers. *Journal of Chemical Education, 88*, 49–52. http://dx.doi.org/10.1021/ed100614f

Blonder, R., & Dinur, M. (2011). Teaching nanotechnology using student-centered pedagogy for increasing students' continuing motivation. *Journal of Nano Education, 3*, 51–61. http://dx.doi.org/10.1166/jne.2011.1016

Blonder, R., Joselevich, E., & Cohen, S. R. (2010). Atomic force microscopy: Opening the teaching laboratory to the nanoworld. *Journal of Chemical Education, 87*, 1290–1293. http://dx.doi.org/10.1021/ed100963z

Blonder, R., & Mamlok-Naaman, R. (2016). Learning about teaching the extracurricular topic of nanotechnology as a vehicle for achieving a sustainable change in science education. *International Journal of Science and Mathematics Education, 14*, 345–372. http://dx.doi.org/10.1007/s10763-014-9579-0

Blonder, R., Mamlok-Naaman, R., & Hofstein, A. (2008). Analyzing inquiry questions of high-school students in a gas chromatography open-ended laboratory experiment. *Chemistry Education Research and Practice, 9*, 250–258. http://dx.doi.org/10.1039/b812414k

Blonder, R., Parchmann, I., Akaygun, S., & Albe, V. (2014). Nanoeducation: Zooming into teacher professional development programs in nanotechnology in four European countries. In C. Bruguière, A. Tiberghien, & P. Clément (Eds.), *Topics and trends in current science education, Vol. 1* (pp. 159–174). Springer. http://dx.doi.org/10.1007/978-94-007-7281-6_10

Blonder, R., & Sakhnini, S. (2012). Teaching two basic nanotechnology concepts in secondary school by using a variety of teaching methods. *Chemistry Education Research and Practice, 13*, 500–516. http://dx.doi.org/10.1039/c2rp20026k

Blonder, R., & Sakhnini, S. (2015). The making of nanotechnology: Exposing high-school students to behind-the-scenes of nanotechnology by inviting them to a nanotechnology conference. *Nanotechnology Reviews, 4*, 103–116. http://dx.doi.org/10.1515/ntrev-2014-0016

Blonder, R., & Sakhnini, S. (2016). What are the basic concepts of Nanoscale Science and Technology (NST) that should be included in NST educational programs. In K. Winkelmann & B. Bhushan (Eds.), *Global perspectives of nanoscience and engineering education* (pp. 117–127). Springer International Publishing. http://dx.doi.org/10.1007/978-3-319-31833-2_4

Blonder, R., & Sakhnini, S. (2017). Finding the connections between a high-school chemistry curriculum and nano-scale science and technology. *Chemistry Education Research and Practice, 18*, 903–922. http://dx.doi.org/10.1039/c7rp00059f

Bryan, L., & Giordano, N. J. (2015). Special issue on pre-college nanoscale science, engineering, and technology learning. *Nanotechnology Reviews, 4*, 1–6. http://dx.doi.org/10.1515/ntrev-2014-0051

Bryan, L. A., Magana, A. J., & Sederberg, D. (2015). Published research on pre-college students' and teachers' nanoscale science, engineering, and technology learning. *Nanotechnology Reviews, 4*, 7–32. http://dx.doi.org/10.1515/ntrev-2014-0029

Bryan, L. A., Sederberg, D., Daly, S., Sears, D., & Giordano, N. (2012). Facilitating teachers' development of nanoscale science, engineering, and technology content knowledge. *Nanotechnology Reviews, 1*, 85–95. http://dx.doi.org/10.1515/ntrev-2011-0015

Delgado, C., Stevens, S. Y., Shin, N., & Krajcik, J. (2015). A middle school instructional unit for size and scale contextualized in nanotechnology. *Nanotechnology Reviews, 4*, 51–69. http://dx.doi.org/10.1515/ntrev-2014-0023

Drane, D., Swarat, S., Light, G., Hersam, M., & Mason, T. (2009). An evaluation of the efficacy and transferability of a nanoscience module. *Journal of Nano Education, 1*, 8–14. http://dx.doi.org/10.1166/jne.2009.001

Gardner, G., & Jones, M. G. (2014). Exploring pre-service teachers' perceptions of the risks of emergent technologies: Implications for teaching and learning. *Journal of Nano Education, 6*, 39–49. http://dx.doi.org/10.1166/jne.2014.1041

Gorghiu, L. M., & Gorghiu, G. (2012). Teachers' perception related to the promotion of nanotechnology concepts in Romanian science education. *Procedia – Social and Behavioral Sciences, 46*, 4174–4180. http://dx.doi.org/10.1016/j.sbspro.2012.06.221

Huang, C. Y., Hsu, L. R., & Chen, H. C. (2011). A study on the core concepts of nanotechnology for the elementary school. *Journal of National Taichung University: Mathematics, Science & Technology, 25*, 1–22.

Hutchinson, K., Bodner, G. M., & Bryan, L. (2011). Middle-and high-school students' interest in nanoscale science and engineering topics and phenomena. *Journal of*

Pre-College Engineering Education Research, 1(1), 30–39. https://doi.org/10.7771/2157-9288.1028

Jones, M. G., Blonder, R., Gardner, G. E., Albe, V., Falvo, M., & Chevrier, J. (2013). Nanotechnology and nanoscale science: Educational challenges. *International Journal of Science Education, 35*, 1490–1512. http://dx.doi.org/10.1080/09500693.2013.771828

Kähkönen, A. L., Laherto, A., Lindell, A., & Tala, S. (2016). Interdisciplinary nature of nanoscience: Implications for education. In K. Winkelmann & B. Bhushan (Eds.), *Global perspectives of nanoscience and engineering education* (pp. 35–82). Springer International Publishing. http://dx.doi.org/10.1007/978-3-319-31833-2_2

Kapon, S., Ganiel, U., & Eylon, B. S. (2009). Explaining the unexplainable: Translated Scientific Explanations (TSE) in public physics lectures. *International Journal of Science Education, 32*, 245–264. http://dx.doi.org/10.1080/09500690802566632

Laherto, A., Tirre, F., Parchmann, I., Kampschulte, L., & Schwarzer, S. (2018). Scientists' perceptions on the nature of nanoscience and its public communication. *Problems of Education in the 21st Century, 76*, 43–57. http://dx.doi.org/10.33225/pec/18.76.43

Langbeheim, E., Abrashkin, A., Steiner, A., Edri, H., Safran, S., & Yerushalmi, E. (2020). Shifting the learning gears: Redesigning a project-based course on soft matter through the perspective of constructionism. *Physical Review Physics Education Research, 16*(2), 020147. https://doi.org/10.1103/PhysRevPhysEducRes.16.020147

Lin, S.-F., Chen, J.-Y., Shih, K.-Y., Wang, K.-H., & Chang, H.-P. (2015). Science teachers' perceptions of nanotechnology teaching and professional development: A survey study in Taiwan. *Nanotechnology Reviews, 4*, 71–80. http://dx.doi.org/10.1515/ntrev-2014-0019

Mamlok-Naaman, R., Blonder, R., & Hofstein, A. (2010). Providing chemistry teachers with opportunities to enhance their knowledge in contemporary scientific areas: A three-stage model. *Chemistry Education Research and Practice, 11*, 241–252. http://dx.doi.org/10.1039/c0rp90005b

Manou, L., Spyrtou, A., Hatzikraniotis, E., & Kariotoglou, P. (2017). *Primary teachers' conceptions about the content of nanoscience – Nanotechnology* [Paper presentation]. Third International Conference "Education Across Borders," University "St. Kliment Ohridski" Faculty of Education Bitola, North Macedonia. https://core.ac.uk/download/pdf/237499824.pdf

Margel, H., Eylon, B., & Scherz, Z. (2004). "We actually saw atoms with our own eyes." Conceptions and convictions in using the scanning tunneling microscope in junior high school. *Journal of Chemical Education, 81*, 558. https://doi.org/10.1021/ed081p558

Parchmann, I., & Komorek, M. (2008). The model of educational reconstruction – A research model for the investigation of students' and teachers' conceptual ideas. In B. Ralle & I. Eilks (Eds.), *Promoting successful science education – The worth of science education research* (pp. 169–181). Shaker Verlag.

Planinšič, G., & Kovač, P. (2008). Nano goes to school: A teaching model of the atomic force microscope. *Physics Education, 43*, 37–45. http://dx.doi.org/10.1088/0031-9120/43/01/002

Putnam, R. T., & Borko, H. (2000). What do new views of knowledge and thinking have to say about research on teacher learning? *Educational Researcher, 29*, 4–15. http://dx.doi.org/10.3102/0013189x029001004

Sakhnini, S., & Blonder, R. (2015). Essential concepts of nanoscale science and technology for high school students based on a Delphi study by the expert community. *International Journal of Science Education, 37*, 1699–1738. http://dx.doi.org/10.1080/09500693.2015.1035687

Sakhnini, S., & Blonder, R. (2016). Nanotechnology applications as a context for teaching the essential concepts of NST. *International Journal of Science Education, 38*, 521–538. http://dx.doi.org/10.1080/09500693.2016.1152518

Sakhnini, S., & Blonder, R. (2018). Insertion points of the essential Nanoscale Science and Technology (NST) concepts in the Israeli middle school science and technology curriculum. *Nanotechnology Reviews, 7*, 373–391. http://dx.doi.org/10.1515/ntrev-2018-0026

Schummer, J. (2007). Identifying ethical issues of nanotechnologies. In H. ten Have (Ed.), *Nanotechnologies, ethics and politics* (pp. 79–98). UNESCO.

Schwarzer, S., Akaygün, S., Sagun-Goko, B., Anderson, S., & Blonder, R. (2015). Using Atomic Force Microscopy in out-of-school settings: Two case studies investigating knowledge and understanding of high school students. *Journal of Nano Education, 7*, 10–27. http://dx.doi.org/10.1166/jne.2015.1079

Srisawasdi, N. (2015). Evaluation of motivational impact of a computer-based nanotechnology inquiry learning module on the gender gap. *Journal of Nano Education, 7*, 28–37. http://dx.doi.org/10.1166/jne.2015.1075

Stamer, I., Kubsch, M., Thiele, M., Höffler, T., Schwarzer, S., & Parchmann, I. (2019). Scientists, their work, and how others perceive them: Self-perceptions of scientists and students' stereotypes. *Research in Subject-Matter Teaching and Learning, 2*, 85–101.

Stevens, S., Sutherland, L. M., & Krajcik, J. S. (2009). *The big ideas of nanoscale science and engineering: A guidebook for secondary teachers*. NSTA Press. http://dx.doi.org/10.2505/9781935155072

Sweeney, A. E. (2006). Social and ethical dimensions of nanoscale science and engineering research. *Science and Engineering Ethics, 12*, 435–464. http://dx.doi.org/10.1007/s11948-006-0044-5

Tomasik, J. H., Jin, S., Hamers, R. J., & Moore, J. W. (2009). Design and initial evaluation of an online nanoscience course for teachers. *Journal of Nano Education, 1*, 48–67. http://dx.doi.org/10.1166/jne.2009.003

Wansom, S., Mason, T. O., Hersam, M. C., Drane, D., Light, G., Cormia, R., Stevens, S., & Bodner, G. (2009). A rubric for post-secondary degree programs in nanoscience and nanotechnology. *International Journal of Engineering Education, 25*, 615–627.

Yarden, A. (2009). Reading scientific texts: Adapting primary literature for promoting scientific literacy. *Research in Science Education, 39*, 307–311. http://dx.doi.org/10.1007/s11165-009-9124-2

Yonai, E., & Blonder, R. (2020). Scientists suggest insertion of nanoscience and technology into middle school physics. *Physical Review Physics Education Research, 16*(1), 010110. https://doi.org/10.1103/PhysRevPhysEducRes.16.010110

CHAPTER 3

Promoting Self-Regulated Learning by Designing a Chemistry Online Blended Learning Environment

Rachel Rosanne Eidelman and Yael Shwartz

Abstract

E-learning is becoming a necessary skill, calling for familiarity with learning management systems. This chapter describes the construction process of the Chemistry Online Blended Learning Environment (COBLE) – a 3-year chemistry course for high-school students. The research that accompanied the COBLE was a detailed 3-year longitudinal study aimed at 23 grade 10–12 students who wished to study chemistry but could not do so in their schools. Since the founding of COBLE, four cohorts have already finished successfully, while students are enrolling for the 7th year. This chapter addresses the dynamic environment's design and redevelopment, which succeeded to cope with rapid growth in student numbers and massive curriculum changes due to a national reform, bearing in mind that the aim was to improve self-regulated learning (SRL) of chemistry. Findings show that the design affected students' level of SRL and constituted a major factor in their achievements and overall success. The novelty of this study is primarily related to the extent to which the environmental design influenced the students over the 3-year course, and in particular, their SRL improvement over time.

Keywords

chemistry education – design-based research – e-learning – self-regulated learning – virtual learning environment

1 Introduction

Chemistry is not an obligatory subject in Israeli high schools; it is an optional high-level science choice for students who are interested in deepening their knowledge of the subject.

The main purpose of developing the Chemistry Online Blended Learning Environment (COBLE) was to introduce a new and appealing way to study

 | DOI: 10.1163/9789004503625_003

chemistry for high-school students, and in doing so, upgrading and reinventing chemistry teaching for students living in a technological world that have not been offered the opportunity to study chemistry at their school.

Self-regulated learning (SRL) skills are vital and may pose great difficulties in the learning progression when they are lacking. Disciplinary content must be tied to the rising trend of distance learning, so thought was given to the ability to convey content knowledge and to support the development of SRL skills in a virtual environment, by creating well-designed and focused tasks. The COBLE was designed as a 3-year high school level chemistry blended classroom based on the national curriculum. The program was divided into years (10th, 11th and 12th grades), and weekly, synchronous lessons (two academic hours) were taught regularly. There were also weekly tutorial lessons, and weekly asynchronous homework assignments. Chemistry laboratories were conducted in three different ways:

- *Home-laboratory kits*: Students received a kit with the relevant equipment to execute simple (but exciting!) laboratory experiments at home.
- *Virtual laboratories*: Students were given assignments that sometimes involved short movies, applets or processed virtual laboratories.
- *Face-to-face laboratories* at the Weizmann Institute of Science: These were primarily held 2–3 times a year, mostly during holiday breaks as part of science camp.

In this paper, we will describe the design of the COBLE as an educational reconstruction process (Duit, 2007; Duit et al., 1997). The literature review below refers to the relevant topics of virtual teaching, designed-based research and SRL.

1.1 *Virtual Teaching*

Any learning that is electronically mediated and/or facilitated by transactional software is regarded as e-learning via the internet (Zemsky & Massy, 2004). The International Association for K–12 Online Learning (iNACOL) defined online learning as "education in which instruction and content are delivered primarily via the internet" and blended learning as "learning that combines two modes of instruction, online and face-to-face, but at potentially different points in time" (Barbour et al., 2011; Horn & Staker, 2011). Blended courses combine e-learning and frontal components, as in our case, where students also participated in face-to-face chemistry inquiry laboratory activities. E-learning has the potential to influence the way learners all over the world are educated, providing access to the best teachers, the best international resources, and subjects that are not otherwise offered, provided that the following culture, policy, and support structures are congruent (McNaught et al., 2000).

Several researchers have tackled the issues that emerge when students encounter e-learning. Tallent-Runnels et al. (2006) reviewed 76 papers and found that e-learners were more successful when the course was well-designed and emphasized the importance of the designer's role in determining the educational design theory used and in the overall success of the students taking the course. They also addressed four main categories that emerged when students encountered e-learning: (1) course environment (classroom culture, structural assistance, success factors, interaction online, and evaluations), (2) learners' outcomes (understanding teaching and learning processes in the virtual environment), (3) learners' characteristics (motivation to take a virtual course, learner's goals and needs), and (4) institutional and administrative factors (clear policies for virtual courses, such as a support system). They concluded that some insights could be drawn although no comprehensive theories or models could be derived regarding instruction online: students preferred the flexibility, convenience and autonomy of individual pacing, although it required self-management. Computer-skilled students had a more positive attitude toward e-learning than others who were less proficient. Boelens et al. (2017) reviewed 20 studies on the design of blended learning environments and discovered four key challenges: incorporating flexibility, stimulating interaction, facilitating students' learning process, and fostering an effective learning climate. They concluded their review by stating that social interaction deserves more attention in future designs because it enhances the students' sense of belonging (to a school or class).

Face-to-face and online components are generally used for different purposes. Online components are used more by motivated students, whereas less motivated students need more stimulation. Some researchers attempted to compare students' learning in virtual and traditional environments: test scores, course grades and performance tasks were used in order to evaluate learning, but no significant differences were found between the two groups.

Picciano (2014) identified a series of four waves of online and blended learning, from the 1990s to the present. According to Picciano, blended learning technologies allow faculty interaction, and incorporate a variety of pedagogical approaches using multiple formats and instructional tools. There are several models representing blended learning, and it is up to every developer to select a model and adapt it to their vision in order to create a unique blended environment of their own. The blended form attempts to deliver "the best of both worlds," trying to combine the advantages of online learning with all of the benefits of the traditional classroom. Furthermore, the existing blended models for learning do not pose a major disruption to the traditional classroom. If, and when the model becomes highly disruptive, it will transform the classroom model and become an engine of change (Christensen et al., 2013).

E-learning was once regarded by many as a negative form of learning, since both students and teachers believed that technology had a negative effect on their studies (Li, 2007; Oxford Group, 2013; Sturgill et al., 1999; Tao, 2008). Today, there seems to be a more positive attitude toward e-learning, and there is an understanding that this form of learning is beneficial in the long term (Allen & Seaman, 2014).

1.2 *Design-Based Research* (DBR)

DBR of technology-enhanced learning environments (TELES) describes the process of development, investigation and refinement of an educational learning environment.

Design experiments are a continuous process evolving from engineering a working environment based on input from class ethos, teacher/student research, curriculum, etc., while maintaining a bilateral relationship with learning theory contributions and dissemination, and ending with output in the form of assessment of the right components and accountability (Collins et al., 2004). Different learning environment design principles can affect dependent variables in educational research (Brown, 1992; Collins et al., 1992; Duit, 2007; Peterson & Herrington, 2005; Piccoli et al., 2001; Van Laer & Elen, 2017). Therefore, as opposed to learning environments based exclusively on theoretical principles derived from prior research, the design is applied and revised according to malfunctions detected along the way.

DBR relies on a mixed-method approach: partially deductive "top-down" and partially inductive "bottom-up." Designers have to select a learning and instructional theory so that interventions can be determined (Edelson, 2002; Reiser, 2001); thus, the underlying theory chosen for the study described here was the active and interactive learning theory which is a learner-centered, active–constructive–interactive framework, where students actively learn by engaging and exploring the virtual environment. Students actively construct new knowledge experience by solving relevant problems and by experimenting, rather than merely building upon previously acquired knowledge (Chi, 2009). Van Laer and Elen (2017) reviewed 95 papers and isolated seven attributes of blended learning for self-regulation, and while all seven rarely appeared in any given blended learning environment, designers should aspire to incorporating as many as possible in their designs. One important attribute is fading scaffolding, i.e., slowly handing over responsibility to the students (Berglas-Shapiro, 2015; Lynch & Dembo, 2004). The term "scaffolding" was first used in the context of education by Wood et al. (1976): (1) recruitment: the tutor introduces the problem and requirements of the task; (2) reduction in degrees of freedom: simplifying the task by reducing the number of constituent actions required to reach the solution; (3) direction maintenance: the tutor has to ensure that students continue to pursue a particular objective; (4) marking critical features: the tutor emphasizes relevant features of the task; (5) frustration control: minimizing tutor dependency; (6) demonstration: the tutor "models" solutions to a task, "imitating" an idealized form of the solution. The best scaffolding will eventually cause learners to internalize the processes that they had to accomplish (Rogoff, 1990; Wang & Hannafin, 2005). It is challenging, yet possible, to address the differences in a blended learning environment so as to maximize student engagement in the learning process. Berglas-Shapiro (2015) developed a technology-enhanced SRL and problem-solving environment and followed middle-school science students. The results reflected the need for a TELE that offers different types of scaffolding to students with different profiles.

Another important design feature is the creation of junctions for interactions and involvement of all sorts (personal involvement in the lessons, tasks and environment, group socializing during assignments, face-to-face meetings, teacher and tutor crossing points, etc.). Lack of interaction can result in disengagement and increase the number of student dropouts (Artino, 2009; DuBois et al., 2008).

Relevance is also necessary; providing a sense of importance to what the students are learning and incorporating real-time issues will maintain a high interest level that encourages students to be motivated and make the required effort so that they can experience success.

Finally, it is imperative to collect feedback and create opportunities for reflection so that improvements can take place and students can evaluate their own achievements.

1.3 *Self-Regulated Learning* (SRL)

Self-regulated learners are those who proactively seek out information, and take the necessary steps to master it (Zimmerman, 1990). They are conceptualized as metacognitive, since they plan, set goals, organize, self-monitor, and self-evaluate several times during the learning process; they are motivated, maintain high levels of self-efficacy, engage in self-attribution, have intrinsic task interest, and are active participants in their learning processes (Pintrich & De Groot, 1990; Zimmerman, 1989, 1990, 2008). SRL is not necessarily intentional, and therefore, is not necessarily a conscious process (Boekaerts & Cascallar, 2006). SRL skills are especially important in a virtual learning environment, as it does not provide the immediate ability to seek help from teachers (Cho, 2004; O'Neill et al., 2004). It is regarded as essential to be a self-regulated learner in order to succeed through e-learning (Tsai, 2011), although McManus (2000) reported that students with low SRL skills learned better than students with medium or high SRL skills, contradicting most other researchers' findings. Teaching students to self-regulate their academic learning is a time- and energy-consuming, complicated task, successful only when students experience the benefits of SRL (Zimmerman et al., 1996).

Four design principles have been suggested to promote SRL skills: (1) explicit presentation of SRL activities; (2) inclusion of opportunities to use SRL strategies; (3) mandatory SRL skill interventions; (4) experience of success (Ley & Young, 2001; Zimmerman et al., 1996). While planning the environmental design for the study described herein, special care was taken to incorporate these design principles, as the main goal was to promote students' SRL through their application, and to be able to measure their level of SRL. This resulted in a dynamic environment that served as more than a task-hosting site and that enabled a constant evaluation of skills attained during the 3-year course period. Some of the results regarding the SRL study can be found in a separate publication (Eidelman et al., 2019).

2 Objectives

The objective of this study was to describe and characterize the process of development of a COBLE. We describe the initial design, changes, final revisions and fine-tuning conducted through DBR as a consequence of the students' attitudes toward learning chemistry and toward the learning environment, including the pedagogy, platform and organizational components.

3 Research Questions

Q1 a. What were the initial pedagogical features of the COBLE?
b. How, based on students' learning, did those features change and/or redevelop over time?

Q2 a. What were the initial LMS and organizational features of the COBLE?
b. How, based on students' learning, did those features change and/or redevelop over time?

Q3 What were the students' attitudes toward learning chemistry and toward the learning environment?

4 Methods

4.1 *Participants*

This study included 23 chemistry students, aged 15–18 years, who studied the 3-year chemistry course via the virtual environment of the COBLE. There were students who completed their studies (i.e., remaining students) and dropouts who did not complete their studies (i.e., dropouts). Students were academically capable of studying high-level chemistry and studied other high-level science-based subjects, as well as high-level English and Math, at school.

4.2 *Tools*

The tools used to collect the data were:

- *In-depth interviews*: The purpose of using in-depth interviews was to apply changes and corrections in the learning materials, update the course contents, and better understand the students' difficulties. The interviews were recorded, transcribed and analyzed qualitatively (Chi, 1997; Shkedi, 2003); the transcripts and recordings were read and heard several times, and some main ideas were derived from them. One independent interviewer interviewed the students (to avoid bias); 15 remaining students and 5 dropouts were interviewed: half of the students were interviewed in the middle of the 3-year program and the other half at the end. In each round, heterogeneous interviewees were chosen (weak, medium and strong students according to their scores). Each group had different guiding interview questions, which covered the following topics: (1) general information, (2) opinion of chemistry and the learning environment, (3) SRL, (4) learning strategies, and (5) administrative and technical issues. The interviews also provided information about the success and failure factors, the causes for student dropout, and the means to support SRL.
- *A feedback task question* was added to every asynchronous task. The feedback question itself was a result of the information collected in the first round of interviews and therefore, is acknowledged as a change of design, as well as a contributor to additional changes incorporated in the course design. This question was obligatory and awarded the students with points that were part of the task score. Information collected from the responses to the feedback questions helped improve tasks and pinpoint students' difficulties therein. This resulted in the implementation of changes in the tasks or other learning materials. In total, we analyzed 30 different feedback questions (402 student responses in total).

5 Results

5.1 *Q1a What Were the Initial Pedagogical Features of the COBLE (2014)?*

5.1.1 General

The initial decisions regarding course design were based on the literature, and on the experience of three chemistry teachers. Careful attention was payed to

SRL, theoretically driven and used to explain and justify the decisions made regarding the environmental design. It was also important to (1) present the content knowledge according to the official chemistry curriculum (Ministry of Education, 2014), (2) develop independent learning and learning skills, and (3) develop inquiry skills and encourage peer learning.

5.1.2 Curriculum

In Israel, high-level chemistry studies are an optional high-level science choice for students who are interested in deepening their knowledge of the subject. In most cases, students study chemistry for 3 years. The official chemistry curriculum (Ministry of Education, 2014) is composed of a variety of topics: structure and chemical bonds, stoichiometry, reduction and oxidation, acids and bases, carbohydrates, fats and vitamins, scientific text reading and understanding, basic energy, kinetics and equilibrium processes, and one more topic, subject to the teacher's discretion (from: bromide compounds, environmental chemistry, nanochemistry, organic chemistry, biochemistry or thermodynamics). Students also completed their studies of the inquiry laboratory subprogram. Students' final scores are based on external matriculation exams (70%) and on teachers' internal assessments (30%).

5.1.3 Principles of Course Design

The course development was based on three foundation stones: (1) cognitive – the active and interactive learning theory (Chi, 2009); (2) design – according to lesson plans and virtual environments (Collison et al., 2000; Elbaum et al., 2002; Pallof & Pratt, 2001); (3) content – according to the Israeli curriculum (Ministry of Education, 2014).

In addition, careful consideration was given to the introduction of a range of assignments that created opportunities for students to use, and reuse their SRL skills, improving them as they went.

5.1.4 Principles of Design for E-learning Materials

The design principles for developing materials or adapting existing materials were:

- *Diagnostics*: Coming from different schools, students' diverse preliminary knowledge needed to be acknowledged. The first unit was constructed in a gradual manner, and basic scientific concepts were taught to create a platform for future learning. Diagnostic assignments were based on students' misconceptions, and ways to prevent them from making errors in the process of problem solving, either in tutorials or when engaged in their homework assignments.

- *Diverse learning styles*: Several teaching methodologies were used to ensure that every student would be engaged in the learning process. Computerized and noncomputerized methods were included, to create a rich, blended environment that would enable every student to experience learning in many ways and to have an opportunity to demonstrate their abilities, according to their SRL profiles (Eidelman et al., 2019).
- *Development of independence and responsibility*: To enhance independent learning, weekly asynchronous lessons followed the synchronous lessons. The important aspect of transfer of responsibility is that the student has not only learned the content but has also abstracted the process of completing the particular task (Puntambekar, 2009). During the first year, all asynchronous assignments included explanations (additional and different from those administered in the synchronous lessons) to enable an easier understanding of the lesson content. During the second year, this practice gradually stopped, and homework tasks included only exercises (implementation of the material learned in the synchronous lessons). This final feature of fading scaffolding was incorporated to reduce the support provided to learners, so that they were encouraged to take responsibility for their learning.
- *Peer-learning promotion*: A student forum and a WhatsApp group were established, in which the teacher did not have a central role. Students were encouraged to take an active role and answer their peers, share experiences, and react to other students' comments.

5.1.5 Principles of Virtual Environmental Design

The design principles for developing the virtual learning environment are presented in Table 3.1.

5.1.6 The Initial Course Features (2014)

Course topics were divided into units; each unit contained all learning materials, exercises and answers. Within each learning unit, there were 2–3 options to answer a self-test, which served the interested students as an aid to evaluate their knowledge level.

It was planned that during the first year (10th grade), approximately half of the lessons would be synchronous (recorded for future student revision) and the rest of the lessons would be asynchronous. During the following years (grades 11 and 12), the number of synchronous lessons would decrease to about one-third of the lessons, and the students would learn by asynchronous assignments.

Furthermore, students would receive laboratory tasks (home laboratory kits or virtual laboratories via the computer) to be carried out independently, in

TABLE 3.1 Design principles for development of the virtual environment

Pedagogical feature	Reason for assimilation of feature	Learning environment features
Orientation	Frustration can cause students to dropout	Easy navigation of learning materials
Synchronous lesson presentation	An identical lesson design served as an organizer and road map for the students so that they knew at any given moment where they stood with respect to the course flow	Identical lesson presentation format: lesson topic, "what have we learned so far?," "previous knowledge needed," acquisition of new learning material, exercising implementation, "summary," additional enrichment materials, relevant links, and homework
Asynchronous lesson presentation	To enhance connectivity, most features were parallel to the synchronous lesson, such as lesson topic, "what have we learned so far?," etc.	Most asynchronous lessons were summarized, and directly related to the synchronous lesson that had previously been taught
Learning aids	All students were expected to participate in all of the lessons and tutorials, use all course components and be active learners	All learning aids were available throughout the course: synchronous lesson presentations, lesson recordings and self-tests, as well as group and personal tutorial sessions

addition to the two science camps that were set up. A few laboratory sessions took place, which included instructions for writing a basic laboratory report. Students would do the required laboratory work in groups, by participating in the science camp held at the Weizmann Institute during spring break. And finally, Students received a detailed explanation of the LMS (Moodle) before the beginning of the school year and experienced their first lesson together.

– *Virtual components*: The LMS Moodle 1.8 was used as the learning environment. All lessons were recorded and uploaded onto the course site. Asynchronous lessons (homework tasks) were presented on the course site, and students could choose a suitable time to complete them. Each homework assignment could be answered twice to improve the final score. Synchronous tutoring sessions were held weekly. Attendance at the tutorial sessions

TABLE 3.2 The initial course features

Virtual course components	Non-virtual course components
Obligatory	*Obligatory*
– Weekly synchronic lessons with teacher	– Weekly a-synchronic homework assignments
– Weekly synchronic lessons with tutor (11th–12th grades)	– Home-lab reports (using a home-lab kit)
– Computerized tests (in each unit, during the synchronic lessons)	– Project (10% of the 30% alternative evaluation-11th grade)
	– Attendance in science camp activities (during school breaks) including face-to-face lab work
	– Written tests (performed during science camps)
Non-obligatory	*Non-obligatory*
– Weekly synchronic lessons with tutor (10th grade)	– Computerized self-tests

was optional in the 10th grade, but was obligatory for students in the 11th and 12th grades. In the 12th grade, some students had personal tutors as well.

- *Non-virtual laboratories*: Laboratory assignments were performed during the face-to-face science camps or by using the home-laboratory kit.
- *Course pedagogy*: All assignments throughout the course were designed with consideration of the development and progress of SRL. Self-tests were given throughout the learning process, and computerized tests were given at the end of each subunit or unit.
- *Course evaluation*: Assignments were checked by the Moodle computerized system and by the course tutor (for answers that could not be evaluated otherwise, such as explanations). The course teacher checked laboratory reports, as well as written tests. Internal assessment (30% of the final score) included: assessment of some topics from the curriculum, some inquiry laboratories and an independent obligatory project, part of a national chemistry competition that enabled them to present their views of a chemical phenomenon in one of five ways: poster, short movie, article, photograph or inquiry laboratory (Sharaabi-Naor et al., 2014).

5.2 *Q1b: How Did the Initial Features Change and/or Redevelop Over Time (2017)?*

Changes were implemented following interviews, feedback questions and teacher observations throughout the 3-year program.

Changes of SRL components. As the course continued, we faced two contradictory trends: on the one hand, the students found it difficult to plan and control their time, and to submit the tasks on time. This was especially reflected in the asynchronous part of the course; on the other, the students enjoyed more freedom, by choosing their own project topics or by picking their own laboratory experiment. According to the literature, time management is a crucial factor in learning. Weinstein et al. (2002) included it as part of 10 categories of a SRL inventory. Time management and task submission in a timely manner are even more complicated for students in e-learning. These are important, because it is the main way that the teacher can follow the students' learning process (as opposed to only summative assessments). This, combined with the growing academic requirements in the second year of the 3-year course, increased the need for our control. For example: weekly synchronous sessions with a tutor became obligatory, a final submission date was incorporated for each asynchronous homework assignment, and the students were required to submit laboratory reports for home experiments (using the home laboratory kit).

To increase student autonomy and involvement, personal tutorials were offered (10th–12th grades), by student choice only, matriculation-style tests were incorporated for self-practice purposes, additional science camps were offered (to manage the necessary laboratory work) with more options for students to choose the dates and types of experiment they wanted to conduct. In addition, a feedback question became part of each homework assignment and we explicitly referred to students' feedback, so that they felt that their voice was being heard. Submission of a second project to a national chemistry competition was also offered.

5.2.1 Practical Necessities as an Engine for Change

The changes and revisions that were made to the initial course design mainly addressed practical necessities and less often, theoretical incompatibilities. Since the development process was continuous (within years, and from year to year), expanding the contents and units constantly, the conclusions drawn from each year were immediately implemented in the following year's course site.

- *Obligatory features*: Obligatory synchronous tutorials with a tutor were held weekly; for students who enrolled in the program later on, tutorial sessions became obligatory for all. This was a result of conclusions drawn from the first iteration of students studying in the program.
- *Personal tutorials* were incorporated because of students' low grades or as a reaction to what students wrote in the feedback questions or in the interviews. For example:
- Student K.V.: *I found the task very difficult. I did not succeed to answer all of the questions because I did not understand the learning material in depth.*
- *A final submission date* was incorporated into each homework assignment to prevent late submission.

- *Increasing flexibility in performing non-virtual laboratories*: Two additional laboratory days were offered to the students during the school year. Missing the science camps meant that some students barely managed to acquire the minimal number of inquiry laboratories required by the curriculum.
- *Course pedagogy*: All homework tasks now contained a feedback question that reflected the degree of effort needed by the student and difficulties encountered during the task. This question awarded students with points (so that the student was forced to answer and not ignore this particular question). In addition, matriculation-style tests were introduced to help students prepare for the final matriculation exam.
- Unplanned opportunities:
  1. The obligatory independent project was very successful; therefore, an option to re-enter and submit another project to the national chemistry competition was offered, encouraging the students to submit their project in the inquiry-laboratory category (this resulted in a team of students who won the competition, and were awarded a 100% score for their final laboratory-work examination).
  2. The option to be tested for the National Chemistry Olympiad for high-school students was offered to the students (this resulted in one student reaching the final stage of the competition and, in doing so, receiving a 100% score on his matriculation exam and thus an exemption from taking the actual exam).

These unexpected and unplanned opportunities became an integral part of the following years and, as a result, were integrated into the COBLE by 2017.

5.3 *Q2a: What Were the Initial LMS Features of the* COBLE *(2014)?*

The initial LMS of the COBLE was Moodle version 1.8 and since there was only one class, there was only one course site to accommodate the course material. Topics were termed "learning units" and were accessed by clicking on the learning unit itself, revealing all of the learning materials related to the relevant topic. To minimize confusion and frustration, the learning units were exposed to the students as learning progressed (see Figure 3.1).

5.4 *Q2b: How Did the Initial* LMS *and Organizational Features Change and/or Redevelop over Time (2017)?*

The Moodle version was upgraded during the project to 3.3 and in addition to one course site for the 10th grade, as the years progressed, a meta-course was created, accommodating classes of new students (see Figure 3.2) who enrolled in the program. The number of students kept growing, resulting in the opening

FIGURE 3.1
First iteration (10th grade) 'learning units' (translated from Hebrew)

FIGURE 3.2
Teacher's view: 'Chemistry Online' meta-course (translated from Hebrew)

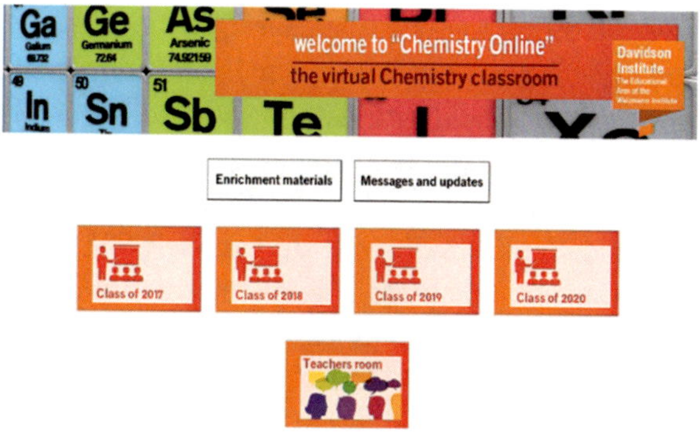

FIGURE 3.3 Student's view: 3-year 'Chemistry Online' (translated from Hebrew)

of several parallel classes; each group had a teacher and a tutor. Each class had their 3 years of material presented, so that each student could access his or her own class and group, and retrieve his or her course material and personal history (Figure 3.3).

5.4.1 Unforeseen Revision and Changes

Contact with the schools played a vital role in students' level of satisfaction with the course. Through experience, we learned that this was an important feature of the course; without it, students dropped out when difficulties occurred.

Access to the infrastructure proved to be a hindering factor that set students back, causing frustration and confusion. This was a serious issue for ultra-Orthodox schools. Such schools usually have limited and controlled access to the internet. Also, girls and boys learn separately. While boys focus on theological and religious studies, girls have more options in choosing their major subject. In the first year (2014), all Ultra-Orthodox students dropped out as a result of this issue, but in 2016 (third iteration), we managed to create and maintain an all-girls Ultra-Orthodox class and minimized this problem.

5.5 *Q3: What Were the Students' Attitudes toward Learning Chemistry and toward the Learning Environment?*

5.5.1 Students' Learning Habits as a Reflection of Their Attitudes

The differences amongst the remaining students (i.e., students who completed the 3-year program) were in the categories that referred to learning habits: not all of them maintained a notebook; the students had different ways of preparing for the test: some preferred to watch the recordings of the lessons and favored audio explanations, whereas some did well with the presentations, and some needed extra help (such as tutorial sessions, peer learning, school science teacher); some students managed their study time during the lessons, whereas others needed extra time after the lessons to grasp the concepts learned during the lessons.

Some students invested greater effort in succeeding by redoing and resending their assignments, trying to solve self-tests (optional and without any scores reported to their schools), and reaching out for help via email or text message; others did not put in the extra work since they understood the learning material very well. Unlike remaining students, all dropout students felt that their lack of sufficient interest and motivation played a vital role in their minimal effort to invest the time, and maintain a continuous learning experience, thus resulting in their decision to leave the program.

Common views shared by the remaining students showed that they were able to demonstrate an on-going and well-maintained interest in chemistry before and after entering the program:

> Quote 1: Chemistry is relevant to everything in our life. When I was in junior high, we studied chemistry, and I was mainly excited about the experiments. (Before entering the program)

> Quote 2: Chemistry is interesting to me. The teacher teaches in an interesting way and links the material to daily life. It makes me want to listen. (After entering the program)

Common views shared by the dropouts showed that they were not able to maintain an interest in chemistry and had a hard time experiencing a sense of belonging:

> Quote 3: I was not interested enough in the content. I was bored, and that is why I decided to drop out.

> Quote 4: In order to study in the virtual class, one needs more motivation.

> Quote 5: My biggest problem was lack of time. I sometimes felt it was almost impossible.

5.5.2 Students' Attitudes toward the Learning Environment

Common views shared by the remaining students included comments on the course site being very well organized and easy to navigate, making it easy to find whatever was needed.

> Quote 6: I can revise whatever I need to, even from years back, since everything is available on the course site in an organized way.

> Quote 7: I liked that all of the learning materials are available as lesson recordings and presentations.

All dropout students expressed the need or preference for face-to-face interaction and contact, and felt uncomfortable when they were deprived of this as they felt it was a necessary feature for success in their studies (interaction/contact with either teacher/students).

> Quote 8: In a virtual lesson, there are no interruptions, which is an advantage. The disadvantage is that the teacher does not see me. There is no eye contact with her [that helps me to listen during the lesson]. A teacher's presence face-to-face in the classroom helps me concentrate.

> Quote 9: It is hard to concentrate for a long period of time in front of the computer screen. If one looks away from the screen during the lesson, one is no longer a part of the lesson. In the face-to-face classroom, the lesson is all around me. It is easier to take off the earphones and turn off the lesson on the computer than when the teacher in front of you.

5.5.3 How Did Students' Performance and Feedback Affect the Course Design?

Revisions were implemented during the 3-year course by detecting the difficulties and a need for change, considering options for the required change, implementing the change and, finally, identifying the overall impact of the change. Changes and revisions were also examined with a consideration of the SRL categories, because a major goal was to promote students' SRL skills over time.

Table 3.3 illustrates the categories for design changes that emerged as result of student's feedback. Specific students' quotes for each category can be found in Appendix 1.

After analyzing students; feedback and prioritizing the need for design changes, we re-designed and inserted changes either in the curriculum, or organizational or structural changes such as adding mentoring, or offering more laboratory days in the Weizmann Institutes.

Table 3.4 illustrates the changes made to the course relating to each category. Detailed students' feedback can be found in Appendix 2.

Another issue that was revised regularly, based on feedback, was the organization of the course site in order to reach an optimal structure. Effort and

TABLE 3.3 Categorization of students' feedback indicating a need for design changes

Category	Why change is important?
Difficulties in conducting home inquiry laboratories	Inquiry laboratories are mandatory in the chemistry curriculum (Ministry of Education, 2014)
Need for face-to-face contact	This is one of two main reasons for dropping out of the course, (Eidelman et al., 2019).
Need for personalized learning	Weak students encountered difficulties keeping up with the class. Strong students felt unchallenged and bored.
Maintaining a high interest level	This is one of two main reasons for dropping out of the course, (Eidelman et al., 2019). Students' attitudes and interests may decrease over time for various reasons
Students; difficulties in time management and preparation for tests	According to the Self-Regulation-Learning theoretical framework, these skills are self-regulation learning skills that are crucial to students learning and achievement any time, but especially in virtual environments.
Interactivity of synchronous lessons	Students did not participate enough during the synchronous lessons

thought were invested so that the time spent in reaching destinations on the course site was minimal and stress-free. The main changes included unifying all topics (learning spaces) regardless of the year in which the students were studying. All learning spaces were presented in one area and a student had an

TABLE 3.4 Design changes made in the course

Category	Changes made in the course
Difficulties in conducting home inquiry laboratories	1. Home-laboratory kits were downgraded: less inquiry-laboratory content, retaining popular and fun laboratories 2. More opportunities for face-to-face laboratories were offered during the summer break:
Need for face-to-face contact	1. More face-to-face laboratories and science camps were offered. 2. Face-to-face exercise meetings before tests were offered. 3. Informal contacts with teachers were established: e.g., a WhatsApp group.
Need for personalized learning	Group/personal tutors: special tutors were assigned to: (a) weak students, assisting them to understand concepts taught; (b) strong students to help them prepare for special high-level competitions (such as the Chemistry Olympiad). 1. Assignment feedback questions became obligatory: the information gained was used to improve assignments, identify unclear topics and gain insights regarding students' states of mind. 2. Special face-to-face learning days: students were offered the opportunity to participate in face-to-face meetings
Maintaining a high interest level	A range of activities were offered to maintain a high level of interest: 1. Chemistry enrichment activities: 2. Competitions: students were offered the opportunity to participate in competitions. 3. Personalization of the lessons: lessons relating to some of the students' interests were constructed (or example: a lesson about drug abuse and hormones in sports was created with a student in mind whose hobby was mountain climbing).
Students' difficulties in time management	1. Tutorial sessions became obligatory for grades 11–12. 2. A 'No lesson cancellation' policy was established 3. students were required to complete the lesson (by watching the recording and completing tasks) if they missed it.

(*cont.*)

TABLE 3.4 Design changes made in the course (*cont.*)

Category	Changes made in the course
Interactivity of synchronous lessons	1. Prompting questions: during the lessons, poll questions were asked to enhance involvement. 2. Homework revision during the synchronous lesson: the teacher used well-written student answers to show other students what a correct answer looks like. 3. Synchronous chat area management: a second teacher was assigned specifically to respond to students' chat questions during the lesson, to minimize disturbance to the natural flow of the lesson.
Preparation for tests	Creation of a question bank resource to supply examples of test questions and well-written answers to them. 1. Self-tests were created for each of the topics learned

overall view of the topics learned for the years they had participated in the course. Students feedback reflected satisfaction with the new site:

> Q32: It's easy to study because all the homework is on the site with the teacher's remarks… I revised for chemistry more than I did for other subjects because I had all the materials, in each year.

> Q33: I can revise whatever I need to, even years back since everything is available on the course site in an organized way.

6 Discussion

Monitoring students' gains involved tracking the changes in their SRL abilities, scores, patterns of website use, homework submission rate and the content of the obligatory feedback questions. As this is a complicated task, we tried to pinpoint, break down, and analyze each of these influential factors, but after this – also generalize and portray a larger picture to shed light on the reasons for the overall changes.

In this chapter, we presented the main building blocks used to construct a novel blended learning environment for high-school students who wish to study chemistry. The construction of the COBLE relied on theories and constraints and continued to evolve over time. Changes are still being implemented, an easy task since the characteristics of a blended environment enable rapid changes (as opposed to parallel programs in print). This kind of blended environment is especially attentive to students' needs and feedback, highlighting a major advantage of online learning courses and in particular, blended learning environments.

We further detailed the changes that were made in numerous aspects. Looking back, we can say that attendance to students' needs was the guiding principle for all of the changes. We did not take into consideration other factors, such as teachers' needs or overload, cost of teaching personnel, etc. This is important, as many times, designers mean well and want to change the learning environment, but changes are not made due to very practical factors. If we need to stress one major factor in designing a virtual learning course, it is to allow time and resources for iterative changes that result from the implementation.

Some changes were made due to combination of theoretical aspects with practical incompatibilities. For example, we noticed that students did not participate enough during the synchronous lessons. According to the active and interactive learning theory, which was the study's framework, it is imperative to be an active learner because students actively learn by engaging and exploring the virtual environment (as opposed to passively viewing the content within). The theory states that new knowledge is actively constructed by students' experience, solving relevant problems and experimenting, rather than merely building upon previously acquired knowledge (Chi, 2009). Another example is the Self-Regulation-Learning theoretical framework (Pintrich & De Groot, 1990; Zimmerman, 1989, 1990, 2008; Zimmerman, Bonner & Kovach, 1996). which implies that time management and test preparation are dimensions that are crucial to students learning and achievement. In both examples – we re-designed the course components to address the challenges as detailed in the results (see Section 5).

However, most changes were made due to practical necessities. There were three leading forces for the changes:

- The teachers' observations: teachers observed the students' difficulties in time management, and in cases where students failed to cope or keep pace with the required level, personal tutoring was offered.
- Students' voice: the feedback questions, which became part of the course culture, as well as the interviews and many informal conversations between the teachers and the students, all became powerful tools in understanding the students' experience. A pertinent example is the students' need to have more interactivity and social relation with peers.
- The topic itself – chemistry: we needed to be attentive to the national curriculum and changes in it, and to the national matriculation exam, and

teach accordingly. In addition, we needed to pay a great deal of attention to the essence of chemistry as an experimental topic. Changes in the way students perform laboratory experiments and write reports were made to retain an authentic flavor of chemistry in our course.

Once more, the triangle: Teacher–Student–Curriculum is the driving force of changing learning and teaching in virtual courses.

According to Tallent-Runnels et al. (2006), virtual course design has a crucial role in students' success. Indeed, during the program, we noted improvements in all of the monitored dimensions of SRL: motivation, attitude and interest, use of support techniques and materials, help-seeking, time management, test strategies and preparation for tests. We also noticed that their laboratory skills and knowledge of chemistry improved, social ties and contact between the students and the teacher strengthened, and students felt free to ask more questions during the lessons and seek help when needed, resulting in diminished anxiety. Since some of the assignments were revised according to students' justified comments, and due to a deeper understanding of students' difficulties with the assignments, the site was reorganized, and students' orientation and navigation improved, as did the percentage of homework submission. We also noted that students who were more involved in the course were more likely to attain higher scores. This finding aligns with Bannert et al. (2014) who found that more regulation event types appear in successful students' behavior, such as preparing activities (orientation and planning) before they process the information to be learned, and deep elaboration of information while reading.

This chapter describes in detail, the design and re-design process during and after, the first iteration of the COBLE 3 year course.

The methodology as well as the specific course components may help other designers to better design a virtual course in general, and in science education in particular.

While we have a well-established course with growing numbers of participants and graduate students, we are well aware of the fact that more redevelopment and refinement of the COBLE will be required in the future, in order to keep addressing student's needs, and in order to preserve high retention numbers.

Acknowledgments

We would like to thank the Meital Fund for helping fund this research. We thank Matan Sinai and Hofit Kindil for their assistance in the design and research process.

References

Allen, E., & Seaman, J. (2014). *Grade change: Tracking online education in the United States*. Babson College Survey Research Group.

Artino, A. R. (2009). Think, feel, act: Motivational and emotional influences on military students' online academic success. *Journal of Computing in Higher Education, 21*, 146–166. http://dx.doi.org/10.1007/s12528-009-9020-9

Bannert, M., Reimann, P., & Sonnenberg, C. (2014). Process mining techniques for analysing patterns and strategies in students' self-regulated learning. *Metacognition and Learning, 9*, 161–185. http://dx.doi.org/10.1007/s11409-013-9107-6

Barbour, M., Brown, R., Waters, L. H., Hoey, R., Hunt, J. L., Kennedy, K., Ounsworth, C., Powell, A., & Trimm, T. (2011). *Online and blended learning: A survey of policy and practice from K-12 schools around the world*. International Association for K-12 Online Learning.

Berglas-Shapiro, T. (2015). *Learning and instruction of science contents and representational skills in a technology-enhanced environment designed to support Self-Regulated Learning (SRL) in junior high school* [Unpublished doctoral dissertation]. Weizmann Institute of Science.

Boekaerts, M., & Cascallar, E. (2006). How far have we moved toward the integration of theory and practice in self-regulation? *Educational Psychology Review, 18*, 199–210. http://dx.doi.org/10.1007/s10648-006-9013-4

Boelens, R., De Wever, B., & Voet, M. (2017). Four key challenges to the design of blended learning: A systematic literature review. *Educational Research Review, 22*, 1–18. http://dx.doi.org/10.1016/j.edurev.2017.06.001

Brown, A. L. (1992). Design experiments: Theoretical and methodological challenges in creating complex interventions. *Journal of Accounting Education of the Learning Sciences, 2*, 141–178. http://dx.doi.org/10.1207/s15327809jls0202_2

Chi, M. T. H. (1997). Quantifying qualitative analyses of verbal data: A practical guide. *Journal of the Learning Sciences, 6*, 271–315. http://dx.doi.org/10.1207/s15327809jls0603_1

Chi, M. T. H. (2009). Active-Constructive-Interactive: A conceptual framework for differentiating learning activities. *Topics in Cognitive Science, 1*, 73–105. http://dx.doi.org/10.1111/j.1756-8765.2008.01005.x

Cho, M.-H. (2004). *The effects of design strategies for promoting students' self-regulated learning skills on students' self-regulation and achievements in online learning environments*. Association for Educational Communications and Technology. https://files.eric.ed.gov/fulltext/ED485062.pdf

Christensen, C. M., Horn, M. B., & Staker, H. (2013). *Is K-12 blended learning disruptive? An introduction of the theory of hybrids*. The Christensen Institute. https://www.christenseninstitute.org/wp-content/uploads/2013/05/Is-K-12-Blended-Learning-Disruptive.pdf

Collins, A., Greeno, J., Resnick, L. B., Berliner, B., & Calfee, R. (1992). Cognition and learning. B. Berliner & R. Calfee (Eds.), *Handbook of educational psychology*. New York, NY: Simon & Shuster Macmillan.

Collins, A., Joseph, D., & Bielaczyc, K. (2004). Design research: Theoretical and methodological issues. *Journal of the Learning Sciences, 13*, 15–42. http://dx.doi.org/10.1207/s15327809jls1301_2

Collison, G., Elbaum, B., Haavind, S., & Tinker, R. (2000). *Facilitating online learning: Effective strategies for moderators*. Atwood Publishing.

DuBois, J. M., Dueker, M. J. M., Anderson, E. E., & Campbell, J. (2008). The development and assessment of an NIH-funded research ethics training program. *Academic Medicine: Journal of the Association of American Medical Colleges, 83*, 596–603. http://doi.org/10.1097/ACM.0b013e3181723095

Duit, R. (2007). Science education research internationally: Conceptions, research methods, domains of research. *Eurasia Journal of Mathematics, Science & Technology Education, 3*, 3–15. http://dx.doi.org/10.12973/ejmste/75369

Duit, R., Komorek, M., & Wilbers, J. (1997). Studies on educational reconstruction of chaos theory. *Research in Science Education, 27*, 339–357. http://dx.doi.org/10.1007/bf02461758

Edelson, D. C. (2002). Design research: What we learn when we engage in design. *Journal of the Learning Sciences, 11*, 105–121. http://dx.doi.org/10.1207/s15327809jls1101_4

Eidelman, R. R., Rosenberg, J. M., & Shwartz, Y. (2019). Assessing the interaction between Self-Regulated Learning (SRL) profiles and actual learning in the Chemistry Online Blended Learning Environment (COBLE). In D. G. Sampson, J. M. Spector, D. Ifenthaler, P. Isaías, & S. Sergis (Eds.), *Learning technologies for transforming large-scale teaching, learning, and assessment* (pp. 231–255). Springer. http://dx.doi.org/10.1007/978-3-030-15130-0_12

Elbaum, B., Mclntyre, C., & Smith, A. (2002). *Essential elements: Prepare, design, and teach your online course*. Atwood Publishing.

Horn, M. B., & Staker, H. (2011). *The rise of K-12 blended learning*. Innosight Institute. http://www.christenseninstitute.org/wp-content/uploads/2013/04/The-rise-of-K-12-blended-learning.pdf

Khalil, H., & Ebner, M. (2014). MOOCs completion rates and possible methods to improve retention – A literature review. *EdMedia: World Conference on Educational Multimedia, Hypermedia and Telecommunications, 1*, 1305–1313.

Ley, K., & Young, D. B. (2001). Instructional principles for self-regulation. *Educational Technology Research and Development, 49*(2), 93–103. http://dx.doi.org/10.1007/bf02504930

Li, Q. (2007). Student and teacher views about technology: A tale of two cities? *Journal of Research on Technology in Education, 39*, 377–397. http://dx.doi.org/10.1080/15391523.2007.10782488

Lynch, R., & Dembo, M. (2004). The relationship between self-regulation and online learning in a blended learning context. *The International Review of Research in Open and Distance Learning, 5*. https://doi.org/10.19173/irrodl.v5i2.189

McManus, T. F. (2000). Individualizing instruction in a Web-based hypermedia learning environment: Nonlinearity, advance organizers, and self-regulated learners. *Journal of Interactive Learning Research, 11*, 219–251.

McNaught, C., Phillips, R., Rossiter, D., & Winn, J. (2000). *Developing a framework for a useable and useful inventory of computer-facilitated learning and support materials in Australian universities*. AusInfo.

Ministry of Education. (2014). *21st century skills*. Israel Ministry of Education (in Hebrew).

O'Neill, K., Singh, G., & O'Donoghue, J. (2004). Implementing e-learning programmes for higher education: A review of the literature. *Journal of Information Technology Education, 3*, 313–323. http://dx.doi.org/10.28945/304

Oxford Group. (2013). *Blended learning – Current use, challenges and best practices*. http://www.kineo.com/m/0/blended-learning-report-202013.pdf

Palloff, R., & Pratt, K. (2001). *Lessons from the cyberspace classroom*. Jossey-Bass Publishers. http://dx.doi.org/10.1145/566891.566895

Peterson, R., & Herrington, J. (2005). The state of the art of design-based research. In *World Conference on E-Learning in Corporate, Government, Healthcare, and Higher Education (ELEARN)*, 24–28 October 2005, Vancouver, Canada.

Picciano, A. G. (2014). *A critical reflection of the current research in online and blended learning*. http://hdl.voced.edu.au/10707/388237

Piccoli, G., Ahmad, R., & Ives, B. (2001). Web-based virtual learning environments: A research framework and a preliminary assessment of effectiveness in basic IT skills training. *Management Information Systems Quarterly, 25*, 401–426. http://dx.doi.org/10.2307/3250989

Pintrich, P. R., & De Groot, E. V. (1990). Motivational and self-regulated learning components of classroom academic performance. *Journal of Educational Psychology, 82*, 33–40. http://dx.doi.org/10.1037/0022-0663.82.1.33

Puntambekar, S. (2009). *Key features of scaffolding*. The Gale Group, Inc. http://www.education.com/reference/article/scaffolding; http://tct-test-referencematerials.yolasite.com/resources/Scaffolding%20_%20Education.com.pdf

Reiser, R. A. (2001). A history of instructional design and technology. Part II: A history of instructional design. *Educational Technology Research and Development, 49*(2), 57–67. http://dx.doi.org/10.1007/bf02504928

Rogoff, B. (1990). *Apprenticeship in thinking: Cognitive development in sociocultural activity*. Oxford University Press. http://dx.doi.org/10.1126/science.249.4969.684

Sharaabi-Naor, Y., Kesner, M., & Shwartz, Y. (2014). Enhancing students' motivation to learn chemistry. *Sisyphus – Journal of Education, 2*(2), 100–123.

Shkedi, A. (2003). *Words of meaning – qualitative research – theory and practice.* Ramot.

Sturgill, A., Martin, W., & Gay, G. (1999). Surviving technology: A study of student use of computer-mediated communication to support technology education. *International Journal of Educational Telecommunications, 5*, 239–259.

Tallent-Runnels, M. K., Thomas, J. A., Lan, W. Y., & Cooper, S. (2006). Teaching courses online: A review of the research. *Review of Educational Research, 76*, 93–135. http://dx.doi.org/10.3102/00346543076001093

Tao, Y. H. (2008). Typology of college student perception on institutional e-learning issues – An extension study of a teacher's typology in Taiwan. *Computers & Education, 50*, 1495–1508. http://dx.doi.org/10.1016/j.compedu.2007.02.002

Tsai, C.-W. (2011). Achieving effective learning effects in the blended course: A combined approach of online self-regulated learning and collaborative learning with initiation. *Cyberpsychology, Behavior, and Social Networking, 14*, 505–510. http://dx.doi.org/10.1089/cyber.2010.0388

Van Laer, S., & Elen, J. (2017). In search of attributes that support self-regulation in blended learning environments. *Education and Information Technologies, 22*, 1395–1454. http://dx.doi.org/10.1007/s10639-016-9505-x

Wang, F., & Hannafin, M. J. (2005). Design-based research and technology-enhanced learning environments. *Educational Technology Research and Development, 53*(4), 5–23. http://dx.doi.org/10.1007/bf02504682

Weinstein, C. E., Palmer, D. R., & Shulte, A. C. (2002). *LASSI: Learning and study strategies inventory* (2nd ed.). H&H Publishing Company, Inc.

Wood, D., Bruner, J. S., & Ross, G. (1976). The role of tutoring in problem solving. *Journal of Child Psychology and Psychiatry, 17*, 89–100. http://dx.doi.org/10.1111/j.1469-7610.1976.tb00381.x

Yang, D., Sinha, T., Adamson, D., & Rosé, C. P. (2013). Turn on, tune in, drop out: Anticipating student dropouts in massive open online courses [Paper presentation]. In *Proceedings of the 2013 NIPS Data-Driven Education Workshop*, Vol. 11 (p. 14).

Zemsky, R., & Massy, W. F. (2004). *Thwarted innovation. What happened to e-learning and why?* Learning Alliance for Higher Education.

Zimmerman, B. J. (1989). A social cognitive view of self-regulated academic learning. *Journal of Educational Psychology 81*, 329–339. http://dx.doi.org/10.1037/0022-0663.81.3.329

Zimmerman, B. J. (1990). Self-regulated learning and academic achievement: An overview. *Educational Psychologist, 25*, 3–17. http://dx.doi.org/10.1207/s15326985ep2501_2

Zimmerman, B. J. (2008). Investigating self-regulation and motivation: Historical background, methodological developments, and future prospects. *American Educational Research Journal, 45*, 166–183. http://dx.doi.org/10.3102/0002831207312909

Zimmerman, B. J., Bonner, S., & Kovach, R. (1996). *Developing self-regulated learners: Beyond achievement to self-efficacy*. APA Books. http://dx.doi.org/10.1037/10213-000

Appendix 1: Examples of students quotes revealing a need for a design change

Category	Students' feedback
Difficulties in conducting home inquiry laboratories	Q10: I do the home labs and find it quite difficult to give in the lab reports since we live in different places. I have not done all my lab work
Need for face-to-face contact	Q13: It is difficult to concentrate for two hours in front of the computer. I find that it's easier for me to concentrate in a face-to-face class.
Need for personalized learning	Q16: I thought it would be easy to catch up with what I missed in a week. It did not work out. If you skip classes in a virtual setting, the consequences are graver than in a face-to-face setting.
Maintaining a high interest level	Q19: I was not interested enough in the content, therefore I decided to drop out.
Students; difficulties in time management	Q23: If I miss lessons, I usually watch the lesson recording and the presentations to close the gaps… I had to learn everything on my own because the lesson times did not suit me.
interactivity of synchronous lessons	Q26: In the virtual classroom, you can choose if you want to participate in the lesson. There is no eye contact.
Preparation for tests	Q30: I usually study alone but at the high school, I sometimes like to join a study group.

Appendix 2: Examples of students quotes responding to a feature in the course

Category	Students' feedback
Difficulties in conducting home inquiry laboratories	Q 11: I also do the home labs. I like them. They are cool. The days at the Weizmann were fun, I met new people, the lectures were interesting and so were the labs. Q15: I liked the days at the Weizmann Institute.

Category	Students' feedback
Need for face-to-face contact	Q14: If I do not understand something, I send a WhatsApp text message to the teacher, tutor or the class WhatsApp group
Need for personalized learning	Q17: The tutoring sessions helped me a lot. I do not think I would have stayed in the program without them.
Maintaining a high interest level	Q20: The teacher teaches in an interesting way and links the material to daily life. It makes me want to listen. Q21: If the virtual lesson is taught in an interesting way, it contributes to my concentration level.
Students 'difficulties in time management	Q24: The option to get help from a tutor is great. It helps me prepare before the exams. The tutor sessions help especially if you miss a lesson. Q25: It's easier to study and understand with videos and presentations… It's easier to complete the missing materials in chemistry than in any other subject I learn in high school.
interactivity of synchronous lessons	Q27: It keeps you on your toes to have to vote during the lesson whenever the teacher gives us a poll question. It makes you keeps us alert. Q28: I understand the homework assignments better after the lesson. I usually wait for the teacher to add explanations or for the other students to receive answers to their questions. Q29: I ask questions in the synchronous lesson chat area during the lesson if I do not understand. I also send emails or text messages.
Preparation for tests	Q31: I answer self-tests after the relevant lesson.

CHAPTER 4

Teaching and Learning Biology Using Authentic Tools and Databases

The Interaction between Scientific Knowledge Elements

Anat Yarden and Ohad Levkovich

Abstract

The strategic vision proposal for the Programme for International Student Assessment in science for the year 2024, as well as of the Framework for K–12 Science Education and the Next Generation Science Standards in the United States, includes the vision that "every young person should be digitally and data literate." Thus, engaging in the practice of analyzing and interpreting data is regarded as an essential experience in the teaching and learning of science. For the last two decades, we have been promoting the idea of using authentic databases for the teaching and learning of biology in high school. The use of such databases requires various proficiencies, including the use of computational tools and databases integrated with biological knowledge. Throughout the research, development and implementation that accompanied the promotion of this idea, we have continuously used various frameworks suggested for the examination of knowledge elements that are involved in the teaching and learning of science. In this chapter, we discuss these various theoretical frameworks of scientific knowledge elements and how they have influenced our research and development efforts to promote the teaching and learning of biology using authentic tools and databases.

Keywords

biology education – biotechnology education – bioinformatics education – high school – authentic tools – authentic databases – knowledge elements – problem solving

1 Introduction

The Organisation for Economic Co-operation and Development's recently published strategic vision proposal for the Programme for International Student Assessment (PISA) in science for the year 2024 states that "every young

 | DOI: 10.1163/9789004503625_004

person should be digitally and data literate at age 15. This includes being familiar with different models for the representation of data, basic computational models and algorithms, as well as any additional areas of procedural knowledge resulting from 'dry lab experiments' (involving large data sets and information structures). Moreover, being digitally and data literate would enable young people to understand AI (Artificial Intelligence) concepts and computational systems at a basic level in order to make important decisions about how to act on information presented to them" (OECD, 2020). This vision is in line with the Framework for K–12 Science Education and the Next Generation Science Standards in the United States (National Research Council, 2012; NGSS Lead States, 2013), which asserts that "analyzing and interpreting data" is one of the core practices required for learning science. According to these documents, the practice of "analyzing and interpreting data" includes the idea that "scientists use a range of tools – including tabulation, graphical interpretation, visualization, and statistical analysis – to identify the significant features and patterns in the data." Moreover, since modern technology has simplified the collection of large datasets, it provides K–12 students with many secondary sources for data analysis (National Research Council, 2012).

Two decades ago, even before the human genome project had been completed, we began to promote the vision of using authentic genomic databases for the teaching and learning of biology in high school (Gelbart & Yarden, 2001). Subsequently, we and others developed learning and teaching materials based on authentic bioinformatics tools and databases (e.g., Gallagher et al., 2011; Levkovich & Yarden, 2017; Lewitter & Bourne, 2011; Machluf et al., 2011). These authentic genomic databases served as the aforementioned secondary sources of data. The use of such databases requires various proficiencies, including the use of computational tools and databases integrated with biological knowledge.

During the research, development and implementation processes accompanying the promotion of this vision, we have been continuously influenced by the seminal review of Alexander and Judy (1988) on the interaction of domain-specific and strategic knowledge in academic performance, as well as by the influential framework suggested by Schoenfeld (1985) for the analysis of mathematical behavior during problem solving. We have also used various other frameworks suggested for the examination of knowledge elements that are involved in the teaching and learning of science (e.g., de Jong & Ferguson-Hessler, 1996; Gott & Roberts, 2008; Shavelson et al., 2005). In this chapter, we discuss these various theoretical frameworks of scientific knowledge elements and how they have influenced our research and development efforts to promote the teaching and learning of biology using authentic tools and databases.

2 Coordination between Knowledge Elements Supports Learning of High-School Genetics

At the turn of this century, we harnessed the genomics research frontier, tools and databases and developed a web-based research simulation that enables high-school biology majors to take part in authentic research in genetics (~6 hours out of the 30 hours devoted to learning genetics in the syllabus, 11th–12th grade, Gelbart & Yarden, 2001, table 1). In the research simulation, the students are introduced to the basic heuristic strategy of correlating the mutated and normal versions of genes with the phenotypes of affected and healthy individuals, respectively. The comparison is carried out at the phenotypic level, using a classical genetics approach, and at the molecular level using laboratory-based molecular biology methods and computer-based bioinformatics tools, similar to the way in which geneticists practice genetics research today. This research simulation resembles the conductance of science per se, and in this sense, we consider it authentic. It includes two bioinformatics tools (*blast* and *blast-2-sequences*), which were downloaded along with the relevant nucleic acid sequences and operate as "stand-alone" software, enabling the simulation to run independently of the scientific tools and databases that are freely accessible on the web.

Chinn and Malhotra (2002) previously differentiated between authentic experiments conducted by scientists, which have numerous intervening events, and simple experiments carried out in schools. The greater complexity of authentic scientific research requires continuous coordination between various stages of the scientific experiment, as well as between different knowledge elements (e.g., declarative, strategic; Falk & Yarden, 2009). Such coordination is not typical of regular school tasks and rarely appears in most learning materials used in schools (Chinn & Malhotra, 2002). Moreover, most school science relates to *what* a phenomenon is, while often ignoring *how* it relates to other phenomena, *why* it is important, and especially *how* this phenomenon evolved (Driver et al., 2000).

Alexander and Judy (1988) previously defined domain-specific knowledge as the declarative, procedural, or conditional knowledge one possesses in a particular field of study. By declarative knowledge, they refer to factual information (*knowing what*), whereas procedural knowledge (or strategies) is the compilation of declarative knowledge into functional units that incorporate domain-specific strategies (*knowing how*), while conditional knowledge entails the understanding of *when* and *where* to access certain facts or employ particular procedures. We adopted this theoretical framework to study the teaching and learning processes that took place while engaging with the web-based research simulation (Gelbart & Yarden, 2001) in high-school biology lessons (Gelbart et al., 2009; Gelbart & Yarden, 2006, 2011). Accordingly, we adopted the view that to engage learners in authentic research practices, they need to use their declarative knowledge (e.g., prior knowledge gained in the course of learning genetics), acquire the procedural knowledge (e.g., use of the bioinformatics tools and the heuristic strategy used by geneticists to compare between phenotypes at various organizational levels), and acquire the conditional knowledge that is required to carry out authentic research (e.g., coordinate the declarative knowledge in genetics with the procedural knowledge to reveal gene function). Since it was unlikely that high-school students would be able to carry out such a coordination without guidance from their teacher, we examined what kind of support the teacher provides during enactment of the research simulation, and how it facilitates students' ability to coordinate between declarative and strategic knowledge.

Analysis of the planning discussions enacted by a high-school biology teacher in her class enabled us to show how she facilitated students' coordination between the heuristic strategy in genetics and the use of the bioinformatics tools that appear in the research simulation. These discussions also facilitated coordination between strategic knowledge and declarative knowledge in genetics in choosing the appropriate tools to carry out the research. In this way, the teacher promoted students' use of conditional knowledge, similar to the use of such knowledge by scientists in the course of performing authentic research. This enabled the teacher to engage high-school biology students in the scientific 'culture' of acquiring new knowledge (Gelbart & Yarden, 2011). Moreover, in this teacher's class, the students coordinated different research steps in the framework of the research design, similar to research-oriented learners, and in contrast to task-oriented learners, who are not constantly involved in the research steps and perceive the research simulation as a set of simple procedural tasks (Gelbart et al., 2009). The research-oriented learners, who consistently recognized the various research practices, used conditional knowledge more often than the task-oriented learners. This suggested that the teacher's support of the use of conditional knowledge enabled her to dictate a research-oriented approach, which may have enabled the learners to be mindful of the actual research instead of focusing on 'doing' and 'performing' the task (namely to using procedural knowledge, Gelbart & Yarden, 2011). The enactment of authentic research simulations in class, along with guidance in the coordination of procedural with declarative knowledge, is especially important for students with a task-oriented approach to learning science. Such students may be encouraged by their teachers to cope with the scientists' steps in the context of the research while participating in the class discourse (Gelbart & Yarden, 2011).

These findings led us to further attempts to promote high-school teachers' awareness of the importance of including various teaching strategies (e.g., discussions, dialogues) that can support acquisition of conditional knowledge, and highlighting learning situations that allow open discussions in high-school biology lessons. Accordingly, we brought the various knowledge elements identified by Alexander and Judy (1988) to the attention of teachers in our various teacher development programs, while making their use explicit in the context of the specific research simulation, as well as in the context of other teaching and learning materials that we developed (see below).

3 Use of Declarative and Strategic Knowledge for Problem Solving in Biotechnology Is Challenging

We subsequently developed a web-based learning environment aimed at introducing bioinformatics into the high-school biotechnology majors' curriculum (60 hours, 12th grade, Machluf et al., 2011, Table 4.1). In the learning environment, students are engaged in scientifically authentic inquiry-based activities in biotechnology, approaching real-world problems using diverse bioinformatics tools and databases, while acquiring and applying modern scientific practices. The bioinformatics tools (*Entrez, Blast-N, Blast-P, ClustalW, Open Reading Frame* (ORF) *Finder, Primer3Plus, Prosite* and *Jmol*) and databases used in this learning environment are freely available on the web and are extensively used by scientists, i.e., they are authentic.

The five teaching and learning activities in the learning environment were developed based on primary research articles, which were tailored and adapted to high-school biotechnology majors' knowledge and cognitive abilities. The topics of these activities focus on authentic investigations that are aimed at improving man's life quality and expectancy. In three of these activities, termed 'in-depth activities,' the students become familiar with using the bioinformatics tools and databases for the first time, and therefore emphasis is placed on promoting understanding via explicit guidance of the procedures required to use the tools and databases through each step of the inquiry process. This guidance includes detailing the considerations for selecting certain bioinformatics tools, and their potential contribution to the inquiry process involved in solving the problem that is presented to the students in each specific 'in-depth' activity, thus providing scaffolds for using the authentic tools and databases. The remaining two activities, termed 'integrated activities,' are based on the learners' previous procedural knowledge and experience with the tools and databases in the 'in-depth' activities. Therefore, the scaffolds are absent, allowing the students to choose and use the tools and databases that are suitable for solving the presented biotechnological problems, thereby mimicking authentic scientific inquiry (Machluf & Yarden, 2013). Throughout the learning process, the students coordinate between different knowledge elements, recall prior content knowledge, apply technical skills in using bioinformatics tools, reason scientifically, make decisions following a strategic plan, and evaluate and justify the scientific process and its steps. Taken together, the bioinformatics learning environment enables high-school students to acquire bioinformatics-specific knowledge and skills, as well as the required research practices to coordinate between them.

Wefer and Anderson (2008) reported that high-school students who integrate factual information and higher order knowledge with procedural and analytical skills perform better in bioinformatics tasks than those who have fundamental deficiencies in factual recall, or are less adept at integrating higher-order skills with specific facts and procedural skills. Other studies, including ours, which examined high-school students' performance in tasks that involve the use of computational skills along with biological content knowledge, pointed to the importance of the learners' ability to integrate factual and procedural knowledge (e.g., Buttigieg, 2010; Gallagher et al., 2011; Gelbart & Yarden, 2011). Moreover, learning bioinformatics was shown to complement and enhance understanding of biological content, such as genetics (Gelbart et al., 2009; Holtzclaw et al., 2006).

In the above studies, we noted that different theoretical perspectives and terminologies relating to knowledge and skills were used to support the overall agreed-upon conclusion that integration of different knowledge elements is required for better performance and understanding. Our previous studies were based on Alexander and Judy's (1988) classification of domain-specific knowledge into declarative (or factual information), procedural (or domain-specific strategies) and conditional knowledge (Gelbart & Yarden, 2011), whereas Wefer and Anderson (2008) referred to 'higher order knowledge,' 'specific knowledge and facts,' 'procedural knowledge' and 'analytical thinking skills.' We looked for a more detailed theoretical framework that might better serve the analysis of the knowledge elements required for learning in the bioinformatics learning environment.

We delved further into the knowledge elements that are required for learning using bioinformatics tools and databases using the classification suggested by de Jong and Ferguson-Hessler (1996) for problem solving in physics. Their classification distinguishes four knowledge elements: conceptual, procedural, strategic, and situational (see Table 4.1). Conceptual and procedural knowledge are in line with the 'knowing what' and 'knowing how,' respectively, previously

TABLE 4.1 The various knowledge elements and the theoretical frameworks used for the analyses of learning and teaching using authentic bioinformatics databases and tools in two different learning environments

	Gelbart and Yarden (2011), following Alexander and Judy (1988)	**Machluf and Yarden (2013), following de Jong and Ferguson-Hessler (1996)**	**Levkovich and Yarden (2021), following Osborne (2014), OECD (2012)**
The research context	*Bioinformatics – Deciphering the Secrets of the Genome* http://stwww.weizmann.ac.il/bioinformatics	*Bioinformatics in the service of biotechnology* https://stwww1.weizmann.ac.il/bioinfo/	Two Jmol tasks from *Bioinformatics in the service of biotechnology* https://stwww1.weizmann.ac.il/bioinfo/
The research population	High-school biology majors, 11th–12th grades	High-school biotechnology majors, 10th–12th grades	High-school biotechnology majors, 10th–12th grades
Knowing what	Declarative knowledge (factual information) – prior knowledge in genetics	Conceptual knowledge (declarative knowledge) – scientific facts, concepts, theories used for problem solving in biotechnology, including prior knowledge in biology	Content knowledge (knowledge of the content of science) – scientific facts, concepts, theories
Knowing how	Procedural knowledge (or strategies) – bioinformatics tools, heuristic strategy	Procedural knowledge – bioinformatics tools and techniques	Procedural knowledge (concepts of evidence) – the procedures used by scientists to establish scientific knowledge
Knowing why	–	–	Epistemic knowledge – the role of specific constructs and features essential to the process of knowledge building in science, and in justifying the knowledge produced by science
Knowing when & where	Conditional knowledge – coordination between declarative and procedural knowledge to reveal gene function	Strategic knowledge – use of heuristics and designing a strategy Situational knowledge – creating a representation of the problem from which additional knowledge (conceptual, procedural) can be invoked	–

identified by Alexander and Judy (1988) and used in our previous studies. However, as de Jong and Ferguson-Hessler (1996) focused on the knowledge elements that are required for problem solving, they highlighted two additional knowledge elements, namely strategic and situational. They defined strategic knowledge as the type of knowledge that helps students organize their problem-solving process by directing which stages they should go through to reach a solution, or knowing the conditions of 'when and where' the knowledge would be applicable. Situational knowledge was suggested to be knowledge about situations as they typically appear in a particular domain, thus serving the learners in creating a representation of the problem from which additional knowledge (e.g., conceptual, procedural) can be invoked (de Jong & Ferguson-Hessler, 1996). We classified the strategic and situational knowledge elements as 'when and where'-type knowledge (Table 4.1), even though we were puzzled by the classification of strategic knowledge into conditional ('when and where'-type) knowledge, whereas Alexander and Judy (1988) included strategic knowledge under procedural knowledge. It seems that indeed, the classification into procedural and conditional (including strategic and situational) knowledge is still open for investigation, and that it might be related to the context of the research.

We examined this classification further, and in particular, whether it might be helpful in our analyses of both the questions included in the learning environment and high-school students' answers to those questions (Machluf et al., 2017; Machluf & Yarden, 2013). The analysis of the cognitive outcomes of high-school biotechnology majors who learned using the bioinformatics learning environment is described briefly in the following to exemplify the use of the de Jong and Ferguson-Hessler (1996) classification and determine whether it can better serve our analysis by allowing a more detailed examination of conditional knowledge.

The analysis was driven by the following research question: whether and to what extent do the bioinformatics activities that are included in the learning environment promote knowledge acquisition and appropriation of the bioinformatics approach? Students' (11th grade, N = 44) answers to questions (N = 63) embedded in two 'integrated activities' from the learning environment were analyzed. High achievement was observed among students' answers to questions that required the use of procedural or situational knowledge, whereas answering questions that required the use of declarative or strategic knowledge was significantly more challenging, as evidenced by lower average student achievement (Machluf et al., 2017). These findings should be discussed in light of the characterization of the questions that are embedded in these two activities from the learning environment, because more than 60% of the questions were multiple choice (Machluf & Yarden, 2013). Providing answers to most of these multiple-choice questions seemed to require the use of procedural knowledge, which stems mainly from the bioinformatics field. In contrast, more than 30% of these questions were open-ended, and providing answers to most of these questions required the use of declarative knowledge, which stems mainly from students prior knowledge in biology. All of the questions that required the use of strategic knowledge were previously reported as open-ended and these were the most challenging questions of all to answer. Taken together, we realized that questions that require the use of declarative or strategic knowledge are more challenging to deal with than those requiring the use of either procedural or situational knowledge, almost totally irrespective of the scientific field they addressed (Machluf et al., 2017).

As noted above, the ability to coordinate between various knowledge elements is at the heart of performing authentic scientific research. It was therefore puzzling to find out that students do not master the use of the knowledge elements that are required for problem solving while learning through the bioinformatics learning environment. We noticed that many of the teachers devoted their effort to teaching the procedural aspects of using the bioinformatics tools and databases, which were new and more challenging to them, and less time to connecting it to the students' prior biological knowledge and to integrating the bioinformatics tools and databases as part of a strategic plan of biological research. We also noticed that referring to the entire 'tool box,' which includes eight different bioinformatics tools in the case of the bioinformatics learning environment used as the basis for these studies, may not have allowed us to explicitly analyze the knowledge elements required for solving specific problems, as those tools are diverse and may require the use of different knowledge elements. We therefore continued by delving into the knowledge elements involved in solving problems using one of these bioinformatics tools: the molecular viewer Jmol.

4 Learning about Protein Structure and Function Using a Molecular Viewer

The molecular viewer Jmol is one of the tools included in the tool box of the learning environment in bioinformatics described above (Machluf et al., 2011). Jmol[1] is an open-source Java viewer for chemical structures in 3D, which was designed for the visualization of macromolecules. Visualizing these macromolecules requires retrieving structure files from the Research Collaboratory for Structural Bioinformatics Protein Data Bank (RCSB PDB) before visualizing them using Jmol. The learning environment includes two in-depth tasks that incorporate Jmol. In one, the students study the structure and function of the enzyme isopenicillin N synthase (IPNS), and in the second, they study the structure and function of the antifreeze protein (AFP). The tasks include numerous representations of the protein molecules (e.g., figures, screenshots, tables). These representations appear in questions, informative segments, and question feedback, and are designed to support the process of learning about the relationship between protein structure and function.

The cognitive skills required for learning and understanding proteins using visual representations of molecular models at the tertiary education level have been previously identified (e.g., Schönborn & Anderson, 2010). Since high-school students have relatively limited prior knowledge about proteins, and since they are less familiar with using visual representations of molecules, we examined what cognitive skills are involved in developing an understanding of protein structure and function while learning using the Jmol tasks from the bioinformatics learning environment mentioned above, which is aimed for high-school biotechnology majors.

Schönborn and Anderson (2010) identified the following cognitive skills for learning using molecular models: (a) *decode* the symbolic language composing the molecular model; (b) *evaluate* the power, limitations and quality of the molecular model; (c) *interpret* and use the molecular model to solve a problem; (d) *spatially manipulate* the molecular model to interpret and explain a concept; (e) *construct* the molecular model to explain a concept or solve a problem; (f) *translate horizontally* across the various molecular models; (g) *translate vertically* between the various molecular models that depict various levels of organization and complexity; and (h) *visualize relative size*, orders of magnitude and scale.

To better understand the actual use of these cognitive skills and their relationship to the knowledge elements required for problem solving using Jmol, we mapped them according to the three knowledge elements identified by the PISA 2015 framework (OECD, 2012; Osborne, 2014): content, procedural and epistemic (Table 4.2). We thought that since the PISA framework is aimed at 15-year-old secondary-school students, it would be highly suitable for the analysis we were performing in our studies carried out in the context of secondary schools. The mapping was done theoretically, as well as while using the questions embedded in the two Jmol tasks from the learning environment in bioinformatics. Herein we present the theoretical mapping, while the analysis of the questions is presented elsewhere (Levkovich & Yarden, 2021).

We carefully examined the eight cognitive skills suggested by Schönborn and Anderson (2010) in light of the classification of the PISA 2015 framework

(OECD, 2012). We noticed that one of these skills can be regarded as epistemic knowledge, namely 'evaluate.' This cognitive skill included students' ability to evaluate the representational power, limitations and overall quality of the molecular model presented to them (Schönborn & Anderson, 2010). Our analysis of the high-school students' discourse while learning using the two Jmol tasks revealed that epistemic knowledge also includes understanding that (a) the molecular model is just a model and not the actual molecule, (b) molecular models emerge from data obtained from scientific experiments, and (c) different displays present different characteristics of the molecules (Levkovich, 2019). We subsequently classified the other seven skills to procedural knowledge. However, we noticed that these seven skills are actually composed of two different kinds of procedural knowledge: (a) visualization of molecular models, namely, the action of observing and understanding the molecular model; and (b) using Jmol software features, namely, the action of turning the molecular model, zooming in and out of the molecular model and copying it, or a more complicated action such as navigating pop-up menus or scripting in a console window. We termed the first type of procedural knowledge – the visualization of molecular models – P1; and the second type of procedural knowledge – the use of Jmol software features – P2 (Table 4.2). This division of the procedural knowledge was determined by the type of action performed by the students while using the Jmol software (Levkovich & Yarden, 2021).

To examine the students' outcomes while learning through the Jmol tasks in the learning environment, knowledge questionnaires were used (N = 70 biotechnology majors). It was found that the use of tasks and Jmol significantly improved the high-school students' understanding of proteins, i.e., students

TABLE 4.2 Combing two theoretical frameworks to represent the knowledge required to learn using Jmol

OECD (2018)	Content knowledge	Procedural knowledge		Epistemic knowledge
Schönborn & Anderson (2010)	Conceptual understanding of structure, function, and process	Decode Interpret Translate horizontally Translate vertically Visualize relative size	Spatially manipulate Construct	Evaluate
Levkovich & Yarden (2021)	C: Structure and function of proteins	P1: Visualizing molecular models	P2: Use of software or applet	E: Evaluating molecular models

acquired content knowledge and procedural knowledge while using the Jmol software and the accompanying tasks. However, in view of the students' performance, the improvement in knowledge is still only relative, and it cannot be concluded that their level of knowledge about proteins is high (Levkovich, 2019).

To characterize the students' acquisition of scientific knowledge more deeply, data were collected from observations and interviews and analyzed qualitatively. In this part of the study, four female students participated in two pairs and served as case studies. The four students were chosen to participate in this study since they were recommended by their teachers due to their high verbal capabilities and they served as a convenience sample. For the most part, the two pairs of students who participated in this part of the study, which focused on the structure and function of IPNS and AFP, showed extensive knowledge of the procedural knowledge component P1 and presented efficient use of the procedural knowledge P2. However, the qualitative analysis of their performance revealed two situations that presented a challenge in acquiring knowledge among the students from both pairs: (i) the acquisition of scientific knowledge that includes only some of the components of knowledge required to give a complete answer to a question; (ii) the use of incorrect scientific knowledge in one of the components of scientific knowledge in response to a question. It follows from this that although learning through Jmol tasks can provide an opportunity to acquire authentic scientific knowledge about proteins, the discourse reveals complexity in students' learning processes, and the acquisition and development of students' conceptual scientific knowledge about proteins does not necessarily occur fully during the task response (Levkovich, 2019).

We provide one example from this qualitative analysis that highlights the complexity of using the epistemic knowledge element 'evaluate.' In this example, one pair of students (Shelly and Betty, pseudonyms) attempt to solve one of the questions. The students are learning in class, sitting in pairs in front of a computer. Their conversation is audio-recorded and their computer screen is video-recorded, but their faces and identity are invisible. The pair of students attempt to solve one of the questions from the IPNS task of the bioinformatics learning environment (see question in Figure 4.1). In this question, students are asked to demonstrate their ability to use epistemic knowledge: specifically, they must understand that different representations can present different characteristics of the same molecule, and that the molecular model is not the actual protein molecule, to answer the question correctly. In addition, they need to use their prior content knowledge about protein tertiary structure, procedural knowledge P1, and specifically decode the information they

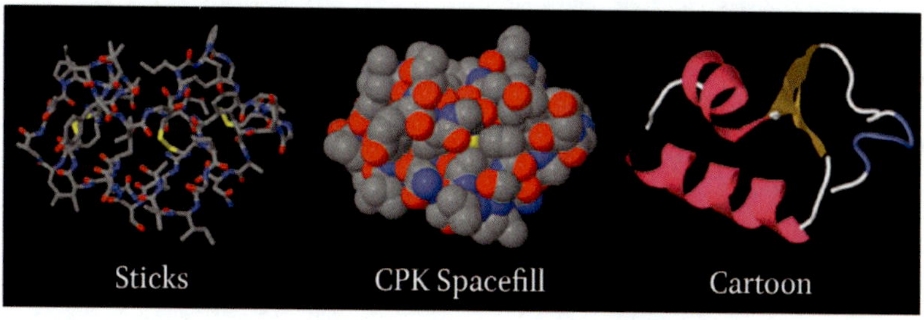

FIGURE 4.1 Display of molecular models in Jmol for students answering the following question that appears in the IPNS task: "Before you are three different display options of the same protein. Which of these options displays the protein structure as it is in reality?"

observe from the protein images and translate horizontally, as all three images represent different characteristics of the same molecule. Procedural knowledge P2 is not used while answering this question, since the presentation does not require any spatial manipulation or construction. When the two students were looking at the display that is shown in Figure 4.1, the following discourse took place:

Betty: In reality, it is the CPK space fill, right? No… Have a look for a second. What do you think it actually looks like? It is… Right? Right?
Shelly: Yes
Betty: Why?
Shelly: Since it shows us the volume of the atoms, right?
Betty (writing): The central display shows the protein as it actually appears in reality because it shows the entire volume of the protein?
Shelly: The volume of the atoms, the volume of the protein?
Betty: Where?
Shelly: I don't know. They say something like that.
Betty: Protein, OK.

From this conversation between the two students, it is not completely clear what led them to think that the CPK (Corey, Pauling, Koltun [the inventors of the color coding]) space-filling model is what the protein molecule actually looks like, but subsequent interviews with the two students revealed differences in the way each of them understood the nature of models. Shelly was not sure if the cartoon display or the CPK model shows what the protein molecule actually looks like. In her individual interview, she said: "I am not saying that it [the protein] looks like this. I just don't know what to choose. I am one of those who don't choose [laughing]. It seems like atomic volume to me but I don't know." In contrast, Betty stayed with the CPK space-filling model. In her individual interview, she said that in the other two presentations, the atoms do not look like balls and therefore they are not suitable. The interviews with the two students showed that both held erroneous epistemic knowledge, which was different from the authentic scientific way of looking into molecular models. However, their determination to choose one of the displays may have stemmed from their familiarity with school tasks and their wording: if they are asked "Which of these options displays the protein structure as it is in reality?" they understand this to mean that one of the displays should be correct. A negative answer, i.e., that none is correct, has to be wrong. In addition, the students' difficulties in understanding the nature of molecular models may have stemmed from the fact that they had never seen molecules with their own eyes and therefore, their ability to imagine the way they might actually look in reality is limited. Moreover, secondary-school students are well-known to have difficulty grasping the various biological levels of organization, and especially the micro level (e.g., Marbach-Ad & Stavy, 2000), and this may also have played a role in the students' difficulties in answering this question. The possible clash between understanding the nature of the term 'model' and the fact that representations of objects at the macro level (e.g., ecological models) and at the micro level (e.g., cells, molecules) are both models is not so easy to comprehend. In addition, school students are often required to build models, but projecting from these models to reality is not a simple task. Indeed, science teachers and students do not hold coherent epistemological views regarding models (Grosslight et al., 1991; Treagust et al., 2002).

5 Concluding Remarks and Discussion

It has been argued that relying on any of the knowledge elements presented above in isolation "misses the point" (Driver et al., 2000). Indeed, in our recent study, we realized that there is a hierarchy in their actual use. This hierarchy does not show the significance or complexity of one knowledge element relative to another, but it does show the inevitable requirement to use a specific knowledge element together with the others. Specifically, content knowledge is a basic requirement and without it, other knowledge elements cannot be used. This is the only knowledge element that can be used in isolation, and use of the procedural knowledge element P1 is not possible without content knowledge. Moreover, use of procedural knowledge P2, or epistemic knowledge, is not possible without content knowledge and procedural knowledge P1 (Levkovich & Yarden, 2021).

Thus, it appears that content knowledge is the only knowledge element that can be used alone while answering certain questions that appear in the bioinformatics learning environment described above. Answering questions that involve either procedural knowledge, P1 and P2, or epistemic knowledge is completely dependent on mastering the relevant content knowledge. Interestingly, learning solely scientific content knowledge is the actual common practice in the learning and teaching of science, which is often studied as a collection of facts. This commonly practiced mode of learning is in complete contrast to the way science is practiced by the academic community (Driver et al., 2000). Thus, use of the other knowledge elements discussed here is essential for meeting the challenge of change that appears in numerous policy documents around the world (e.g., National Research Council, 2012). Accordingly, we need to find means to allow high-school students to practice these other knowledge elements so that they will develop as scientifically literate citizens.

Further research is required to verify whether procedural and epistemic knowledge is also dependent on content knowledge when problem solving is carried out using other bioinformatics tools and databases, as well as in other problem-solving and learning contexts. It is commonly assumed that some procedural knowledge is domain-specific, while some is transferable across domains (e.g., OECD, 2018). We are not referring here to the possible transfer of procedural or epistemic knowledge across domains (Dori & Sasson, 2013), but rather to the dependency of use of these knowledge elements on content knowledge, which was identified in our study and needs further investigation to be generalized.

It should also be borne in mind that our studies in this field are consistently based on the interaction between the domain-specific and strategic knowledge suggested by Alexander and Judy (1988). It is interesting to look into the knowledge elements that we used for the analyses of problem solving in biology and biotechnology as presented in this chapter, in light of the categories previously suggested by Schoenfeld (1985) for problem solving in mathematics. Schoenfeld suggested that the knowledge necessary for adequate mathematics problem-solving performance is composed of 'resources,' 'heuristics,' and 'control.' The first category, 'resources,' includes "facts" and it seems to correspond to declarative/conceptual/content knowledge, *knowing what* (Table 4.1) (Alexander & Judy, 1988; de Jong & Ferguson-Hessler, 1996; OECD, 2012). In the second category, 'heuristics,' Schoenfeld included "general problem solving techniques," such as "drawing figures, introducing suitable notations, exploiting related problems, reformulating problems, working backwards, testing and verification procedures" (Schoenfeld, 1985, p. 15, table 1.1). These techniques seem to be included under procedural knowledge (strategies), *knowing how*

(Table 4.1). In the category 'control,' Schoenfeld included "global decisions regarding the selection and implementation of resources and strategies, including planning, monitoring and assessment, decision-making, conscious metacognitive acts" (Schoenfeld, 1985). These components can be included under conditional knowledge, *knowing when and where* (Table 4.1). Moreover, Schoenfeld suggested in a later study that "self-regulation, or monitoring and control, is one of three broad arenas encompassed under the umbrella term metacognition" (Schoenfeld, 2016), where metacognition was suggested as one of the multifaceted constructs of epistemic thinking (Barzilai & Zohar, 2014). Taken together, the framework suggested by Schoenfeld (1985) for problem solving in mathematics can be aligned with the other frameworks presented here for problem solving in biology and biotechnology. It should be noted that in the suggested framework for problem solving in mathematics, Schoenfeld also included the learner's belief system. Alexander also considered that learner's interest plays an important role in academic performance (e.g., Alexander & Murphy, 1998). However, learner's interest and motivation were not the focus of the work presented here.

6 Future Directions

The learning and teaching of science using authentic databases and tools is a tempting, albeit challenging task. We are currently pursuing this initiative using databases that are very different from the ones used in the studies described here, namely those that include data of various molecules (e.g., nucleic acids, proteins). We are embarking on exploring the use of 'big data' obtained from biology research that was carried out mostly at the macro level. Specifically, we are collaborating with various natural history museums in Israel and the United States that have made some of their databases available for high-school student inquiry. For example, we are developing teaching and learning activities, and looking into high-school students' open inquiry of (a) grizzly bear migration in North America in the last 200 years; (b) birds' migration in Israel (in collaboration with the Steinhardt Museum of Natural History at Tel Aviv University); (c) human impact on the environment through the connection between sea turtle nesting and light pollution, and more (Carmel Bar, PhD thesis, in preparation). All of these 'big data'-driven activities are located on the newly established Moodle-based platform, PeTeL (for Personalized Teaching and Learning), at the Department of Science Teaching, Weizmann Institute of Science. The PeTeL platform is designed to continuously collect data on students' performance while using the platform, from the amount of time a student is connected to the platform, to every answer provided in the assignments and test performance.[2]

Acknowledgments

We are thankful to all of the members of the Biology Group in the Department of Science Teaching, Weizmann Institute of Science, who contributed their insightful thoughts and experiences in numerous meaningful discussions that greatly promoted our thinking. We are especially thankful to Hadas Gelbart and Yossy Machluf with whom we shared many hours of discussion and data analyses of the above described research. We are thankful to the dedicated biology and biotechnology teachers who participated in these studies.

Notes

1 http://www.jmol.org/
2 https://petel.weizmann.ac.il/prototypes/biology/login/index.php

References

Alexander, P. A., & Judy, E. J. (1988). The interaction of domain-specific and strategic knowledge in academic performance. *Review of Educational Research, 58*, 375–404. http://dx.doi.org/10.3102/00346543058004375

Alexander, P. A., & Murphy, P. K. (1998). Profiling the differences in students' knowledge, interest, and strategic processing. *Journal of Educational Psychology, 90*, 435–447. http://dx.doi.org/10.1037/0022-0663.90.3.435

Barzilai, S., & Zohar, A. (2014). Reconsidering personal epistemology as metacognition: A multifaceted approach to the analysis of epistemic thinking. *Educational Psychologist, 49*, 13–35. doi:10.1080/00461520.2013.863265

Buttigieg, P. L. (2010). Perspectives on presentation and pedagogy in aid of bioinformatics education. *Briefings in Bioinformatics, 11*, 587–597. doi:10.1093/bib/bbq062

Chinn, C. A., & Malhotra, B. A. (2002). Epistemologically authentic inquiry in schools: A theoretical framework for evaluating inquiry tasks. *Science Education, 86*, 175–218. http://dx.doi.org/10.1002/sce.10001

de Jong, T., & Ferguson-Hessler, M. G. M. (1996). Types and qualities of knowledge. *Educational Psychologist, 31*, 105–113. http://dx.doi.org/10.1207/s15326985ep3102_2

Dori, Y. J., & Sasson, I. (2013). A three-attribute transfer skills framework – Part I: Establishing the model and its relation to chemical education. *Chemistry Education Research and Practice, 14*, 363–375. doi:10.1039/C3RP20093K

Driver, R., Newton, P., & Osborne, J. (2000). Establishing the norms of scientific argumentation in classrooms. *Science Education, 84*, 287–312. http://dx.doi.org/10.1002/(sici)1098-237x(200005)84:3<287::aid-sce1>3.0.co;2-a

Falk, H., & Yarden, A. (2009). "Here the scientists explain what I said." Coordination practices elicited during the enactment of the Results and Discussion sections of adapted primary literature. *Research in Science Education, 39*, 349–383. http://dx.doi.org/10.1007/s11165-008-9114-9

Gallagher, S. R., Coon, W., Donley, K., Scott, A., & Goldberg, D. S. (2011). A first attempt to bring computational biology into advanced high school biology classrooms. *PLoS Computational Biology, 7*, e1002244. doi:10.1371/journal.pcbi.1002244

Gelbart, H., Brill, G., & Yarden, A. (2009). The impact of a web-based research simulation in bioinformatics on students' understanding of genetics. *Research in Science Education, 39*, 725–751. http://dx.doi.org/10.1007/s11165-008-9101-1

Gelbart, H., & Yarden, A. (2001). *Bioinformatics – Deciphering the secrets of the genome.* The Amos de-Shalit Center for Science Teaching (in Hebrew). http://stwww.weizmann.ac.il/bioinformatics

Gelbart, H., & Yarden, A. (2006). Learning genetics through an authentic research simulation in bioinformatics. *Journal of Biological Education, 40*, 107–112. http://dx.doi.org/10.1080/00219266.2006.9656026

Gelbart, H., & Yarden, A. (2011). Supporting learning of high-school genetics using authentic research practices: The teacher's role. *Journal of Biological Education, 45*, 129–135. http://dx.doi.org/10.1080/00219266.2011.580771

Gott, R., & Roberts, R. (2008). *Concepts of evidence and their role in open-ended practical investigations and scientific literacy; background to published papers* [Master's thesis]. Durham University. http://community.dur.ac.uk/rosalyn.roberts/Evidence/Gott%20&%20Roberts%20(2008)%20Research%20Report.pdf

Grosslight, L., Unger, C., Jay, E., & Smith, C. L. (1991). Understanding models and their use in science: Conceptions of middle and high school students and experts. *Journal of Research in Science Teaching, 28*, 799–822. https://doi.org/10.1002/tea.3660280907

Holtzclaw, J. D., Eisen, A., Whitney, E. M., Penumetcha, M., Hoey, J. J., & Kimbro, K. S. (2006). Incorporating a new bioinformatics component into genetics at a historically black college: Outcomes and lessons. *CBE Life Sciences Education, 5*, 52–64. doi:10.1187/cbe.05-04-0071

Levkovich, O. (2019). *Using computer-based Jmol tasks for molecular modeling of proteins by high-school students: Development of conceptual framework, examination of learning processes and perceptions* [Unpublished doctoral dissertation]. Weizmann Institute of Science.

Levkovich, O., & Yarden, A. (2017). *Learning about proteins using Jmol 3-D molecule viewer: Teachers and students views* [Paper presentation]. The Chais Conference on Instructional Technologies Research: Learning in the Technological Era, Raanana, Israel.

Levkovich, O., & Yarden, A. (2021). *Conceptualizing learning about proteins with a molecular viewer in high school based on the integration of two theoretical frameworks* [Manuscript submitted for publication].

Lewitter, F., & Bourne, P. E. (2011). Teaching bioinformatics at the secondary school level. *PLoS Computational Biology, 7*, e1002242. doi:10.1371/journal.pcbi.1002242

Machluf, Y., Dahan, O., Shpalter-Avidan, C., Mitchel, A., & Yarden, A. (2011). *Bioinformatics in the service of biotechnology* (*a web-based learning environment https://stwww1.weizmann.ac.il/bioinfo/, The Amos de-Shalit Israeli Center for Science Teaching, grades 11–12*). http://www.weizmann.ac.il/ScienceTeaching/Yarden/sites/ScienceTeaching.Yarden/files/uploads/Bioinformatics-in-the-service-of-biotechnology.pdf

Machluf, Y., Gelbart, H., Ben-Dor, S., & Yarden, A. (2017). Making authentic science accessible – the benefits and challenges of integrating bioinformatics into a high-school science curriculum. *Briefings in Bioinformatics, 18*, 145–159. doi:10.1093/bib/bbv113

Machluf, Y., & Yarden, A. (2013). Integrating bioinformatics into senior high school: Design principles and implications. *Briefings in Bioinformatics, 14*, 648–660. doi:10.1093/bib/bbt030

Marbach-Ad, G., & Stavy, R. (2000). Students' cellular and molecular explanations of genetics phenomena. *Journal of Biological Education, 34*, 200–205. http://dx.doi.org/10.1080/00219266.2000.9655718

National Research Council. (2012). *A framework for K-12 science education: Practices, crosscutting concepts, and core ideas*. https://www.nap.edu/catalog/13165/a-framework-for-k-12-science-education-practices-crosscutting-concepts.

NGSS Lead States. (2013). *Next Generation Science Standards: For states, by states*. https://www.nap.edu/catalog/18290/next-generation-science-standards-for-states-by-states.

OECD. (2012). *The PISA 2015 Assessment Framework: Key competencies in reading, mathematics and science*. http://www.oecd.org/pisa/pisaproducts/pisa2015draftframeworks.htm

OECD. (2018). *The future of education and skills – Education 2030: The future we want*. https://www.oecd.org/education/2030/E2030%20Position%20Paper%20(05.04.2018).pdf

OECD. (2020). *Strategic vision proposal for PISA 2024 Science*. https://www.oecd.org/pisa/publications/PISA-2024-Science-Strategic-Vision-Proposal.pdf

Osborne, J. (2014). Teaching scientific practices: Meeting the challenge of change. *Journal of Science Teacher Education, 25*, 177–196. doi:10.1007/s10972-014-9384-1

Schoenfeld, A. H. (1985). A framework for the analysis of mathematical behaviour. In *Mathematical problem solving* (pp. 11–45). Academic Press, Inc./Harcourt Brace Jovanovich, Pub. http://dx.doi.org/10.1016/b978-0-12-628870-4.50007-4

Schoenfeld, A. H. (2016). Learning to think mathematically: Problem solving, metacognition, and sense making in mathematics. *Journal of Education, 196*(2), 1–38. doi:10.1177/002205741619600202

Schönborn, K. J., & Anderson, T. R. (2010). Bridging the educational research-teaching practice gap. *Biochemistry and Molecular Biology Education, 38*, 347–354. doi:10.1002/bmb.20436

Shavelson, R., Ruiz-Primo, M., & Wiley, E. (2005). Windows into the mind. *Higher Education, 49*, 413–430. doi:10.1007/s10734-004-9448-9

Treagust, D. F., Chittleborough, G., & Mamiala, T. L. (2002). Students' understanding of the role of scientific models in learning science. *International Journal of Science Education, 24*, 357–368. http://dx.doi.org/10.1080/09500690110066485

Wefer, S. H., & Anderson, O. R. (2008). Identification of students' content mastery and cognitive and affective percepts of a bioinformatics miniunit: A case study with recommendations for teacher education. *Journal of Science Teacher Education, 19*, 355–373. http://dx.doi.org/10.1007/s10972-008-9099-2

CHAPTER 5

Evolution of Four Decades of Research

From Cognition to Emotion Paradigm

Nir Orion

Abstract

This chapter describes the milestones of 36 years of research, presented as a combination monograph, biography and scientific articles. The focus of the chapter is the evolution of the Earth Science Education (ESE) Group in the Department of Science Teaching at the Weizmann Institute of Science, Israel. This evolution is presented and analyzed against the background of educational developments and changes within the Ministry of Education in Israel and within the global science teaching discipline. The analysis is based on quantitative and qualitative data derived from dozens of studies. It describes the development of the holistic earth systems educational approach that incorporates integration of the outdoor learning environment as a central component of the learning sequence; a model for the integration of learning environments; the development of environmental insight through a holistic earth systems approach; development of a layered systems thinking model; and the notion of learning as an instinct. Integration of these components led to the development of the learning instinct theory, which contradicts the essentialist–reductionist paradigm.

Keywords

earth science education – earth systems education – inquiry-based learning – outdoor learning environment – holistic learning environments approach – learning instinct

1 Introduction: The Past Is the Key to the Future

This chapter is a combination monograph and autobiography. It describes the developmental milestones of the Earth Science Education (ESE) Group in the Department of Science Teaching at the Weizmann Institute of Science along four decades of research. This development is portrayed in the context of the science education paradigm and contrasted with the policy of the Israeli Ministry of Education during this long period.

 | DOI: 10.1163/9789004503625_005

The evolutionary process results from the reaction and interaction between an organism's genetic code and its environment. The term evolution is used as a metaphor in the title of this chapter, which describes the development of a research program as a result of interactions between a subconscious "educational code" and educational research paradigms, and between the former and the reality of the Ministry of Education and school environments.

Although the uploading of my "educational code" started about 60 years ago, I still remember most of the events that shaped it. One of them happened on a hot summer day in July 1973. It was the day of my last matriculation exam. I do not remember the subject of that exam, as I do not remember anything of any other exam, but I clearly remember that I finished it quite quickly and immediately went home.

Once there, I went to my room, collected my notebooks, took them into the yard and set them on fire. Today, I regret this act somewhat, but back in the 1970s, global warming was unknown and no one was aware of the influence of burning organic materials on the greenhouse effect. In any event, my conscience is clear because in all honesty, I had only one notebook, with only a few pages to burn.

My reason for having only one notebook at the end of high school was my tendency to limit my visits to the school. Of course, at least once a semester, I had a serious talk with my homeroom teacher, who refused to accept "boring" as a valid explanation for my absence from classes and would say: "This is school, not a club! You come here to study, not to enjoy." During one of our talks, I answered: "when I grow up, I will prove to you that school does not have to be a place where children get bored and suffer. I will show you that learning in school can and should be an enjoyable thing." This promise, made by a scared and confused 17-year-old, became etched in my soul and has accompanied me ever since.

During my military service, I "discovered" nature. The joy of climbing a high mountain, the beauty of the landscape, the rocks, the flora, the fauna. When I finished my service, I worked as a field guide and once I started to guide, I never stopped asking questions or looking for answers. And one day, the boy who swore that after graduating high school, he would never again set foot in a learning institution, found himself sitting in the library of the Hebrew University of Jerusalem's Geology Department reading Master's and PhD dissertations about the geology of Sinai. The need to understand had stimulated my learning instinct. This natural instinct, which had been suppressed throughout my school years, had just burst out of me.

A year later, I started my formal geoscience studies at the Hebrew University. I began my studies in a cloud of anxiety, because my mathematical and scientific background was shaky at best. Very soon, however, I realized that I had missed nothing by missing high school. My university studies included many geological field trips, most of which I found ineffective: I failed to understand the idea of driving for hours to see a geological phenomenon, then listening to a long theoretical lecture about what we could not see there anyway, instead of listening to this lecture in an air-conditioned classroom. After completing my geology degree, I became a field guide in a field school of the Society for the Protection of Nature, where I mainly worked with school students. It did not take me long to identify the limitations of informal education. I realized that neither I nor the other field guides had any methodological tools to educate. We focused on transforming our broad but shallow knowledge and on our charisma as storytellers. However, this was not enough to influence the children's attitudes toward their natural environment, or to stimulate their need to expand their knowledge and understanding of it. I realized that being a professional amateur, a jack of all trades, was not enough to educate children. Therefore, if I wanted to live up to my promise, given as a hopeless teenager, about the joy of learning, I had to go back to the scene of the crime – the formal education arena.

In 1982, by the time I started my MSc studies in the Department of Science Teaching at the Weizmann Institute of Science, all of the information needed for the evolutionary potential of the future ESE Group had already been uploaded into my educational DNA. The knowledge source was there, but most of it was raw or subconscious.

This chapter describes the milestones and key findings along the evolutionary process of shaping that raw knowledge into the current research program, educational perception and most importantly, practical educational work plan of the ESE Group.

2 The 1980s: The Quantitative Era

The formal evolution of the ESE Group began in 1982, when I began my MSc work. The focus of the Department of Science Teaching at that time was curriculum development. The research paradigm in the 1980s was quantitative. The science education discipline had been established during the 1960s by scientists and in the 1980s, it was still in its early days as a discipline. During that period, the focus and research program of science education were still strongly influenced by scientists. The vast majority of those scientists had come to this field as saviors of scientific education, but without understanding the nature of education and without school teaching experience. Therefore, the research methodology of science education was a duplication of the scientific methodology: quantitative studies with an experimental group "tube" and a control group "tube." The Department of Science Teaching was highly influenced by scientists and each research group had a scientific patron.

The ESE Group was initiated by the geoscientist Prof. Emmanuel Mazor, about 10 years after the establishment of the Department of Science Teaching. Prof. Mazor belonged to that unique, small group of scientists who perceive public communication as an integral part of their scientific work. Moreover, although he was a scientist, he did not refer only to scientific content; he realized that science education is not a unidirectional system. It includes not only information transfer (teaching), but also absorption and internalization of information (learning). In addition, he understood the complexity and limitations of educational research and unlike many scientists, who disregarded the educational research methodology, he respected it and chose to focus on the scientific aspects and not to interfere with what he was not expert at.

During the 1980s, the ESE Group had only one member, but the MSc and PhD studies that I conducted under the supervision of Prof. Avi Hofstein and Prof. Mazor paved the way for the establishment of earth sciences as an independent discipline in the science curricula of schools in the educational system, and for the expansion of the ESE Group (Orion, 1989, 1993; Orion & Hofstein, 1994; Orion et al., 1986).

Those studies formed the following pillars of the evolution of the earth science Teaching group (Figure 5.1): the inquiry-based pillar, which was then, "hands-on activities"; the outdoor learning environment pillar, with the

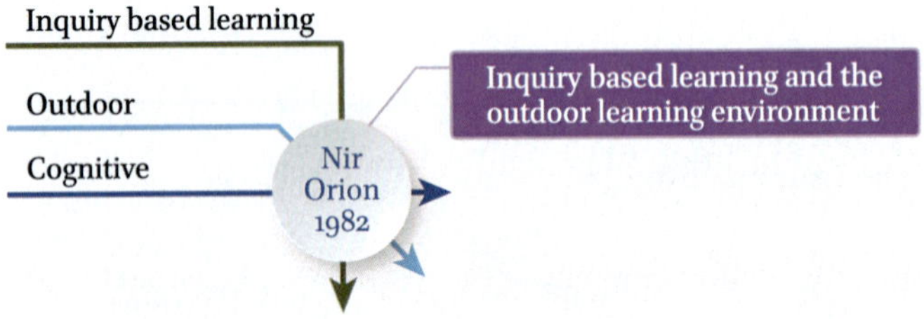

FIGURE 5.1 The first stage of the ESE Group's evolution

integrated learning environments (outdoor and indoor); the cognitive aspects of learning earth sciences, including the emotional aspects of learning earth sciences (e.g., the novelty space).

3 The 1990s: The Era of Constructivism

The 1990s were the golden age of science education – the era of constructivism. The constructivism paradigm influenced both the perception of curriculum development and the research methodology. The focus of curriculum development shifted from the teacher-centered approach to a learner-center approach, and the research methodology shifted from the quantitative paradigm to one of qualitative and mixed approaches. However, the development of science education has never followed a gradual linear line (Frelindich, 1998). Rather, it goes through a series of reforms, which arise in cycles (Hurd, 1986). As these reforms do not cause punctual development, they are characterized by a so-called pendulum effect. This means that rather than following a pattern of linear progression, in each decade, before the concurrent reform can reach maturation, it is replaced by a new reform that drives the science education field towards a different direction. The "pendulum" swings between the educational paradigms end points of essentialism and progressiveness. While the essentialism paradigm is based on the conservative reductionist philosophy, the progressive paradigm perceives learning holistically in terms of connecting emotions and cognition, integrating learning environments, and taking an interdisciplinary approach. Thus, the constructivist reform of the 1990s required that the science education establishment moves from the perspective of disciplinary-driven schooling, with the main goal of preparing a nation's new generation of scientists (reductionism) to that of integration and systems, with attention focused on educating students for lives of social responsibility within democratic societies (holism).

The 1990s constructivist science education reform, named "Tomorrow 95," introduced the earth sciences, for the first time, as an independent discipline in the high school curricula and as an integral part of the "Science for All" curricula for the elementary and junior-high school levels. The "Tomorrow 95" reform opened the door for the establishment of the ESE Group within the Science Teaching Department. This enabled the introduction of the earth sciences as an integral part of the Israeli scientific curricula.

However, since no curriculum materials existed at that time, the 1990s were characterized by the intensive development of a learning curriculum within an academic framework of design-based research. The curriculum development was unique in relation to what existed at that time worldwide in the following aspects:

a. The holistic multidisciplinary earth systems approach (Ben-Zvi Assaraf & Orion, 2005a; Ben-Zvi-Assaraf et al., 2008; Gudovitch & Orion, 2001; Orion, 2002, 2007; Orion & Fortner, 2003)
b. The holistic learning environments approach: laboratory–outdoor–computer–classroom (Orion, 2003a, 2007)
c. The holistic cognition–emotions learning approach (Orion, 2003a; Orion & Ault, 2007; Orion et al., 2007)
d. The holistic research–curriculum implementation spiral (design-based) approach (Ben-Zvi Assaraf & Orion, 2009; Orion & Cohen, 2007).

The dozens of K–12 earth systems-based units developed from the 1990s onward had the common goal of developing environmental insight, first mentioned and defined by Orion (1996, 1997) as the ability to perceive the following three principles or ideas:

a. We live in a cyclic world that is built upon a series of subsystems: geosphere, hydrosphere, biosphere and atmosphere, which all interact through an exchange of energy and materials
b. Humans are part of nature, and thus must act in harmony with nature's laws of cycling
c. The deep-time perception of earth indicates that earth and its subsystems (including the biosphere) have no environmental crises. Throughout the geological history of the earth, species have gone extinct and new species have evolved.

To achieve the goal of student acquisition of environmental insight, most of the earth systems units were developed within the geocycles framework; e.g., the rock cycle, the water cycle, the carbon cycle; these programs included content and activities that focused on recognizing and understanding the following concepts:

– The reciprocal relations of the transfer of energy and matter within and between the earth subsystems, including the biosphere
– The place of the human system as part of the earth systems
– The causes of natural hazards and their interrelationships with human activity on earth.

Moreover, the perception of this insight required the development of higher-thinking skills, such as logic thinking, spatial thinking, temporal thinking, cyclic thinking, and systems thinking. These cognitive abilities were explored

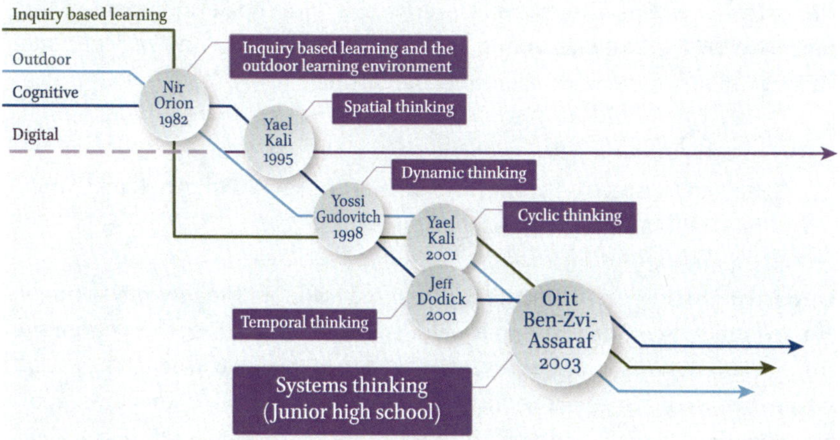

FIGURE 5.2 The milestones of the ESE Group's evolution during the 1990s

for two decades through a series of MSc theses and PhD dissertations (Ben-Zvi Assaraf & Orion, 2005a; Dodick & Orion, 2003; Gudovitch & Orion, 2001; Kali & Orion, 1996; Kali et al., 2003; Orion & Kali, 2005; Orion et al., 1997) (Figure 5.2).

The dozens of curriculum units that were developed following the above designed-based studies shared the following characteristics:

- Each program was developed in a context-based (authentic), clear cover story (Ben-Zvi-Assaraf & Orion, 2005b)
- The learning sequences of each program gradually shifted from the concrete to the abstract (Orion, 2002)
- The outdoor learning environment served as a central component of each program (Orion, 2003a; Orion & Basis, 2008; Orion & Hofstein, 1994; Yunker et al., 2011)
- Each program was based on active inquiry learning, both indoors and outdoors (Orion, 2007)
- The earth systems approach served as a platform for learning basic scientific concepts of physics, chemistry, and biology (a cross-curricular approach) (Orion & Cohen, 2007)
- The learning process was adjusted to learners' varying abilities (Orion et al., 2007)
- The emotional aspect was used as a key for developing cognitive abilities by integrating the metacognitive aspect as an integral part of the learning process (Ben-David & Orion, 2012; Orion et al., 2007; Yunker et al., 2011).

The main progression of the ESE Group in the 1990s was along the cognitive axis. However, this progress was intertwined with the development of the other pillars of the ESE Group: inquiry-based learning, the outdoor learning environment, and the emotional aspect of learning.

4 The 21st Century – Reductionism and Conservatism Are Back: The Standardization and "Back to Basics" Era

The constructivism period lasted less than a decade and made only a ripple in the overall educational research field. In as early as 2000, the pendulum swung back to the conservative, essentialist edge of its range, where it has been stuck for two decades now. The last two decades have been characterized by standardization, globalization and a "back to basics" policy. Since 2000, K–12 schools have been directed toward testing and scaling through national and international tests. This sharp backward swing of the pendulum wiped away most of the progressive buds that had begun to sprout in the 1990s, especially at the junior high level.

The return of the reductionist testing-oriented era has created a toxic environment for the expansion of the ESE Group, but it has not caused its extinction; rather, it has limited the research and implementation of earth science learning efforts to the high school and elementary school levels.

4.1 *The Systems Thinking Hierarchy (STH) Model*

The main research effort of the ESE Group during the first decade of this century was toward expanding the systems thinking study to the high school (Orion & Basis, 2008) and elementary school (Ben-Zvi Assaraf & Orion, 2010) levels (Figure 5.3).

The hierarchic and pyramidal systems thinking structure emerged from an analysis of the data, conducted by Orion and Libarkin (2014), from all relevant studies (Figure 5.4). After earth systems inquiry-based instruction almost all of the students were able to analyze the components and processes of the system; fewer students could identify cycles of matter and energy, understand subsurface processes, or think backwards and forwards in time. Students seemed to move through three stages in their development as systems thinkers. At the analytical ability stage, students could recognize components and processes in a system. Development of the ability to identify simple relationships between a few variables and to represent a system as a network of variables and processes (cyclic thinking) occurred as students moved into the synthesis ability stage. At the final, problem-solving stage, students could identify patterns within a

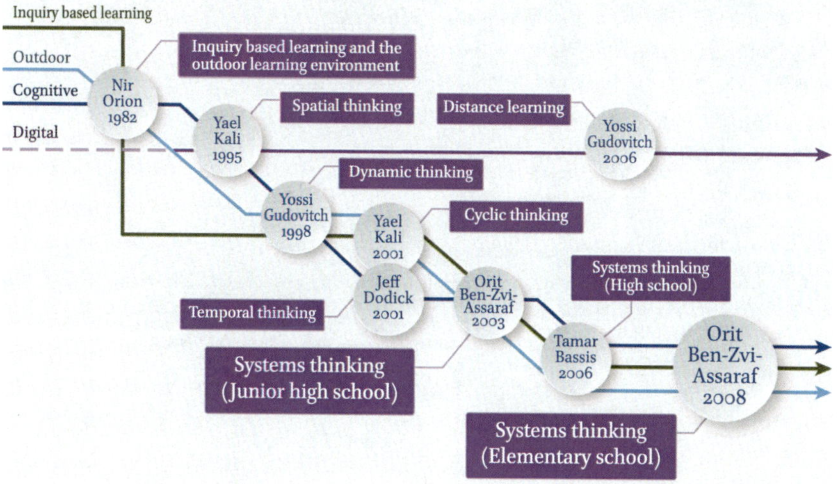

FIGURE 5.3 The milestones of the ESE Group's evolution during the first decade of the 21st century

system, generalize across systems, and transform a system forwards (prediction) and backwards (retrodiction) in time. These identified stages were very well aligned with other research (e.g., Evagorou et al., 2009). In addition, the student learning outcomes realized here were well aligned with the learning goals discussed earlier in this chapter. Although those goals were developed in the United States, the strong alignment of these outcomes in Israel with the desired outcomes in the United States suggests that this or a similar curriculum could be transferred effectively. For example, the ability to recognize patterns in a system, as well as to understand how systems change over time (prediction and retrodiction) are themes identified here that have been identified as cross-cutting themes within the Next Generation Science Standards (National Research Council, 2012). Earth science education might be the ideal venue for building stronger international collaborations and ties.

However, this STH model ignored a very important component of systems thinking: the ability to identify feedback loops in a system (Ossimitz, 2000). This aspect does not appear in this review, since no attention has been paid to this ability in any of the studies, even at the high school level. This important ability should be tested in future studies. Moreover, it can serve as a predictor for the STH model since, according to the hierarchical nature of this model, it should be located at the higher levels of the abilities pyramid.

Orion and Libarkin (2014) noted the direct link between developing systems thinking skills and the ability to develop environmental insight. Orion (2016),

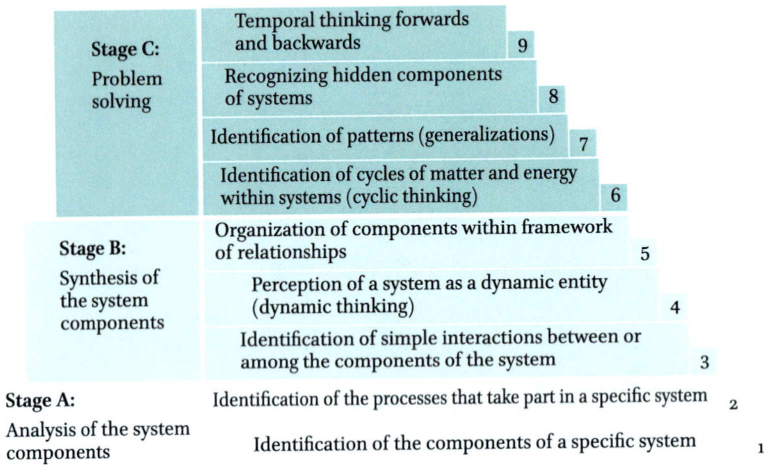

FIGURE 5.4 The systems thinking hierarchy (STH) model

using a comparative study, showed that the systems thinking abilities of high school students participating in an earth systems program, which included all of the components described above, were significantly higher than those of students from the same schools who did not study the earth systems program. In addition, the environmental behavior of this earth systems group of students was significantly higher than that of the other students, including students who had studied a traditional environmental science program. The earth systems holistic model was also found to be a useful platform to illustrate and understand chemical, physical, and biological principles (Orion & Cohen, 2007; Orion et al., 2007).

4.2 *The Outdoor Learning Environment*

All of the cognitive studies of the ESE Group, without exception, highlighted the central role of outdoor learning events that were developed according to Orion's holistic model to serve as a conceptual anchor for students to make linkages to the content learned in the classroom, both before and after the field trip, and for creating a concrete relevant framework for the construction of higher-order thinking skills, such as the ability to discern among observations, conclusions, and assumptions; thinking in a geological time frame (deep time); spatial thinking; three-dimensional thinking; and systems thinking (Orion & Basis, 2008; Yunker et al., 2011). The development of thinking processes and of connections between students and their physical (natural and non-natural) environment need to be considered simultaneously. The relationship with the immediate environment begins with authentic questions that are related to the students themselves, and enhances their awareness and insight regarding their environment. Later, the students can experience their environment through activities that are based on the intake of stimuli for all of the senses. Moreover, all of the cognitive studies highlighted the role of those outdoor learning events in encouraging learners to cooperate and engage in inquiry-based learning.

5 Closing the Cycle: The Emotional–Social Component and the Learning Instinct Theory

A dualism between cognition and affect emerged from several studies of earth systems education at the elementary level (Ben-Zvi Assaraf & Orion, 2010; Yunker et al., 2011), the junior high level (Ben-Zvi Assaraf & Orion, 2009; Orion et al., 2007) and the high school level (Orion & Basis, 2008; Orion & Cohen, 2007). Orion (2007) suggested that the earth systems approach should emphasize the development of both thinking skills and affective responses. However, the research milestone that highlighted the central place of the emotional aspect of the learning process was the MSc study of Merhav (2013) (Figure 5.5).

That study examined the engagement of high-school earth science students in writing field-trip reports. This assignment required students to demonstrate the above variety of higher-order thinking skills. Therefore, the research hypothesis was that the students' initial cognitive abilities while participating in the learning process would be the central factor influencing the performance

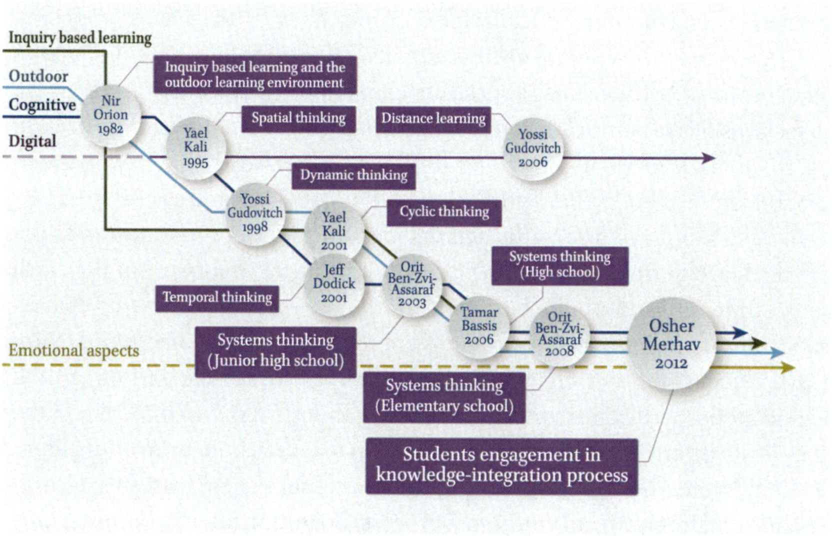

FIGURE 5.5 The emergence of the emotional axis

level for this task. However, the findings indicated no significant correlation between initial thinking skills (such as systems thinking and logical thinking) and the students' engagement and performance in writing about the logical sequences and the earth systems interrelationships in their field reports. In contrast, engagement and students' cognitive abilities were found to be mainly influenced by emotional aspects.

Inquiry-based learning in small groups at school is embedded in the earth systems education approach, in both indoor and outdoor learning environments. Thus, the earth systems approach creates numerous opportunities for social interaction and depends on students' social ability to interact with their peers in a learning process, and on the teachers' ability to deal with this social aspect. For example, teachers must be able to adjust the laboratory space to allow students to move between different groups, thereby facilitating their interactions, and encouraging spontaneous social interactions.

Eyov (2017) presented a mechanism of interactions in which a positive social situation that includes social connections, or a sense of belonging that stems from the existence of these relationships, constitutes a fundamental factor for the development of independent learning skills. That study indicated that the earth systems teaching approach that had been developed and implemented by the ESE Group had rendered the terminology of formal vs. informal learning meaningless. This finding was also a result of the ability to develop a digital environment as a joint connecting the inquiry-based learning in the indoor and outdoor learning environments (Liberty, 2018).

Schechter (2020) took Eyov's (2017) study one step further and explored the interrelationships between social well-a high-school earth science program. There are several fundamental needs that must be met for the academic success of students in school, including a sense of belonging, connectedness and security. This social aspect is part of a broad domain called "social well-being." Since learning in school takes place in a social environment, social well-being is expected to be a main factor affecting the optimal emotional state for learning (Figure 5.6).

Schechter's (2020) study confirmed the relationships between social well-being and engagement in the learning process. The social well-being of the earth science students was found to be positively influenced by the following characteristics of the progressive earth systems approach: (a) the inquiry-based learning that encourages and creates opportunities for social interaction; (b) the teaching model in the outdoor learning environment; (c) the architecture of the indoor learning environment, and (d) the open teacher–student relationships.

The emergence and development of the emotional axis indicated that learning is, first and foremost, an emotional process. Cognition joins the process only

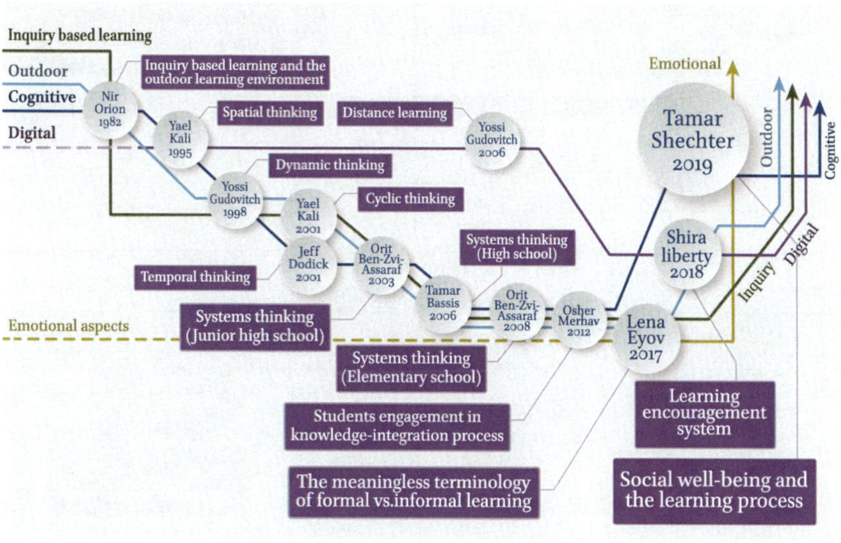

FIGURE 5.6 The development of the emotional–social well-being axis

after the emotional need has been met. The teaching method (inquiry-based learning) and the learning environments (indoor, outdoor, and digital) are tools to ignite the emotional need and then develop and scaffold the cognitive abilities, thereby maintaining the emotional–social aspects of learning.

Thus, all five paths that I started to walk, seemingly independently, at the end of the 20th century intersected, about 30 years later, into the unified learning instinct theory (Figure 5.7).

5.1 *The Learning Instinct Theory*

Learning is a natural process, an instinct. Like any instinct, the urge to learn is only called into play by a stimulus or a need. The inborn abilities to learn and teach are not the exclusive domain of the human species; they are also naturally inherent in animals. For example, the lioness and her cubs have innate characteristics that allow them to teach and learn how to hunt for prey.

The learning mechanism in humans, as in other animals, is instinctive, and therefore occurs in response to stimulation. Possibly, the difference between humans and other species lies in the relationship between learning and the characteristics of the natural and intrinsic motivation for learning. For humans, learning has evolved far beyond the most basic existential survival; it also serves humans' natural curiosity and inborn tendency to seek novelty and challenges. Thus, as already noted, in humans, the main stimulus for learning is emotional, and the cognition follows this emotional need. Unfortunately,

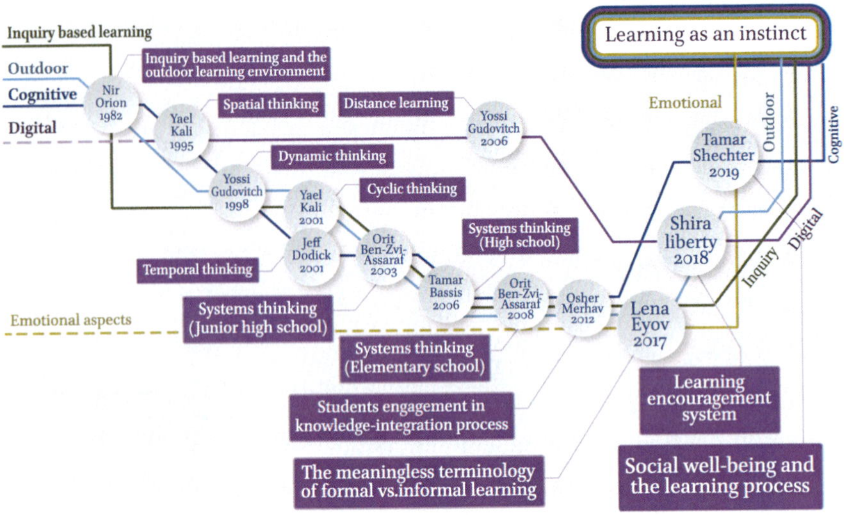

FIGURE 5.7 The intersection of the research directions of the ESE Group to construct the learning instinct theory

the traditional classroom stifles this natural instinct, consequently encouraging boredom, absenteeism, and rebellion among the students.

6 The Professional Change Venue

The earth systems approach is the opposite of the traditional approach to teaching that has been adopted in schools and universities. The traditional approach focuses mainly on the transmission of information from teachers to students, who must memorize it and give it back through a one-time event called an 'examination.' In contrast, the earth systems approach is based on the construction of knowledge by learners through the mediation of their teacher, and is therefore based on a close engagement of the learner in the learning process. In practice, the teaching strategies of the earth systems-based science program are quite different from the traditional way of teaching science in the following practical aspects (Table 5.1).

For many traditional science teachers the world over, implementation of the earth systems approach is not just a professional development. The meaning of professional development is that the subject of the development, in our case the teachers, have a very solid professional core from which they can grow and expand. However, for teachers to move from the left column in Table 5.1 to the right column, even in relation to some of the parameters, they have to change

TABLE 5.1 Comparison between traditional science teaching and earth systems teaching

Traditional science teaching	Earth systems teaching
The main purpose is to prepare society's future scientists	The main purpose is to prepare society's future citizens
Discipline-centered teaching (reductionism)	Multidisciplinary teaching
Learning is a mechanical process (essentialism)	Learning is an emotional–social process (instinct of learning)
Teacher-centered teaching (essentialism)	Student-centered teaching (instinct of learning)
Content-based teaching	Integration of skills within contents
The teacher is a source for knowledge/information	The teacher is a mediator for triggering the learning instinct
"Chalk and talk" or PowerPoint presentation-based teaching	Inquiry-based teaching
Almost ignoring the outdoor learning environment	The outdoor learning environment is an essential and central learning environment
School-based learning	Multiple learning environments: classroom, laboratory, outdoors, and computer
Teaching that is derived from the scientific world	Authentic-based teaching that is derived from the real world
Traditional assessment	Alternative assessment

their goals, contents, ways and philosophy of teaching. Thus, the shift from a traditional science teacher to an earth systems teacher is not just developmental; rather, it is a major reform or even a revolution: a professional change.

Therefore, along with the already mentioned research venues, much effort has been invested by the ESE Group in exploring teachers' ability to apply the earth systems approach in schools (Kapulnik et al., 2004; Midyan & Orion, 2003; Orion, 2003b; Orion et al., 2007; Shalom, 2013). These studies indicated that although it is very difficult to change teachers' habits and perceptions of science teaching, it is possible, even for senior teachers with over 20 years of teaching experience. Such teachers changed their science content focus and taught earth science subjects that were completely new to them. They began to teach in the outdoor learning environment. They changed their ways of teaching and changed their views on the purpose of science teaching. This professional change was achieved through long-term in-service programs conducted in the schools with close support and assistance, including both professional and emotional support. A paradigm shift in learning is basically a psychological process, and therefore science educators should be equipped with psychological knowledge and skills to deal with reservations and opposition, which are the result of a fear of change.

However, our findings also suggested that even the most powerful and effective in-service program alone cannot guarantee a long-term sustainable reform. Unfortunately, education in many countries is mainly controlled by economic and political decisions and less by pedagogical ones. Thus, to generate such a paradigm shift, a large amount of resources needs to be invested over a long period, at least 10 years. Unfortunately, a genuine conceptual change cycle is much longer than a political cycle (the time from election to election) and therefore, the process never comes close to maturation.

7 Back to the Future

The evolution of the ESE Group started with a frustrated, confused, and scared youngster, who could not stand the oppressive pressure of the essentialist school; a boy who instinctively felt that learning should be an enjoyable event, and that a teacher must serve as a positive, encouraging model, and not as a distant and frightening figure.

Forty years of research evolution and evolving implementation indicate that the natural instincts of that youngster, and probably billions of children worldwide, are not just the misconception of a spoiled child. Learning is an instinct that is stimulated by an emotional trigger. Therefore, the oppression felt by that youngster so many years ago, and likely by youngsters the world over, is reasonable. Moreover, four decades of research and implementation have shown, beyond a shadow of a doubt, that there is no inherent contradiction between learning and enjoyment. On the contrary.

Today, the ESE Group of the Department of Science Teaching at the Weizmann Institute of Science is the leading ESE group worldwide. The ESE Group has conducted earth systems education-based studies all over the world (e.g., Argentina, Brazil, Chile, China, Ethiopia, Germany, India, Peru, Portugal, Spain, Uruguay, and the United States) and to date, the learning units of the ESE Group have been translated into five languages (Arabic, English, Chinese, Spanish, and Portuguese). Thus, over the years, a great number of students in Israel and worldwide have experienced positive, enjoyable learning through the study of earth systems education units developed by the ESE Group.

The child who promised his teacher that he would prove that school learning can be an enjoyable experience can feel satisfied in having fulfilled this promise. The research evolution of the ESE Group indicates that the earth systems approach has great potential to stimulate students' learning instinct by helping them see the relevance of what they are learning to their own daily lives. This statement is based on the earth systems content and the existing ESE research, which highlights the central role of the outdoor learning environment in creating personal relevance. The latter is expected to stimulate the learning instinct mechanism and, once this instinct is active, students will cooperate and engage in the inquiry-based learning. Consequently, with the right program, students can develop higher-order thinking skills, such as the ability to discern between an observation, a conclusion and an assumption, to think on a geological time scale (deep time), and to engage in spatial thinking, three-dimensional thinking and systems thinking.

However, the feeling of satisfaction is still only partial.

Essentialism and reductionism still control and dominate schools today in Israel and in most other countries, as they have done since the establishment of public schools in the 18th century. Under this oppressive conservative regime, the earth systems education approach can only survive in small niches.

Education systems everywhere focus on the needs of the society, nation, and economy, among others. They know how to transform these needs into syllabuses, curricula, guidelines, textbooks, and standards, national tests and international tests. They prefer to stick to the traditional essentialism model, which is much cheaper, but mainly because it maintains social hierarchies.

The gap between the traditional essentialist schooling paradigm and the natural instinct of learning is a central reason for the worldwide phenomenon of children's reluctance to attend school and their struggle to learn there. Children must find their own meaning and relevance in what they learn in school, since this sense of relevance is likely to stimulate their interest in the subject matter, thus tapping into their learning instinct.

World attention became focused on science education with the launch of Sputnik in 1957. Since that "wake-up" call, science education policy worldwide has focused on the need for new curricula, new instructional materials, new reforms, and new approaches to learning and teaching science (Bybee & DeBoer, 1994; Yager, 2000). However, these reforms do not cause punctual development, since they are characterized by the so-called pendulum effect. This means that they lack any pattern of linear progression. Rather, in each decade, before the concurrent reform can come to fruition, it is replaced by a new reform that moves the field of science education in a different direction.

Depending on one's point of view, the failure of the science education reforms is either a painful failure of science education leadership or its great success.

The past and present of the ESE Group have evolved alongside the past and present of ESE worldwide. However, the future is still questionable. Although humanity is jeopardized by the public's lack of awareness of earth systems concepts and lack of environmental insight, the profile of ESE in schools worldwide is low, and the number of currently active academic ESE leaders is limited as well. This situation is a direct result of the essentialism–reductionism conservative regime.

In education, as in many other fields, quantity is not a predictive measure of success. The only key to success is quality. The learning instinct theory, which is embedded in the earth systems approach, can provide ESE with a high-quality tool for breaking through the walls of the reductionist ghetto.

At the age of 16, during the summer vacation between 10th and 11th grade, I saw a book in my sister's room (she was already attending university) with a strange name: "Summerhill." I don't know what made me start looking at it, but from the minute I started reading it, I could not put the book down. And when I finished it, I was no longer the same boy. This book gave me the justifications for my internal reluctance to attend school and my internal power to stand up to my parents and teachers (schooling in Israel is compulsory) and make the promise, which has directed my whole life since.

Evolutionary process is a result of reaction and interaction between a living organism's genetic code and its environment. The trigger for the ESE Group was the interaction of Dr. Neill's life story (Summerhill) with the preface of my own life story.

I have no doubt that somewhere during the thousands of interactions of the ESE Group with young students all over the world, there are already some whose life stories interconnect with that of the ESE Group. These random interactions of life stories will ultimately create the critical mass needed to break down the essentialism–reductionism walls and to make school an enjoyable, supportive environment for children.

Finally, it is essential to clarify that the strong criticism of this article is only against the educational essentialist-reductionism approach and not about attending schools. Unfortunately, the Essential education approach that tightly controls most educational systems worldwide is suitable for some children, but harmful for many others. However, different educational philosophies like the progressive and existentialist receive very partly supported and are often ignored by most governments worldwide. Thus, the impression or insight I would like this article to leave is that it is the responsibility of academic educationalists, including the science education leaders, to work to open the education system in their country to a pluralism of educational philosophies. Furthermore, it is their responsibility that parents would have the right to choose their children's school upon the the school's educational philosophy approach.

References

Ben-David, A., & Orion, N. (2012). Teachers' voices on integrating metacognition into science education. *International Journal of Science Education, 12*, 1–33. http://dx.doi.org/10.1080/09500693.2012.697208

Ben-Zvi Assaraf, O., & Orion, N. (2005a). Development of systems thinking skills in the context of earth system education. *Journal of Research in Science Teaching, 42*, 1–43. http://dx.doi.org/10.1002/tea.20061

Ben-Zvi-Assaraf, O., & Orion, N. (2005b). A study of junior high students' perceptions of the water cycle. *Journal of Geosciences Education, 53*(4), 366–373. http://dx.doi.org/10.5408/1089-9995-53.4.366

Ben-Zvi Assaraf, O., & Orion, N. (2009). A design-based research of an earth systems-based environmental curriculum. *Eurasia Journal of Mathematics, Science & Technology Education, 5*, 197–214. http://dx.doi.org/10.12973/ejmste/75256

Ben-Zvi Assaraf, O., & Orion, N. (2010). Systems thinking skills at the elementary school level. *Journal of Research in Science Teaching, 47*, 540–563. http://dx.doi.org/10.1002/tea.20351

Ben-Zvi Assaraf, O., Orion, N., & Ronen, D. (2008). The Blue Planet Earth Systems Approach (BEPESA) for the study of water related systems. In C. A. Brebbia (Ed.), *Environmental problems in coastal regions, VII* (pp. 161–168). WIT Press. http://dx.doi.org/10.2495/cenv080151

Bybee, R. W., & DeBoer, G. E. (1994). Research on goals for the science curriculum. In D. L. Gabel (Ed.), *Handbook of research on science teaching and learning* (pp. 357–387). Macmillan.

Dodick, J., & Orion, N. (2003). Cognitive factors affecting student understanding of geological time. *Journal of Research in Science Teaching, 40*, 415–442. http://dx.doi.org/10.1002/tea.10083

Evagorou, M., Korfiatis, K., Nicolaou, C., & Constantinou, C. (2009). An investigation of the potential of interactive simulations for developing systems thinking skills in elementary school: A case study with fifth graders and sixth graders. *International Journal of Science Education, 31*, 655–674. http://dx.doi.org/10.1080/09500690701749313

Eyov, L. (2017). *The earth science cross-country class as an intersection point between formal and informal education* [Unpublished master's thesis]. Weizmann Institute of Science.

Frelindich, N. (1998). From Sputnik to TIMSS: Reforms in science education make headway despite setbacks. *Harvard Education Letters, 14*(5).

Gudovitch, Y., & Orion, N. (2001). The carbon cycle and the Earth systems – Studying the carbon cycle in an environmental multidisciplinary context. In *Proceedings of the 1st IOSTE Symposium in Southern Europe*, Paralimni, Cyprus.

Hurd, P. D. (1986). Perspectives for the reform of science education. *Phi Delta Kappan, 67*, 353–358.

Kapulnik, E., Orion, N., & Ganiel, U. (2004). *In-service training programs in science and technology: What changes do teachers undergo?* [Paper presentation]. The National Association for Research in Science Teaching (NARST) Symposium, Vancouver, BC, Canada.

Liberty, S. (2018). *Designing a digital space to host learning* [Unpublished master's thesis]. Weizmann Institute of Science.

Merhav, O. (2013). *High-school students' engagement in knowledge integration process, based on logical thinking and systems thinking* [Unpublished master's thesis]. Weizmann Institute of Science.

Midyan, Y., & Orion, N. (2003). *Attitudes of Israeli elementary science teachers towards the implementation of outdoor learning activities as an integral part of an earth science unit* [Paper presentation]. The 3rd International Conference on Geoscience Education, Calgary, Canada.

National Research Council. (2012). *A framework for K-12 science education: Practices, crosscutting concepts, and core ideas*. The National Academies Press. http://dx.doi.org/10.17226/13165

Orion, N. (1989). Development of a high school geology course based on field trips. *Journal of Geological Education, 37*, 13–17.

Orion, N. (1993). A model for the development and implementation of field trips, as an integral part of the science curriculum. *School Science and Mathematics, 93*, 325–331.

Orion, N. (1996). A holistic approach to introduce geoscience into schools: The Israeli model – From practice to theory. In D. A. Stow & G. J. H. McCall (Eds.), *Geosciences education and training: In schools and universities, for industry and public awareness* (AGID special publication series, No. 19). A.A. Balkema Publishers.

Orion, N. (1997). *Earth science education + environmental education = Earth systems education* [Paper presentation]. The Second International Conference on Geoscience Education, University of Hawaii at Hilo, HI, USA.

Orion, N. (2002). An earth systems curriculum development model. In V. J. Mayer (Ed.), *Global science literacy* (pp. 159–168). Kluwer. http://dx.doi.org/10.1007/978-1-4020-5818-9_11

Orion, N. (2003a). The outdoor as a central learning environment in the global science literacy framework: From theory to practice. In V. J. Mayer (Ed.), *Implementing global science literacy* (pp. 33–66). Ohio State University Press.

Orion, N. (2003b). Teaching global science literacy: A professional development or a professional change. In V. J. Mayer (Ed.), *Implementing global science literacy* (pp. 279–286). Ohio State University Press.

Orion, N. (2007). A holistic approach for science education for all. *Eurasia Journal for Mathematics, Science and Technology Education, 3*, 99–106. http://dx.doi.org/10.12973/ejmste/75382

Orion, N. (2016). Earth systems education and the development of environmental insight. In C. Vasconcelos (Ed.), *Geoscience education: Indoor and outdoor* (pp. 59–72). Springer International Publishing. http://dx.doi.org/10.1007/978-3-319-43319-6_4

Orion, N., & Ault, C. (2007). Learning earth sciences. In S. Abell & N. Lederman (Eds.), *Handbook of research on science teaching and learning* (pp. 653–688). Lawrence Erlbaum Associates.

Orion, N., & Basis, T. (2008). *Characterization of high school students' systems thinking skills in the context of Earth systems* [Paper presentation]. The National Association for Research in Science Teaching, (NARST) Symposium, Baltimore, MD, USA.

Orion, N., & Cohen, C. (2007). A design-based research of an oceanography module as a part of the Israeli high school earth sciences program. *Journal of Geographie und ihre Didaktik, 4*, 246–259.

Orion, N., & Fortner, W. R. (2003). Mediterranean models for integrating environmental education and earth sciences through earth systems education. *Mediterranean Journal of Educational Studies, 8*, 97–111.

Orion, N., & Hofstein, A. (1994). Factors that influence learning during a scientific field trip in a natural environment. *Journal of Research in Science Teaching, 31*, 1097–1119. http://dx.doi.org/10.1002/tea.3660311005

Orion, N., Hofstein, A., & Mazor, E. (1986). A field-based high school geology course: Igneous and metamorphic terrain, an Israeli experience. *Geology Teaching, 11*, 16–20.

Orion, N., Ben-Chaim, D., & Kali, Y. (1997). Relationship between earth science education and spatial visualization. *Journal of Geoscience Education, 45*, 129–132. http://dx.doi.org/10.5408/1089-9995-45.2.129

Orion, N., Ben-Menacham, O., & Shur, Y. (2007). Raising scholastic achievement in minority-reached classes through earth systems teaching. *Journal of Geosciences Education, 55*, 469–477. http://dx.doi.org/10.5408/1089-9995-55.6.469

Orion, N., & Libarkin, J. (2014). Earth systems education. In S. Abell & N. Lederman (Eds.), *Handbook of research on science teaching and learning* (pp. 481–496). Lawrence Erlbaum Associates.

Ossimitz, G. (2000). Teaching system dynamics and systems thinking in Austria and Germany. In *Proceedings of the 18th International Conference of the System Dynamics Society*, Bergen, Norway.

Schechter, T. (2020). *The interrelationships between social well-being and the learning process in the high school earth science program* [Unpublished master's thesis]. Weizmann Institute of Science.

Shalom, M. (2013). *What factors promote and inhibit teachers making changes in their methods of teaching?* [Unpublished master's thesis]. Weizmann Institute of Science]

Yager, R. E. (2000). The history and future of science education reform. *The Clearing House: A Journal of Educational Strategies, Issues and Ideas, 74*, 51–54. http://dx.doi.org/10.1080/00098655.2000.11478641

Yunker, M., Orion, N., & Lernau, H. (2011). Merging playfulness with the formal science curriculum in an outdoor learning environment. *Children, Youth and Environments, 21*, 271–293.

CHAPTER 6

Learning Skills for Science (LSS) – An Israel-UK Collaborative Program

Models, Dissemination, and Impact

Zahava Scherz and Bat-Sheva Eylon

Abstract

Attainment of higher-order skills should be a fundamental part of school science education in the 21st century and is imperative for the development of independent learning. These skills include inquiry and problem-solving skills, thinking skills and learning skills. This chapter relates to the program Learning Skills for Science (LSS), which was developed in the late 1990s for schools in Israel and later extended for UK secondary schools through a 10-year collaboration with the Gatsby-SEP (Science Enhancement Programme). We describe the objectives and characteristics of the LSS program, and present models for its usage in science and technology education. We elaborate on LSS learning activities, teacher development and dissemination frameworks.

Research and evaluation findings from Israel and the UK indicate that explicit and spiral instruction of LSS skills, integrated into a variety of scientific contexts and tasks, promote students' performances in compound science learning activities. Participating teachers were instrumental and resourceful in integrating LSS into their schemes of work. The LSS program was successfully adapted by key reforms in Israel, UK and had impact additional countries.

Keywords

Learning Skills for Science (LSS) – Science and Technology – independent learning – higher order skills – secondary school science

1 Background

Science and technology are central to people's lives in modern world (Next Generation Science Standards, 2020) and therefore, science education should be a foremost part of the education of all school students. Science education

 | DOI: 10.1163/9789004503625_006

aims to prepare all students for life in a world of rapid scientific and technological change and to prepare a smaller number of them for highly specialized science-oriented professions. Science education today is facing an endless struggle between the vast number of topics that have to be taught in school science and the need to develop independent learners, as a lifetime habit, who must master a variety of higher-order skills (Berliner, 1992; Biggs & Collis, 1982; Bybee, 1997; Bybee & Ben-Zvi, 1998; Campbell et al., 1993; Eylon & Linn, 1988; Next Generation Science Standards, 2020; OECD [Organisation for Economic Co-operation and Development], 2018a; Osborn, 2006).

Towards the beginning of the new millennium reforms in science and technology education were thrived in many countries (e.g. American Association for the Advancement of Science, 1993; National Research Council,1996; Next Generation Science Standards, 2020) to fit the rapidly changing world and the technological demands (DeBoer, 2000). Those reforms, were also based on the view that learning happens throughout one's life, as the previous notion of a divided lifetime – education followed by work – ceased to be tenable. In fact, learning has become an integral part of adult activities, referred to as 'lifelong learning' (Aspin & Chapman, 2007; Jarvis, 2009).

These conceptions also reflect the overall goal of helping students integrate what they learn in the science classroom into their daily lives. This goal can be achieved by creating a multidisciplinary curriculum and replacing the traditional frontal instruction with instruction that is more inquiry-based, involving teamwork, interactive workshops, apprenticeships, and individual projects (Bereiter & Scardamalia, 1989; Bybee, 1997; Linn et al., 1994). For students to learn independently and autonomously, as a lifelong habit, they have to be able to successfully implement higher-order skills (Berliner, 1992; Biggs & Collis, 1982; Bybee & Ben-Zvi, 1998; Eylon & Linn, 1988). In view of these requirements, it is necessary to equip the teachers with new instructional methods and materials that foster the development of such skills in the classroom (Spektor-Levy et al., 2002).

The importance of learning-skills instruction is strengthened by studies that have found a positive correlation between students' performance in several learning skills and their academic achievement (Carns & Carns, 1991; Segal et al., 1985) Interestingly, these findings referred to high-school students (Onwuegbuzie et al., 2001; Slate et al., 1993), undergraduates (Jones et al., 1993), and pre-academic students with disadvantaged backgrounds (Scherz et al., 1985, 1986). However, even students who acquire and implement learning skills will use those skills regularly only if they are demanded by their instructors, mentors or career (Oosterhuis-Geers, 1993). Programs for the learning and implementation of learning skills in secondary school and even earlier, lay the foundation for learning capabilities that will help students throughout their future studies and changing careers.

Assessments should reward students' engagement in inquiry activities, as opposed to simply memorizing content knowledge. This shift in goals has led to reforms in science education in many countries which reflect the overall tendency of replacing traditional transmission instruction with more student-centered learning; these require higher-order skills and active learning processes. Consequently, worldwide science education reforms tuned to the 21st century have changed the curriculum of Science & Technology studies to a flexible framework, with rich opportunities to select subtopics and sequences of instruction. These reforms also advocate a gradual move toward a curriculum based on higher-order skills and authentic scientific contexts. These trends form the underlying rationale for influential educational authorities and policymakers who promote and convey changes in the curriculum (National Research Council, 2012; OECD, 2018a, 2018b; Partnership for 21st Century Learning Framework, 2019; Rotherham & Willingham, 2009; Shamos, 1995).

We believe that in high-quality science education students should develop an in-depth understanding of scientific concepts and main ideas, as well as key higher-order skills, i.e., learning, inquiry, problem-solving and thinking skills (Figure 6.1a).

2 Description of the LSS Program

The LSS program was first developed in Israel (Scherz et al., 1986; Spektor-Levy & Scherz, 1999, 2001) and was implemented in Israeli Junior High Schools (JHSs) in the late 1990s and into the 2000s. In this chapter, we describe the objectives and characteristics of the LSS program, and present models for the program's learning and instruction in Science & Technology education. We briefly describe several LSS learning activities, as well as LSS teacher development and dissemination frameworks. In particular, we comment on selected research and evaluation findings from Israel and the UK that refer to the impact of the LSS program on student learning and future instruction.

The LSS program was introduced to UK science education scholars in the years 2003–2004 as part of a collaborative project between three academic groups from the Weizmann Institute of Science in Israel and three academic groups from the UK as an initiative of the Gatsby-SEP Foundation to support "Evidence-Based Professional Development of Science Teachers" in the two countries (Harrison et al., 2008). In 2004, the Gatsby-SEP -Foundation chose to further support the LSS team in adapting the LSS program to the needs of the UK science education system. Consequently, a UK–Israel LSS program was developed in a three-way lateral collaboration between the Weizmann, the Gatsby-SEP and the Nuffield Curriculum Centre, for school levels 14–15. Latter this was followed by an advanced LSS program for post-16 students taking A-level science. The overall goal of the LSS project was declared as follows: "The program specifically aims to foster the development of skills considered necessary for enhancing science learning and to provide a good foundation on which science learning can take place" (Price et al., 2008; Scherz & Spektor-Levy, 2006; Scherz et al., 2005; Spektor-Levy et al., 2008).

Higher-order skills for science are an integral part of appropriate science education. They include inquiry and problem-solving skills, thinking skills and learning skills (see Figure 6.1a), and they are essential for the development of independent learners. The LSS program focuses on learning skills, and further divides them into six subareas (Figure 6.1b). Today, a learner in the knowledge era is expected to deal with knowledge-based episodes as a *knowledge consumer* or *knowledge creator*. As a consumer, one needs to use skills such as information retrieval, reading, listening and observing, to benefit from a variety of resources (left three branches in Figure 6.1b). A knowledge creator should use skills such as data analysis and representation, scientific writing, and knowledge presentation (right three branches Figure 6.1b). The LSS program aims to advance all six skill areas to develop the desired learning skills.

2.1 *The Goals of the Program*

The primary goals of the LSS program are:
- To enhance learning skills for science among secondary school students
- To provide teachers with resources that can be easily integrated into a variety of scientific subjects
- To design flexible teaching and learning tasks suitable for different levels of students and a variety of learning styles.

2.2 *The Instructional Model*

The model of LSS instruction and learning is based on our accumulated research and practice and is grounded in assumptions and principles of learning sciences theories.

Memory load: the amount of new information one can learn, remember and understand is limited to the amount that the working memory can manage, termed cognitive load. If material to be learned is too complex, or overloading or too demanding (high cognitive load), then learning will be inhibited. LSS provides strategies to decrease the extraneous cognitive load, by developing

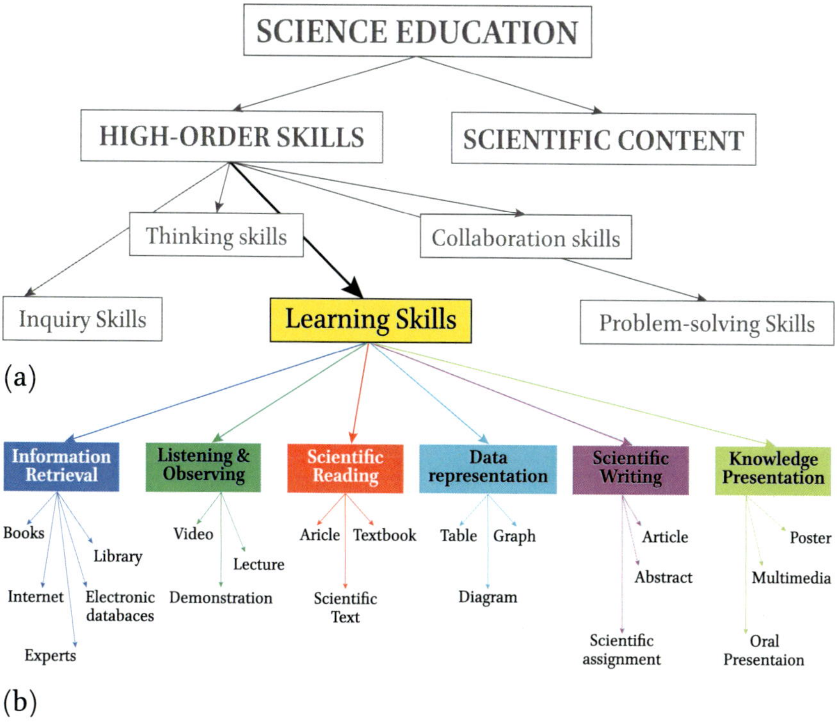

FIGURE 6.1 Components of science education

learning strategies, e.g., chunking, organizing, and constructing (Mayer et al., 1999; Mousavi et al., 1995; Spiegel & Barufaldi, 1994). Excess load can be due to the nature of the information, quantity of the text, language used and/or complexity of the visual presentations. The explicit teaching of skills in LSS supports students by providing them with strategies to recognize and process information irrespective of how it is presented. These strategies are learned and automated, providing more processing capability to deal with complex disciplinary concepts or compound ideas.

Explication: skills usually do not develop spontaneously. Even motor skills such as swimming need to be taught and practiced over time. In order to develop high-quality learning skills they must be taught explicitly, in a well-planned manner (Prawat, 1989).

Integration: the teaching of learning skills should be integrated and infused with content learning in science and technology; they should not be taught as a separate content-free subject (Ennis, 1989; Spektor-Levy et al., 2008; Zohar & Dori, 2003).

Intentional learning: to master higher-order skills, the student should experience meaningful learning, via a constructivist instructional approaches for student-centered learning (Brown et al., 1989; Cakir, 2008; Mayer, 1999; Mousavi et al., 1995).

Spiral learning and transfer: all learning skills should be applied repeatedly in a variety of domains and contexts throughout the curriculum; they should not be taught as a 'one-shot' experience. Every subskill should be attained in three cycles: basic instruction, practice and application in different subjects (Scherz & Spektor-Levy, 2006; Spektor-Levy et al., 2008).

These assumptions guided us in designing a general model for skills instruction that provides the science teacher with instructional strategies to be implemented in the science and Science & Technology classrooms. A practical representation of the LSS instructional model appears in Table 6.1.

TABLE 6.1 LSS instructional model

Characteristics	Explication
Explicit instruction	The instruction of skills and subskills is evident and is emphasized explicitly using metacognitive reflections and discussions. Students are aware of the process of skill acquisition.
Active learning	Learning takes place through diverse activities (e.g., independent learning, team work); and students are immediately requested to use the learned skill in their science assignments.
Framework	The instructional materials consist of a generic framework of many common activities that can be used in conjunction with different science topics. These activities are designed to practice the different learning skills and subskills in any given area in science (e.g., employing scientific reading activities in science tasks).
Integration	Teachers/curriculum developers should tailor the general activities to specific content areas according to the students' levels and needs. For several topics, integrated activities are provided through 'interface' materials that have been developed as examples. A growing collection of interfaces is presented on the LSS website.
Spiral instruction	Throughout the school year, the students practice the six skill areas. Each year students are introduced to different subskills, which they learn in depth. They continue to practice them during the course of their studies.
Flexibility and modularity	The instructional materials are flexible and modular so that every year, specific, appropriate skills and activities can be implemented. Activities can be adjusted to the students' levels and needs.

2.3 *Example Activities*

For each of the six skill areas, we developed 5–12 generic activities according to our model. Figure 6.2 outlines six example of these generic activities, one for each skill area.

2.3.1 Information Retrieval: Advertising a Scientific Journal

This activity helps students become familiar with scientific journals that are suited to their level. Working in teams, students are given samples of a scientific journal. They have to explore the journal according to specific instructions, introduce the journal to the class, and prepare an attractive advertisement to encourage others to use this journal in the future. In doing so, they present the structure of the journal, its goals, its different sections, and they describe the level of the journal and its target audience. In preparing the advertisement,

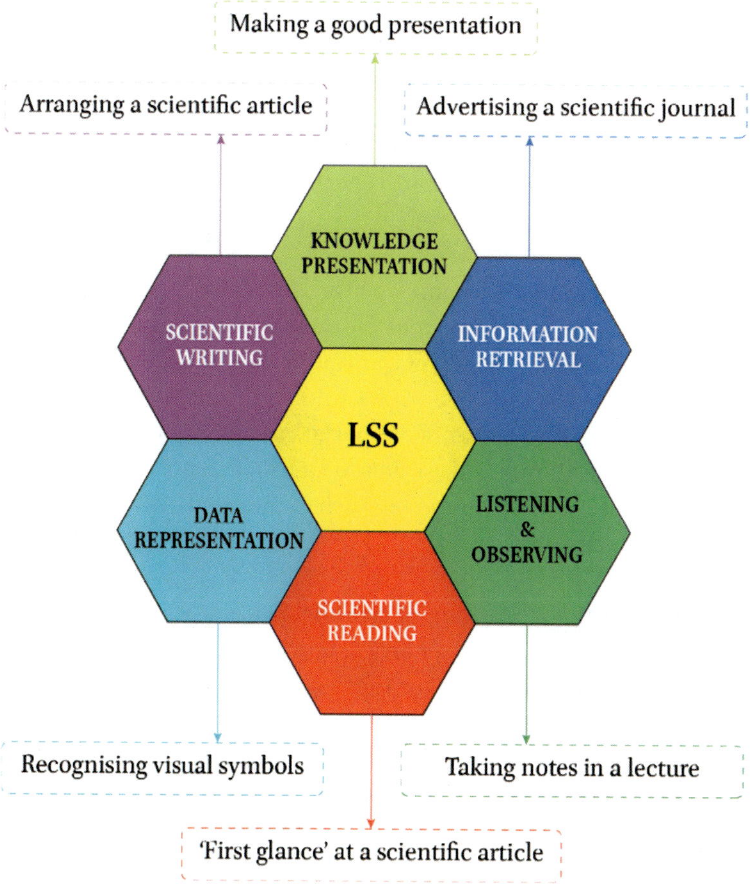

FIGURE 6.2 LSS skill areas and examples of activities

the students utilize their creativity to compose jingles, draw posters, and write slogans.

2.3.2 Listening and Observing: Taking Notes in a Lecture

In this activity, students gain experience in summarizing and documenting information transmitted orally through a lecture, a discussion, etc. The student is given guided instruction on how to summarize the information transmitted in a lecture. After the lecture, they are asked to think and self-evaluate in terms of whether they succeeded in concentrating and listening to the lecture, and how they accomplished the task.

2.3.3 Scientific Reading: The 'First Glance' into a Scientific Article

In this activity, students acquire the skills of browsing and sorting scientific articles to find those that are suitable, relevant and credible for a specific assignment. 'First glance' refers to skimming through an article, while drawing information from it and becoming acquainted with it. The aim is to decide whether an article is relevant for the reader's aims and thus worth reading in greater depth. In general, after a 'first glance,' the initial selection of articles can be reduced by around 80%. Following the activity, the readers should know whether they are interested in the article in terms of its suitability to the assignment at hand and its scientific level.

2.3.4 Data Representation: Recognizing Visual Symbols

In this activity, students are given a map of the climatic regions of the world, without a color key, and asked to interpret the significance of the colors on the map. If necessary, they can be provided with a number of aids – weather-forecast icons at various points on the map, a symbol key, a color key, or a map title. The activity demonstrates the need to use aids to interpret an unfamiliar visual representation, as well as the contribution of each of these aids, which include standard symbols from daily life.

2.3.5 Scientific Writing: Arranging a Scientific Article

Students are asked to correctly order an article in which the pages have been shuffled. To make things a little easier for them, certain words are marked in bold in the text to give a clue as to the nature of the section, i.e., the introduction, the methods, etc. After they have identified the various sections, students are asked to arrange the article in the standard order. The activity ends with the students being asked to answer a number of questions, as a check on whether they have understood the article and its central message.

2.3.6 Knowledge Presentation: Preparing a Good Presentation

In this activity, the students are required to prepare a brief presentation of knowledge after having read a short scientific article. The teacher then asks several students to present what they have prepared. The other students listen to the lectures, while drawing up a list of criteria and tips for preparing a scientific lecture and presenting it to an audience. The immediate product of the activity is a set of criteria for a good lecture. This may also be varied by creating an acronym (based on the first letters of the formulated criteria), or a series of illustrations, which provide students with a humorous reminder of what they have to remember when presenting information.

2.4 *LSS Learning Materials*

The UK LSS learning materials (14–16) consisted of :

- *An extended guide for the teacher* – a booklet that includes relevant theoretical background information about the skills and their teaching along with guidance, examples and tips for the implementation of the activities.
- *An activity workbook for the students* – a folder of worksheets for all six modules with instructions for the classroom activities. These can be download or photocopied.
- *Interfaces* – a website providing supporting resources such as scientific articles and texts, and worksheets that can be downloaded for modification and reproduction. It also includes a notice board for exchange of good practices among teachers using the program.

2.5 *LSS Teacher Professional Development*

Introductory and continuing LSS professional development for teachers has been disseminated across England using a multilevel professional development model. The model consists of two dimensions: a continuing professional development (CPD) program for teachers and trainers, and scaled-up implementation. During 2004–2005, the SEP in the UK established a teaching program to fit with the curriculum in that country. Two teachers from each of eight schools were trained in the use of the LSS activities. Those teachers then tried different ways of implementing the LSS tasks in their science classes. Feedback from this pilot was encouraging and a larger LSS teacher development program was initiated in 2006. The CPD program includes a 2-hour 'taster' session, a 2-day teacher development workshop, a 2-day 'training the trainers' workshop, and a departmental teacher meeting (Figure 6.3).

Professional development were carried on through teacher development organizations such as the SEP, the Nuffield Curriculum Centre and the regional science learning centers.

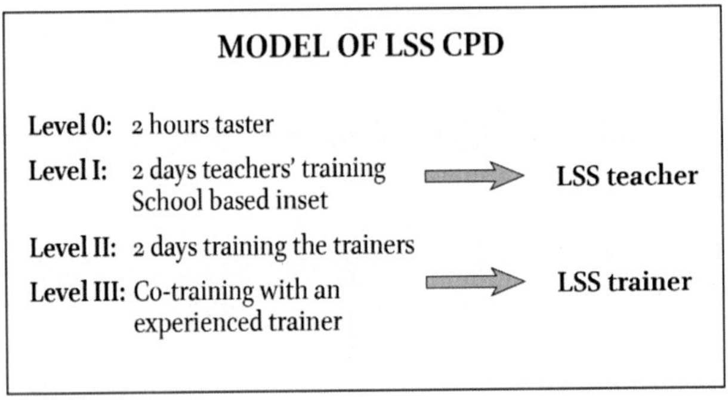

FIGURE 6.3 LSS CPD program for teachers: three-level model

Scaling-up of implementation: this was comprised of three stages: (a) first pilot – 6 schools (2004–2005); (b) extended pilot – 60 schools (2005–2006); (c) wide dissemination – integration into 'Twenty-First Century Science' in the UK and other new specifications (GCSE Criteria for Science, 2006). The LSS CPD model was farther implemented in various cycles of professional development.

3 Research and Evaluation

The development of the LSS program was followed by research and formative evaluation aimed at refining it and studying its impact on students' learning, performance and attitudes. This section refers to research carried out in Israel and in the UK in various stages of LSS development and implementation. It is important to emphasize that the research efforts reported in this chapter were performed by LSS academic scholars from both countries, who were responsive to each other's research results and methods. However, the research design and performance were carried out separately and in different periods of LSS implementation. In this chapter we focus on selected findings and conclusions from research efforts that influenced the development of advanced LSS versions and assisted us in consolidating evolving models of LSS instruction and dissemination.

3.1 *The Case of Israel*

One of the declared goals of Israeli Science & Technology national curricular programs is the development of higher-order skills. However, few of the learning materials provide pedagogical guidance on how to impart these skills to students assuming that "skill attainment" happens spontaneously during school learning.

The first edition of the LSS program began to be integrated in Science & Technology classes in Israel at the beginning of 2000. During the years 2002–2004, we performed a 2-year longitudinal study of JHS students (grades 7 and

8) and their science teachers. During that period, version 1 of the LSS program ("Scientific Communication" in Hebrew) was published as a set of generic activities with examples of integration with Science & Technology contents for JHSs (Spektor-Levy & Scherz, 1999, 2001). The assumption was that the teachers would integrate the generic LSS tasks with various STEM contents of the school/national curriculum. A study was designed to examine students' and teachers' performance and attitudes with respect to the LSS program.

3.2 *Research Goals*

The 1st goal was to examine *students' skill-learning* performance from two perspectives:
- What skills do students report having acquired during their Science & Technology studies?
- How does LSS instruction influence students' performance and achievements.

The 2nd goal examined *teachers' instruction* of LSS:
- How did the teachers customize the LSS instructional model?
- How complex were the various LSS activities?
- How do the teachers feel about the potential use of the LSS activities?

3.3 *Methodology, Results and Discussion*

The following are extractions from research studies of our LSS group in Israel (Scherz et al., 2005, 2008, 2011; Scherz & Spektor-Levy, 2006; Spektor-Levy et al., 2008).

3.3.1 Students' Skill-Learning

What skills do students report having acquired during their Science & Technology studies? The research followed LSS implementation in grades 7 and 8 in Israel. At the end of the 8th grade, about 450 of the Israeli students were asked to indicate, in an open-ended question, which skills and capabilities they had acquired during their Science & Technology studies in JHS. The sample included students who did not study learning skills explicitly in their Science & Technology class or elsewhere (reference group) and LSS students who did study learning skills through the LSS program (intervention groups). The skills that were mentioned by the students were listed and categorized. The students who studied the LSS program indicated acquiring a larger variety of skills and capabilities than the reference group. Moreover, each of the skills was mentioned by a significantly higher percentage of the students than in the reference group. It was also found that students who experienced the LSS program better explicated and described their implementation of learning skills than

Channel 100 – This prestigious channel is looking for investigators: young, enthusiastic, with high motivation, knowledgeable!

You are invited to send a sample 5-minute TV "Update Report" about your research on air pollution. The report must include a general review on air pollution and its causes, and then focus on one pollutant or associated phenomena.
Prepare a 5-minute TV broadcast: an oral report (up to three pages of text) accompanied by up to five slides/transparencies that show relevant pictures, figures, graphs, tables, etc.

FIGURE 6.4 Complex performance task "Update Report"

those who did not. These students could detail their moves and decision-making considerations while implementing the learning skills.

How does LSS *instruction influence students' performance and achievements?* students' performance and achievements were diagnosed by a complex assessment task ("Update Report," Figure 6.4) at the end of the 8th grade; 206 students participated in the study (164 from the LSS intervention groups and 42 from the reference group). The LSS intervention groups performed significantly better than the reference group, who did not learn the LSS program. Performance was linked to three main measured criteria: (a) knowledge, (b) learning skills, and (c) products and outcomes (Table 6.2).

3.3.2 Teachers' Instruction of LSS

How did the teachers customize the LSS *instructional model? How complex were the various* LSS *activities? How do the teachers feel about the potential use of the* LSS *activities?* Interview and questionnaire results showed that (a) teachers customized the program and conducted a variety of sequences and patterns of instruction; (b) most teachers claimed that they practiced a spiral implementation; (c) teachers usually planned the instruction as teamwork with their colleagues in school; (d) teachers realized that the skills differed in their level of complexity and therefore distributed the instruction of certain skills accordingly in the different grade levels (Spektor-Levy et al., 2008, 2009).

Our study indicated that the development of learning skills may occur to some extent through experience or ordinary studies, even without formal instruction. However, formal and structured teaching and learning are necessary to make a significant difference. We showed that explicit and spiral instruction of skills, integrated into scientific contents, along with a continuous demand for implementation in various contexts and tasks, promotes meaningful development of LSS skills.

TABLE 6.2 Student performance on the complex performance task "Update Report"

Category	Criteria	LSS N = 42 Mean (SD)	Reference N = 164 Mean (SD)	P
a. Knowledge	– Information about pollutant. – Main concepts & terms. – Chemical processes. – The air as a mixture of gases. – Change of phases in matter. – Effects of air pollution on man and environment. – Ways to decrease pollution.	48 (3.4)	64 (1.8)	***
b. Learning skills	– Information: variety of sources. – Reliable and relevant. – Text: clear & professional. – Representation of quantitative data. – Computerized presentation.	44 (3.4)	64 (1.8)	***
c. Products and outcomes	Additional criteria (not included in a & b).	41.6 (2.8)	60.7(1.6)	***

*** $P < 0.001$

3.4 *The Case of the UK*

In 2004, the UK Gatsby-SEP Foundation decided to establish a project with the Weizmann Institute of Science in Israel aimed to translate, adapt and, if necessary, expand the initial LSS program for the needs of the UK science education system. Altogether, the project was developed and implemented under SEP during 10 years and continues to be used today. It went through several stages of development, accompanied by research and evaluation.

Stage 1. The first version of LSS materials 14–16 took a year to develop and involved extensive translation and adaptation effort carried out by the mixed Israeli–UK team. The team conducted a CPD program for six science teachers from different schools in the London area, followed by a first pilot of UK class implementation as well as an evaluation headed by Prof. Jonathan Osborne from King's College London. The evaluation revealed much enthusiasm and commitment from the teachers (Osborne & Manning, 2006). They enjoyed their LSS in service training and were keen to use the materials more widely in the future. The main recommendations of this evaluation were: (a) to revise some of the LSS materials and develop more activities for visual representations in science and in technology, (b) to carry out a scaled-up implementation comprised of steps: initial step – 6 schools (2004–2005); extended step – 60 schools (2005–2006); wide dissemination – integration into the 'Twenty-First Century Science' and other new UK secondary school specifications (2006–2011).

Stage 2. In 2008, after 2 years of CPD and dissemination in the UK, a larger-scale formative evaluation project for the LSS program was carried out by the London UCL Institute of Education (Price et al., 2008). The primary goal of this evaluation was to ascertain the impact of the LSS program on the teaching and learning of science in UK secondary schools, and in particular, its impact on teachers, students, professional development and dissemination.

Use of LSS *materials and resources*: The LSS activities and materials were described as "generally excellent," and, despite the remarked need for improvements (particularly related to differentiation), they were, on the whole, "highly commended."

Professional development and dissemination: Four main methods were observed:

a. developing the individual teacher, then dissemination to individuals in that teacher's school science department
b. developing the individual teacher, then dissemination to the whole school science department
c. formal LSS development, for the entire science department during a school teacher development day
d. outreach dissemination where LSS is disseminated across other departments within the school, e.g., English, mathematics, or to other schools in the area.

Teachers: All teachers were extremely positive about LSS as an approach for supporting more skills-based development. LSS was perceived as a very good teaching tool with great potential, and considered invaluable for students as both future citizens and potential scientists. In particular, the teachers' opinion was that adoption practices are influenced to some degree by dissemination practice, and that successful adaptation of LSS is dependent on a number of factors, including: the degree of adoption within the school science department; resource and material development; extra time for teachers' lesson preparation, planning and writing into schemes of work; plus some level of external support and community interaction. At a general level, two different teacher perspectives on LSS emerged: as a 'skills' set of resources or as a 'method' of teaching. As a skills set, it was seen, and expected to be, an 'off-the-shelf' set of resources that could be inserted into the teaching program as an extra lesson or learning activity. As a method of teaching, the focus is on attaining an awareness of the skills required by students, and an expectation of either adapting the LSS activities themselves or incorporating the activities into teaching. Collectively across schools, LSS was reported to be useful for various purposes, e.g., to introduce new science content, as a revision mechanism, and simply as skills development. On the whole, participating teachers believed that it is possible for LSS to be adopted and adapted within all of the science curricula and across key stages 3, 4 and 5. However, teachers consistently reported that LSS materials and tasks are not suitably differentiated to be of general use.

Students: The main data about LSS students was collected from their task reports and teacher interviews served as evidence for the LSS CPD programs (Scherz et al., 2011). We learned the following:

Engagement – Several students reported enjoying LSS activities and/or finding them particular productive. Teachers explicitly identified reasons for positive student engagement with LSS: the introduction of something 'fresh' and different from their normal lesson; the use of different kinds of activities; activities with time limits can create a 'fun' challenge; achieving something new; and the opportunity for students to express their own opinions. On the other hand, a number of adverse responses to LSS were encountered, particularly with the reading and graphing activities.

Pedagogically related aspects – Generally students had mixed perceptions of the value of LSS for them. Some groups of students did not see the relationship between the LSS activity and science. Some students pointed out that working in groups was quite difficult, especially as they had never done group work before.

Student skill development – Assessment instruments developed by the Weizmann Institute were given, in both hard and electronic copies, to the main contact teacher in all participating schools. However, many teachers (21 of the 22) did not use the assessment activities because of lack of time required for implementing the tasks, together with the view that LSS development could be assessed through coursework. Our evaluation suggests that most teachers were able to comment on students' skills development by discussing their everyday work in the classroom and looking at their coursework. Thirteen out of sixteen teachers from seven of the schools identified instances where they considered that students showed improved skill proficiency.

Stage 3. The favorable evaluation findings resulted in supporting revisions and further development of new LSS materials. As a result, the following materials were developed:

A revised collection of LSS *materials* (*14–16*), comprising additional activities to develop students' scientific communication skills; resources and pedagogy that can be easily integrated into a variety of scientific subjects; flexible teaching and assessment tasks suitable for different student levels; a guidebook "Training the trainers" with CPD sessions for LSS providers.

Learning skills for post-16 sciences: recognizing the need to prepare students for higher education and employment, the "Advanced Learning Skills for Post-16 Sciences" program was developed, comprising of activities and resources that were specifically mapped to the contents in Biology, Chemistry, Physics, Applied Science and Science in Society.

Ideally, the activities meant to be fully integrated into the work schemes. Because the science content is usually covered along with development of a particular skill, the activities should not require substantial additional curriculum time. The assumption was that time devoted to development of these skills in the early part of an advanced course, will be made up for as students will be able to use these skills in their learning experience.

In 2009, LSS activities were chosen to complement the teaching of the new Extended Project Qualification which was offered by 900 centers to 17.5 thousand students with interest increasing annually. Since 2011, LSS activities have been incorporated into key texts which support the core units of the GCSE science specifications in Twenty-First Century Science.

4 Overall LSS Impact

4.1 *Israel*

The LSS skills became a central part of two consecutive reforms of the Science & Technology curriculum in Israel: (a) MATMON 1996–2008, where the six main skills were published as generic activities with examples of integration into science contents, and (b) MATMON HADASH 2010, where the learning skills and other science-oriented skills were integrated with different contents across the 1-year science curriculum. This approach liberated teachers from the need to integrate the skill activity with a science content; rather, they received already integrated activities as part of the LSS materials.

4.2 *UK*

Since 2004, the LSS program has been translated to English, expanded and adapted to the needs of the British education system as part of a collaborative project between the Weizmann Institute of Science, the Gatsby-SEP and the

Nuffield Curriculum Centre. An estimated 12,000 teachers and science consultants across the UK have undergone to teach using LSS in the years 2006–2009. The program was rolled out through science learning centers, and more broadly through in-service development delivered to school science departments. It was then adapted by the National Science Learning Centre in York and was integrated into the 21st century science program. In 2008, the LSS program (14–16) was disseminated to about 3000 classes across the UK.

The LSS program was considered particularly helpful for students preparing for 'Twenty-First Century Science' and other new GCSE (General Certificate of Secondary Education) specifications (Millar, 2006). In 2009, LSS activities were chosen to complement the teaching of the new Extended Project Qualification. Since 2011, LSS activities have been incorporated into key texts which support the core units of the GCSE science specifications in Twenty-First Century Science.

LSS teacher development was firmly established in a regular in-service run by the national network of science learning centers. Participants qualifying for the science and discovery center Techniques are responsible for the imminent roll out of LSS teacher development to Welsh school teachers. The LSS materials were translated into Welsh and the in-service teacher development has been used as part of a wider initiative to address numeracy and literacy skills.

4.3 *International*

For five years (2005–2010), LSS teacher development has contributed 2 out of 10 days of an annual international teacher leaders seminar led by the Weizmann Institute to a global audience.

- *Singapore.* In 2009, we sent an expert team from Israel and the UK to co-deliver in-service development to 50 science teachers from the Raffles Institution in Singapore. Representatives from the Singapore Ministry of Education observed the teacher development sessions and were keen to incorporate LSS into their science education program. LSS activities have now been integrated into the teaching schemes of the institute and its feeder schools.
- *Brazil.* In 2010, we were invited to present LSS and to support teacher development in Brazil. The work in Brazil has resulted in the translation of the LSS materials into Portuguese and Spanish and a planned LSS implementation in Sao-Paulo and Buenos-Aires (2017–2020); CPD workshops were begun toward the end of 2011. Building on the experience in the UK, LSS is gradually becoming embedded within the Brazilian schools' curriculum.
- *Other countries.* Over the years, LSS teacher development and workshops have also been carried out successfully in Canada, Germany and Latvia, as well as some places in the United States.

5 Concluding Remarks

There is no doubt that students and individuals who want to be independent lifelong learners and to be prepared for the changing world of the 21st century need to develop higher-order learning skills. In this chapter, we presented the LSS program, which was developed and implemented to enhance learning capabilities. We also presented findings indicating quality, efficiency, and impact of LSS.

COVID-19 Pandemic started to penetrate to our lives last year. Distance learning using synchronic and a-synchronic online media became part of school students' daily life. Independent learning skills happened to be essential for successful learning more than ever, and LSS program suggests valuable solutions for this unmet need. We envision several directions for further advances and applications of the LSS program in the future:

- *Applying* the LSS model and pedagogy to additional higher-order cognitive skills, such as critical-thinking skills, inquiry skills and problem-solving skills, as well as socio-psychological skills such as inter- and intrapersonal skills, collaboration and communication skills.
- *Extending and adapting* the LSS program to non-scientific disciplines such as history, art or economy.
- *Extending the scope* of the LSS program to additional educational levels – from elementary schools at one end, to higher education levels (college and university students) at the other.
- *Developing a sophisticated digital* LSS platform which will enable a growing collection of applications and student-based uses such as self-learning supported by personal tutoring.

We believe that in this era of immense technological development and unexpected global changes, these proposed advances are possible and important for the future of education.

Acknowledgments

We thank our partners in Israel: Ornit Spektor-Levy (Bar-Ilan University) for contributing to LSS learning materials, research and implementation; Dr. Liora Bialer (Weizmann Institute) for research and teacher development; Yahavit Loria (Meigal) for evaluation tasks and editing in Hebrew. We thank the UK collaborators: Sally Johnson for major contribution in all stages and Jill Scarce for the dissemination; Johnathan Osborn and Alex Manning (Kings College), and Sara Price and Michael Reiss (University of London) for project evaluation; Andrew Hunt and Angela Hall (Nuffield Curriculum Centre) for their trust and professional contribution to the LSS design. We thank the Gatsby-SEP foundation (UK) for granting and supporting the LSS project and the directors Rachid Rkaina and Nigel Thomas.

References

American Association for the Advancement of Science. (1993). *Benchmarks for science literacy, project 2061*. Oxford University Press.

Aspin, D. N., & Chapman, J. D. (2007). Lifelong learning concepts and conceptions. In D. N. Aspin (Ed.), *Philosophical perspectives on lifelong learning* (pp. 19–38). Springer. http://dx.doi.org/10.1007/978-1-4020-6193-6_1

Bereiter, C., & Scardamalia, M. (1989). Intentional learning as a goal of instruction. In L. Resnick (Ed.), *Knowing, learning and instruction* (pp. 361–392). Lawrence Erlbaum Associates. http://dx.doi.org/10.4324/9781315044408-12

Berliner, D. C. (1992). Redesigning classroom activities for the future. *Educational Technology, 32*, 7–13.

Biggs, J. B., & Collis, K. F. (1982). *Evaluating the quality of learning: The SOLO taxonomy*. Academic Press.

Brown, J. S., Collins, A., & Duguid, P. (1989). Situated cognition and the culture of learning. *Educational Researcher, 18*(1), 32–42. http://dx.doi.org/10.3102/0013189x018001032

Bybee, R. W. (1997). *Achieving scientific literacy: From purpose to practice*. Heinemann.

Bybee, R. W., & Ben-Zvi, N. (1998). Science curriculum: Transforming goals to practices. In B. J. Fraser & K. Tobin (Eds.), *International handbook of science education* (pp. 487–498). Kluwer Academic Publishers. http://dx.doi.org/10.1007/978-94-011-4940-2_28

Cakir, M. (2008). Constructivist approaches to learning in science and their implications for science pedagogy: A literature review. *International Journal of Environmental & Science Education, 3*, 193–206.

Campbell, J. P., McCloy, R. A., Oppler, S. H., & Sager, C. E. (1993). A theory of performance. In N. Schmitt & W. C. Borman (Eds.), *Personnel selection in organizations* (pp. 35–70). Jossey-Bass.

Carns, A. W., & Carns, M. R. (1991). Teaching study skills, cognitive strategies and metacognitive skills through self-diagnosed learning styles. *The School Counselor, 38*, 341–346.

DeBoer, G. E. (2000). Scientific literacy: Another look at its historical and contemporary meaning and its relationship to science education reform. *Journal of Research in Science Teaching, 37*, 582–601. http://dx.doi.org/10.1002/1098-2736(200008)37:6<582::aid-tea5>3.0.co;2-l

Ennis, R. H. (1989). Critical thinking and subject specificity: Clarification and needed research. *Educational Researcher, 18*(3), 4–10. http://dx.doi.org/10.3102/0013189x018003004

Eylon, B., & Linn, M. C. (1988). Learning and instruction: An examination of four research perspectives in science education. *Review of Educational Research, 58*, 251–301. http://dx.doi.org/10.3102/00346543058003251

Harari, H. (1992). *Tomorrow 98*. Report of the Supreme Committee for Scientific and Technological Education. Israel Ministry of Education.

Harrison, C., Hofstein, A., Eylon, B., & Simon, S. (2008). Evidence-based professional development of science teachers in two countries. *International Journal of Science Education, 30*, 577–591. http://dx.doi.org/10.1080/09500690701854832

Jarvis, P. (2009). *The Routledge international handbook of lifelong learning*. Routledge. http://dx.doi.org/10.4324/9780203870549

Linn, M. C., diSessa, A., Pea, R. D., & Songer, N. B. (1994). Can research on science learning and instruction inform standards for science education? *Journal of Science Education and Technology, 3*, 7–15. http://dx.doi.org/10.1007/bf01575812

Mayer, R. E., Moreno, R., Boire, M., & Vagge, S. (1999). Maximizing constructivist learning from multimedia communications by minimizing cognitive load. *Journal of Educational Psychology, 91*, 638–643. http://dx.doi.org/10.1037/0022-0663.91.4.638

Millar, R. (2006). *Twenty First Century Science*: Insights from the design and implementation of a scientific literacy approach in school science. *International Journal of Science Education, 28*, 1499–1521. http://dx.doi.org/10.1080/09500690600718344

Millar, R., & Osborne, J. (1998). *Beyond 2000: Science education for the future. A report with ten recommendations*. King's College London.

Mousavi, S. Y., Low, R., & Sweller, J. (1995). Reducing cognitive load by mixing auditory and visual presentation modes. *Journal of Educational Psychology, 87*, 319–334. http://dx.doi.org/10.1037/0022-0663.87.2.319

National Research Council. (1996). *National science education standards*. National Research Council. http://dx.doi.org/10.17226/4962

National Research Council. (2012). *Framework* for *K-12 science education, new generation of science studies*. The National Academies Press. https://doi.org/10.17226/13165

Next Generation Science Standards. (2020). https://www.nextgenscience.org/

OECD. (2018a). *PISA for development assessment and analytical framework: Reading, mathematics and science*. OECD Publishing.

OECD. (2018b). *The future of education and skills: Education 2030*. https://www.voced.edu.au/content/ngv:79286

Onwuegbuzie, A. J., Slate, J. R., & Schwartz, R. A. (2001). Role of study skills in graduate-level educational research courses. *The Journal of Educational Research, 94*, 238–246. http://dx.doi.org/10.1080/00220670109598757

Oosterhuis-Geers, J. (1993). *PROcedure to Promote Effective and Efficient Study Skills (PROPES) with PA-students* [Paper presentation]. Annual Meeting of the American Educational Research Association, Atlanta, GA, USA.

Osborne, J., & Manning, A. (2006). *An evaluation of the Science Enhancement Programme's (SEP) Learning Skills for Science (LSS) initial pilot funded by Gatsby Technical Education Projects.* King's College, University of London.

Partnership for 21st Century Learning Framework. (2019). https://www.battelleforkids.org/learning-hub/learning-hub-item/framework-for-21st-century-learning

Prawat, R. (1989). Promoting access to knowledge, strategy and disposition in students: A research synthesis. *Review of Educational Research, 59*, 1–41. http://dx.doi.org/10.3102/00346543059001001

Price, S., Kolokitha, M., & Reiss M. (2008). *Learning skills for science evaluation project, final report.* Institute of Education, University of London. Private Communication.

Rotherham, A. J., & Willingham, D. (2009). 21st Century Skills: The challenges ahead. *Educational Leadership, 67*(1), 16–21.

Scherz, Z., Bialer, L., & Eylon, B. (2008). Learning about teachers' accomplishment in 'Learning Skills for Science' practice: The use of portfolios in an evidence-based continuous professional development programme. *International Journal of Science Education, 30*, 643–667. http://dx.doi.org/10.1080/09500690701854865

Scherz, Z., Bialer, L., & Eylon, B. (2011). Towards accomplished practice in Learning Skills for Science (LSS): The synergy between design and evaluation methodology in a reflective CPD programme. *Research in Science & Technological Education, 29*, 49–69. http://dx.doi.org/10.1080/02635143.2011.543799

Scherz, Z., Michman, M., & Tamir, P. (1985). Preparing academically disadvantaged students. *Journal of College Science Teaching, 14*, 395–401.

Scherz, Z., Michman, M., & Tamir, P. (1986). Attitudes of university candidates towards learning activities aimed at preparation for science studies. *Research in Science & Technological Education, 4*, 183–194. http://dx.doi.org/10.1080/0263514860040208

Scherz, Z., & Spektor-Levy, O. (2006). *Learning skills for science: Activity book and teachers' guide.* Gatsby Science Enhancement Programme, Weizmann Institute of Science and Nuffield Curriculum Center.

Scherz, Z., Spektor-Levy, O., & Eylon, B. (2005). "Scientific communication": An instructional program for high-order learning skills and its impact on students' performance. In K. Boersma, M. Goedhart, O. de-Jong, & H. Eijkelhof (Eds.), *Research and the quality of science education* (pp. 231–243). Springer. http://dx.doi.org/10.1007/1-4020-3673-6_19

Scherz, Z., Spektor-Levy, O., & Eylon, B. (2008). Teaching communication skills in science: Tracing teacher change. *Teaching and Teacher Education, 24*, 462–477. http://dx.doi.org/10.1016/j.tate.2006.10.009

Schneider, R. M., Krajcik, J., Marx, R. W., & Soloway, E. (2002). Performance of students in Project-Based Science classrooms on a national measure of science achievement. *Journal of Research in Science Teaching, 39*, 410–422. http://dx.doi.org/10.1002/tea.10029

Segal, J. W., Chipman, S., & Glaser, R. (1985). *Thinking and learning skills, 1: Relating instruction to basic research.* Erlbaum.

Shamos, M. H. (1995). *The myth of scientific literacy.* Rutgers University Press.

Slate, J. R., Jones, C., & Dawson, P. (1993). Academic skills of high school students as a function of grade, gender, and academic track. *The High School Journal, 76*(4), 245–251.

Spektor-Levy, O., Eylon, B., & Scherz, Z. (2008). Teaching communication skills in science: Tracing teacher change. *Teaching and Teacher Education, 24*, 462–477. http://dx.doi.org/10.1016/j.tate.2006.10.009

Spektor-Levy, O., Eylon, B., & Scherz, Z. (2009). Teaching scientific communication skills in science studies – Does it make a difference? *International Journal of Science and Mathematics Education, 7*, 875–903. http://dx.doi.org/10.1007/s10763-009-9150-6

Spektor-Levy, O., & Scherz, Z. (1999). *Scientific communication.* Weizmann Institute of Science (in Hebrew).

Spektor-Levy, O., & Scherz, Z. (2001). *Scientific communication: Teacher guide.* Weizmann Institute of Science (in Hebrew).

Spektor-Levy, O., & Scherz, Z. (2005). *Learning skills for science – Activity book and teacher guide.* Weizmann Institute of Science, Gatsby Enhancement Program & Nuffield Curriculum Centre.

Spektor-Levy, O., Scherz, Z., & Eylon, B. (2002). The "Scientific Communication" program: How do science teachers implement a modular program of learning skills acquisition? In *Proceedings of the 2nd International Conference on Science Education* (pp. 497–503). The Cyprus Pedagogical Institute.

Spiegel, G. F. Jr., & Barufaldi, J. P. (1994). The effect of a combination of text structure awareness and graphic post organizers on recall and retention of science knowledge. *Journal of Research in Science Teaching, 31*, 913–932. http://dx.doi.org/10.1002/tea.3660310907

Von Glasersfeld, E. (1998). Cognition, construction of knowledge, and teaching. In M. R. Matthews (Ed.), *Constructivism in science education* (pp. 11–30). Dordrecht: Springer. http://dx.doi.org/10.1007/978-94-011-5032-3_2

Zohar, A., & Dori, J. (2003). Higher order thinking skills and low-achieving students: Are they mutually exclusive? *Journal of the Learning Sciences, 12*, 145–181. http://dx.doi.org/10.1207/s15327809jls1202_1

CHAPTER 7

Importing from a Young Educational Discipline

The Case of Computational Thinking

Michal Armoni

Abstract

Computer science (CS) is a young discipline. Its theoretical facet can be traced back to the 1930s, to recursion theory and proof theory, and the work of mathematicians such as Gödel and Turing. Its physical facet, related to digital computers and programming, is a little younger. In fact, the identity of CS is still debated, within and outside the discipline. Naturally, the field of computer science education (CSE) is even younger and has yet to grow and mature, in practice and in research.

Despite its short history, the merit of exporting from CSE to other educational fields is now almost a consensus. Many, including educational stakeholders at the highest global and national levels, strongly believe that *computational thinking* is a set of skills that should be acquired by all students. However, this position should be taken with a grain of salt. In particular, a deep understanding of the term 'computational thinking' and its relation to CS is necessary before embarking on such curricular initiatives. This chapter discusses the current trend that calls for teaching computational thinking to all students. Building on my research, I argue that current approaches for integrating the teaching of computational thinking into K–12 curricula may not be effective, and suggest another perspective on computational thinking and on teaching it.

Keywords

computer science – computational thinking – abstraction – K-12 education – nature of computer science

1 Introduction

Computer science (CS) is a very young discipline, certainly compared to classic disciplines such as mathematics, physics, art and medicine, but also compared to younger disciplines such as economics or psychology. As with many other disciplines, principles, ideas, theories, and practices of CS emerged, formed,

 | DOI: 10.1163/9789004503625_007

were conceptualized, or developed even before the identity of the discipline had been shaped and recognized. In fact, even today, some scholars of other disciplines do not acknowledge CS as an academic discipline, let alone science. Moreover, its nature and identity, including its relationships with other disciplines, are still debated, even among CS experts in academia and in the industry.

This is the first stumbling block that a CS educator encounters, or at least should encounter. Before designing a curriculum, and certainly before conducting research on learning and understanding, one should know what the discipline is – what its major themes, ideas, and thinking patterns are, and what the expertise of seasoned scholars or practitioners of the discipline is. This derives the contents of the curriculum, in terms of the disciplinary knowledge that it includes, as well as the image of the nature of the discipline that it aims to portray. It also induces paths of educational research.

Hence, I see this as an important, somewhat philosophical facet of computer science education (CSE) research: identifying, characterizing and understanding the identity and nature of the discipline. It is especially important today, when educational endeavors involving CS are becoming increasingly prevalent in Israel and worldwide, and significant efforts tapping massive financial and human resources have been implemented to develop K–12 CS or CS-related curricula (e.g., Armoni & Gal-Ezer, 2007; Armoni et al., 2010; Bell et al., 2014; Brown et al., 2014; Gal-Ezer & Harel, 1999; Gal-Ezer & Stephenson, 2014; Meerbaum-Salant et al., 2012).

In line with this, the nature of CS, which is at the center of my research work, is a major theme of this chapter. Through this theme, I explore some aspects of the reciprocal relationship between CSE and other educational disciplines. The following two sections lay the groundwork, discussing the nature of CS. Then I focus on teaching CS in school, from several perspectives, and conclude.

2 What Is CS?

Scholars and educators of CS have been discussing and debating this question since the early days of CS as an academic profession. Universities began granting degrees in CS in the 1960s. At some universities, CS programs were part of the electrical engineering department, whereas at others, they were offered by departments of mathematics. This expressed the duality of the field, rooted in two very different disciplines. Some of its facets are rooted in mathematics, from as early as the 1930s, specifically in the work of Gödel, Turing, Kleen, Church, Post and others, dealing with recursion (or computability) theory, a branch of mathematical logic that focuses on computable functions and models of computations (such as Turing machine or λ-calculus). Other facets are rooted in electrical engineering, where the design of the early digital computers took place, in the 1940s, and the field of communicating with these computers (aka programming) came to life. The two academic affiliations of the field have also been a source of confusion regarding its nature. In fact, the emergence of digital computing was both a blessing and a curse of the discipline. It facilitated its development, paving its way to academic independence. It also created strong ties between the discipline and technology, starting with the meager choice of the name *computer science*, "which, actually, is like referring to surgery as 'knife science,' as has been sharply put by Dijkstra (1986), thus fostering a wrong image of the discipline. This confusion was strengthened by the sporadic disciplinary origins of the early professionals (e.g., physicists or chemists), who were motivated by the contribution of the new technology to their practice (Dijkstra, 1986).

Generally speaking, the confusion still exists. The term 'computer science' is prevalent, and the widespread use of computers, in almost every part of our daily lives, has caused the formation of alternative conceptualizations of CS, which are often very far from the truth. Moreover, in many cases, these are very obstinate conceptualizations. Presumably, most laypeople would acknowledge the fact they do not really know what nuclear physics is or what a nuclear physicist does. However, many of these same people are quite certain that they know what CS is and what a computer scientist does (although many of them are wrong about this) (Lewis et al., 2016; Schulte & Knobelsdorf, 2007; Taub et al., 2012; Yardi & Bruckman, 2007). Among laypeople, a reliable conceptualization of CS is hard to find, but wrong or inaccurate images of CS are common, even among non-experts who have some background or education in CS.

So, what is the real nature of CS? Perhaps it is easier to start with the wrong images, and clarify what CS is not. It is not about the machine (just as surgery is not about the knives, echoing Dijkstra). Specifically, it is not about designing computers (this is done by hardware engineers) or about constructing them and fixing hardware problems (the expertise of hardware technicians). It is also not about installing software and applications or recovering accidentally deleted files, or about using applications (e.g., for sending emails, writing documents, or preparing presentations).

Another common misconception equates CS with programming. In the 1960s and '70s, this was also a common view among CS educators, as evidenced by the curricula of undergraduate programs, which mostly included programming courses (Atchison et al., 1968; Austing et al., 1979). However, programming is only one aspect of CS. It is the action of communicating with computers, using formal languages to formulate sequences of instructions as objects (programs) that can be executed by computers. The challenges of CS mostly concern coming up with the appropriate sequences of instructions rather than translating (programming) them into executable objects. As the discipline matured, the dissonance became apparent, and a task force was appointed in 1986 for the purpose of defining CS as a separate discipline. Their report explicitly stated that CS does not equal programming. The discipline of CS was defined as "the systematic study of algorithmic processes that describe and transform information; their theory, analysis, design, efficiency, implementation and application" (Denning et al., 1989, p. 12). Programming is there ("implementation and application"), but there is much more.

While this definition is rather concise and reflects major facets of CS, it also has flaws. First, it focuses on algorithmic processes. However, algorithmic processes are the outcome of using algorithms (referred to above as *sequences of instructions*), and algorithms are not independent entities; rather, they are solutions to problems. Moreover, focusing on algorithmic processes or even algorithms seems to overshadow some facets of the discipline that focus on problems rather than algorithms.

I prefer to see CS as *a science of problems*. This view may seem too general. After all, problems lie at the heart of all disciplines. This is what disciplinary experts do: they use their disciplinary knowledge to analyze and solve problems. For example, among other things, mathematicians are experts in proving theorems. They formulate (or receive) a mathematical statement and solve the problem of finding a mathematical proof that establishes its correctness. A physicist may face a problem that requires the analysis of a certain physical system.

Nevertheless, there is a material difference between the roles of problems in CS and in other disciplines. In most disciplines, solving problems is the way to advance the discipline. By proving theorems, mathematical knowledge grows. Discovering the function and behavior of a certain gene enhances biology knowledge. The same holds for CS, which also uses problems to advance the science. However, in CS, problems play another, more substantial role. CS is *about* problems, just like chemistry is about substances. Computer scientists study problems, just like chemists study substances. More accurately, computer scientists study *computational* problems. These are problems whose solutions are *algorithms*, that is, methods or general recipes for doing certain things. For example, how do we sort a long list of items? The solution to this problem is a method, an algorithm, for sorting. By definition, these solutions are intended for obedient agents, namely, they tell you exactly what to do. Following them meticulously constitutes a process that is bound to lead to the desired outcome. Such a process is called *computation*. For example, employing a solution for the sorting problem with a given list of items yields a process that sorts the list, or in other words, computes the sorted list. Note that the meaning of the term *computation* here is wider than *calculation*, which is the standard mathematical meaning of this term. Rather, calculations are very specific cases of computations. Moreover, computations are not limited to the numerical context. For example, for the sorting problem, the resulting computations are not necessarily numerical, since the sorted items are not necessarily numbers. They need only be comparable, for example, English words that can be sorted according to lexicographic order.

In what sense do computer scientists study and analyze computational problems? They may devise solutions (algorithms) to such problems or use mathematical reasoning to prove that they cannot be solved. They may use the same kind of mathematical reasoning to determine the problems' inherent level of complexity, to produce solutions that are efficient as possible and prove their correctness. They also identify connections between problems and classify them by their solvability and difficulty. Namely, computer scientists are experts of problems.

As experts of computational problems, computer scientists can handle different kinds of computational problems, from all areas. Photography experts may require a method for replacing the background of a digital image with another one. Police detectives may require a method for face recognition, so that they can check whether a certain person is already documented in their list of known criminals. Schools may require a method for designing an optimal weekly timetable for all classes. Computer scientists can use their expertise to devise solutions to problems, but as noted above, their knowledge of problems and of reasoning about problems is even wider and deeper. For example, as an expert of computational problems, a computer scientist will probably realize that designing an optimal school timetable is a very difficult problem. In fact, this problem belongs to a large set of very difficult problems, for which no efficient solution (method) has been found to date, and the existence of such solutions is an open question. This CS expert can then inform a school principal of the inherent difficulty of the problem, and advise the school to settle for a method that does not guarantee an optimal solution, unless they are ready to wait for many years until the computation ends and provides an optimal timetable (and that would be the case even if the method were employed by the most advanced computer instead of a school staff member).

In particular, the problems computer scientists deal with may also come from computer engineering, computer applications, or other computer-related areas, including programming. For example, verifying the correctness of the design of a new component of a digital computer is a very important problem that computer engineers face and that computer scientists study. In fact, the general version of this problem has been proven by computer scientists to be unsolvable, but some restricted, albeit useful versions of this problem can be solved. Similarly, searching for a sequence of characters in a document (such as files created by applications such as Microsoft Word or Google Docs) is a computational problem from the field of computer applications, and the problem of checking whether a computer program adheres to the rules of the programming language is a computational problem from the field of computer programming. However, this does not mean that designing computers or using computer applications is CS, or that CS equals programming, just as CS is not biology, even though computer scientists handle problems related to the human genome. At the same time, solving such problems may advance CS. For example, the need for tools to verify programs and hardware led to the development of the CS field of formal verification, the challenge of secure digital communication promoted the CS field of modern cryptography, and the challenge of biological problems initiated and promoted the CS field of computational biology.

3 CS as a Discipline

Accepting a definition of CS does not necessarily mean acknowledging it as a distinct academic discipline. To acknowledge that, one has to agree that it has a specific accumulated body of knowledge, theories that organize this knowledge, specific concepts, terminology, research methods, procedures, culture, and ways of thinking that, together, generate coherence and distinction (Klein, 1990; Krishnan, 2009).

Is this the case for CS? Apparently, this is not a consensus among the general public, including experts from other disciplines. For those who perceive CS as equal to programming, it is often considered a pragmatic profession concerning only practitioners, rather than an academic discipline, since they believe that among the components listed above, it is lacking theory and research methods. Others do not see coherence, but rather fragments taken from other fields (e.g., mathematics and engineering). Mathematicians may feel ownership of some parts of it that they consider to be mathematics, and at the same time feel alienated from other parts (Dijkstra, 1986). After all, they say, we have been doing computations for ages, and have developed numerous algorithms.

These arguments were indeed valid in the early days of CS. Similar to economics, CS started as a collection of sometimes unrelated subjects, some taken from other disciplines, and some new. But then gradually, a few things happened: computer scientists studied these subjects, developed deeper insights into them and expanded them, and eventually their expertise in these subjects was far greater than that of the original owners. For example, branches of recursion theory developed into computability and then complexity theories, which have largely expanded beyond the days of Turing, and modern cryptography flourished and grew around number theory, exploiting and expanding its knowledge into new directions to produce a wider, yet focused theory. Then, by gaining a deeper understanding of these subjects, computer scientists developed overarching views, principles, and themes of theory and practice that connected these parts into a coherent entity. The coherent entity grew and expanded, enhancing its theory, adding knowledge, developing habits of mind and ways of thinking, and thus became a discipline.

Today, CS undoubtedly satisfies all of the characteristics of an academic discipline (Klein, 1990; Krishnan, 2009). It has a distinct and coherent theory that reasons about formal models which may vary in their mode of computation (e.g., sequential, parallel, distributed, random, or non-deterministic) or their resources (e.g., time and space). It studies the solvability of problems (computability theory), formalizing concepts such as *solution* and *computation*. It studies the difficulty of problems (complexity theory), formalizing concepts such as *complexity*, *efficiency*, and *tractability*. It studies algorithms and data, using methods of mathematical logic, such as structural induction and formal verification methods based on temporal logic (developed by computer scientists) to establish the correctness of an algorithm, formalizing concepts such as *correctness* and *specification*.

Its knowledge includes, among other things, representations of data and abstract data structures, classical algorithms, problem-solving strategies, problem-solving paradigms and corresponding programming languages, formalizing concepts such as *program* or *language*. CS also has characteristics and unique habits of mind and ways of thinking, including, among others, specialized forms of abstraction, decomposition, reversing, approximation, and reduction.

4 On Teaching CS in Schools

From an educational point of view, after establishing CS as an academic discipline, the next natural question would be: should CS be taught in schools? For the purpose of this chapter, I will focus on including CS as a mandatory school subject.

There are several justifications for including a specific subject as part of the mandatory school curriculum. The most basic one is the relevance and importance of the subject: will children need these knowledge or skills outside the school and throughout their lives? For example, it is widely agreed that everyone should know how to perform arithmetic calculations. To this end, the mathematics curriculum in the lower grades focuses on arithmetic. This knowledge also serves as a basis for mathematics at higher grade levels. Similarly, science curricula include topics that are considered basic general knowledge, such as the human body and the solar system.

Another justification, which is more vague and yet quite common, is the improvement of cognitive abilities – "it develops their mind" or "it enriches their thinking." The underlying rationale is simple: if a certain subject is characterized by certain habits of mind, then teaching this subject can serve as a means to develop these habits of minds (Cuoco et al., 1996). For example, learning science may develop scientific habits of minds, such as formulating informed hypotheses and checking them (Duschl et al., 2007), and engaging in mathematical argumentation when learning mathematics may develop habits of minds such as deductive reasoning, including coherent inference and reasoning about abstract objects.

Any of these two justifications may be sufficient for including certain topics as part of school curricula. For example, most students will not need the skill of proving geometric theorems once they graduate from high school; however, this skill satisfies the second justification, because by learning and practicing proof challenges, they may acquire mathematical methods and strategies (Hanna & Barbeau, 2008).

Do either of these two justifications hold for CS? In other words, we are actually asking two questions: (1) Which factual knowledge of CS, if any, does one need outside of school and throughout one's life? (2) Which important general habits of mind can one acquire by learning CS in school?

As for the first question, there is no single agreed-upon answer. However, in many countries, stakeholders currently believe that programming is a skill and factual knowledge that everyone should have, and thus aim at teaching programming to all students. While CS does not equal programming (just like mathematics does not equal arithmetic), the knowledge and skills relevant to programming can be included in the subject of CS, among other topics, thus satisfying this agenda. However, using this as the only justification for teaching CS in school may lead to unwanted results, because it may reduce the teaching of CS to the teaching of programming, thus fostering the misconception of "CS = programming." This may be parallelized with issues concerning mathematics education. If acquiring some concrete necessary knowledge is the only justification for including mathematics in school, there is a risk of reducing school mathematics to teaching arithmetic or basic algebra, thus fostering a misconception of the nature of mathematics.

This brings us to the second question, concerning CS habits of mind. This question is in fact quite complex, and includes three components:
- Are CS's ways of thinking beneficial in contexts outside CS?
- Can one learn some of CS's ways of thinking by learning CS in school?
- Is learning CS in school the only way to learn these ways of thinking?

The third component is important, because even if the answers to components 1 and 2 are positive, this does not necessarily justify CS as a mandatory school subject. Perhaps some modifications or additions to other school subjects can achieve the goal of teaching these ways of thinking. Alternatively, they may be taught through a stand-alone subject that is different from CS.

To address this threefold question, we will start by discussing these ways of thinking, also referred to by many as *computational thinking*. After the nature and meaning of computational thinking is established, we will return to this complex question.

5 Computational Thinking

The term computational thinking was used by Papert in his seminal book, Mindstorms (Papert, 1980). He argued that by engaging with CS, students acquire powerful ways of representing ideas that make them better constructors of their own knowledge. Namely, Papert provided a positive answer to the second question posed in the previous section, regarding the educational value of CS habits of mind. Although Papert was credited with being the first to use this term, the general terminology was not new. Any discipline has its own ways of thinking, so talking about computational thinking was as natural as talking about mathematical thinking or scientific thinking, and just as vague. A few decades later, Wing (2006) used this term as the title of her influential paper. Her position was very strong: the kind of thinking that characterizes the work of computer scientists is important for everyone and should be taught to everyone. Apparently, she was also very convincing and had better timing than Papert. Her paper initiated an educational wave that is still gaining momentum. Educational decision-makers the world over are promoting the teaching of computational thinking, and educators are looking for effective ways to achieve it. Wing's timing was better because of that "original sin" – the root of confusion – the ties made between the discipline and the machine.

Stakeholders and decision-makers were readily convinced, because after all, computers are everywhere, it just makes sense that teaching computational thinking is important.

However, at that point, things took a rather peculiar turn. Those stakeholders and decision-makers were not satisfied with the vague term "computational thinking." They were looking for a definition – what is it that should be taught to everyone?

By nature, disciplinary thinking, namely, the ways of thinking in a specific discipline, cannot be reduced to a short and concise definition. An academic discipline has a depth and breadth that make any attempt to capture it in a few lines inconceivable. One can hardly be more accurate than defining it as the ways of thinking (or practices) that characterize the work of an expert in the discipline. One can provide examples for specific ways of thinking, but such a list can hardly be expected to be exhaustive. For example, Schoenfeld (1992) described mathematical thinking as follows: "learning to think mathematically means (a) developing a mathematical point of view – valuing the processes of mathematization and abstraction and having the predilection to apply them, and (b) developing competence with the tools of the trade and using those tools in the service of the goal of understanding structure – mathematical sense-making" (p. 335). Kuhn (2010) simply described scientific thinking as "knowledge seeking," encompassing "any instance of purposeful thinking that has the objective of enhancing the seeker's knowledge" (p. 497).

Wing described computational thinking with a similar flavor (Wing, 2006, p. 33): "Computational thinking involves solving problems, designing systems, and understanding human behavior, by drawing on the concepts fundamental to computer science. Computational thinking includes a range of *mental tools* that reflect the breadth of the field of computer science" (emphasis added. Hereafter, I use "mental tool" in the sense used by Wing in this definition). In the rest of the paper, she provided a long list of major habits of mind that underlie the work of computer scientists (such as abstraction, recursion, modeling, representation, or nondeterminism), and general characteristics of computational thinking. But her list would not do – the type of self-referential vague definitions-by-inclusion used in other disciplines deemed insufficient in the case of computational thinking. The "original sin" is again to blame. Of course, if one does not understand what CS is, one cannot be expected to understand what computational thinking is, and hence a definition is warranted.

From that point on, the tale of teaching computational thinking became entangled. Many educators (including Wing) were trying to come up with a definition for computational thinking that could serve as a basis for a computational thinking curriculum, and considerable work has been done in this direction (e.g., National Research Council, 2010, 2011). Some definitions are rather general and far from being operational, thus failing to meet the goals that motivated the quest for a definition in the first place. Others are very detailed. There are far too many to discuss all of them here, but I will elaborate on some of them, to depict the evolution of the image of computational thinking. Specifically, I will refer to three aspects that are reflected in these definitions: concreteness, execution, and abstraction.

5.1 *The Aspect of Concreteness*

As already noted, stakeholders and educational decision-makers were looking for a concrete, exhaustive, and concise definition for computational thinking, as opposed to Wing's first presentation of this term (Wing, 2006), which was very general, referring to fundamental concepts and mental tools of CS and exemplifying them through a long list of such tools. In this section, I will follow the evolution of the aspect of concreteness in several of the definitions of computational thinking.

In 2008, Wing published another position paper, in which she added to her original description of computational thinking (cited above), the following general sentences:

> Computational thinking is a kind of analytical thinking. It shares with mathematical thinking in the general ways in which we might approach solving a problem. It shares with engineering thinking in the general ways in which we might approach designing and evaluating a large, complex system that operates within the constraints of the real world. It shares with scientific thinking in the general ways in which we might approach understanding computability, intelligence, the mind and human behavior. (Wing, 2008, p. 3717)

Then she focused on abstraction (which she referred to as the essence of computational thinking) and automation (as a tool to turn abstractions into computational processes, i.e., computations). This portrait of computational thinking was still vague, maintaining its identity as the mental reflection of CS. Later, Wing, together with Cuny and Snyder, came up with a more concise, albeit still general definition: "Computational thinking is the thought processes involved in formulating problems and their solutions so that the solutions are represented in a form that can be effectively carried out by an information-processing agent" (Wing, 2010, p. 1).

Another definition of computational thinking, presented as an "operational definition," was composed by the International Society for Technology in

Education (ISTE) and the Computer Science Teachers Association (CSTA). It defines computational thinking as "a problem-solving process that includes (but is not limited to)," and then follows a list of six characteristics (ISTE/CSTA, 2011). This definition seems to aim to a higher level of concreteness (compared to Wing's definitions), which necessarily limits its scope. Computational thinking was reduced from thought processes or mental tools (in the plural form) that are *involved in* problem solving to one process *of* problem solving. In addition, although this definition enables the inclusion of additional characteristics, it is obvious that the six short and concise items are considered to be an extract, the essential constituents. Somewhere along the road, the need to distill a definition reduced the rich reflection of a deep and broad discipline to a very small and non-impressive set of skills. Different definitions that share the same nature were composed by the British community Computing at School (CAS, 2015) and ISTE (2016).

Another widely used definition of computational thinking was presented by Brennan and Resnick (2012). It consists of three dimensions: computational concepts, computational practices, and computational perspectives. The first dimension includes seven concrete concepts (e.g., sequences, loops, conditionals, and operators). The second includes four practices: being incremental and iterative, testing and debugging, reusing and remixing, and abstracting and modularizing. The last dimension includes three perspectives: expressing, connecting and questioning. As is often the case, when decomposing a forest to its trees, the forest is lost; the detailed definition, obtained from breaking down the general definition into details, seems to lose the original unified upper-level appeal of Wing's description.

5.2 *The Aspect of Execution – Obedient Agents*

The different definitions also vary in their treatment of *execution*. If computational thinking is about coming up with solutions intended for obedient agents (i.e., those who meticulously perform the instructions given to them), who is to carry out these solutions? Who are the obedient agents to whom the solutions should be communicated?

Throughout her series of computational thinking papers, Wing stressed that the solutions to problems need not necessarily be executed by machines. Indeed, the use of algorithms is not restricted to computers. For example, young students who calculate the multiplication of two 3-digit numbers can be looked upon as obedient agents that follow a method, a simple algorithm, for multiplication. Similarly, a librarian may follow a method, an algorithm, for sorting when organizing books on the shelves.

However, this seems to be a delicate point, as manifested by the back and forth of the different wordings over the years. In 2008, Wing used the term 'computer' but explicitly emphasized that a computer can be a physical device, a human, or a combination of both. In the definition presented in 2010, this entity, whether a machine or a human, is referred to as an "information-processing agent," but later, Wing slightly changed this definition and the information-processing agent again became "a computer – human or machine" (Wing, 2014).

This is an important issue, which concerns and challenges the image of the discipline. Although the word 'computer' is an obvious choice, its natural interpretation as a physical device might reinforce the confusion regarding the nature of CS, strengthening the ties between CS and technology. It might also reinforce the image of CS as programming, because when the executing entity is a machine, a physical device, communication is made via programs, thereby necessitating the involvement of programming and programming languages. In contrast, when the information-processing agent is a human, algorithms described in natural language are sufficient for communicating solutions and there is no need for programming or programming languages.

This range, from humans to machines, from algorithms to programs, was also reflected in other general definitions (e.g., Aho, 2011). However, as the definitions evolved, this range narrowed. In the definition of ISTE/CSTA (2011), the agent became "a computer or other tools" and at the same time, its role grew, from a passive obedient entity that carries out solutions to an active contributor that can help in solving the given problems. That is, the meaning of 'solution' was extended beyond the concept of an algorithm, now also including the representation of an algorithm (i.e., programming it) as well as its execution by the computer. The definition of Brennan and Resnick (2012) went even further, becoming all about programming (indeed, their framework emerged from engaging with programming for and by children).

The emphasis on programming becomes even more evident when using the perspective of assessment: almost all of the diagnostic tools developed for assessing computational thinking among K–12 students have been designed to evaluate programming artifacts (e.g., Román-González, 2015; Seiter & Foreman, 2013). In other words, in most cases, the work of computer scientists as characterized by Wing's rich set of mental tools and thought processes has been, once again, reduced to programming.

5.3 *The Aspect of Abstraction*

From the early days of the discipline, abstraction has been acknowledged as the essence of CS (Aho & Ullman, 1992; Dijkstra, 1972, 1975; Knuth, in Hartmanis, 1994) and as a deep, multifaceted idea. CS experts constantly employ abstraction for solving problems, starting with using abstractions for reformulating given problems to represent them as computational problems, for modeling the problem space, and for representing data, and then using abstractions to devise the solutions. Furthermore, CS experts are knowledgeable about different *paradigms* for solving problems (e.g., functional, imperative, procedural, event-driven, object-oriented, and logical), each coming with a different form of abstraction. When dealing with a computational problem, CS experts can choose and employ the appropriate paradigm for the problem at hand, and use the corresponding type of abstraction to solve the problem. During the solution process, CS experts work at multiple levels of abstraction while constantly moving between them as appropriate. Because of its major role, teaching CS abstraction should be an important part of any CS teaching program (see Armoni, 2013 for a discussion of CS abstraction from the perspective of CS education).

As a fundamental idea of CS that plays such a significant role, abstraction is certainly a major component of computational thinking. In her paper from 2008, Wing focused on, analyzed, and discussed this complex mental tool, explicitly acknowledging it as the essence of computational thinking.

Consequently, abstraction is present in any detailed definition of computational thinking. However, in this case as well, the need to capture computational thinking within a concise definition fostered a narrow interpretation of abstraction, making it one among a set of skills. In the ISTE/CSTA definition (2011), the rich mental tool of abstraction was reduced to a tool for representing data by means of models and simulations, although other parts of the definition are also manifestations of abstraction (e.g., formulating problems, generalizing and transferring). Similarly, in the CAS definition (2015), abstraction stands for choosing appropriate representations, even though their definition also includes decomposition, generalizations, and identifying and making use of patterns, all of which are clear manifestations of abstraction. In Brennan and Resnick's (2012) definition, abstraction is perceived only as a tool for decomposition and modularization. Tools for assessing computational thinking take it a few steps further. They look for the demonstration of abstraction in the context of programming through specific programming constructs and program components (e.g., Román-González, 2015; Seiter & Forman, 2013; Warner et al., 2012), thus demoting this rich and powerful habit of mind to low-level practice.

6 On Teaching Computational Thinking in Schools

After introducing and discussing the concept of computational thinking and its different interpretations, we can now return to our threefold question, rewording it in terms of computational thinking:

1. Is computational thinking beneficial in other contexts outside CS?
2. Can one learn components of computational thinking by learning CS in school?
3. Is learning CS in school the only way to learn computational thinking?

According to Wing (2006, 2008), the answer to part 1 is yes, computational thinking is important to everyone, also outside the context of CS. Does that mean that everyone should think like a computer scientist? Not necessarily. It only means that these disciplinary habits of mind have merit in general contexts and situations. Furthermore, it does not mean that each and every mental tool that is attributed to computational thinking is unique to CS or "owned" by it. If that were the case, these mental tools would not be beneficial in other contexts.

Why, then, should CS be considered an educational source for these habits of minds? Because in the context of CS, most of these habits of mind and mental tools have been enhanced to become more powerful and effective.

For example, data analysis and organization are relevant in many contexts outside CS, and experts in other disciplines are proficient in organizing data in various forms. However, computer scientists are proficient in coming up with methods of organization (*data structures*) that optimize the work with the data, even for huge amounts of data. They consider the actions and manipulations that should be performed on the data (e.g., adding new items, combining sets of items) and the information that should be extracted from the data, and then choose, accordingly, the best way to represent the data and the best method to organize it.

Similarly, modeling has long been employed in the natural sciences, e.g., to simulate chemical processes or model physical systems. However, computer scientists are familiar with various methods of modeling and can choose the best fit. Consider, for example, modeling a system with different kinds of players, each with its unique role and attributes, and each communicating with and activating the others. To model such a system, computer scientists will probably use the object-oriented paradigm that encapsulates design thinking. For modeling processes (such as human blood circulation), they will probably choose the procedural paradigm (featuring procedural thinking), which enables the modeling of complex processes as simpler processes that activate other processes; it also enables encapsulating processes within processes and focusing on different levels, as appropriate; for example, moving from the level of blood circulation as a whole to the level of one erythrocyte, or even lower levels. The event-driven paradigm can be used to simulate systems whose components respond to triggering events (such as closed chemical equilibrium systems in which molecules react to collision events). Other paradigms (rule-based, scenario-based, functional and more) will best fit other kinds of situations.

Thus, engaging with CS is characterized by the continuous use of a unique blend of all of these mental tools, and therefore engaging with CS constantly offers opportunities to practice stronger variations of these tools and become proficient in using them. This is the ultimate goal of teaching computational thinking and its major intended contribution.

But is this feasible? That is, does teaching CS indeed lead to the development of computational thinking? This is part 2 of the threefold question. To contextualize our answer, let us start with a quick snapshot of the current state of affairs regarding teaching computational thinking, and then discuss the effectiveness of specific trends in computational thinking education.

Fourteen years after Wing's call for teaching computational thinking to everyone, its effects are apparent. Computational thinking is present in the K–12 curricula of many countries. Most of these countries (e.g., New Zealand, UK, and Scotland) have mandatory K–12 CS curricula (sometimes termed computing or informatics) that set the development of computational thinking as a learning goal (whether explicitly or not). In a few other countries (e.g., Taiwan), there are designated mandatory computational thinking curricula, but these are usually based on teaching topics of CS. In some places, components of computational thinking are integrated into other school subjects, such as mathematics (e.g., Benton et al., 2016). In addition to state curricula, there are also independent endeavors to teach computational thinking, for example, outreach projects of universities, or courses developed by educational organizations such as code.org.

Most curricula that relate to computational thinking are based on its operational definitions, which limit its scope and hence also its richness, in the spirit of the ISTE/CSTA's 2011 operational definition. Almost all of these curricula and activities narrow the interpretation of computational thinking even more, by revolving around or even amounting to programming (sometimes using the term 'coding'). Which of these kinds of curricula and activities are appropriate for teaching computational thinking?

To answer this, we refer to three aspects that, together, address parts 2 and 3 of our threefold question:

- *Context*: Teaching computational thinking as a stand-alone subject, teaching it through teaching the subject of CS, or integrating it in other school subjects.
- *Content*: What should computational thinking teaching cover?

- *Means*: Can programming-centered curricula be effective in teaching aspects of computational thinking? Do they promote the acquisition of the transferrable components of computational thinking?

These are not independent aspects, but I will address them separately, and refer to specific connections explicitly.

6.1 *The Context of Computational Thinking Education*

Teaching computational thinking as a stand-alone subject (apart from or instead of CS) necessitates the extraction and disconnection of computational thinking from CS. To allow this, an operational definition of computational thinking is required, to serve as a basis for curricular design. However, as argued earlier, it seems that the quest for a definition of computational thinking to guide its teaching has narrowed its essence, resulting in a shadow of the original entity.

Therefore, it seems natural to turn to the second approach, teaching CS to everyone, as a means of teaching computational thinking, relying on the development of computational thinking as a result of the exposure to and engagement in CS. This is in line with current efforts for teaching computational thinking and with the arguments of several CS educators. For example, Nardelli (2019) argued that while the acknowledgment of computational thinking is important to justify its learning, it should be used to support and promote the teaching of CS.

There are several counterarguments for teaching CS to everyone. First, this may be overdoing it. If we are only interested in computational thinking for everyone, perhaps teaching CS to everyone is too much, and might be too demanding or frustrating for some students. Second, can the teaching of CS at the school level guarantee sufficient exposure to computational thinking? Perhaps the cognitive characteristics of young students prevent teaching CS at a sufficient level of depth, providing little opportunity to meaningfully exploit computational thinking skills? Third, since the goal is that students acquire skills that can serve them in other contexts, teaching CS might be insufficient to meet this goal, unless transfer from CS to other contexts is achieved.

The first argument is not unique to CS. For example, mathematics is known to be a challenging subject, which may be frustrating for some students, provoking anxiety, low self-esteem, and other negative feelings (Gellert et al., 2001) that may even lead to passive avoidance. Nevertheless (Gates & Vistro-Yu, 2003), mathematics educators believe that these problems can be solved by using appropriate teaching methods, by careful design of curricula, and by using research to investigate teaching and learning processes. The same holds true for CS.

As for the second argument, providing sufficient opportunities for engaging with computational thinking is mainly related to content as well as means, and will be discussed further on.

The issue of transfer is a crucial one, and it may therefore constitute a compelling argument against teaching computational thinking through CS. As pointed out by Denning (2017), there is no evidence that teaching programming contributes to enhancing general problem-solving skills which can be employed in other contexts. However, as mentioned several times throughout this chapter, teaching programming is not the same as teaching CS. In addition, such curricula can be enhanced by strategies that explicitly direct toward transfer. Further on, when discussing the methods and means for teaching computational thinking, I will also discuss transfer in the context of teaching computational thinking through CS.

Nevertheless, one may argue that the stumbling block of transfer can be resolved by the third approach: integrating the teaching of computational thinking into other school subjects instead of teaching computational thinking or CS as stand-alone subjects. However, this approach has two substantial drawbacks.

First, although practicing and exploiting computational thinking in different school subjects can potentially develop computational thinking skills relevant to different contexts, this does not necessarily mean that the students will spontaneously connect these learning events and generalize the skills, thus allowing their use in new contexts beyond these subjects, or even outside the school.

Second, this approach requires that teachers of other subjects be knowledgeable about computational thinking and its reflections or manifestations in their discipline and consequently, in their school-subject curriculum. In particular, they should have a sufficient understanding of CS as well as its ideas, habits of mind, and patterns of thinking. Unfortunately, this is not an easy or even realistic requirement. Although there are educators who have a sufficiently strong CS background, the majority do not. Specifically, many of them hold the widespread misconceptions regarding the nature of CS. Consequently, their ability to take advantage of the full power of computational thinking, as well as their appreciation of its potential, are limited. Not surprisingly, many of them tend to identify computational thinking with programming.

This obstacle may lead to using what is supposed to be computational thinking but is actually programming when teaching other school subjects, with an agenda that is very different from that envisioned by Wing. The differences are subtle, and yet substantial. In such cases, instead of using programming to promote the development of computational thinking, it is often perceived as scaffolding, as a (sophisticated) teaching aid to facilitate the learning of the concepts of the school subject at hand (similar to concrete mathematical reference systems in the form of different-sized blocks for learning about numbers). For example, in the ScratchMaths project (Benton et al., 2016), which builds on constructionism, students start by learning to program in Scratch; programming in Scratch then helps them to better understand mathematical concepts, such as numbers and geometry concepts. Once these concepts are properly learned, and the disciplinary learning goals are achieved, the tool of programming is no longer necessary. This is very different from treating the skills encompassed in computational thinking as valuable learning goals that are relevant for school mathematics graduates, as arithmetic skills and geometry concepts are. In fact, this perception of Scratch as a tool for learning mathematics fails to fully exploit opportunities for effective teaching of computational thinking. For example, the authors mention user-defined blocks in Scratch (referred to as an "under-used component of Scratch"), claiming in passing that they reduce complexity and aid readability, and then say that they encourage the students to use user-defined blocks to help them explain their artifacts. However, user-defined blocks are not merely a technical tool for reducing complexity and scaffolding for explaining. They are a clear manifestation of abstraction and this is exactly why they support explaining, since they help students form explanations with the appropriate level of detailing. Hence, user-defined blocks can be used to explicitly learn and develop the skill of abstraction, a main idea of computational thinking, but ScratchMaths seems to ignore this opportunity.

Other teaching approaches may use programming as a technical aid for practicing a subject. For example, diSessa (2020) demonstrates how programming proficiency may help in analyzing a natural phenomenon (the spread of Covid-19) mathematically. In this context, programming is a tool for performing actions that would otherwise be too cumbersome to perform. Using this tool may allow students, or people in general, to perform more sophisticated analyses and reasoning since they can "outsource" some of the technical work to computers, provided they know how to communicate with them. However, although diSessa refers to computational thinking only within the programming phase, it is actually exploited also in other parts of his example. Moreover, many of the higher-level stages in his example utilize computational thinking skills and thus this example could serve to identify and characterize these skills, so that they can be used in other (not necessarily mathematical) contexts, but in this case as well, an opportunity to promote meaningful learning of computational thinking was missed.

Bottom line, I believe that teaching computational thinking should be done mainly (though not solely) through the teaching of CS as a stand-alone subject.

Next, I will discuss the content as well as the means and methods for implementing such an approach.

6.2 *The Curricular Content for Teaching CS toward Computational Thinking*

By nature, K–12 curricula are limited in the disciplinary breadth and depth that they can cover. This stems from time constraints as well as the cognitive abilities of young learners. However, to achieve meaningful learning of computational thinking, K–12 CS curricula should encompass sufficient manifestations of CS's habits of mind and mental tools. Is this feasible?

As in other cases, insights from mathematics education may prove to be relevant. In the context of mathematics, the term *mathematical thinking* has been brought forward because educators had reached the conclusion that school mathematics does not lead to the development of mathematical thinking (Schoenfeld, 1992). This might happen when school mathematics is not a reliable image of the discipline of mathematics. School mathematics is often about *using* mathematics (e.g., using known rules to calculate the derivative of a function), rather than *doing* mathematics (solving authentic mathematical problems, for example, "discovering" such rules). Changing the way mathematics is taught in schools can provide students with opportunities to experience the work of a mathematician and consequently, facilitate the development of mathematical thinking (Cuoco et al., 1996; Schoenfeld, 1992).

Similarly, if CS is taught in a manner that is consistent with its nature as the science of computational problems, it is more likely that its teaching will facilitate the development of computational thinking. Achieving that while adhering to the inherent limitations of K–12 school curricula is not at all simple. Bruner's (1960) work is very relevant in this context. In his own words, "any subject can be taught effectively in some intellectually honest form to any child in any stage of development" (p. 33). That is, even difficult habits of mind can be taught at school, provided that their learning is carefully designed to be age-appropriate and effective. The integration of CS fundamental ideas and habits of mind in CS curricula is a central theme of my research work (e.g., Alexandron et al., 2014; Armoni, 2013; Statter and Armoni, 2020, regarding the idea of abstraction; Alexandron et al., 2016 and Armoni & Gal-Ezer, 2007, regarding the idea of non-determinism; and Armoni & Gal-Ezer, 2005, regarding the idea of reduction). For example, in Statter and Armoni (2020), we used a framework for introducing CS abstraction to novices (Armoni, 2013), and we showed how the challenging idea of CS abstraction can be effectively taught to 7th-graders in the context of an introductory CS course that utilizes the Scratch programming language for learning CS ideas and concepts. Interestingly, the required extra teaching effort was minimal, and it mainly called for the teachers to understand the concept of algorithmic abstraction and the manner in which it should be taught. Indeed, curricula that reflect the authentic nature of a discipline need not necessarily be overloaded. The same material may be taught differently and new material may replace some parts of the old material, bringing forward habits of minds and fundamental ideas.

Thus, it is recommended to use a problem-based curriculum that is designed around CS habits of mind.

6.3 *Methods and Means for Teaching Computational Thinking through CS*

The misconception of CS = programming was revisited throughout this chapter from various angles; for instance, in the context of teaching computational thinking by integrating it into other school subjects. It is just as relevant when considering the teaching of computational thinking through CS as a standalone subject, since as noted above, most corresponding curricula focus on programming, and even identify teaching computational thinking with teaching programming (e.g., Brennan & Resnick, 2012; Denning, 2017; Seiter & Foreman, 2013). This approach is bound to reinforce the misconception.

In addition, the effectiveness of such curricula may be limited. A standard teaching of programming does not lend itself easily to many computational mental tools. For example, when abstraction (in its full essence) is not given sufficient attention and emphasis, its learning is very limited and at best, it is reduced to some specific programming manifestations (Román-González, 2015; Seiter & Foreman, 2013; Statter & Armoni, 2020).

Finally, although programming does utilize certain aspects of computational thinking, this is almost always done the same way: the students are given a task and their solutions constitute computer programs as artifacts. Throughout the teaching process, the difficulty of the tasks gradually increases, and additional programming constructs are introduced, but all tasks share the same flavor. This increases the distance between the context in which computational aspects are present in the teaching process of CS and the other contexts, in which these aspects may be used in other school subjects, thus making transfer a very difficult, perhaps even impossible challenge.

Several pedagogical principles may serve to overcome these flaws:

- Rise above programming, exploiting the full extent of the problem-solving process in which programming is just one phase, and focusing specifically on problems and algorithms, as demonstrated in Statter and Armoni (2020).

This way, the students experience hands-on learning and enjoy the creation of concrete, fully operable artifacts in the form of programs, but at the same time, they are exposed to a more authentic nature of the discipline.

- Devise tasks that lend themselves to additional mental tools, such as reduction, reversing, problem representation, and data manipulation. Since these mental tools are general and abstract by nature, in line with Bruner (1960), their effective teaching requires explicit treatment in different contexts (such as different kinds of tasks), while making the necessary connections to foster their generalization.
- Use different kinds of tasks, including those that do not involve programming at all. These may include analyzing and formulating problems, unplugged activities (e.g., CS Unplugged[1]) that deal with different topics (e.g., cryptography, computational biology, and computational models[2]), and discussing the correctness of algorithms (by means of argumentation).
- Use tasks anchored in different domains and disciplines. This can also support far (nonspecific) transfer (Bruner, 1960), and foster the creation of a more authentic image of CS as the science of computational problems.
- Cooperate with teachers of other school subjects to integrate activities and tasks that encompass computational thinking in other contexts. Some tasks may involve algorithmization and programming, whereas others should necessitate the use of different computational thinking habits of mind for solving tasks that are supposedly unrelated to CS.

The last recommendation does not contradict the position, stated earlier in this chapter, against teaching computational thinking through integration in other subjects. Rather, it calls for enhancing the teaching of computational thinking through CS (as a stand-alone subject) and increasing its effectiveness by means of integrated activities. The cooperation with teachers from other school subjects can address the arguments posited against both of these approaches. First, it can contribute to achieving transfer. Second, it can foster a correct image of CS among educators of other subjects, causing them to acknowledge that computer scientists (or educators) are experts of problems. Last, cooperation can produce tasks or activities that optimize the exploitation of computational thinking and hence are more effective in developing computational thinking skills.

7 Summary

Computational thinking encapsulates the ways of thinking, mental tools, and habits of mind of computer scientists. These are often improved, enhanced, or stronger variations of skills used in other disciplines. Hence, acquiring computational thinking can potentially promote the acquisition of these skills and therefore has substantial merit for everyone.

Computational thinking can be acquired by learning CS, provided that CS is taught in a way that is consistent with the nature of the discipline – as the science of computational problems that exploits CS habits of mind and is not limited to programming.

To support transfer from the context of CS to other contexts, the teaching of CS should involve different kinds of problems from various domains. In addition, activities that utilize computational thinking should be integrated into other school subjects, by means of cooperation between CS teachers and those of other disciplines.

Notes

1 https://csunplugged.org/en/
2 In the context of CS, *computational models* are not computerized models in the sense of computational science, but rather formal (mathematically flavored) descriptions representing different kinds of computational entities.

References

Aho, A. V. (2011). Computation and computational thinking. *Ubiquity*, *11*(1), 1–8.

Aho, A. V., & Ullman, J. D. (1992). *Foundations of computer science.* Computer Science Press.

Alexandron, G., Armoni, M., Gordon, M., & Harel, D. (2014). Scenario-based programming: Reducing the cognitive load, fostering abstract thinking. In *Proceedings of the 36th International Conference on Software Engineering* (ICSE'14) (pp. 311–320). http://dx.doi.org/10.1145/2591062.2591167

Alexandron, G., Armoni, M., Gordon, M., & Harel, D. (2016). Teaching nondeterminism through programming. *Informatics in Education*, *15*, 1–23. http://dx.doi.org/10.15388/infedu.2016.01

Armoni, M. (2013). On teaching abstraction in CS to novices. *Journal of Computers in Mathematics and Science Teaching*, *32*, 265–284.

Armoni, M., & Gal-Ezer, J. (2005). Teaching reductive thinking. *Mathematics and Computer Education*, *39*, 131–142.

Armoni, M., & Gal-Ezer, J. (2007). Non-determinism: An abstract concept in computer science studies. *Computer Science Education*, *17*, 243–262. http://dx.doi.org/10.1080/08993400701442885

Armoni, M., Benaya, T., Ginat, D., & Zur, E. (2010). Didactics of introduction to computer science in high school. In J. Hromkovic, R. Královic, & J. Vahrenhold (Eds.), *Lecture notes in computer science, 5941* (pp. 36–48). Berlin, Germany: Springer. http://dx.doi.org/10.1007/978-3-642-11376-5_5

Atchison, W. F., Schweppe, E. J., Viavant, W., Young, D. M. Jr., Conte, S. D., Hamblen, J. W., Hull, T. E., Keenan, T. A., Kehl, W. B., McCluskey, E. J., Navarro, S. O., & Rheinboldt, W. C. (1968). Curriculum 68: Recommendations for academic programs in computer science. *Communications of the ACM, 11*(3), 151–197. http://dx.doi.org/10.1145/362929.362976

Austing, R. H., Barnes, B. H., Bonnette, D. T., Engel, G. L., & Stokes, G. (1979). Curriculum 78: Recommendations for the undergraduate program in computer science. *Communications of the ACM, 22*(3), 147–166. http://dx.doi.org/10.1145/359080.359083

Bell, T., Andreae, P., & Robins, A. (2014). A case study of the introduction of computer science in NZ schools. *ACM Transactions on Computing Education, 14*(2), 1–31. http://dx.doi.org/10.1145/2602485

Benton, L., Hoyles, C., Kalas, I., & Noss, R. (2016). Building mathematical knowledge with programming: Insights from the ScratchMaths project. In *Proceedings of the Constructionism in Action Conference* (pp. 26–33).

Brennan, K., & Resnick, M. (2012). New frameworks for studying and assessing the development of computational thinking. In *Proceedings of the 2012 Annual Meeting of the American Educational Research Association* (pp. 1–25).

Brown, N. C. C, Sentance, S., Crick, T., & Humphreys, S. (2014). Restart: The resurgence of computer science in UK schools. *ACM Transactions on Computing Education, 14*(2), 1–22. http://dx.doi.org/10.1145/2602484

Bruner, J. S. (1960). *The process of education*. Harvard University Press. http://dx.doi.org/10.1002/bs.3830090108

CAS (Computing at School). (2015). *Computational thinking: A guide for teachers*. https://community.computingatschool.org.uk/resources/2324/single

Cuoco, A. E., Goldenberg, P., & Mark, J. (1996). Habits of mind: An organizing principle for mathematics curricula. *The Journal of Mathematical Behavior, 15*, 375–402. http://dx.doi.org/10.1016/s0732-3123(96)90023-1

Denning, P. J. (2017). Remaining trouble spots with computational thinking. *Communications of the ACM, 60*(6), 33–39. http://dx.doi.org/10.1145/2998438

Denning, P. J., Comer, D. E., Gries, D., Mulder, M. C., Tucker, A., Turner, A. J., & Young, P. R. (1989). Computing as a discipline: ACM Curriculum Committee on Computer Science. *Communications of the ACM, 32*(1), 9–23. http://dx.doi.org/10.1145/63238.63239

Dijkstra, E. W. (1972). The humble programmer. *Communications of the ACM, 15*(10), 859–866. http://dx.doi.org/10.1145/355604.361591

Dijkstra, E. W. (1975). About robustness and the like. EWD 452. *The archive of Dijkstra's manuscripts*. http://www.cs.utexas.edu/users/EWD/

Dijkstra, E. W. (1986). On a cultural gap. *The Mathematical Intelligencer, 8*(1), 48–52. http://dx.doi.org/10.1007/bf03023921

diSessa, A. (2020). Computational literacy in the time of Covid-19. Appendix in Li, Y., Schoenfeld, A. H., diSessa, A., Graesser, A. C., Benson, L. C. English, L. D., & Duschl, R. A. (2020), Computational thinking is more about thinking than computing. *Journal for STEM Education Research, 3*, 11–16.

Duschl, R. A., Schweingruber, H. A., Shouse, A. W., & National Research Council. (2007). *Taking science to school: Learning and teaching science in grades K-8*. National Academies Press.

Gal-Ezer, J., & Harel, D. (1999). Curriculum and course syllabi for a high-school CS program. *Computer Science Education, 9*, 114–147. http://dx.doi.org/10.1076/csed.9.2.114.3807

Gal-Ezer, J., & Stephenson, C. (2014). A tale of two countries: Successes and challenges in K–12 computer science education in Israel and the United States. *ACM Transactions on Computing Education, 14*(2), 1–18. http://dx.doi.org/10.1145/2602483

Gates, P., & Vistro-Yu, C. P. (2003). Is mathematics for all? In A. J. Bishop, M. A. Clements, C. Keitel, J. Kilpatrick, & F. K. S. Leung (Eds.), *Second international handbook of mathematics education* (pp. 31–73). Springer.

Gellert, U., Jablonka, E., & Keitel, C. (2001). Mathematical literacy and common sense in mathematics education. In B. Atweh, H. Forgasz, & B. Nebres (Eds.), *Sociocultural research in mathematics education: An international perspective* (pp. 57–76). Lawrence Erlbaum Associates.

Hanna, G., & Barbeau, E. (2008). Proofs as bearers of mathematical knowledge. *ZDM – Mathematics Education, 40*, 345–353. http://dx.doi.org/10.1007/s11858-008-0080-5

Hartmanis, J. (1994). Turing award lecture on computational complexity and the nature of computer science. *Communications of the ACM, 37*(10), 37–43. http://dx.doi.org/10.1145/194313.214781

ISTE (International Society for Technology in Education). (2016). *ISTE standards for students*. http://www.iste.org/standards/standards/for-students-2016

ISTE/CSTA (International Society for Technology in Education/Computer Science Teachers Association). (2011). *Operational definition of computational thinking for K–12 education*. https://cdn.iste.org/www-root/ct-documents/computational-thinking-operational-definition-flyer.pdf?sfvrs

Klein, J. T. (1990). *Interdisciplinarity: History, theory and practice*. Wayne State University Press.

Krishnan, A. (2009). *What are academic disciplines? Some observations on the disciplinarity vs. interdisciplinarity debate*. ESRC National Centre for Research Methods, University of Southampton.

Kuhn, D. (2010). What is scientific thinking and how does it develop? In U. Goswami (Ed.), *The Wiley-Blackwell handbook of childhood cognitive development* (2nd ed., pp. 497–553). Wiley-Blackwell. http://dx.doi.org/10.1002/9781444325485.ch19

Lewis, C. M., Anderson, R. E., & Yashuara, K. (2016). "I don't code all day": Fitting in computer science when the stereotypes don't fit. In *Proceedings of the 2016 ACM Conference on International Computing Education Research* (ICER'16) (pp. 23–32). http://dx.doi.org/10.1145/2960310.2960332

Meerbaum-Salant, O., Armoni, M., & Ben-Ari, M. (2013). Learning computer science concepts with Scratch. *Computer Science Education, 23*, 239–264. http://dx.doi.org/10.1080/08993408.2013.832022

Nardelli, E. (2019). Do we really need computational thinking? *Communications of the ACM, 62*(2), 32–35. http://dx.doi.org/10.1145/3231587

National Research Council. (2010). *Report of a workshop on the scope and nature of computational thinking*. National Academies Press. http://dx.doi.org/10.17226/12840

National Research Council. (2011). *Report of a workshop on pedagogical aspects of computational thinking*. National Academies Press. http://dx.doi.org/10.17226/13170

Papert, S. (1980). *Mindstorms: Children, computing, and powerful ideas*. Basic Books, Inc. Publishing.

Román-González, M. (2015). Computational thinking test: Design guidelines and content validation. In *Proceedings of the 7th Annual International Conference on Education and New Learning Technologies* (EDULEARN) (pp. 2436–2444).

Schoenfeld, A. H. (1992). Learning to think mathematically: Problem solving, metacognition, and sense making in mathematics. In D. A. Grouws (Ed.), *NCTM handbook of research on mathematics teaching and learning* (pp. 334–368). Macmillan.

Schulte, C., & Knobelsdorf, M. (2007). Attitudes towards computer science-computing experiences as a starting point and barrier to computer science. In *Proceedings of the 3rd International Workshop on Computing Education Research* (ICER'07) (pp. 27–38). http://dx.doi.org/10.1145/1288580.1288585

Seiter, L., & Foreman, B. (2013). Modeling the learning progressions of computational thinking of primary grade students. In *Proceedings of the 9th ACM Conference on International Computing Education Research* (ICER'13) (pp. 59–66). http://dx.doi.org/10.1145/2493394.2493403

Statter, D., & Armoni, M. (2020). Teaching abstraction in computer science to 7th grade students. *ACM Transactions on Computing Education, 20*(1), 1–37. http://dx.doi.org/10.1145/3372143

Taub, R., Armoni, M., & Ben-Ari, M. (2012). CS unplugged and middle-school students' views, attitudes, and intentions regarding CS. *ACM Transactions on Computing Education, 14*(2), 1–29. http://dx.doi.org/10.1145/2160547.2160551

Warner, L., Denner, J., Campe, S., & Kawamato, D. C. (2012). The fairy performance assessment: Measuring computational thinking in middle schools. In *Proceedings of the 43rd ACM Technical Symposium on Computer Science Education* (SIGCSE12) (pp. 215–220). http://dx.doi.org/10.1145/2157136.2157200

Wing, J. M. (2006). Computational thinking. *Communications of the ACM, 49*(3), 33–35. http://dx.doi.org/10.1145/1118178.1118215

Wing, J. M. (2008). Computational thinking and thinking about computing. *Philosophical Transactions of the Royal Society, 366*, 3717–3725.

Wing, J. M. (2010). *Computational thinking: What and why.* https://www.cs.cmu.edu/link/research-notebook-computational-thinking-what-and-why

Wing, J. M. (2014). *Computational thinking benefits society.* http://socialissues.cs.toronto.edu/2014/01/computational-thinking/

Yardi, S., & Bruckman, A. (2007). What is computing? Bridging the gap between teenagers' perceptions and graduate students' experiences. In *Proceedings of the 3rd International Workshop on Computing Education Research (ICER'07)* (pp. 39–50). http://dx.doi.org/10.1145/1288580.1288586

CHAPTER 8

Areas of Concern in the Design of a Mathematics Curriculum

The Case of Five Curriculum Projects

Alex Friedlander, Nurit Hadas, Rina Hershkowitz and Michal Tabach

Abstract

This chapter relates to some of the numerous attempts to implement the Mathematics Group's original mission to cater to the cognitive and affective needs of the Israeli student population by developing a wide variety of mathematical learning materials. To describe some of the issues considered throughout a period of more than 50 years of curriculum development, we organized this chapter around five areas of concern in the design of mathematical learning materials: changing the nature of mathematical content, promoting context-based activities, promoting multiple representations, supporting students' learning processes and reflecting intended teaching and learning processes. Different projects related to these design concerns in different ways, according to their goals and rationale, and provided correspondingly varied answers. In this paper, each area of concern is discussed in the context of one curriculum project that considered this particular area to be one of its main goals. The discussion provides some details about the project's background, a rationale for the selected area of concern, and illustrative examples of project tasks.

Keywords

design concerns – curriculum projects – context-based tasks – multiple representations – informal problem solving strategies – intended teaching processes

1 Introduction

The Mathematics Group was established as a section of the Department of Science Teaching at the Weizmann Institute of Science more than 50 years ago, with the original scope of creating and implementing learning materials for students learning mathematics in the newly established educational frame

DOI: 10.1163/9789004503625_008

of junior high schools (for more background details – see the next section). Throughout the years, the activities of the group diversified, but curriculum design remained a central component in and of itself, and also became a source and basis for other domains of activity – such as research, graduate studies in math education, in-service teacher education, and student-assessment projects.

This chapter relates to some of the quite numerous attempts to implement the Mathematics Group's original mission to cater to the cognitive and affective needs of the Israeli student population by developing a wide variety of mathematical learning materials. During those years, the domain of curriculum design underwent considerable changes, due to developments in the national and international scene of math education, a growing volume of research findings, changes in the structure of the Israeli student population, newly designed technological tools, and even personnel changes in the Group's staff.

The scope of this chapter does not allow a systematic survey of the numerous curriculum projects conducted during this period, or a detailed description of several selected projects. To describe some of the issues considered throughout this long period of time, we organized this chapter around five areas of concern in the design of mathematical learning materials, with each of these areas discussed in the context of a curriculum project that considered this particular area to be one of its main goals. Each section was written by a leading figure from the corresponding project's staff. Table 8.1 presents the structure of this chapter.

TABLE 8.1 Areas of concern in curriculum design and corresponding example projects

Area of concern	Example curriculum project
Changing the nature of mathematical content	The Rehovot Program
Promoting context-based activities	Seeing and Doing Geometry
Promoting multiple representations	The CompuMath Project
Supporting students' learning processes	The 3U (Shai) Project
Reflecting intended teaching and learning processes	The Integrated Mathematics Project

2 Changing the Nature of Mathematical Content: The Case of the *Rehovot Program*

In this section, we describe some aspects of the emergence of new mathematical contents in a reform curriculum, and the attempts made by its designers to cater to the needs and characteristics of the student population of a newly created educational system and to a new approach to school mathematics.

A reform in the structure of the Israeli educational system was formally declared in 1967, involving a gradual transition from a system of 8 years of elementary and 4 years of high school, to a system of 6-3-3, which created a new junior-high school entity. With regard to the teaching of mathematics (and possibly other domains as well), this reform set two main goals for itself: (1) introducing professionally qualified teachers at the formerly elementary 7th- and 8th-grade levels, and (2) introducing more advanced topics at an earlier stage – for example, starting the learning of algebra in grade 7 rather than 9.

The first goal raised the need to adapt the mathematical background of former elementary teachers, and the pedagogical background of former high-school teachers, to fit the needs of the newly established junior high schools. The achievement of this goal obviously involved a rather complex and lengthy process (Hershkowitz & Israeli, 1981).

The implementation of the second goal required the creation of a new syllabus, and then the development of a new curriculum. A brief (compulsory) syllabus containing the list of required mathematical topics for grades 7–9 was quickly created in 1967 by a committee nominated by the Ministry of Education comprising a majority of mathematicians. However, the new curriculum had to transform the vision of a few mathematicians into an official program for all grade 7–9 students. The complexity of this task ended up involving the investment of considerable effort, funds and professional ingenuity (Dreyfus et al., 1987).

At a slightly earlier stage, in the late 1950s, a reform movement in mathematics learning and teaching (labeled the New Math movement) had begun (Howson et al., 1981). Thus, for example, the *School Mathematics Study Group* (SMSG) project was founded in the United States in 1958, and the *School Mathematics Project* (SMP) was founded in England at about the same time. The SMSG was developed by mathematicians and experienced mathematics teachers, whereas the SMP was designed and carried out mainly by mathematics teachers.

It is under these circumstances that the Mathematics Group of the Science Teaching Department was founded at the Weizmann Institute (also known as "the Rehovot Mathematics Group") as part of a national effort to provide solutions to the challenges in curriculum development and teacher preparation posed by the reform in mathematics education. Thus, the founding of the junior-high school system, the consequent new national mathematics syllabus and the New Math reform movement had a quite fundamental influence on the activities of the Mathematics Group in general, and on the mathematical contents of the Group's curriculum in particular. From the very beginning, the

Mathematics Group's work was based on an underlying philosophy that considered curriculum development and implementation as a continuous long-term activity involving many aspects: developing textbook sequences, promoting students' active learning, classroom implementation of curriculum materials, in-service teacher training, research, and dissemination of information.

In the following, we focus on the mathematical contents of the new textbook sequences that were developed at three levels – also known as the *Rehovot Program*. We relate to (1) the structure of the 7th-grade mathematical topics in number sets and algebra, and (2) some innovative task formats catering to the junior-high school student population.

2.1 *The Structure of Topics in Number Sets and Algebra*

The contents related to number sets and algebra in the *Rehovot Program*'s textbooks followed the outline of the national syllabus at its three levels. Thus, for example, the grade 7 syllabus on number sets included the topics of number bases, laws and conventions of arithmetic, positive and negative numbers, and the coordinate system and graphs, whereas the topics related to beginning algebra were algebraic expressions, introduction to equations and inequalities, and basic concepts in set theory. The transition from this outline to a corresponding curriculum required a drastic change in the traditional perception of the nature of school mathematics and the corresponding learning materials for this age level. With respect to the domain of task design, the project staff chose the English SMP and the American SMSG learning materials as its main sources of inspiration. The SMSG textbooks had a rigorous formal approach to mathematics (for example, symbolic notations, formal definitions and formal algebraic concepts), whereas the SMP tended to be less formal and to employ concrete manipulatives and context-based situations. The *Rehovot Program*'s staff aimed to create tasks that allow for students' construction of knowledge through active learning and maximal student involvement. Consequently, the SMSG learning materials served as a model for structuring the mathematical content according to the new syllabus outline, and for defining the corresponding algebraic concepts, whereas the SMP frequently served as a model for the pedagogical approach used in the presentation of concepts. This integration of terminology and structure on the one hand, and pedagogy on the other, aimed to promote a dynamic, generalized and interconnected view of arithmetic and algebra.

For example, the concepts of number name, open phrase (algebraic expressions) and open sentence (equations and inequalities) aimed to emphasize the connections between different arithmetical and algebraic concepts:

– *a number name* was defined as one of many possible representations of the same number;

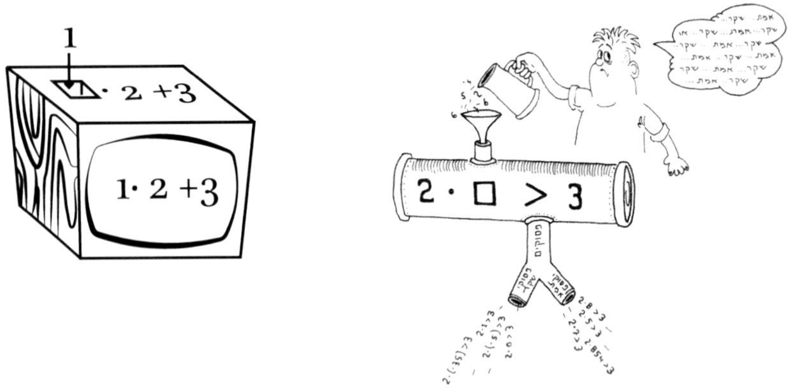

(a) (b)

FIGURE 8.1 Illustrative representations of an *open phrase* (a) and an *open sentence* (b) in the *Rehovot Program's* grade 7 beginning algebra book

- *an open phrase* was presented as a "machine" with an "open slot," where the substitution of different numbers produces a variety of numerical results (see Figure 8.1a);
- *an open sentence* was presented as a "machine" where the substitution of different numbers produces a variety of either true or false sentences (see Figure 8.1b).

According to this approach, the variable and open phrase represent a set of numbers, whereas an open sentence represents a set of some true, and some false sentences, and consequently has the potential of having none to an infinite number of solutions that form its *truth set*.

The topic of positive and negative numbers would be another example of curricular change in terms of conceptualization and pedagogy. Following the SMP approach, the *Rehovot Program* staff labeled these numbers as *shift numbers*, where each number was characterized by a length and a direction that determined a corresponding shift on the number line. Consequently, consecutive shifts of two numbers allowed students to find the sum or the difference of the corresponding numbers. At a more advanced stage, this notation was extended to the topic of powers (Dreyfus et al., 1987) and scientific notation (Arcavi & Hadas, 1989).

2.2 *Catering to the Needs of the Junior-High School Student Population*

Due to the heterogeneity of the junior-high school student population, the Ministry of Education decided to stream the teaching of mathematics into three levels, each level learning from specially designed textbooks. However, streaming did not solve all of the problems – particularly not the problems of the low achievers. About one-third of the student population was defined according to nationally standardized socioeconomic criteria as "socially deprived." Most of these students lacked motivation for learning mathematics, and received little support from their family and social environment.

The Mathematics Group designed and evaluated various learning materials and teaching strategies aimed at overcoming some of the learning difficulties and the psychological barriers of the junior-high school student population in general, and of the low achievers in particular. We would like to mention in this context the games and remedial programs.

Mathematical games – such as board games, card games and puzzles, turned out to be particularly useful for those places in the curriculum where the process of mastering a particular skill is lengthy (Friedlander, 1977; Taizi, 1979). The game strategies were usually designed in such a way as to require students to apply higher-order thinking, to practice the skill to be learned, to provide external motivation and to promote student teamwork.

The remedial learning materials (*Links*) were developed as collections of topic-related worksheets (for example, *Links in Fractions* and *Links in Decimals*). The development of these materials was the result of classroom observations and need-assessment surveys that showed that at the entrance to junior high school, a sizable part of the student population in general, and the socially deprived population in particular, lacked mastery of basic computational skills (Hershkowitz, 1979; Israeli & Hershkowitz, 1979). Consequently, several collections of short worksheets ("chains of links") were designed to overcome difficulties caused by the diagnosed lack of basic knowledge. Most worksheets were designed to provide students with quick feedback to their work – such as finding a path through a labyrinth, reaching a given target, and deciphering a hidden code (see, for example, Figure 8.2). The *Links*' implementation scheme was based on diagnostic pre–post testing, differential treatment of individual students, and minimal disturbance to the teaching of the regular junior-high school curriculum.

Initially, each game was used, evaluated and published as a separate entity, whereas the design format of the *Links* tasks was designed and evaluated as part of a remedial project. Both formats were gradually incorporated as integral parts of a "second generation" of textbooks at all three levels. The *Links* format of worksheet sequences was also adopted in the design of learning materials for several less central curriculum topics, for example, *Estimation* (Markovits et al., 1987) and *Calculators*.

Finally, we note in hindsight that the first 20 years of the Weizmann Mathematics Group were a period of intensive curriculum development. However,

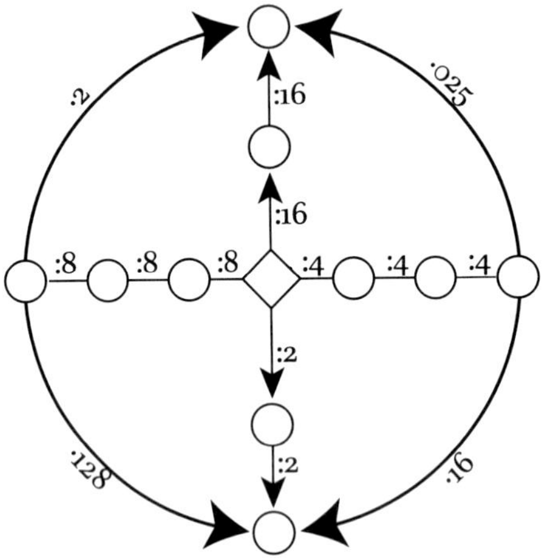

FIGURE 8.2
Example of a *Links* worksheet (*Decimals*)

with regard to the role of the mathematical content as an agent of change, we note that content received major attention and investment of design efforts during the first half of this period. Once the nature of the mathematical topics, the definitions and the teaching sequences of the relevant concepts were established, we can distinguish a shift of emphasis to students' cognitive and affective needs, and as a result, a shift to searching for new formats of tasks that aimed to cater to those needs. During the following years, the efforts of the Rehovot Mathematics Group were directed to designing a curriculum for learning mathematics in a technological environment (see Section 4), and a curriculum for learning mathematics in heterogeneous classes.

3 Promoting Context-Based Activities: The Case of *Seeing and Doing Geometry*

Employing a context-based approach in curriculum design seems to have both immediate and more general advantages (Tabach & Friedlander, 2008):
- It facilitates learning processes by providing a real or concrete meaning to an otherwise abstract concept or algorithm
- It provides points of reference that students can review at a more advanced stage of learning, when work is performed at a more abstract level
- It raises student motivation and willingness to become engaged in the learning activity
- It emphasizes the potential of using mathematical models and skills in other fields.

Traditionally, if context problems in mathematics curricula were used at all, they consisted of applying a pure mathematical topic after it had been studied (Gravemeijer & Doorman, 1999). These problems referred to a real situation borrowed (as is or edited) from any academic field outside of mathematics or from everyday life, and they served several educational goals. Some problems were used to illustrate the usefulness of mathematics, others to teach the ins and outs of mathematical modeling and yet others to simply motivate students.

Three "levels of embeddedness of context" (Stillman, 1998, p. 246) can be distinguished for such problems: *border*, *wrapper* and *tapestry* problems. In *border* problems, the context is a mere wrapping story, some kind of excuse to present a mathematical exercise; it is not related in any way to the understanding or solving of the problem. In *wrapper* problems, the solver needs to dig into the context to uncover hidden mathematics, but after that, the context can be ignored, since it is not needed for working out a solution; nevertheless, the context may become useful again to check whether the result makes sense in terms of the situation. In *tapestry* problems, the context and the mathematics are interrelated and the process of solving the problem may require going back and forth between the contextual situation and the mathematics, because both are interdependent as solving resources.

In any case, mathematical modeling presupposes

> knowledge of pure mathematics which must be properly invoked and applied in order to make a model of a given real situation, solve it mathematically and reinterpret the results in terms of the situation being modelled. This implies that knowing pure mathematics comes before its applications… (Arcavi, 2020, p. 88)

However, *tapestry* problems allow for the inversion of the mathematics-first–applications-later chronology as follows: intriguing real-world situations can be the departure point for mathematization, and rich contexts can serve as a source and departure point for learning new mathematics (e.g., Treffers, 1993) rather than applying it.

Consider, for example, the *Grilled Fish* activity presented in Figure 8.3 (taken from Arcavi, 2020). The idea of this task is to connect the real-world concern of grilling all of the fish at the same time while all get the same heat, and to realize that if they are arranged in a square some fish will be closer to the fire than others. This task may be used in both modes – to apply the definition of a circumference (as the set of points equidistant from a center), if known, or alternatively to motivate its geometrical definition. The situational needs and intentions and the implicit mathematical idea are closely interwoven.

The picture shows fish being grilled around a fire.

Why do you think the fish are arranged in a circle and not in a square?

FIGURE 8.3 The *Grilled Fish* activity

In most curricula around the world, the study of geometry, beyond elementary school, focuses on definitions, axioms and theorems to be proven using logical deduction. In some cases, where dynamic geometry is introduced, students are also challenged to explore and pose hypotheses for investigation (e.g., Hadas et al., 2002). In any case, the study of geometry remains entirely within the realm of "pure mathematics."

In this section, we describe a curriculum program designed for junior high school in which the study of geometry is embedded in real-life situations, such as the activity illustrated in Figure 8.3. The *Seeing and Doing Geometry Project* was mostly aimed at non-mathematically oriented students for whom the study of deductive geometry may be uninteresting, unmotivating, or even difficult. The main goals of these real-world geometry learning materials were:

- To involve students in activities in which their experiences with real-world situations, their common sense and intuitions are valid resources, and thus have the potential to enhance motivation and engagement
- To get acquainted with geometrical shapes and objects, their properties and some of the basic theorems as they emerge from practical activities, from daily life situations and even games
- To support the development of a "mathematical gaze" at the world surrounding us by getting used to looking deeper at situations that are usually taken for granted or left unnoticed. Students may learn to ask questions whose answers are opportunities to use or to produce geometrical knowledge by posing problems and gaining new insights (Arcavi, 2020).

Thus, for example, the two tasks presented in Figures 8.4 and 8.5 are aimed at the first two goals of "sensing" and understanding geometrical concepts. The idea of the *Placing Dice* activity (Figure 8.4) is to resort to "sight lines" (rather than resorting to axioms or postulates) to convey in an experiential way some properties related to straight lines. In this case, students are expected to understand that two points determine one line (the "vision line") as well as to experience the notion of co-linearity.

- Place two dice on your desk. Close one of your eyes, and move around keeping your eyes at the desktop level until you can spot only one of the dice.
- Now, place on the desk a third die, so that looking from the same position, you can still see only one of these three dice.
- Can you place a fourth and then a fifth die, and still see only one of these dice?
- Can you recommend a way to place several dice on a desk, and see only one of them?

FIGURE 8.4 The *Placing Dice* activity – "sensing" the concept of a straight line

The second example, the *Breaking a Stick* game (Figure 8.5), was designed to allow students to experience and understand a main property of the sides of a triangle – the triangle inequality. The goal of the game is to break a given stick into three pieces such that the players can build a triangle. By the end of the game, a winning strategy is discussed, and students may generalize the conditions for three sides to build up a triangle, i.e., the triangle inequality.

The *Road Sign* activity (Figure 8.6) addresses the third goal of promoting the development of a "mathematical gaze" at the world. The activity provides opportunities for learning about the geometrical appearances of the concept of slope and the ways to measure them.

The idea behind this activity is twofold: to habituate students to open their eyes to the world around them and to discern "mathematical opportunities" to think about, extract information from, and draw conclusions. Developing a mathematical gaze is indeed one of the goals for inserting a contextual, authentic and interesting real-world situation. Another goal is to use real authentic situations as triggers for mathematization, i.e., to learn new mathematics, and at the same time to convey the feeling of the utility of mathematics for a better understanding of the world around us.

In each round:
- The first player takes a breakable stick, cuts out a piece, keeps it, and hands over the remaining piece to the second player.
- The second player breaks the remaining piece into two parts.
- If the three available pieces can form a triangle, the second player receives a point. If the three pieces do not fit to make a triangle, the first player receives the point.

In the next round, the two players switch roles.
The winner of the game is declared after playing several rounds.

FIGURE 8.5 The *Breaking a Stick* game – "sensing" the triangle inequality

- Tell a story about what you see in the picture at your right.
- What do you think is the message of the black triangle?
- What do you think is the message of 12 percent?
- Do you think that the 12 percent fits the drawing?
- Can you draw on a grid paper a triangle that would fit the message of 12 percent?
- Can you draw on a grid paper a triangle that would fit the message of 100%?

FIGURE 8.6 The *Road Sign* activity – promoting a "mathematical gaze" at the world

This section focused on the rationale and examples of context-based activities from the *Seeing and Doing Geometry* curriculum project. The designers of these tasks took special care to engage students' common sense, previous knowledge (of mathematics or of real-world experiences), intuition, curiosity and visual cues. However, some words of caution are in place, referring to at least two potential challenges: sociocultural and cognitive (e.g., Arcavi, 2003). From a sociocultural–affective point of view, students might dismiss some of these tasks as being "not mathematical," regard them as an "adaptation" for low achievers, and thus refuse to become meaningfully engaged. Context-based activities aim to promote classroom norms and practices that value sense-making activities, and lead to sound mathematical ideas, even if the solution methods are not fully formal. From a cognitive point of view, challenges refer to an appropriate invocation of intuition, common sense, relevant previous knowledge, visual noticing and reasoning, recognition of relevant and irrelevant features of a given context, and a flexible back-and-forth transition from contextual features to the mathematical language and procedures. These capabilities should be nurtured through repeated (non-algorithmic) practice.

4 Promoting Multiple Representations: The Case of *the CompuMath Project*

Mathematics is a highly abstract domain in terms of the involved concepts and the relations among them. Hence, the way in which mathematical ideas are represented is fundamental to how people learn and use them (Heinze et al., 2009). According to the *Principles and Standards* document issued by the National Council of Teachers in Mathematics (NCTM, 2000), a *representation* refers "to the act of capturing a mathematical concept or relationship in some form and to the form itself" (p. 4). In other words, representations refer to both processes and products of learning and doing mathematics.

Representations of mathematical concepts are an integral part of doing mathematics and an important aspect of teaching and learning mathematics. We see representations as a means for recording and communicating information and processes, thinking about and developing mathematical ideas and practices, and then understanding and expressing them. Since any representation has its strengths and limitations, we see the work with multiple representations as necessary for developing students' understanding of mathematical concepts, and for catering to students' individual thinking styles (Friedlander & Tabach, 2001). Kaput (1992) pointed out that in the presence of dynamic software environments, notation systems that are static in other environments become dynamic. As a consequence, the gap between a symbolic notation system and others (such as numerical and graphical ones) becomes less significant.

The *CompuMath Project* was initiated in 1993 by the Mathematics Group, as part of a national effort to support the intensive use of technological tools in the teaching and learning of mathematics and science. The project's main goal was to promote meaningful learning of junior-high school mathematics in an environment supported by technological tools, and it developed a complete curriculum for junior-high school mathematics requiring the use of computerized tools on a weekly basis. The activities of this project evolved through cycles of design, implementation, reflection and re-design of the learning materials, and was accompanied by research throughout each of these cycles (Hershkowitz & Tabach, 2018; Hershkowitz et al., 2002).

This section is an attempt to investigate the potential of a technological learning environment to promote the multiple representations of algebraic concepts, as reflected in the *CompuMath* curriculum. The project's approach to early algebra was based on a functional view, and was supported at that stage by spreadsheets as a digital tool. As stated by Yerushalmy (2009), a functional approach to algebra in a technological environment "provides students with opportunities to investigate algebraic ideas by linking the symbolic representation of functions and symbolic manipulations with their numeric and graphic representations" (p. 56). The use of spreadsheets as a main tool was based on the familiarity of beginning algebra students with a numerical representation on the one hand, and on its use of the symbolic representation of a relation (by "dragging down" a formula along a column) on the other (for a detailed description, see Tabach et al., 2008).

In the following, we analyze the structure of two *CompuMath* activities, and give some relevant excerpts from students' work, to illustrate the use of multiple representations to promote these claims.

Savings is a sequence of three 90-minute-long activities. The three activities exemplify the design and implementation of a functional approach to algebra, in which growth and change can be expressed by symbolic or "semi-symbolic" rules with, or without, using spreadsheets. We will relate here to the first part of this sequence. In this part, students are required to explore changes in four different weekly savings over a period of 52 weeks, and to represent them in mathematical language. In the process, students have to consider the roles and meanings of constants and variables in a context-based situation, use multiple (verbal, numerical, graphical and symbolic) representations, and compare a variety of growth processes.

The *Savings* activity (in one of the three *CompuMath* 7th-grade beginning algebra textbooks) presents the cumulative processes of change in the savings of four children, as a result of receiving a weekly allowance (see Figure 8.7). Each of these four process is presented in a different representation. The designers' choice to present each process in a different representation was made for several reasons: it encourages flexibility in students' choice of representations in their solution path, it increases their awareness of their solution style, it legitimizes the use of multiple representations in a solution process, and it requires students to actually perform frequent transitions between representations and perceive them as a natural need, rather than as an arbitrary requirement. Posing a problem in several representations is a particularly suitable design strategy for situations that require the parallel investigation of several methods, quantities, etc. (Friedlander & Tabach, 2001). In these situations, to compare the given entities, students must make transitions between the given representation and another one.

In the *Savings* activity, the need to map information from one representation to another provides students with opportunities to increase their understanding of each representation separately, and of the problem situation as a whole. Students may choose their "favorite" representation, and use it for comparing the four saving schemes. Dolev (1996) found that students who could flexibly change representations while solving a problem were more successful than their peers who used only one representation systematically to solve the same problem. In experimental classes, the students' work on the *Savings* activity was usually followed by whole-class discussions regarding the advantages and disadvantages of a certain representation in their solution of a particular question.

One of the main concerns expressed by teachers with regard to allowing a free choice of representations was that such a design strategy may lead to students' choice of a familiar, but more time-consuming and error-prone solution method (e.g., working with a numerical representation when analyzing a global

The savings of Dina, Yonni, Moshon and Danny changed during the last year, as described below. The numbers indicate amounts of money in NIS at the end of each week.
Dina: *The table shows how much money Dina had saved at the end of each week. The table continues in the same way for the rest of the year.*

Week	*1*	*2*	*3*	*4*	*5*	*...6*
Amount	*7*	*14*	*21*	*28*	*35*	*...42*

Yoni: *Yoni kept his savings at 300 NIS throughout the year.*
Moshon: *The graph describes Moshon's savings at the end of each of the first 20 weeks.*
The graph continues in the same way for the rest of the year.

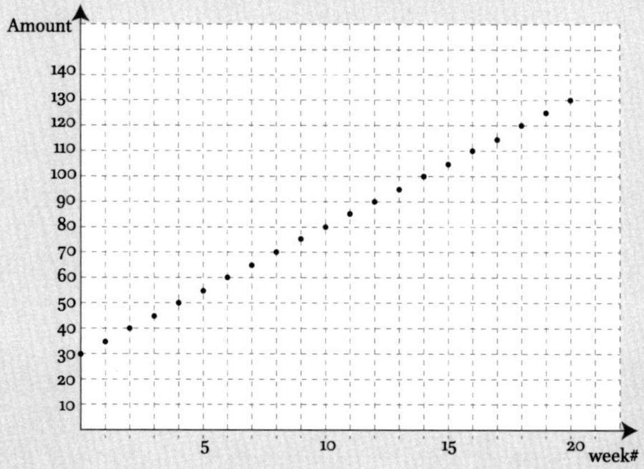

Danny: *Danny's savings can be described by the expression 300 – 5x, where x stands for the number of weeks.*

FIGURE 8.7 The *Savings* activity

phenomenon), and to a lack of motivation for employing a more general and mathematically advanced method (e.g., working with a symbolic or graphical representation in a similar circumstance). However, work with a technological tool considerably lessens the relevance of this argument. Our observations of students' work on *CompuMath* activities indicated that in most cases, the use of a technological tool makes the construction of any representation equally accessible. As a result, the choice of a certain representation usually depends on the nature of the question involved, and on each student's personal cognitive preference, rather than on the effort involved in its construction. Moreover, as mentioned in the discussion above on the advantages of using spreadsheets when learning beginning algebra, the choice of a certain representation frequently involves the use of other representations as well. Thus, for example, to obtain a list of numerical data with spreadsheets, or to draw a graph with a graph generator, students must use algebraic expressions as well.

In the *Improving Grades* activity (in one of the four *CompuMath* 9th-grade algebra textbooks), the students were presented with a situation of three grading schemes being considered by a teacher to retroactively improve her students' low grades obtained in a rather difficult test (Figure 8.8). Initially, the

On an unusually difficult test, the grades were so low that the teacher offered the class the opportunity to choose between three schemes for improving grades:

Scheme A: Add 10 points to the original grade.

Scheme B: Add to the original grade one-fourth of it.

Scheme C: Make the average of the original grade and 100.

Construct the representations below, and use them to answer the following questions.

Numbers

Original grade	Scheme A:	Scheme A:	Scheme A:
10			
30			
x			

Symbols → x

Graphs →

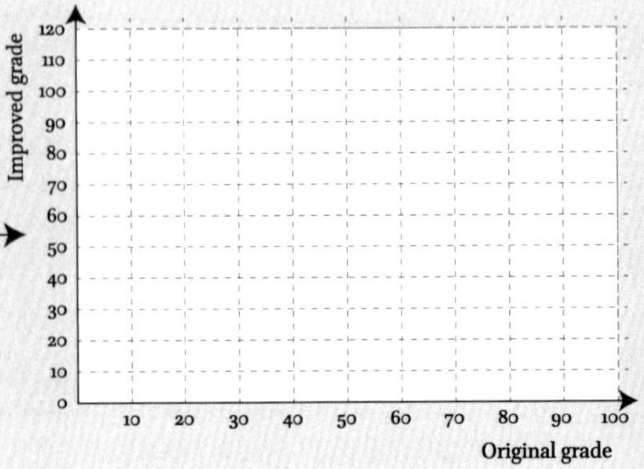

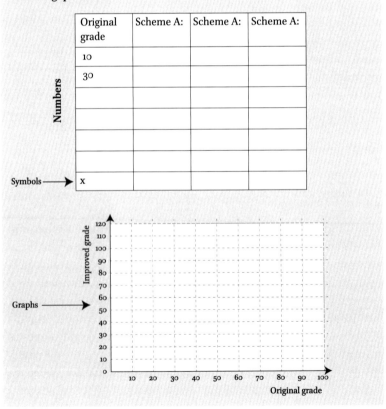

FIGURE 8.8 The *Improving Grades* activity

three schemes were presented verbally, and the students were required first to create corresponding numerical, graphical and symbolic representations, and then to answer several questions that required a comparison of the three schemes.

An analysis of the representations used by 61 grade 8 students (Tabach & Friedlander, 2012) showed that the students' choice of representation in their response to the activity's various questions depended on the nature of the task. Thus, most students chose a numerical representation when working on questions related to a local aspect of a particular grading scheme (for example, questions involving a particular grade according to a particular scheme), but chose a graphical or a symbolic representation when working on questions related to global aspects of this problem situation (e.g., questions that required finding a range of grades, or advancing general recommendations).

To conclude, the design of the *CompuMath* curriculum project in general, and its focus on multiple representations in particular, were initially guided by research findings and by the Mathematics Group's experience accumulated in previous curriculum projects. Classroom observations and additional research that accompanied the implementation of the *CompuMath* learning materials provided further support for the designers' predictions, showing an increase in the students' awareness and ability to choose and work in various representations, and consequently improving their flexibility as problem solvers, and their autonomy as mathematics learners.

5 Supporting Students' Learning Processes: The Case of *the 3U (Shai) Project*

Under the Israeli mathematics education system, high-school students (grades 10–12) are streamed into three tracks leading to three levels (3, 4 and 5 units(of matriculation exams in mathematics. This section relates to aspects of designing a curriculum for students who are studying at the lower level of 3 units (3U).

Traditionally, most of the mathematics learned by these students is based on drill and practice of basic procedures, with less emphasis on understanding their meaning and the need for their use. As a result, these students usually regard mathematics as a technical activity that does not require any sense-making, and cannot be a source of enjoyable experiences. Many 3U students tend to rely on their short-term memory (rather than on reasoning), and give up when encountering even the smallest difficulty. Moreover, many of these students drop out of their mathematics courses altogether, and some others fail to pass the 3U matriculation exam.

The *3U* (*Shai*) curriculum project was initiated in 1991 by the Mathematics Group as an attempt to cater to the needs of this target population. The main goals of the project team were to develop curriculum materials that were compatible with the concurrent national syllabus on the one hand, and to harness low-achieving students' capabilities and eschew obstacles that may harm their learning and motivation on the other. The *3U* approach emphasized students' intuitive, qualitative, and visual thinking based on their common sense, and consequently downplayed technical and formal manipulations. Estimated results, and visual and numerical approximations were legitimized, and qualitative and informal reasoning was preferred over technical and symbolic treatments.

As a result, most *3U* activities departed from situations in which common sense is engaged, and based students' learning experiences on multiple representations as different ways to envision the same idea. An attempt was made to link students' thinking to their acting in order to help them make sense out of what they were doing. While solving *3U* tasks, students were encouraged to use any available strategies, tools and connections. The problems were built in a way that allowed students to go back and forth between the "big picture" and the "small details" – i.e., between global and local processing (Tall & Thomas, 1991).

Thus, the process of designing the *3U* curriculum was based on the following three factors: (1) the project team's beliefs about what mathematics is and what a mathematical activity should be, (2) the team's theoretical biases about learning and teaching issues, and (3) its awareness of the characteristics and needs of the project's target population. These factors delineated and inspired the scope of the mathematics, the internal consistency and flow of a learning module, and the design of each problem situation.

The design process itself followed several phases. The first stage consisted of a careful design of tasks, their sequencing within an unfolding story, and their critical reading by fellow members of the team. Next, scrutinized classroom trials were conducted in at least two classrooms to collect and analyze feedback, and to redesign tasks where needed. Finally, a larger-scale dissemination was performed through teacher courses (Arcavi et al., 1994).

In the next two sections, we illustrate the *3U Project*'s approach to curriculum design and student learning, by describing and analyzing (1) the design process of a sequence of tasks related to the topic of linear functions, and (2) an example of the strategies advanced by the *3U Project* and employed in a student's solution of a mathematical task.

5.1 *An Example of Task Design*

The first step in the process of designing a sequence of tasks related to a specific topic involved "inspecting" the relevant mathematics. In this particular example, we focus on the underlying ideas and concepts related to the topic of linear functions. Thus, the idea that "a point is on the graph of a function (or a relation) if and only if the coordinates of the point satisfy the equation" seems very simple, but has several entailments and multiple contexts that students may not be fully aware of (e.g., Schoenfeld et al., 1993). Applying this idea to tasks and problems implies moving back and forth between the symbolic and graphical representations of functions.

Let us consider the task of finding the equation of the line that is parallel to $y = 2x - 5$ and goes through the point (1, 4). This is a rather traditional task which requires some understanding and ability to apply concepts related to the domains of algebra, analytical geometry and calculus. Moschkovich et al. (1993) extensively analyzed the difficulties involved in this task, and reported that the success rate in tasks of this kind, as reflected in United States national surveys, is quite low. In its present format, the problem has an analytical-symbolic point of departure, and can be very difficult for non-mathematically oriented students.

The *3U* learning materials encourage students to consider and use multiple representations, practical tools, visual thinking and common sense. The following practices are recommended in the context of graphing linear functions:

- Using an intuitive interpretation of the slope of a linear function as "rise over run," and representing it graphically by counting units on a Cartesian grid
- Placing the frequently used tool of a physical "cut-out" line on a Cartesian grid through (0, 0), obtaining the graph of a line of the form $y = ax$ according to the coordinates of corresponding points, and identifying the slope with the *a* parameter
- Identifying the *b* parameter in the equation $y = ax + b$ as the vertical translation of a line of the form $y = ax$. For example, to obtain the graph of the line $y = 2x + 3$, identify 3 as the *y*-coordinate of the point which was originally at (0, 0), and slide the line $y = 2x$ three units upward from the origin (0, 0).

This kind of practice allows students to draw the graphs of linear functions in a practical, visual and sense-making way. Now the original problem of finding the equation of the line according to the equation of one of its parallels and one of its points becomes a graphical activity that leads to finding the symbolic representation of the required line.

Next, we illustrate this interplay between geometrical and algebraic representations by presenting a sequence of *3U* tasks that follow this path. In the first part (Figure 8.9), students investigate possible ways of placing three lines relative to each other.

After identifying the possibilities of intersecting and parallel pairs of lines, students in the project's experimental classes used the graphical and algebraic interplay to conclude that equations with the same *a* parameter represent

1. Identify the possible relative positions of two lines and write symbolic expressions for each pair.
2. Work with your peers:
   - draw all possible locations of three lines relatively to each other
   - in each case, write down corresponding equations for the three lines.
3. Write the equations of three lines that intersect at the point (2, 3).

FIGURE 8.9 A sequence of *3U* tasks – Part One

parallel lines, whereas equations with the same *b* parameter represent intersecting lines.

In Question 2, students had no difficulty identifying the four possible situations (Figure 8.10), or finding equations for the first three situations by extending their conclusions from the case of two lines.

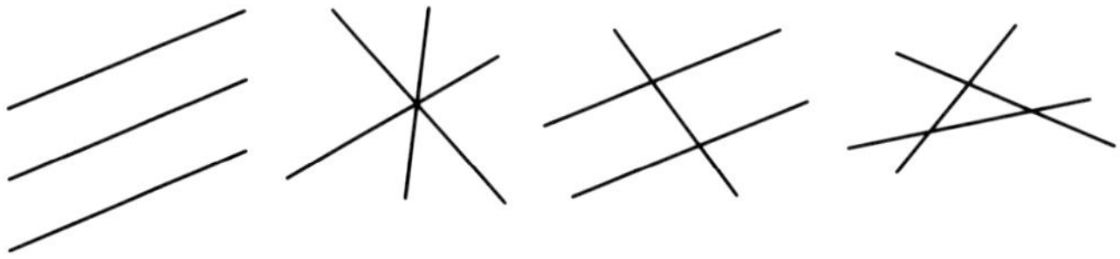

FIGURE 8.10 Possible positions of three lines on a plane

However, finding equations for three lines with three intersecting points was less straightforward. Many students chose three equations with different *a* and *b* parameters as the solution for this case as well. The main goal of Question 3 was to allow students to realize that equations with different *a* and *b* parameters do not necessarily yield three intersection points. As a result, students revised their inaccurate conjecture and, relying on their acquired tools and strategies, they placed three lines on the grid and deduced the corresponding equations.

The second part of this sequence (Figure 8.11) was aimed to allow students to use the acquired tools and strategies to solve a system of two linear equations in a graphical, rather than algebraic way.

Students in the *3U* experimental classes positioned physical cut-out lines on a Cartesian grid according to the given equations, and found the solution of the system by reading the coordinates of the intersection point, and checking their answer by algebraic substitution.

5.2 *An Example of a 3U Student's Problem-Solving Strategies*

Data collected from experimental 3U classrooms indicated that non-mathematically oriented students learning with the project's approach tended to avoid difficulties posed by formal symbolic solution methods, and were able to

1. Draw two lines that intersect at the point (3, 5), write their equations, and check whether the coordinates of the intersection point satisfy the two equations.
2. Find the solution of the system formed by the two equations that you used in the previous question.
3. Find the solution of the system: $\begin{cases} y=2x-1 \\ y=x+4 \end{cases}$

FIGURE 8.11 A sequence of *3U* tasks – Part Two

construct meaningful mathematical knowledge by basing themselves on common sense, informal reasoning and practical tools. For many non-mathematically oriented students, a formal solution method of algebraic tasks is both meaningless and prone to error – due to their tendency to incorrectly recall formulas or to incorrectly handle algebraic procedures.

The following problem (Figure 8.12) and student solution (Figure 8.13) illustrate this point. The expected and traditional solution of this problem involves applying the formulas for the general term and the sum of terms, and constructing and solving a system of two equations.

The tenth term of an arithmetic sequence is 20, and the sum of the first ten terms is 65.
Find the first term and the constant difference of this sequence.

FIGURE 8.12 Example of a number sequence problem

The *3U* unit on arithmetic sequences emphasizes the use of properties (rather than formulas) when dealing with this kind of problem. Thus, for example, students learn that the sum of the terms of an arithmetic sequence can be found by using the constant sum of any pair of sequence terms situated in symmetrical positions. The *3U* student's solution of the number sequence problem (Figure 8.13) illustrates this approach.

The student explained his solution as follows:

> 5 arcs [two of these were drawn above the numbers] are 65, so one arc equals $\frac{65}{5} = 13$.
>
> Since each arc equals 13 and the tenth term is 20, the first term is −7. The number of jumps [the small arcs beneath the numbers] from −7 to 20 is 9, the distance between them is 27. Divide $\frac{27}{9} = 3$. The difference: b = 3.

To conclude this section, we note that the work of the *3U Project* in general, and the examples described here in particular, seem to indicate that designing

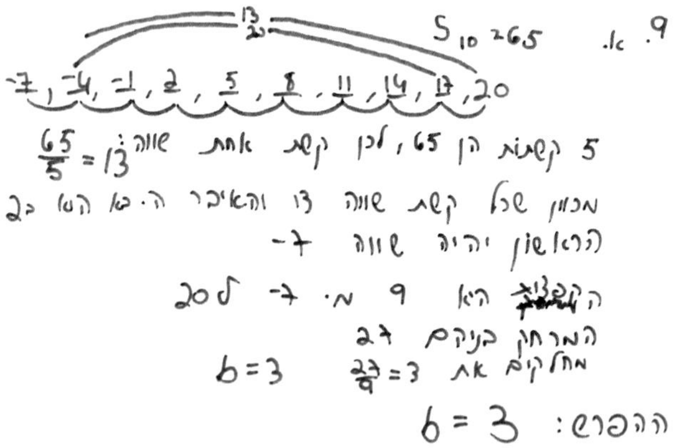

FIGURE 8.13 A student's solution of a number sequence problem

a mathematics curriculum in a qualitative and visual way, and emphasizing interconnecting ideas and representations, allow for more effective, meaningful and enjoyable learning for the non-mathematically-oriented student population. Further examples of low-achieving students' preference and ability to produce informal solutions can be found in Karsenty et al. (2007).

6 Reflecting Intended Teaching and Learning Processes: The Case of *the Integrated Mathematics Project*

In this section, we consider some aspects of the connection between the structure and contents of a textbook and the teaching and learning processes intended by the textbook designers. *The Integrated Mathematics Project* (IMP) serves as an exemplary case for illustrating some of the attempts made by this project's design team to reflect and support certain teaching and learning processes through their textbooks.

The *IMP* is a comprehensive junior-high school (grades 7–9) mathematics curriculum program, developed in response to introducing a new national curriculum. The project team set as one of its main goals the promotion of a gradual and meaningful construction of mathematical concepts and tools (Friedlander et al., 2018). The complete sequence of seven textbooks was developed at two levels, started in 2009, and required 7 years of intensive work. Initially, the textbooks were written in Hebrew, then translated to Arabic, and also converted to a version suitable for the ultra-Orthodox Jewish community. A teacher's guide and other accompanying resources (e.g., collections of activities for advanced students, assessment items, additional activities, and applets) resulted in a volume of about 10,000 pages.

6.1 *Supporting Teaching and Learning through Textbook Structure*

In general, mathematics textbooks are divided into units, each unit relating mainly to one specific mathematical topic. To ensure a particular teaching and learning sequence, the units are further subdivided into four or five lessons. Moreover, the sequence of tasks within the IMP lessons follows an instructional model that consists of four main parts:

- *Introductory discussion.* At the beginning of each textbook lesson, an introductory problem is presented. The aim of this problem is to motivate students (i.e., to stimulate curiosity and create a need for learning a new concept), "to set the scene" (i.e., present a context), and to provide a "larger picture" for a new concept or tool to be acquired during the lesson. No final solutions or solution methods are provided or discussed at this stage.
- *Student work.* At this stage, two sets of tasks are presented in this order: (1) tasks that lead to the formalization of a new concept or tool – based on students' previous knowledge and intuitive thinking, and (2) tasks that require students to use and apply various aspects of the formalized concept.
- *Summary discussion.* This part is conducted as a whole-class discussion, and is described in the teacher's guide. The summary is dedicated to gathering and comparing solution methods and results, making conjectures, drawing conclusions and possibly, making extensions. Note that this part of the model is based on student work, but is not addressed in specific textbook tasks. The teacher's guides provide the relevant recommendations.
- *Work on additional tasks.* The main goal of these tasks is consolidation of the newly acquired knowledge; they can be employed as an integral part of the lesson or as homework. To allow, or even ensure differential use of these tasks according to individual students' mathematical abilities, almost every consolidation task was designed and is presented in the IMP textbooks as consecutive triplets of the same basic task posed at three levels of difficulty, and explicitly marked accordingly.

6.2 *Supporting Teaching and Learning through Textbook Contents*

Besides teacher actions, the nature of the learning tasks posed to the students is crucial in the construction of their mathematical knowledge. To achieve one of the IMP's main goals of promoting a gradual and meaningful construction of mathematical concepts and tools, the design team invested considerable effort in systematically integrating – throughout the textbooks – algorithmic procedural tasks and tasks that require higher-order thinking. With regard to the "drill-and-practice" procedural tasks, we only note that a considerable limitation of the "volume" of routine practice tasks is one of the characteristics of the IMP textbooks.

Next we present a sample of three types of tasks that require higher-order thinking skills, and occur quite frequently throughout the *IMP* textbooks.

- *Integrative tasks.* The integration of the domains of algebraic procedures, higher-order thinking, and conceptual understanding within the same task is described and recommended by Friedlander and Arcavi (2012, 2017). Figure 8.14 presents an example of an integrative procedural *IMP* task that requires students to create, rather than solve, a multiple-choice quiz. For each quiz item, students are expected to provide several expressions that are equivalent to a given one (i.e., correct answers) and some other expressions that reflect errors that might be made in this context (i.e., distractors). Besides employing procedural knowledge, the task also aims to raise students' awareness of potential errors related to simplifying algebraic expressions, and to promote higher-order thinking skills, such as divergent thinking, generating examples, reverse thinking, and monitoring one's own or others' work.
- *Multiple-solution tasks.* The goal of promoting multiple solutions for the same task can be pursued in a textbook by posing problems that allow for, or explicitly request more than one solution method, or by presenting several alternative solutions and requesting students to analyze and interpret them. Multiple-solution tasks encourage cognitive flexibility and a deeper

Create distractors and correct answers for each quiz item.
Try to give more than one correct answer and some "attractive" distractors.
Give your quiz to one of your classmates and check the answers.

Example: $6 - 3 \cdot (7x - 1) =$

a) $3(7x - 1)$ *b)* $21x - 9$ {*c)* $6 - 21x + 3$ *d)* $-21x + 9$

1. $\frac{x}{2} + 2x =$

a) *b)* *c)* *d)*

2. $10 - \frac{1}{4}x + \frac{x}{2} =$

a) *b)* *c)* *d)*

3. $1 - x - \frac{2}{3} =$

a) *b)* *c)* *d)*

FIGURE 8.14
Create a Quiz – an integrative task

understanding of concepts and procedures, and allow for meaningful learning of problem-solving strategies. Thus, for example, the *IMP* task in Figure 8.15 provides three equations as alternative algebraic models for the same word problem, and requests students to connect these equations and the expressions that form them to their meaning in the context of the problem situation. This example also emphasizes the need to make frequent connections between the context of a problem and its algebraic model throughout the whole solution process.

- *Error-detection tasks.* In this type of task, several solutions of a problem are given (each solution possibly labeled under the name of a fictitious student), and students are required to identify correct and incorrect solutions, and describe their reasoning. Thus, for example, the goal of the *Two Solutions* task presented in Figure 8.16 is to encourage students to compare two given solutions of the same equation, to determine whether a given procedural solution and its result are correct, and to justify their answers. Besides its also being an integrative task according to the definition above, the task addresses the common error of not multiplying all terms by the common denominator in solving an equation that contains algebraic fractions. This type of task encourages students to employ the metacognitive skill of monitoring, i.e., inspecting, criticizing and commenting on one's own and others' work.

Doron prepared a fruit salad of 288 calories.
An orange has 32 calories, and a banana – 56 calories.
The salad contained twice as many bananas as oranges.
The following three equations describe algebraically the situation presented in this problem.
Find the meaning of the x variable in each of these equations.

$\frac{x}{32} - 2 = \frac{288 - x}{56}$ $\qquad 32 \cdot \frac{x}{2} + 56x = 288$ $\qquad 32x + 56 \cdot 2x = 288$

FIGURE 8.15 *Fruit Salad* – a multiple solution task

Shay and Assaf were asked to solve the equation $\frac{3x}{7} - 4 = \frac{2x}{7}$

Shay's solution:	**Assaf's solution:**
$\frac{3x}{7} - 4 = \frac{2x}{7} \quad / \cdot 7$	$\frac{3x}{7} - 4 = \frac{2x}{7} \quad / \cdot 7$
$3x - 28 = 2x$	$3x - 4 = 2x$
$x = 28$	$x = 4$

Whose solution is correct? What error has been made in the other solution?

FIGURE 8.16 *Two Solutions* – an error-detection task

As mentioned above, the common goal of these, and possibly other types of tasks is to support and promote both students' procedural knowledge and their ability to employ a wide variety of higher-order cognitive and metacognitive skills.

Finally, we would like to make a cautionary remark. This section focused on the potential of a curriculum textbook to convey its designers' beliefs and goals with regard to certain teaching and learning processes. However, we note that a large body of research indicates that learning materials in and of themselves do *not* necessarily ensure classroom implementation of the designers' original intentions. To support the classroom implementation of a curriculum project, continuous teacher support, such as teacher's guide booklets, teacher workshops, summer courses, and website and discussion forums, is strongly needed.

7 Conclusion

This chapter presents five areas of concern related to the complex process of curriculum design and exemplifies them with five out of the many mathematics curriculum projects created by the staff of the Weizmann Institute's Department of Science Teaching during the 50 years of the Mathematics Group's existence. We discuss each of the selected areas of concern in the context of a curriculum project that considered this particular area to be one of its main goals.

The decision of structuring this paper according to a one-to-one mapping between areas of concern and curriculum projects is a result of space limitation. In actuality, each of these areas was considered and pursued as a goal by each project, and the relationship can be illustrated as a five-by-five matrix, where each term represents a particular project's way of attaining a particular goal. Thus, for example, in addition to its goal of emphasizing the issue of representations analyzed in this paper, the *CompuMath Project* related and found some characteristic ways to pursue other domains of concern as well:

- The nature of its mathematical contents was influenced by the use of technological tools.
- Most of its activities were based on contexts that are external to mathematics.
- Many of its activities allow students a free choice of solution methods and tools that were aimed to support meaningful and conceptual learning.
- Learning materials were structured along long-term and complex activities that reflect the designers' intention to promote open-ended investigative learning.

As a result, different projects related to the design concerns mentioned above in different ways, according to their goals and rationale, and provided correspondingly varied answers. In the following, we mention some of the issues that had to be resolved by the designers of a curriculum project with regard to these areas of concern – some of them exemplified in this paper.

- *Nature of mathematical content*: innovative terminology and mathematical structure (*Rehovot Program, CompuMath, Seeing and Doing Geometry*) or more traditional school mathematics (*3U Project, IMP*)
- *Context*: mathematical context (*Rehovot Program*), mainly external context (*CompuMath, Seeing and Doing Geometry*) or mixed contexts (*3U Project, IMP*)
- *Representations*: multiple representations for most tasks (*CompuMath, 3U Project*), multiple representations for some of the tasks (*IMP*), or a single representation for most tasks (*Rehovot Program, Seeing and Doing Geometry*)
- *Student's learning processess*: addressing different ability levels within the same textbook (*IMP*) or addressing one ability level within the same textbook (*Rehovot Program, Seeing and Doing Geometry, CompuMath, 3U Project*)
- *Intended learning and teaching*: textbook reflecting a certain teaching and learning style (*CompuMath, Seeing and Doing Geometry, 3U Project, IMP*) or textbook that can be adapted to various teaching and learning styles (*Rehovot Program*).

As a final remark, we note that the goals, design strategies, experimental classroom observations, accompanying research and implementation schemes of each separate project were based on the cumulative experience and knowledge acquired in previous and simultaneously conducted projects. We hope that this chapter allows a glimpse into the body of knowledge acquired during 50 years of the Mathematics Group's activities in curriculum design.

Acknowledgment

We would like to express our appreciation and thanks to Professor Abraham Arcavi for his helpful comments and contribution to the writing of this chapter.

References

Arcavi, A. (2003). The role of visual representations in the teaching and learning of mathematics. *Educational Studies in Mathematics*, *52*, 215–241. http://dx.doi.org/10.1023/a:1024312321077

Arcavi, A. (2020). Learning to look at the world through mathematical spectacles – A personal tribute to Realistic Mathematics Education. In M. V. D. Heuvel-Panhuizen (Ed.), *Reflections from abroad on the Netherlands didactic tradition in mathematics education* (pp. 83–95). Springer. http://dx.doi.org/10.1007/978-3-030-20223-1_6

Arcavi, A., & Hadas, N. (1989). Large numbers and calculators: A classroom activity. *School, Science and Mathematics, 5*, 412–417. http://dx.doi.org/10.1111/j.1949-8594.1989.tb11938.x

Arcavi, A., Hadas, N., & Dreyfus, T. (1994). Engineering curriculum tasks on the basis of theoretical and empirical findings. In J. P. da Ponte & J. P. Matos (Eds.), *Proceedings of the 18th International Conference on the Psychology of Mathematics, Vol. II* (pp. 280–287). Lisbon, Portugal.

Dolev, O. (1996). *Transitions between representations as an action of characterizing student's learning in an interactive computer based environment* [Unpublished doctoral dissertation]. The Hebrew University of Jerusalem.

Dreyfus, T., Hershkowitz, R., & Bruckheimer, M. (1987). Processes in the transition from syllabus to curriculum. *ZDM – Mathematics Education, 87*, 19–25.

Friedlander, A. (1977). The steeplechase. *Mathematics Teaching, 80*, 37–39.

Friedlander, A., & Arcavi, A. (2012). Practicing algebraic skills: A conceptual approach. *Mathematics Teacher, 105*, 608–614. http://dx.doi.org/10.5951/mathteacher.105.8.0608

Friedlander, A., & Arcavi, A. (2017). *Tasks and competencies in the teaching and learning of algebra*. National Council of Teachers of Mathematics.

Friedlander, A., Even, R., & Robinson, N. (2018). Designing mathematics textbooks: The case of the Integrated Mathematics Curriculum Program. In N. Movshovitz-Hadar (Ed.), *K-12 mathematics education in Israel* (pp. 209–216). World Scientific. http://dx.doi.org/10.1142/9789813231191_0022

Friedlander, A., & Tabach, M. (2001). Promoting multiple representations in algebra. In A. A. Cuoco & F. R. Curcio (Eds.), *The roles of representation in school mathematics. 2001 yearbook* (pp. 173–185). The National Council of Teachers of Mathematics.

Gravemeijer, K., & Doorman, M. (1999). Context problems in realistic mathematics education. *Educational Studies in Mathematics, 39*, 111–129.

Hadas, N., Hershkowitz, R., & Schwarz, B. B. (2002). Analyses of activity design in geometry in the light of student actions. *Canadian Journal of Science Mathematics and Technology Education, 2*, 529–552. http://dx.doi.org/10.1080/14926150209556539

Heinze, A., Star, J. R., & Verschaffel, L. (2009). Flexible and adaptive use of strategies and representations in mathematics education. *ZDM – Mathematics Education, 41*, 535–540. http://dx.doi.org/10.1007/s11858-009-0214-4

Hershkowitz, R. (1979). Entry behavior: The first false assumption. In D. Tall (Ed.), *Proceedings of the Third International Conference for the Psychology of Mathematics Education* (pp. 108–112). Mathematics Education Research Center.

Hershkowitz, R., Dreyfus, T., Ben-Zvi, D., Friedlander, A., Hadas, N., Resnick, N., Tabach M., & Schwarz, B. B. (2002). Mathematics curriculum development for computerized environments: A designer-researcher-learner-activity. In L. D. English (Ed.), *Handbook of international research in mathematics education* (pp. 657–694). Lawrence Erlbaum Associates. http://dx.doi.org/10.4324/9781410602541-24

Hershkowitz, R., & Israeli, R. (1981). *Who is the mathematics teacher in Grades 7, 8 and 9?* Technical Report M 81/4. Department of Science Teaching, The Weizmann Institute of Science.

Hershkowitz, R., & Tabach, M. (2018). Junior-high school mathematics curriculum based on the power of open technological tools: The case of CompuMath project. In N. Movshovitz-Hadar (Ed.), *K-12 mathematics education in Israel – Issues and challenges* (pp. 135–143). World Scientific Publication.

Howson, G., Keitel, C., & Kilpatrick, J. (1981). *Curriculum development in mathematics.* Cambridge University Press. http://dx.doi.org/10.1017/cbo9780511569722

Israeli, R., & Hershkowitz, R. (1979). *A study of achievement in basic skills and its application to the development of a remedial program.* Technical Report M 79/10. Department of Science Teaching, The Weizmann Institute of Science.

Kaput, J. (1992). Technology and mathematics education. In D. A. Grouws (Ed.), *Handbook of research on mathematics teaching and learning* (pp. 515–556). National Council of Teachers of Mathematics.

Karsenty, R., Arcavi, A., & Hadas, N. (2007). Exploring informal mathematical products of low achievers at the secondary school level. *Journal of Mathematical Behavior, 16*, 156–177. http://dx.doi.org/10.1016/j.jmathb.2007.05.003

Markovits, Z., Hershkowitz, R., & Bruckheimer, M. (1987). Estimation activities: Developing solving skills and qualitative thinking. *Mathematics Teacher, 80*, 461–468. http://dx.doi.org/10.5951/mt.80.6.0461

Moschkovich, J., Schoenfeld, A. H., & Arcavi, A. (1993). Aspects of understanding: On multiple perspectives and representations of linear relations, and connections among them. In T. A. Romberg, E. Fennema, & T. P. Carpenter (Eds.), *Integrating research on the graphical representation of function* (pp. 69–100). Lawrence Erlbaum Associates.

NCTM (National Council of Teachers of Mathematics). (2000). *Principles and standards for school mathematics.* NCTM.

Schoenfeld, A. H., Smith, J., & Arcavi, A. (1993). Learning: The microgenetic analysis of one student's evolving understanding of a complex subject matter domain. In R. Glaser (Ed.), *Advances in instructional psychology, Vol. 4* (pp. 55–175). Lawrence Erlbaum Associates. http://dx.doi.org/10.4324/9781315864341-2

Stillman, G. (1998). The emperor's new clothes? Teaching and assessment of mathematical applications at the senior level. In P. Galbraith, W. Blum, G. Booker, & D. Huntley (Eds.), *Mathematical modelling: Teaching and assessment in a technology-rich world* (pp. 243–253). Horwood Publishing.

Tabach, M., Arcavi, A., & Hershkowitz, R. (2008). Transitions among different symbolic generalizations by algebra beginners in a computer intensive environment. *Educational Studies in Mathematics, 69*, 53–71. http://dx.doi.org/10.1007/s10649-008-9125-5

Tabach, M., & Friedlander, A. (2008). The role of context in learning beginning algebra. In C. E. Greens & R. Rubenstein (Eds.), *70th Yearbook of the National Council of the Teachers of Mathematics: Algebra and algebraic thinking in school mathematics* (pp. 223–232). NCTM.

Tabach, M., & Friedlander, A. (2012). Five considerations in task design – The case of improving grades. *Investigations in Mathematics Learning, 4*(3), 32–49. http://dx.doi.org/10.1080/24727466.2012.11790315

Taizi, N. (1979). Two Sides to Zero: An arithmetic game with integers. *Mathematics Teacher, 72*, 88–90. http://dx.doi.org/10.5951/mt.72.2.0088

Tall, D., & Thomas, M. (1991). Encouraging versatile thinking using the computer. *Educational Studies in Mathematics, 22*, 125–147. http://dx.doi.org/10.1007/bf00555720

Treffers, A. (1993). Wiskobas and Freudenthal realistic mathematics education. *Educational Studies in Mathematics, 25*, 89–108. http://dx.doi.org/10.1007/bf01274104

Yerushalmy, M. (2009). Technology-based algebra learning: Epistemological discontinuities and curricular implications. In B. B. Schwarz, T. Dreyfus, & R. Hershkowitz (Eds.), *Transformation of knowledge through classroom interaction* (pp. 60–69). Routledge.

CHAPTER 9

Using Assessment to Inform Instructional Decisions

The Story of a Three-Decade Research and Development Journey

Ruhama Even

Abstract

This chapter tells the story of a three-decade research and development journey addressing the problem of using assessment to inform instructional decisions. The story is situated in mathematics education. The first part of the chapter highlights three milestones in our study of the challenges associated with eliciting, interpreting and acting on evidence of student learning of mathematics. They are related to teachers' knowledge about students' learning of mathematics, the complexity inherent in interpreting students' talk and actions, and ways of addressing students' errors in mathematics. The second part of the chapter presents two approaches that we designed for addressing these challenges: the MANOR approach and the MesiMatica approach. Finally, the chapter demonstrates the way the different facets of this work were often interwoven, contributing to, and building on, each other, displaying the personal story as a case of the developmental process of a long-term research and development program.

Keywords

formative assessment – teacher knowledge – teaching practices – evidence of students' learning – addressing students' errors – long-term research and development program

1 Introduction

In an algebra lesson, a student performed the following transformations:

$10 + 3a = 13a$
$7s + 2s + s + 6 = 16s$
$7x + 4 = 11x = 11$

 | DOI: 10.1163/9789004503625_009

What do you think the student had in mine? How would you respond? Most experienced math teachers would not be surprised by such student answers. They are all too familiar. But why do students tend to "oversimplify" algebraic expressions? And what would be suitable teacher responses?

The literature suggests that teachers' use of formative assessment, that is, eliciting, interpreting, and acting on evidence of student learning (Goos, 2020), is a critical component in the teaching–learning process (Black & Wiliam, 2009; Thompson et al., 2018). Yet, in contrast to the use of summative assessment, formative assessment is not commonly incorporated into mathematics classrooms (Burkhardt & Schoenfeld, 2018). This chapter tells the story of a three-decade research and development journey addressing the problem of using assessment to inform instructional decisions.

To tell the story, I draw on a comprehensive research and development work on formative assessment that I conducted in collaboration with colleagues and students. The chapter consists of two main parts. The first scrutinizes the challenges associated with eliciting, interpreting and acting on evidence of student learning, demonstrating our evolving construing of these challenges. The second presents two approaches that we designed and investigated to address these challenges. One is the MANOR approach for developing teachers' competencies to elicit and interpret evidence of student learning; the other is the MesiMatica approach, which addresses all three principles associated with formative assessment (Goos, 2020): eliciting evidence of student learning, interpreting evidence of student learning, and acting on evidence of student learning.

2 Challenges Associated with Eliciting, Interpreting and Acting on Evidence of Student Learning

This part of the chapter highlights three milestones in our study of the challenges associated with incorporating formative assessment in classroom instruction. They are related to (1) teachers' knowledge about students' learning of mathematics, (2) the complexity inherent in interpreting students' talk and actions, and (3) ways of addressing students' errors in mathematics. The first two milestones are related to challenges associated with eliciting and interpreting evidence of student learning; the third, with acting on evidence of student learning.

2.1 *Teachers' Knowledge about Students' Learning of Mathematics*

My first attempt to address the problem of using assessment to inform instructional decisions was made at the end of the 1980s (Even, 1989). Inspired by

Shulman's (1986) introduction of the construct of pedagogical content knowledge and the Cognitively Guided Instruction approach (e.g., Carpenter & Fennema, 1992), I began a research and development program that centered on teacher awareness and knowledge of students' conceptions and learning processes.

A significant impetus for the work was the identification of a surprising and somewhat disturbing gap in the mathematics education literature: research on student conceptions and learning processes in mathematics, and research on teachers and teaching were almost totally unconnected at that time (Romberg & Carpenter, 1986). The then flourishing literature on mathematics learning provided important information on students' ideas, conceptions and processes of learning central mathematical concepts and topics, such as function, algebra, geometry, etc., showing how students construct their knowledge in ways that are not necessarily identical to the instruction and the discipline (e.g., Nesher & Kilpatrick, 1990). Yet, there was hardly any information regarding teacher awareness and knowledge of those student conceptions and learning processes – a critical aspect of pedagogical content knowledge (Shulman, 1986).

This gap in the literature served as the point of departure for a comprehensive research and development program that integrated knowledge from both bodies of work, using the research literature on students' mathematics learning as a basis for conducting research on mathematics teachers' knowledge, its role in instruction, and its development (for detailed information about this set of studies, see Even & Markovits, 1993, 1995; Even & Tirosh, 1995, 2002, 2008; Markovits & Even, 1999a, 1999b; Tirosh et al., 1998).

Our research findings revealed great variation among teachers in terms of their attention to students' ways of thinking, their knowledge about students' common conceptions and errors, and their acquaintance with possible sources of student ideas and the reasoning behind them. This variation is illustrated in the following, using teachers' responses to the scenario in Figure 9.1, which was presented to numerous groups of teachers (e.g., Even, 1989; Even & Markovits, 1993; Even & Tirosh, 1995). The scenario was designed to reflect the widely documented student tendency to improperly use linear reasoning (e.g., De Bock et al., 2002):

When asked to find the equation of the straight line that goes through points A and the origin O (Figure 9.1 – left side), a student suggested using the line $y = x$ as a reference (Figure 9.1 – right side). She claimed that since the slope of the line $y = x$ is 1, the slope of line AO will be close to 2. The student then concluded that the equation of line AO is about $y = 1.9x$.

What do you think the student had in mind? How would you respond?

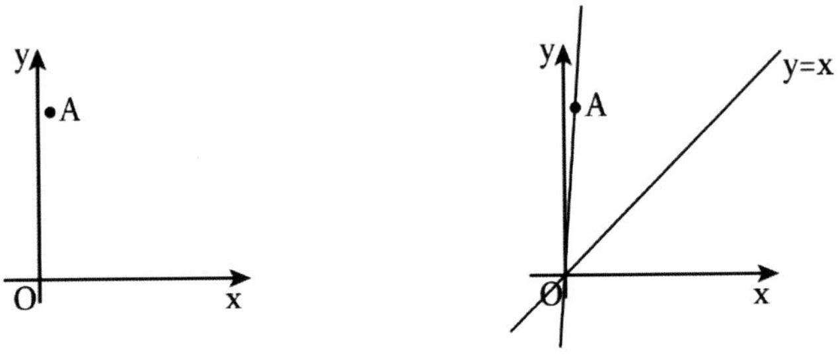

FIGURE 9.1 Equation of the straight line through points A and O

In their responses, some teachers focused on the erroneous assumption that the student appeared to have made about the relation between angles and slopes, i.e., that the slope of a linear function is directly proportional to the angle between the line and the x-axis. For instance, one teacher said: "The student meant that the angle between line AO and the x-axis is almost twice the angle between the line y = x and the x-axis, and by mistake mixed up angles and slopes."

Yet, there were quite a few teachers who disregarded the erroneous relation between angles and slopes that the student presumably made. Some of them evaluated the student's answer only as right or wrong. For instance, "The student wanted to use the slope to find the equation, but she didn't do it right." Others attended to the student's reasoning and described it as estimation. For instance, "She had the right idea but she was off in her gross approximation of y = 2x." While the student's reasoning was indeed comprised of estimation, these teachers did not attend to the erroneous assumption about the relation between angles and slopes that appeared to serve as the basis for the student's estimation.

Classroom observations enabled us to provide empirical evidence for the central role that teachers' acquaintance with common student conceptions and ways of thinking in mathematics plays in shaping classroom teaching (Even & Tirosh, 2002, 2008; Tirosh et al., 1998). This is exemplified below in the context of algebra teaching.

A widely documented finding in the literature on algebra learning is students' tendency to "oversimplify" algebraic expressions. For instance, as was demonstrated in the introduction of this chapter, when dealing with expressions such as 7x + 4, students often assert that it equals 11x (or even 11). The literature suggests various sources for this common mistake. For example: students' previous experience in arithmetic, which centered on performing operations when dealing with arithmetical expressions that comprise signs, such as "+," and on reaching single-term final answers (e.g., Booth, 1988; Davis, 1975; Tall & Thomas, 1991); and cognitive difficulty in conceiving the dual nature of algebraic expressions as both processes and objects (Davis, 1975; Sfard, 1991; Tall

& Thomas, 1991) – students often view algebraic expressions as processes only, interpreting signs, such as "+" in 7x + 4, as a signal for performing an operation.

The following episodes exemplify the contribution of awareness of students' tendency to "oversimplify" algebraic expressions to shaping classroom instruction. The teaching episodes are drawn from lessons of three 7th-grade teachers – two experienced and one novice – who used the same algebra textbook to teach the topic of equivalent algebraic expressions, a large part of which consists of manipulating and simplifying these expressions (for detailed information on this study, see Tirosh et al., 1998).

Analysis of the teachers' lesson plans and pre- and post-lesson interviews suggested that the two experienced teachers were aware of students' tendency to "oversimplify" algebraic expressions before teaching the observed lessons. For instance, "I expect difficulties in problematic cases [such as] 2x + 3 = 5x." Similar to the literature, these teachers described the source of this students' tendency as: "They need to get an answer, it does not seem finished to them," and "They tend to 'finish' it." In contrast to these teachers, the third teacher did not mention this common student error when asked to describe students' difficulties related to learning algebraic expressions, nor did he address it in his lesson plans, or later on.

The two teachers who were aware of the students' difficulty and its possible sources purposely addressed it when planning the teaching of equivalent algebraic expressions and when actually teaching it in the classroom. One teacher designed a complete unit on identifying and collecting like terms. She then devoted an extensive period of time to teaching it, and to practicing the collection of like terms and the differentiation between like and unlike terms. Only after students mastered those skills did the teacher progress to teaching how to simplify algebraic expressions, building on the 'collecting like terms' and 'differentiating between like and unlike terms' skills as the foundation and reference whenever students "oversimplified," which seldom occurred. The other teacher addressed the anticipated student difficulty using a range of strategies aimed at creating a cognitive conflict whenever students "oversimplified" algebraic expressions. For example, when a student suggested that 3 + 4x equals 7x, the teacher proposed to check the claim by substituting a specific number, such as x = 5, which revealed that 3 + 4 × 5 (= 23) does not equal 7 × 5 (= 35). Other times, she used the idea of order of operations, leading the students to conclude that the claim was wrong because multiplication (the operation between 4 and x in 3 + 4x) precedes addition (the operation between 3 and 4x). Alternatively, she directed students to work backwards, starting from the erroneous proposed answer of, say, 7x, and expressing it as the sum of 3x (as opposed to the error of proposing 3) and 4x.

In contrast to these two experienced teachers, the novice teacher, who was unaware of the students' tendency to "oversimplify" algebraic expressions, planned to provide his students with a rule for simplifying algebraic expressions: "Adding numbers separately and adding letters separately." Following his plan, he started teaching by stating the rule and demonstrating how to apply it. When students erroneously "oversimplified" algebraic expressions, such as suggesting that $5a + 2 = 7a$, the teacher looked surprised. His response to such errors – which frequently occurred – was to state that the answer was wrong, and to repeat the rule. In his reflection on the lesson, the teacher explained that he sensed a problem but he did not understand its source.

As illustrated, teachers' knowledge about students' common conceptions and errors, and their acquaintance with possible sources of students' ideas and the reasoning behind them, play an important role in teachers' competencies to elicit and interpret evidence of student learning. (They also play an important role in teachers' competencies to act on evidence of student learning – an issue that I discuss further on.) However, the issue of eliciting and interpreting evidence of student learning cannot be confined to attending solely to teacher knowledge about common student conceptions and ways of reasoning in mathematics – or to teacher knowledge in general – as elaborated in the next section which centers on the second milestone in our study of the challenges associated with incorporating formative assessment into classroom instruction.

2.2 *The Complexity Inherent in Attending to and Interpreting Students' Talk and Action*

Attending to and interpreting students' talk and action are critical for assessing students' understanding, knowledge and learning of mathematics. However, our research indicated that the process of teacher interpretation of students' talk and action has inherent complexity due to the very nature of the teaching practice. This is demonstrated below, using three cases of teacher–student interactions in which teachers did not attend to, or misunderstood, things said or done by students (for detailed information on this set of studies, see Even, 2005a; Even & Wallach, 2004; Wallach & Even, 2005).

The first case of teacher–student interaction was documented in Robinson (1993). It illustrates how lesson preparation might interfere with the teacher's ability to attend to students' talk and action. When preparing an early algebra lesson, a novice 7th-grade teacher planned to motivate the learning of simplifying algebraic expressions by providing his students with the experience of substituting numerical values into a pair of equivalent expressions: one "complicated" and the other "simple." Such an experience, he assumed, would demonstrate that it is easier to substitute numerical values into simplified expressions, and consequently, the need to learn how to simplify algebraic expressions.

Accordingly, the teacher started the lesson by asking his students to substitute ½ in each of the two equivalent expressions: $4a + 3$ and $\frac{3a+6+5a}{2}$. However, he neglected to state that these two expressions are equivalent. Instead, when a student responded and said that he got the same results, the teacher further deviated from his lesson plan and asked the class: "Are the algebraic expressions equivalent?" This question led to an insightful mathematical debate among the students regarding the validity of using substitution of numerical values as a means of determining whether two algebraic expressions are equivalent, and how one can decide that two algebraic expressions are equivalent. Whereas these are important mathematical questions in the context of learning algebra, they were unrelated to the teacher's original goal for the lesson, which centered on understanding why it is worth learning how to simplify algebraic expressions.

After several students expressed their opinions, the teacher interrupted the students' debate and returned to his original goal, opening with the phrase, "We can conclude," as if it was a natural conclusion of the students' debate, even though it was completely unrelated to it, "that it is difficult to substitute numbers into a complicated expression and therefore, we should find a simpler equivalent expression."

In his reflection on the lesson, the teacher reported sensing that the lesson had not gone as planned, and pointed out that attending to students' talk when it deviated from his lesson plan was difficult for him: "I prepare my objective and the exercises I want to give the students, and it is very confusing for me when they suddenly ask something that is not according to my planning."

The second case of teacher–student interaction was documented in Goldenberg (2000). It illustrates how a teacher's general acquaintance with her students, and in particular with their mathematical achievements, might limit her ability to interpret students' talk and action. After teaching her students how to find the whole when a fraction is known, a 5th-grade teacher gave her class a quiz that included the following problem: 3/5 of a number is 12. Calculate the number. One student submitted the following solution:

$$12 \times 2 = 24$$
$$24 : 6 = 4$$
$$24 - 4 = 20$$

which did not follow the conventional procedure taught in class:
$12 : \frac{3}{5} = \frac{12 \cdot 5}{3} = 20$.

Solution	Explanation
12 X 2 = 24	If $\frac{3}{5}$ is 12 then 24 is $\frac{6}{5}$
24 : 6 = 4	The value of $\frac{1}{5}$ is 24 : 6 = 4
24 − 4 = 20	The number is 24 − 4 = 20

FIGURE 9.2 A student's innovative solution

The teacher marked the student's solution as wrong, explaining: "He reached a correct answer but I didn't understand what he did. It didn't seem right… [he] usually has difficulties with homework." When the student protested and insisted that his solution was correct, the teacher did not think it could be, but eventually she relented and allowed the student to explain his solution. And so he did (shown in Figure 9.2).

Based on her acquaintance with the student and his previous mathematical achievements, the teacher did not believe that there was something worth attending to in this student's solution. Thus, she was not tuned into interpreting the student's method of solution. This was coupled with the student's unconventional method of solution and the teacher's expectation that a correct solution would follow the conventional method taught in class.

Teacher expectation regarding methods of solution is also related to the third case of teacher–student interaction, which was documented in Wallach (2005). This case illustrates how having a specific mathematics solution in mind – not necessarily one that uses a conventional school procedure – might constrain the teacher's ability to interpret students' talk and action. A 4th-grade teacher presented her students with a task as follows. First, she told the students that it is impossible to divide a group of 15 players into two teams, so that on one team there are 4 players less than on the other team. She then asked the students to change the total number of players, so that it would be possible to fulfill the requirement of one team having 4 players less than the other team.

A couple of students solved the problem by building up two teams, using a drawing of 15 "players" lined up. First they marked 4 players at the left end of the line of 15 players. Then they built one team of 7 players by "adding" to the marked 4 players the 3 players closest to them. Finally, they built the other team by marking the next 3 players, explaining: "Here are 7 players [one team] and here are 3 [the other team], so 10 players; 7 and 3 makes 10; And 7 minus 3 is 4, so 10 players."

The teacher was puzzled by this solution. She realized that the students had reached a correct solution – a total number of 10 players – but she could not understand the reasoning behind it: "She just said 10 off the top of her head... I was really surprised that they changed to 10, [that they] removed 5... Remove 1... it seemed to me that you need to remove 1 and try." This interpretation of the students' solution reflected the teacher's own method of solution, which used the strategy of removing a minimal number of players to reach an even number of players, leading to a total number of 14 players. The teacher's strategy of *removing* players was qualitatively different from the students' strategy of *building up* two teams that satisfy the requirement. This discrepancy between the two strategies limited the teacher's ability to interpret the students' reasoning, because she used her own method of solution as a lens for interpreting theirs.

As the three cases demonstrate, interpreting students' talk and action, like any other type of interpretation, cannot be an accurate reflection of what was actually said or done. Teachers interpret what students say or do "through" various factors that act as semi-transparent screens. These "screens" include the teachers' own knowledge of mathematics, their beliefs about mathematics learning and knowing, their understanding of mathematics teaching, their dispositions toward the teacher's role, feelings about students, expectations from students, the context in which the interpretation takes place, and so on.

Moreover, in contrast with the previous section that focused on teacher awareness and knowledge of students' conceptions and learning processes, the cases above show that ignoring or misinterpreting what students say or do is not necessarily associated with deficiencies; with what teachers should do, but do not do. That is, they are not necessarily associated with not knowing about students' common conceptions, not preparing lessons, not understanding the mathematics, not listening to students, etc. Difficulties in attending to and interpreting what students say and do are also associated with professional teaching practices; with what teachers should do, and indeed do; i.e., with working out the mathematics, anticipating students' answers, knowing about their students' background, and so on. Teacher interpretation of students' talk and action is an active process that draws on a rich base of knowledge, beliefs, and attitudes. Consequently, by its very nature, this process involves ambiguity and difficulties.

2.3 *Ways of Addressing Students' Errors in Mathematics*

The previous two sections focused on challenges associated with eliciting and interpreting evidence of students' learning. The third milestone in our study of the challenges associated with incorporating formative assessment into classroom instruction emerged as our study progressed. We realized that, independent of the challenges discussed earlier, there were also challenges associated with the third principle of formative assessment, that is, with acting on evidence of students' learning. These challenges concerned teacher responses to students' errors in ways that did not seem to have the potential to advance mathematical understanding (for more information on this set of studies, see Even, 2005a; Even & Markovits, 1993, 1995; Even & Tirosh, 2002, 2008; Markovits & Even, 1999a, 1999b; Tirosh et al., 1998).

Our findings revealed a tendency in quite a few teachers' responses to students' errors to ignore the specific errors and the reasoning that led to them. Instead, when students made mistakes, teachers often chose to respond by going over the general mathematics topic and reminding students of how to apply previously taught school procedures. This kind of response is exemplified below by illustrations of two contrasting types of teacher responses to the student in the scenario in Figure 9.1 (e.g., Even, 1989; Even & Markovits, 1993, 1995).

Some teachers proposed responses that addressed the student's idea regarding the connection between angles and slopes. For instance, to use squared paper and check whether, for every horizontal step on the required line, there were two vertical steps, or "In order to clarify for him the difference between angle and slope, I would draw several examples: $y = x$, $y = 2x$, $y = 3x$. Thus, the student will understand the difference between slope and angle." In contrast, a number of teachers ignored the student's erroneous assumption about the relation between slopes and angles, and proposed to review the topic of slope and the standard procedure for calculating it. For instance, a teacher suggested telling the student that "this is not the way one finds the slope; the way to find slopes is by using the method of differences." And another teacher said, "There is a need to explain the topic of slopes again, and how to calculate them." Still another teacher's response: "I would send him back to the material that we have learned, to see how we calculate a slope."

Reviewing the general mathematics topic and focusing students' attention on using previously taught school procedures in cases such as those described above do not seem to have the potential to help students develop an understanding of what was wrong with their method or with the reasoning behind it. Moreover, we often found in our studies (e.g., Even, 2005a; Even & Markovits, 1993) that there was no indication in the students' answers, to which the teachers responded, that the students did not understand the general topic (e.g., slope) or did not know how to use the previously taught conventional school procedure (e.g., for calculating slopes). Thus, not only is the potential of such teacher responses to advance students' understanding of specific mathematical content questionable, but they may also very well be signaling to the students that they are not expected to reason about mathematics, but instead, should follow procedures taught in class.

Related to this was a tendency of quite a few teachers observed in our studies to act on evidence of students' learning using teaching approaches that incorporated characteristics of *teaching for mechanistic answer finding*. That is,

> …teaching that aims to help students obtain correct answers with no attention to developing understanding…devoting considerable class time to performing fragmentary, individual, small rituals…emphasis is put on mechanistic answer-finding…it is the teacher who provides explanations, asks questions, and evaluates students' short answers…directing students to a "predetermined solution procedure preferred by the teacher." (Even & Kvatinsky, 2009, p. 958)

The teaching episodes described earlier in the section *Teachers' knowledge about students' learning of mathematics* exemplify such characteristics. For instance, considerable time in the observed lessons was devoted to practicing the manipulation of algebraic expressions by following rules with no connection to problem solving. Lessons were structured so that it was mainly the teacher who asked questions and evaluated students' short answers, commonly using the Initiate–Response–Evaluate discourse pattern (Mehan, 1979) or the "funnel pattern" (Bauersfeld, 1988; Wood, 1994), where the teacher's questions are aimed at directing students to a predetermined solution procedure.

While concentrating on achieving the goal of mastering the skill of manipulating algebraic expressions – which the teachers who were aware of students' tendency to "oversimplify" algebraic expressions achieved to a large extent – they, as many other teachers observed in our studies, rarely used teaching approaches that incorporated characteristics of *teaching for understanding*. That is,

> … teaching that aims to develop understanding… devoting considerable class time to solving problems, proposing and justifying alternative solutions, and critically evaluating alternative courses of action… students are expected and encouraged to make conjectures, explain their reasoning, validate their assertions, discuss and question their own thinking and the thinking of others, and argue about what is mathematically true… the teacher's questions are aimed at helping students focus on the important aspects of the mathematics problem. (Even & Kvatinsky, 2009, pp. 957–958)

As demonstrated in this section, the problem of using assessment to inform instructional decisions not only requires addressing challenges associated with eliciting and interpreting evidence of student learning; it also requires careful consideration of the "next step," of ways of addressing challenges related to acting on evidence of students' learning in ways that advance students' mathematical understanding.

3 Developing Teachers' Competencies to Elicit, Interpret and Act on Evidence of Student Learning

In the first part of this chapter, I highlighted three milestones in our study of the challenges associated with incorporating formative assessment into classroom instruction. The first two milestones were related to challenges associated with eliciting and interpreting evidence of student learning, namely, teachers' knowledge about students' learning of mathematics, and the complexity inherent in interpreting students' talk and action. The third milestone was related to challenges associated with acting on evidence of student learning, namely, ways of addressing students' errors in mathematics. Below I describe the MANOR and MesiMatica approaches, which we designed to address these challenges.

3.1 *The MANOR Approach*

The first two milestones in our study of the challenges associated with incorporating formative assessment into classroom instruction revealed that interpreting what students are saying and doing should neither be regarded as a nonproblematic task nor as something that can be certain. However, our research findings showed that teachers can improve their sensitivity to, and sense making of, students' talk and action, and consequently, their competencies to elicit and interpret evidence of student learning (e.g., Even & Tirosh, 2002, 2008; Markovits & Even, 1999b).

A multistage activity that we designed as part of the MANOR Program for the preparation of teacher leaders and educators (Even, 1999a, 2005b) exemplifies this. The activity was carefully studied in the context of three cohorts of secondary-school teachers, who participated in the MANOR Program in the 1990s (for detailed information about this set of studies, see Even, 1999a, 1999b, 2005b, 2008). Variations of the activity were later successfully enacted with numerous groups of teachers.

The MANOR activity was designed to provide secondary-school mathematics teachers with an opportunity to advance their knowledge about research-based common student conceptions and ways of learning and knowing mathematics. The activity also aimed to promote the development of teachers' appreciation of the idea that students construct their knowledge in ways that are not necessarily identical to the instruction, and that inquiry into student learning of mathematics is important for teaching. To support such development of knowledge and dispositions, the MANOR activity centered on promoting a synthesis of academic and practical sources of knowledge as a means of challenging teachers' existing conceptions and beliefs about students' learning of mathematics, and enhancing their understanding of what the constructivist view on learning mathematics might mean in a practical context of secondary-school mathematics teaching and learning.

The first stage of the MANOR activity focused on developing academic knowledge related to students' conceptions, classroom culture, and ways of learning mathematics in the domains of real numbers, algebra, analysis, geometry, probability and statistics. Such academic knowledge was (and often still is) new and unexplored terrain for many secondary-school mathematics teachers in Israel. This stage included reading, presentations and discussions of theoretical and empirical research articles that focused on learning related to central mathematics topics and concepts from the secondary-school curriculum (e.g., irrational number, variable, algebraic expression, function, derivative, circle, probability, proof).

Our research findings showed that at this stage, the participating teachers were often astounded to learn that students "were able" to think in the ways reported in the research articles. They then began to seize the idea that students construct their knowledge in ways that do not necessarily mirror instruction. The development of such academic knowledge also contributed, in some cases, to conceptualizing and making explicit what was previously naive and implicit teacher knowledge about students' conceptions and ways of learning and thinking in mathematics.

The second stage of the MANOR activity centered on making connections between the newly acquired academic knowledge and the teachers' experience-based practical knowledge. At this stage, the participating teachers conducted a mini-replication of a published empirical study. They selected a study reported in one of the research articles that they had read in the first stage of the activity, and replicated it (or a variation of it) with their own students. Next, they wrote a reflective report describing their students' ways of thinking and difficulties, and compared their findings with the findings of the original study. Finally, the teachers presented their mini-replication of a study to their colleagues and to other mathematics educators.

Our research findings revealed two types of contribution of the mini-replication of a study. One was theoretical/academic. Conducting the mini-replication with real students provided teachers with an opportunity to examine theoretical matters (e.g., constructivism, linear reasoning, the dual nature of mathematical notions) by particularizing them in a concrete context. In this way, replicating a study expanded the teachers' theoretical knowledge, and helped them develop a better understanding of the theoretical issues presented and discussed during the first stage of the activity, realizing that learning processes are complicated, no matter how "clear" the instruction.

The other type of contribution of the mini-replication reflected an integration of knowledge learned in the academy with knowledge learned in practice. It involved teachers' learning about real students in a situation authentic to the teachers' practice. The requirement to write and present a reflective report regarding their students' conceptions and ways of thinking, and to compare their findings with the findings of the original study, encouraged the teachers to examine their experience-based knowledge in light of their newly acquired academic/theoretical knowledge. In doing so, many of the teachers were surprised by the results of this examination, realizing that their judgement of their students' knowledge and understanding was not as valid as they had previously believed.

Interestingly, some teachers learned that their students could do more, whereas others discovered that their students could do less than they expected. For example, after replicating a study on algebra learning, an experienced teacher enthusiastically wrote in her reflective report that

> Even though I have worked for 30 years as a teacher, I was surprised by some of the things we found... The students reached much higher levels of thinking than what I would have given them credit for.

In contrast, a teacher who replicated a study on university students' knowledge of irrational numbers wrote in her reflective report,

> Simply, I was amazed by the results... I said, OK, no problem. Our [9th-grade] students, for sure, would know better than those students at the university. And we were shocked that actually with us it was the same as there.

As illustrated above, the MANOR activity provided teachers with an opportunity to advance their knowledge about students' common conceptions and ways of learning and knowing mathematics in different mathematical domains. Consequently, it served as a powerful means to develop teacher competencies to elicit and interpret evidence of student learning. To support large-scale professional development of this kind, students' conceptions and ways of learning and thinking were included as a major theme in each of the MANOR resource files we developed for use by mathematics teacher educators (Even, 2000, 2005b).

Furthermore, our research showed that some teachers used their newly acquired knowledge on students' mathematics learning to make instructional decisions. For instance, following her mini-replication of a study that focused on students' tendency to "oversimplify" algebraic expressions, one of the teachers decided to work with the other mathematics teachers in her school on this issue. First, she worked with them on examining the extent of this phenomenon in their classrooms. Next, the team collaborated on analyzing the textbooks they were using with respect to their potential to address this student error. Finally, the team modified the curriculum that they had traditionally enacted in previous years by modifying the selection of textbook tasks to be used in class to address the outcome of the textbook analysis they conducted.

Nevertheless, our research revealed that, in general, teachers' competencies to act on evidence of student learning were not effectively developed by the MANOR activity. Becoming more sensitive to, and knowledgeable about, students' conceptions and ways of reasoning in mathematics was not enough. Addressing the aforedescribed challenges associated with acting on evidence of student learning, namely, ways of addressing students' errors in mathematics, appeared to require explicit attention.

3.2 *The MesiMatica Approach*

The MesiMatica project is our most recent attempt to address the problem of integrating formative assessment into the teaching of secondary-school mathematics classrooms. The project was started in 2014, in collaboration with the Trump Family Foundation and the National Authority for Measurement and Evaluation in Education (RAMA), and is in its final year at the time of this writing. Building on insights gained from our studies of the challenges associated with incorporating formative assessment into classroom instruction, the project centers on developing research-, theory- and practice-based formative assessment materials that attend to all three overarching principles associated with formative assessment (Goos, 2020): (1) eliciting evidence of student learning, (2) interpreting evidence of student learning, and (3) acting on evidence of student learning.

The MesiMatica materials are designed in the form of a series of several dozens of formative assessment resource files in the domains of algebra, geometry and analysis, available free of charge on the MesiMatica website.[1] The development of the files follows principles of design research "in which a product… is envisaged, designed, developed, and refined through cycles of enactment, observation, analysis, and redesign, with systematic feedback from end users" (Swan, 2020, p. 192). It is being carried out by a team of experienced secondary-school teachers, expert curriculum developers, researchers in mathematics education, and a mathematician, led by the author of this chapter who serves as chief editor of the files.

The MesiMatica files are designed to assess mathematics that is important and worth knowing, significant in the secondary-school mathematics curriculum, and for which student difficulties are known from research and practice. Thus, in line with current views of classroom assessment (Suurtamm et al., 2016), the materials attend to mathematics content, as well as to mathematical practices, processes, proficiencies, and competencies, focusing on aspects of problem solving, modeling, and reasoning. The following examples illustrate selected foci of the MesiMatica resource files in each of the domains of algebra, geometry and analysis.

The first illustration is from the collection of algebra files, whose lead developers are Alex Friedlander, Omri Nave, Naomi Robinson and Zippora Resnick. A cluster of algebra files focus on fundamental aspects of mathematical modeling, for example, identifying and considering constraints; constructing equations or functions as mathematical models for problems situated in mathematical and non-mathematical contexts; identifying different possibilities for defining variables, and considering their implications for the solution of the problem; connecting and distinguishing between the solution of the mathematical model and the solution of the problem, etc.

The second illustration is from the geometry files, whose lead developers are Nurit Hadas, Reut Parasha, and Orna Shoham-Cohen. A cluster of geometry files focus on key aspects of mathematical argumentation and proof, for example, connecting the use of specific examples and proving/refuting claims; using a suitable theorem and not its inverse; identifying what is given and what needs to be proved; using geometrical considerations to justify presumed properties; rejecting assumptions regarding properties that are based only on the appearance of a drawing, etc.

The third illustration is from the analysis files, whose lead developers are Menucha Farber, Galia Gonen, Na'ama Tal, and Zippora Resnick. A cluster of analysis files focus on important aspects of the function–derivative connections, for example, connecting the behavior of a function and the behavior of its derivative; connecting attributes of the graphs of a function and its antiderivatives, etc.

The structure of all MesiMatica resource files is the same. In accordance with the three formative assessment principles, each file contains three main components. The first component comprises assessment tasks that focus on assessing aspects of problem solving and reasoning related to the specific topic of the file. For instance, Figure 9.3 presents one of the assessment tasks included in the MesiMatica file "Same problem – different definitions of the variable." The task requires students to evaluate the correctness of two correct solution paths for a given problem, each based on a different definition of the variable used to construct the equation that serves as the mathematical model.

The second main component comprises a user-friendly assessment chart to be filled out by the teacher, so that the overall performance of the classroom, as well as individual students' difficulties, are clearly exhibited. The headings of the columns in the assessment charts correspond to the students' competencies that are the focus of the file. Examples of real students' solutions are

Task 1: Consecutive numbers

In the presented frame, there is a problem and then a description of **Anna's** and **Dorit's** ways of solving it.

You have to decide which way of solving it is correct, or whether both are correct/wrong.

Given are three consecutive numbers.

The product of the two larger numbers is larger by 20 than the product of the two smaller numbers.

What are the three numbers?

Description of Anna's and Dorit's solution methods:

Anna said: I constructed the equation $(x - 1)\,x = (x - 2)\,(x - 1) + 20$.
I solved it and got $x = 11$. Then I found the other two numbers.

Dorit said: I constructed the equation $(x + 1)\,(x + 2) = x\,(x + 1) + 20$.
I solved it and got $x = 9$. Then I found the other two numbers.

Circle the correct claim:

- Only **Anna's** way of solving is correct.
- Only **Dorit's** way of solving is correct.
- Both students' ways of solving are correct.
- Both students' ways of solving are wrong.

Explain your choice:

____

____

FIGURE 9.3 Example of a MesiMatica assessment task

Assessment of students' work

You may use the following chart to assess students' work and sort their answers.

Student's name	Correct answers	Difficulty regarding different definitions of the variable	Relating to the equation solution as the problem solution	Remarks
Total				

FIGURE 9.4
Example of a MesiMatica assessment chart

also provided. Figure 9.4 presents the assessment chart suggested in the MesiMatica file "Same problem – different definitions of the variable."

The third main component comprises different follow-up teaching activities, designed to support personalized teaching by enabling the matching of different teaching activities to different groups of students, in accordance with their performance and detected difficulties. These follow-up teaching activities focus on promoting the learning of the assessed aspects of problem solving and reasoning related to the topic of the file. Figure 9.5 presents an excerpt from one of the follow-up teaching activities suggested in the MesiMatica file "Same problem – different definitions of the variable." It highlights the importance of wisely choosing how to define the variables for the mathematical model.

Accompanying the three main components of a MesiMatica file is a teachers' guide that provides information on the goals of the file, background on the mathematics and on students' difficulties that are the focus of the file, links to other MesiMatica files that deal with the same mathematical idea or student difficulties, and practical suggestions for using the file.

To date, more than 600 secondary-school mathematics teachers have participated in the year-long MesiMatica professional development (PD) activities, in which they worked on ways of incorporating formative assessment into their classroom teaching. These PD activities focus on developing teachers' competencies to elicit, interpret, and act on evidence of student learning. The PD activities use the MesiMatica files to support teachers' learning about what formative assessment entails; for them to try the different files' components in their own classrooms, and to collaboratively discuss their and their colleagues' experiences; and eventually for teachers to devise ways to incorporate

Worksheet part c: *Is it worth it?*

In the presented frame is a problem, followed by the beginning of Rachel's solution.

Given are three consecutive natural numbers whose product is 15 times greater than the middle number of the three.

What are the three numbers?

Rachel's solution:

x represents the smallest of the three numbers ($x \geq 1$, x is a natural number).

The corresponding equation: $x (x + 1) (x + 2) = 15 (x + 1)$

After simplifying I got: $x^3 + 3x^2 - 13x - 15 = 0$

I don't know how to solve this kind of equation.

Michael suggested choosing the variable this way: x represents the middle number instead of the smallest.

Follow Michael's suggestion and check whether it is worth representing the variable that way.

a. What equation will one get? ________________

b. What are the equation solutions? ____________

c. What are the three numbers? _______________

FIGURE 9.5 Excerpt from a MesiMatica follow-up teaching activity

formative assessment into their teaching on a regular basis. Preliminary examination suggests that the MesiMatica files have the potential to serve as a useful tool for assisting teachers in this endeavor, as illustrated by the teachers' descriptions of their experiences via questionnaires or conference presentations. For example, at a recent national MesiMatica conference concluding a year-long participation in MesiMatica PD activities in various places in the country, one of the presenting teachers reflected on her experiences in a MesiMatica community of learning:

> The participation in the community of learning and trying out the assessment tasks made me internalize how important the assessment methods are; how important it is to precisely identify students' competencies, even when it seems to us that the topic is easy and students understand it. Therefore, next year, I will change the way I handle assessment. I plan

> to use MesiMatica files as much as I can, because I saw that sometimes we mistakenly think that students understand, and when attempting to identify their competencies, it is revealed that they have essential and fundamental difficulties that will make it difficult for them in the future.

4 Conclusion

This chapter tells the story of a personal journey through three decades of research and development to address the problem of using assessment to inform instructional decisions, conducted in collaboration with colleagues and students. The story can serve as a case of the developmental process of a long-term research and development program. It highlights three milestones in the study of the challenges associated with eliciting, interpreting and acting on evidence of student learning, and two approaches that we designed and investigated to address these challenges. These different facets of our work were often interwoven, contributing to, and building on, each other.

The first milestone emerged from identifying, and then bridging, a gap between research on student learning in mathematics and research on teachers and teaching. This milestone shed light on the important role played by teachers' knowledge about students' common conceptions and errors, and their acquaintance with possible sources of students' ideas and the reasoning behind them, in teachers' competencies to elicit and interpret evidence of student learning.

The second milestone evolved from gradually acknowledging the need to expand the study of the challenges associated with eliciting and interpreting evidence of student learning beyond knowledge per se. This milestone marked our developing the understanding that teacher interpretation of students' talk and action, by its very nature, involves ambiguity and difficulties. Thus, whereas the first milestone highlighted, to some extent, potential deficiencies that might be "fixable" (i.e., lack of teacher knowledge), the second milestone indicated that difficulties in eliciting and interpreting evidence of student learning are associated not only with knowledge, and not necessarily with deficiencies, but also with teaching practices conducted in a professional manner.

The MANOR activity was originally designed to address the challenges associated with the first milestone. Later, as the second milestone evolved, the aim was expanded to address the challenges associated with both milestones. The MANOR activity provided teachers with an opportunity to advance their knowledge of common student conceptions and ways of learning and reasoning in different mathematical domains. This served as a powerful means to improve teachers' sensitivity to, and sense making of, students' talk and action, and consequently, their competencies to elicit and interpret evidence of student learning.

The third milestone was, in a way, an outcome of insights developed during our attempts to address the challenges associated with the first two milestones. This third milestone denoted our realization that improving teachers' competencies to elicit and interpret evidence of student learning is important, but it is not enough. Consideration should also be given to the "next step," i.e., acting on evidence of students' learning in ways that advance students' mathematical understanding.

Building on all of the above, the MesiMatica resource files, which we continue to develop at the time of writing this chapter, address all three overarching principles associated with formative assessment (Goos, 2020), that is, eliciting, interpreting, and acting on evidence of student learning. The files are designed in line with current recommendations for classroom assessment that reflects the complex nature of mathematics (Suurtamm et al., 2016), attending to mathematics content, as well as to mathematical practices, processes, proficiencies, and competencies. The files focus on aspects of problem solving, modeling, and reasoning – aspects that are not commonly addressed in assessment materials – reflecting what is important to assess and thus, to learn. Initial examination suggests that the MesiMatica resource files have the potential to serve as a useful tool for teachers to incorporate formative assessment into the mathematics classrooms; i.e., to use assessment to inform instructional decisions in ways that advance students' understanding.

This brings us to the end of our story, but the work is definitely not done. I look forward to seeing the next milestones in the study of the challenges associated with eliciting, interpreting and acting on evidence of student learning; and what approaches will be designed to address them. Based on our work at MANOR, a promising direction would be to focus research and development work on the integration of knowledge and practice; integration that I term knowtice (Even, 2008) to signify that this integration is related to the elements that create it (knowledge and practice), but that the product is a new object. In other words, using the construct of knowtice as a lens to capture the essence of what teachers need to learn and develop in order to use assessment to inform instructional decisions in ways that advance students' understanding.

Finally, whereas the story recounts a personal journey, this journey did not occur in a vacuum. Rather it was situated in, and continuously dialectically interacted with the corresponding global journey of the international community of mathematics education.

Note

1 https://stwww1.weizmann.ac.il/mesimatika/ (in Hebrew).

References

Bauersfeld, H. (1988). Interaction, construction, and knowledge: Alternative perspectives for mathematics education. In D. A. Grouws & T. J. Cooney (Eds.), *Effective mathematics teaching* (pp. 27–46). Erlbaum.

Black, P., & Wiliam, D. (2009). Developing the theory of formative assessment. *Educational Assessment, Evaluation and Accountability, 21*, 5–31. http://dx.doi.org/10.1007/s11092-008-9068-5

Booth, L. R. (1988). Children's difficulties in beginning algebra. In A. F. Coxford (Ed.), *The ideas of algebra, K-12, National Council of Teachers of Mathematics yearbook* (pp. 20–32). NCTM.

Burkhardt, H., & Schoenfeld, A. (2018). Assessment in the service of learning: Challenges and opportunities or plus ça change, plus c'est la même chose. *ZDM – Mathematics Education, 50*, 571–585. http://dx.doi.org/10.1007/s11858-018-0937-1

Carpenter, T. P., & Fennema, E. (1992). Cognitively guided instruction: Building on the knowledge of students and teachers. *International Journal of Educational Research, 17*, 457–470. http://dx.doi.org/10.1016/s0883-0355(05)80005-9

Davis, R. B. (1975). Cognitive processes involved in solving simple algebraic equations. *Journal of Children's Mathematical Behavior, 1*(3), 7–35.

De Bock, D., Van Dooren, W., Janssens, D., & Verschaffel, L. (2002). Improper use of linear reasoning: An in-depth study of the nature and the irresistibility of secondary school students' errors. *Educational Studies in Mathematics, 50*, 311–334.

Even, R. (1989). *Prospective secondary teachers' knowledge and understanding about mathematical functions* [Unpublished doctoral dissertation]. Michigan State University.

Even, R. (1999a). Integrating academic and practical knowledge in a teacher leaders' development program. *Educational Studies in Mathematics, 38*, 235–252. http://dx.doi.org/10.1007/978-94-017-1584-3_11

Even, R. (1999b). The development of teacher-leaders and inservice teacher educators. *Journal of Mathematics Teacher Education, 2*, 3–24.

Even, R. (2000). The MANOR resource materials for teacher-leaders and educators. In A. Gagatsis & G. Makrides (Eds.), *Proceedings of the 2nd Mediterranean Conference on Mathematics Education, Vol. 2* (pp. 472–479). Cyprus Mathematical Society.

Even, R. (2005a). Using assessment to inform instructional decisions: How hard can it be? *Mathematics Education Research Journal, 17*(3), 45–61. http://dx.doi.org/10.1007/bf03217421

Even, R. (2005b). Integrating knowledge and practice at MANOR in the development of providers of professional development for teachers. *Journal of Mathematics Teacher Education, 8*, 343–357. http://dx.doi.org/10.1007/s10857-005-0855-3

Even, R. (2008). Facing the challenge of educating educators to work with practicing mathematics teachers. In B. Jaworski & T. Wood (Eds.), *The international handbook of mathematics teacher education: The mathematics teacher educator as a developing professional* (pp. 57–73). Sense Publishers. http://dx.doi.org/10.1163/9789087905521_005

Even, R., & Kvatinsky, T. (2009). Approaches to teaching mathematics in lower-achieving classes. *International Journal of Science and Mathematics Education, 7*, 957–985. http://dx.doi.org/10.1007/s10763-008-9141-z

Even, R., & Markovits, Z. (1993). Teachers' pedagogical content knowledge of functions: Characterization and applications. *Journal of Structural Learning, 12*(1), 35–51.

Even, R., & Markovits, Z. (1995). Some aspects of teachers' and students' views on student reasoning and knowledge construction. *International Journal of Mathematics Education in Science and Technology, 26*, 531–544. http://dx.doi.org/10.1080/0020739950260407

Even, R., & Tirosh, D. (1995). Subject-matter knowledge and knowledge about students as sources of teacher presentations of the subject matter. *Educational Studies in Mathematics, 29*, 1–20. http://dx.doi.org/10.1007/bf01273897

Even, R., & Tirosh, D. (2002). Teacher knowledge and understanding of students' mathematical learning. In L. English (Ed.), *Handbook of international research in mathematics education* (pp. 219–240). Erlbaum.

Even, R., & Tirosh, D. (2008). Teacher knowledge and understanding of students' mathematical learning and thinking. In L. English (Ed.), *Handbook of international research in mathematics education* (2nd ed., pp. 202–222). Routledge (updated version of the 2002 chapter). http://dx.doi.org/10.4324/9780203930236.ch10

Even, R., & Wallach, T. (2004). Between student observation and student assessment: A critical reflection. *Canadian Journal of Science, Mathematics, and Technology Education, 4*, 483–495. http://dx.doi.org/10.1080/14926150409556629

Goldenberg, G. (2000). *The portfolio as a means for changing teacher assessment of student knowledge of positive rational numbers* [Unpublished master's thesis]. Tel Aviv University (in Hebrew).

Goos, M. (2020). Mathematics classroom assessment. In S. Lerman (Ed.), *Encyclopedia of mathematics education* (2nd ed., pp. 572–576). Springer Nature Switzerland AG. http://dx.doi.org/10.1007/978-3-030-15789-0_104

Markovits, Z., & Even, R. (1999a). The decimal point situation: A close look at the use of mathematics-classroom-situations in teacher education. *Teaching and Teacher Education, 15*, 653–665. http://dx.doi.org/10.1016/s0742-051x(99)00020-7

Markovits, Z., & Even, R. (1999b). Mathematics classroom situations: In-service course for elementary school teachers. In B. Jaworski, T. Wood, & A. J. Dawson (Eds.), *Mathematics teacher education: Critical international perspectives* (pp. 59–67). Falmer Press.

Mehan, H. (1979). *Learning lessons: Social organization in the classroom.* Harvard University Press. http://dx.doi.org/10.4159/harvard.9780674420106

Nesher, P., & Kilpatrick, J. (1990). *Mathematics and cognition.* Cambridge University Press. http://dx.doi.org/10.1017/cbo9781139013499

Robinson, N. (1993). *Connectedness in teaching: Equivalent algebraic expressions – By expert and novice teachers* [Unpublished master's thesis]. Tel Aviv University (in Hebrew).

Romberg, T. A., & Carpenter, T. P. (1986). Research on teaching and learning mathematics: Two disciplines of scientific inquiry. In M. C. Wittrock (Ed.), *Handbook of research on teaching* (3rd ed., pp. 850–873). Macmillan.

Sfard, A. (1991). On the dual nature of mathematical conceptions: Reflections on processes and objects as different sides of the same coin. *Educational Studies in Mathematics, 22*, 1–36. http://dx.doi.org/10.1007/bf00302715

Shulman, L. S. (1986). Those who understand: Knowledge growth in teaching. *Educational Researcher 15*(2), 4–14. http://dx.doi.org/10.3102/0013189x015002004

Suurtamm, C., Thompson, D. R., Kim, R. Y., Moreno, L. D., Sayac, N., Schukajlow, S., Silver, E., Ufer, S., & Vos, P. (2016). *Assessment in mathematics education: Large-scale assessment and classroom assessment.* Springer. http://dx.doi.org/10.1007/978-3-319-32394-7

Swan, M. (2020). Design research in mathematics education. In S. Lerman (Ed.), *Encyclopedia of mathematics education* (2nd ed., pp. 192–195). Springer Nature Switzerland AG. http://dx.doi.org/10.1007/978-3-030-15789-0_180

Tall, D. O., & Thomas, M. O. J. (1991). Encouraging versatile thinking in algebra using the computer. *Educational Studies in Mathematics, 22*, 125–147. http://dx.doi.org/10.1007/bf00555720

Thompson, D. R., Burton, M., Cusi, A., & Wright, D. (2018). Formative assessment: A critical component in the teaching-learning process. In D. R. Thompson, M. Burton, A. Cusi, & D. Wright (Eds.), *Classroom assessment in mathematics* (pp. 3–8). Springer. http://dx.doi.org/10.1007/978-3-319-73748-5_1

Tirosh, D., Even, R., & Robinson, N. (1998). Simplifying algebraic expressions: Teacher awareness and teaching approaches. *Educational Studies in Mathematics, 35*, 51–64.

Wallach, T. (2005). *Teachers' hearing and interpretation of students' talk and action while they engage in mathematics problem solving* [Unpublished doctoral dissertation]. Weizmann Institute of Science (in Hebrew).

Wallach, T., & Even, R. (2005). Hearing students: The complexity of understanding what they are saying, showing, and doing. *Journal of Mathematics Teacher Education, 8*, 393–417. http://dx.doi.org/10.1007/s10857-005-3849-2

Wood, T. (1994). Patterns of interaction and the culture of mathematics classrooms. In S. Lerman (Ed.), *The culture of the mathematics classroom* (pp. 149–168). Kluwer. 10.1007/978-94-017-1199-9_10

PART 2

Professional Development of Science and Mathematics Teachers

CHAPTER 10

Evolving Approaches to the Professional Development of Teachers

Abraham Arcavi

Abstract

This chapter presents a bird's-eye view of 50 years of academic work on the professional development of mathematics and science teachers, conducted alongside curriculum development and research on teaching and learning at the Department of Science Teaching, Weizmann Institute of Science. It presents the evolving approaches, their rationale, and the accumulated wisdom and experiences which have impacted, and continue to impact the educational system in Israel.

Keywords

professional development – mathematics teachers – professional communities of teachers – curriculum development and implementation – fifty years overview

•••

Dedicated to the memory of Professor Maxim Bruckheimer, Mathematician, educator, leader, teacher and an exceptional human being

∴

1 Background

The Department of Science Teaching (DST) was officially founded on 5 December 1968 on the initiative of Professor Amos de-Shalit (1926–1969), a theoretical physicist who was the General Director of the Weizmann Institute of Science at the time. De-Shalit envisioned science education as a full-fledged academic

 | DOI: 10.1163/9789004503625_010

discipline of inquiry with an impact on the educational system at large, in coordination with the Israeli Ministry of Education (de-Shalit, 1968).

For the five decades since then (and counting), the DST – through its various leaders, scientists and graduate students – has shaped and consolidated its mission and its modus operandi: development and implementation of innovative learning materials and pedagogical models, teacher professional development, and research and evaluation. Each of these activities informs and is informed by the others through iterative cycles that incorporate practical experience, research outcomes, the dynamic evolution of scientific contents (where applicable), the evolution of emerging didactical tools (e.g., digital environments, communication technologies), and changes in social contexts and educational policies.

In this chapter, I present an account of one of the main aspects of the DST's work: teacher professional development (which in the past was called in-service teacher education). The account highlights the centrality assigned – from the very beginning – to the work with and for teachers in mathematics and science education, and how the different perspectives and conceptions of teacher education have evolved toward refined models and activities (in which both curriculum development and research have critical roles) aimed at a system-wide impact. The examples are taken mostly from the area of mathematics teaching, although the main stages of the development were similar in the teaching of all scientific areas at the DST.

2 "Prehistory"

There seems to be wide agreement that a landmark event in the worldwide history of science and mathematics education was the launching of the first artificial Earth satellite (Sputnik) by the Soviet Union, on 4 October 1957. This event had a profound catalytic impact, especially in the United States, in triggering a thorough revision of science education. The United States Congress passed the National Defense Education Act (NDEA, 1958) to support the development of science and mathematics education programs. Other countries followed suit, and many mathematicians and scientists took on the responsibility of designing new curriculum materials, which they believed should become "much more rigorous" (Wissehr et al., 2011, p. 371). It was under this zeitgeist that leading scientists at the Weizmann Institute, concerned with the quality of their children's science education, decided to take their own first steps in science education in the early 1960s (6 years before the founding of the DST). De-Shalit assembled a team of scientists and he selected physics, mathematics and chemistry teachers, who started to work using the Hebrew translation of curriculum materials developed in the United States. From the perspective of teacher development, a main event was the first course for teachers designed and taught by Haim Harari. At the time, Harari was a doctoral student, who became Head of the Department of Science Teaching in the early 1970s and President of the Weizmann Institute in the late 1980s, leading institutional and major national science education projects involving teacher professional development.

This course (Harari, 1964–65) was the first organized activity for junior high school teachers and it was remarkable for many reasons. First, it considered teachers (rather than curriculum materials) as crucial for advancing science education. Thus, following the dismal results of a test with basic science items administered to about 150 students, it was decided that a main step toward improving the quality of science education would be to focus on strengthening the teachers' knowledge (later labeled by Shulman, 1986, as teacher's "content knowledge"). Second, it not only assigned importance to the non-mediated and hands-on work of active science researchers with school teachers, but it also modeled how this work should be done. Third, the nature of the relevant "content knowledge" was conceived as much more than a mere concatenation of science facts and laws; it stressed the nature of science and scientific activity, the tools and processes used by scientists, and even some epistemological issues. For example, the course included: looking at very different phenomena as manifestations of the same physical laws; highlighting the powerful role of mathematics, as well as its potential limitations, in deeply understanding the physics itself; reviewing ways of measuring (especially space and time) and issues of measurement precision; discussing the perils of careless extrapolation and interpolation; use of several ways to represent phenomena and data (tables, graphs), interpreting these representations, and the ways in which they display experimental results. Though the course was not formally evaluated, it was considered successful by both the instructor and the participating teachers. Since then, the spirit of this course – based on strengthening teachers' subject matter knowledge (in its wide conception as described above) and teachers' immersion in sites where authentic science is being done – has been at the core of all teacher development activities in the DST.

This chapter describes how this core evolved and expanded to include other types of knowledge and models to support teachers' professional development, such as: specific pedagogies for science education, acquaintance with and harnessing of student cognition, analysis of the variety of teacher practices in which these types of knowledge are enacted, cognitive and social means to support teachers' reflective practice, learning to collaborate with peers in many educational endeavors and settings, and developing the role and activities of teacher leaders in upscaling innovations.

3 Curriculum Development and Implementation – The Beginnings

Following the worldwide trend, during its first decade (the 1970s), the recently established DST embarked on massive curriculum development in mathematics (grades 7–9), physics, and chemistry (grades 9–12). Although inspired by projects from other countries, the development teams neither adopted nor adapted foreign materials but started anew, attuned to the local educational context and needs (e.g., a thorough national educational reform in 1968–69). Moreover, in the case of mathematics and under the leadership of Professor Maxim Bruckheimer, the development teams took into account two main challenges already faced by other countries. The first was to heed the complaints regarding the content and approaches of the new curricula (widely known as "New Math"). These complaints included, for example, that the content was of interest only to pure mathematicians (e.g., Feynman, 1965), it disregarded "the basics" (e.g., Kline, 1973), and it had bad press coverage (for example, *Time Magazine* included New Math as one of the 100 worst ideas of the century[1]). The second challenge, which is central to our story about teachers and teaching, was the implementation of a new curriculum.

Addressing the first challenge entailed the careful analysis of relevant topics in mathematics, irrespective of their centrality or absence in the "New Math." For example, the notion of function and its importance in almost all areas of mathematics (and at almost all levels) was borrowed from "New Math," but without the formalism of its mathematical definition (Markovits et al., 1986).

As the second, and more complex challenge, curriculum implementation was conceived as the enactment, in classrooms across the country, of the learning and teaching materials (their rationale, their pedagogical approaches and their evaluation practices) developed by the Mathematics Group at the DST. Implementation strived to accomplish the curriculum learning goals, according to the spirit in which they were established, taking into account the characteristics of the target student and teacher populations. Since the 1970s, curriculum developers all over the world have noticed that the implemented curriculum (by the teachers) can differ considerably from the intended curriculum (by the designers) on the one hand, and from the attained curriculum on the other, as reflected in evaluations (e.g., Thompson & Usiskin, 2014).

Professor Maxim Bruckheimer, who headed the DST for a decade (from the mid-1970s to the mid-1980s) and the Mathematics Group for more than two decades, was very aware of, and concerned with the complexities of implementation. First and foremost, he strived to change a reality in which "generally, [new] curricula are simply not implemented" (Bruckheimer, 1979, p. 43). Moreover, he was well aware of the aforementioned disparities between intended, implemented and attained curricula, and he pointed out three main "inhibitors for curriculum implementation": inherent faults in the design, inhibitors within the educational system, and external inhibitors (Bruckheimer, 1979).

These challenges were addressed in several ways. First, it was recognized that implementation is "a phenomenon in its own right" (Fullan & Pomfret, 1977, p. 336). Thus, it "should not be conceived, as a relatively static… but a dynamic process in which the products of the first curriculum development stage are the basic data but they can be manipulated, added to and adapted." Moreover, "the implementation begins almost simultaneously with the creation of the learning materials, as some of the first drafts begin to be tested" (Bruckheimer, 1979, p. 45) and discussed. Therefore, Bruckheimer proposed that the DST not refer to curriculum development, but to curriculum development *and* implementation as an inseparable dyad.

To defuse some of the inhibitors of curriculum implementation mentioned above, it became clear that curriculum development and implementation should not be confined to academia, but rather should be fully coordinated with the Ministry of Education, following its official syllabus and guidelines (with the DST occasionally exerting some influence in shaping them). Most importantly, since it was clear that teachers are crucial players in any implementation process, much effort was directed at reaching out to them on local and national scales. The inclusion of teachers as partners in curriculum implementation took many forms, one of them being to get deeply acquainted with their professional profiles. "Who is the Mathematics Teacher in Grades 7, 8 and 9?" (Hershkowitz & Israeli, 1981) was a comprehensive survey undertaken to characterize the teacher population (age ranges, academic background, seniority and more). Knowing the potential implementers of the learning materials well was an invaluable resource in designing customized in-service courses around the curriculum for different teacher subpopulations.

Another avenue for teachers' active participation from the early stages of implementation was to create a working model for the design of materials in which teachers were major team players. Thus, curriculum development and implementation involved teachers from the very beginning of the process, so that they could contribute their experience, their needs, their practices, their wisdom and their knowledge of the field and the different contexts of their work (Bruckheimer, 1979). Since the 1970s, a number of teachers have been hired (part-time and in parallel to their work in classrooms) as integral members of the hands-on design of any team. Such intense involvement of teachers provides a powerful "reality check," both a priori (what can be viable and sustainable in classes around the country), as well as in the pilot testing in authentic classrooms (their own or those of their close colleagues). The collective work of teachers, developers, researchers in mathematics education, and mathematics advisors in developing curriculum materials creates a productive synergy. This synergy constitutes a first necessary condition (although certainly not the only one and certainly not sufficient) for potentially successful curriculum implementation by reducing the possible inherent flaws in the design (first inhibitor described above).

The involvement of teachers in the design process turned out be more than an important component in the implementation process, it also became an unintended, but powerful means of professional development for teachers themselves. As active team members, the teachers' involvement in the life of the DST included drafting learning units, getting feedback from colleagues and academicians, attending and leading in-service courses, attending departmental seminars, and sometimes even taking graduate courses; above all, they had frequent interactions with all of the members of the Mathematics Group.

At the beginning of the 2000s, the author of this chapter invited Dr. Susan Magidson, a postdoctoral fellow from the United States, to study the effects of teacher involvement in curriculum design on their professional development as teachers. The study was based on lengthy one-on-one conversations with eight teachers, who at the time were involved in curriculum development in the DST. The findings were very revealing; the learning experienced by the teachers involved in the process of curriculum design within our academic environment was classified into six categories: design of instructional materials, student learning, mathematics content, teaching and pedagogy, teacher leadership, and research and theory. No less important than *what* they learned was *how* they learned it: by creating and experiencing design and getting feedback on their ideas and products, through intensive discussions, by leading in-service courses, and by being exposed to research on teaching and learning in an environment characterized by apprenticeship, mentorship and collaboration with peers and with the academic staff (Magidson, 2004). Clearly, this form of professional development is not sustainable on a large scale because it can only support a small number of teachers at once, and it spans a long period of time. Nevertheless, and given these results, "there are elements that could be adapted for another setting," for example: collaboration, close proximity to academic environments, teaching through design of learning materials, etc. (Magidson, 2004, p. 20).

To scale up and sustain implementation on a nationwide scale, the DST developed several resources (e.g., teacher guides, teacher journals, evaluation models, on-site guidance at schools), established extensive nets of in-service teacher courses and in-school guidance, and later created and ran national and regional teaching centers. During the 1980s and the early 1990s, a large number of in-service activities were conducted throughout the country, spread over the school year and summers (school recess), in a central location (the Weizmann Institute) as well as in other several regions, especially in the geographical and socioeconomic periphery.

From its inception, the DST was well aware of Freudenthal's concerns regarding massive in-service education: "Teachers initially participated in the innovation movement as *listeners* [emphasis added]; perplexed or frightened they listened to revolutionary expositions…" (Freudenthal, 1973, p. 134). Thus, under the widely held assumption (see, for example, Owens, 2013) that teachers tend to replicate the ways in which they themselves were taught, much effort was devoted not only to the contents of the in-service courses but also to the way in which these courses were carried out, by modeling intended classroom pedagogies. Thus, all in-service teacher activities were designed and conducted as active forums for learning and participation. In other words, the main modus operandi was to "teach the teachers as one would wish them to teach, rather than lecturing the teacher on strategies… Most of the time the teacher is active, working, discussing, playing…" (Bruckheimer & Hershkowitz, 1983, p. 134). This implied that the courses were lively workshops in which teachers worked around ad hoc designed worksheets for individual or group work followed by plenary discussions. However, experience showed that this kind of learning was not enough. It soon became clear that teachers' active engagement during a workshop should include awareness of and reflection about their participation, such that teachers were led to explicitly notice and talk about the ways in which they worked, and how this could be applied to their own classrooms.

The contents were not limited to innovative curriculum materials and ways of teaching them. They also included topics chosen to strengthen the mathematical background of the relevant materials in the curriculum, even if these topics were not intended for the classroom. The rationale was that, even for teachers with a strong mathematical background, there was always room for enhancing the foundations and deepening the mathematics that they teach toward insights which were "possible on mature reflection and when the material is seen to be relevant" (Bruckheimer & Hershkowitz, 1983, p. 134). An example of such content is a major course on the conceptual history of the mathematical topics relevant to the curriculum (negative numbers, irrational numbers, and linear and quadratic equations) which was developed, tested and evaluated within the framework of a doctoral dissertation (Arcavi, 1985). These materials offered an opportunity to encounter potential epistemological and cognitive difficulties (as reflected in history), to become acquainted with the evolution of solution approaches to problems, and to learn about the struggles preceding the rigorous definitions of concepts.

Participation in all of the in-service courses became a tradition, attendance was massive, most teachers expressed their satisfaction, and the Ministry of Education endorsed and funded them and applied a reward system for the participants.

In sum, the above moves were aimed at defusing the inhibitors of curriculum implementation; they were well thought out and, to a certain extent, they worked well. However, many questions remained regarding their ultimate success. The massive net of courses conducted by the DST never covered the majority of the teacher population, and many of those who attended the in-service courses neither fully adopted the new curriculum materials nor deeply changed their traditional teaching practices. Even some of those who worked within the Mathematics Group in curriculum design (teachers with above average motivation and knowledge, and a willingness to try alternative approaches and strategies) complained about their loneliness; as one teacher eloquently described it (after leaving the team): "The opposing powers are stronger now… I just go home and I don't have anyone with whom to talk about it" (Magidson, 2004, p. 19).

It was clear that teacher satisfaction after a workshop, and even some success stories, should not lull curriculum developers into a false sense of wide accomplishment. The challenge that remained was to reach the population at large (i.e., "scale up") with long-lasting sustainable effects on teacher practices. This challenge is still ongoing around the world as attested by a recent issue of the prestigious journal *Educational Studies in Mathematics* devoted in its entirety to this topic (e.g. Maass et al., 2019).

4 Teachers' Continuous Professional Development – Beyond the Curriculum

In the 1990s, curriculum development and implementation continued as intensely as before, or even more so. Very large projects were funded by the Ministry of Education to develop learning materials: (a) for junior high school using computerized tools (see, for example, Tabach et al., 2008), (b) for heterogeneous classes in junior high school (Robinson & Taizi, 2000), and (c) for non-mathematically oriented students in high school (Arcavi et al., 1994). Each of these projects established an extensive net of in-service teacher courses. However, it became clear that the focus on teacher development around curriculum development and implementation, no matter how well-conceived and well-applied, was insufficient. What was felt to be missing was the expansion of teacher professional development beyond implementation of curriculum materials and toward "real opportunities to learn about mathematics learning and teaching" (Even, 1999, p. 4). These opportunities could be realized in regional "homes" for mathematics and science teachers, created ad hoc across the country following one of the recommendations of the comprehensive report "Tomorrow 98" (1992) submitted by a committee led by Professor Haim Harari. Teachers learning about learning and teaching, on a large scale, required a cadre of qualified "teachers of teachers" throughout the country. Thus, under the umbrella of the National Teacher Center (created following the Tomorrow 98 report), and under the leadership of Professor Ruhama Even, a special program called MANOR was established. MANOR, a 2-year preparation program, targeted existing mentors, heads of mathematics departments in schools, and staff from curriculum and implementation projects, with the aim of upgrading them to certified teachers of teachers. The mission of these teachers of teachers would consist of initiating, guiding and supporting lifelong teacher learning by leading courses and activities in Regional Teacher Centers throughout the country (for details, see Even, 1999). The MANOR participants worked on the following: analysis of mathematical problems, student conceptions and ways of thinking, acquaintance with theoretical frameworks, hands-on experience replicating small-scale research studies, and what becoming a teacher leader entails. Moreover, MANOR engaged in the large-scale development of materials for teacher educators and conducted regular monthly forums and biannual congresses (Even, 2005). The program was aimed at the personal, professional, and social development of these teacher leaders. It was very successful in creating a degree of status for the profession of teacher leadership; the training gained partial recognition by academic institutions, and resulted in the advancement of professional development activities for teachers in Regional Teacher Centers for several years. These teachers of teachers led many courses and projects throughout the country, and some even took several influential positions of leadership in Israel.

5 Continuous Teacher Professional Development – Beyond Learning about Learning

As noted in the previous section, the National and Regional Teacher Centers provided a boost for teacher professional development that went beyond curriculum implementation. However, the influence of the Tomorrow 98 report underwent "an ongoing process of erosion and diminution of some of its main recommendations" (Bar-Joseph, 2017, p. 18); and the Regional Teacher Centers began to close in the 2000s.

In the absence of the Regional Centers, the National Teacher Centers for science and mathematics began to initiate, support, and sustain the creation of an innovative avenue for continuous professional development: professional learning communities (PLCs) of mathematics and science teachers. The motivation was not only to fill the vacuum left by the Regional Teacher Centers; it was mainly to establish and sustain a more comprehensive conception of teacher professional development. Today, these PLCs are striving to move away from the classical course format (regardless of whether they focus on a particular curriculum or on learning about learning or teaching, or both). These PLCs should function like any other PLC, namely they have to engage their participants in an ongoing study of the profession, continuously rethinking its practice, and striving for ongoing improvement and implementation of innovations. A special characteristic of the PLC is to provide an environment that empowers teachers by fostering and valuing exchanges among peers, mutual cooperation and collaboration, emotional support, personal growth, and a sense of togetherness, in order to achieve what it is more difficult to accomplish alone (Dufour & Eaker, 1998).

Dozens of PLCs are presently operating under the aegis of the DST (or similar academic institutions) with the aim of positioning teachers as respected professionals who, eventually, will "take off" on their own. In the future, PLCs are expected to become well-established self-sustainable institutions (local or regional) with autonomous agendas, and with the role of academia deferring to that of a consultant or a provider of resources and ideas.

The following are the main characteristics/foundations of these PLCs (Arcavi, 2020):

- *discipline-based*, that is to say, deeply rooted in the specifics of mathematics (or the sciences), its concepts and big ideas, its ways of working, its habits of mind, and its ways of sense-making (e.g. National Research Council, 2012), resembling the spirit of the very first teacher in-service course described earlier (Harari, 1964–65);
- *generative*, namely yielding new understandings that in turn lead to enhancing both the subject matter and the pedagogical content knowledge with subsequent changes in practices, dispositions and orientations (e.g., Karsenty & Arcavi, 2017);
- oriented toward the *understanding of students'* idiosyncratic ways of coping with content and searching for ways to build on them to facilitate and support student learning (e.g. Karsenty et al., 2007);

- *resourcefulness* to become aware of and formulate the need for useful resources and the ability to search for and use them appropriately (e.g., Adler, 2012);
- *active* through experimentation, inquiry, collection and discussion of data-based evidence (e.g. Eylon et al., 2008), posing, debating, and resolving dilemmas of practice in productive ways;
- *meta-learning*, namely reflection on one's own learning while working in the PLC both for the sake of one's awareness of possible changes and as a means for the community to review and redirect its agenda (e.g. Arcavi & Karsenty, 2018);
- *collaborative*, such that teachers support each other, complement each other, and develop a sense of professional identity (e.g., Prytula & Weiman, 2012) within a social space of peers, sharing a collective responsibility for themselves and for their students;
- *productive*, by interactively engaging in the collective creation of useful resources (such as lesson plans, proposals for student evaluations and the like), testing them, and eventually redesigning them according to classroom trials, deriving morals and applicable conclusions (similar to the Japanese Lesson Study model, as in Fernandez & Yoshida, 2011);
- driven by *values and norms* of academic civility (Lampert, 2001) in which ample room is provided to respectfully accommodate diversity and dissidence, providing participants with a sense of safety to freely express themselves without the fear of being judged (or, alternatively, handling judgement in productive ways);
- nurturing a *passionate, motivating and pleasant* atmosphere, leading to motivating insights, feeding on curiosity, perseverance, and professional enjoyment;
- *legitimized, appreciated, valued and encouraged* by the educational establishment at large (from the local school establishment to the highest level of policymaking).

At present, PLCs are the main avenue for professional development that is supported and encouraged by the Ministry of Education, and it is the main activity with and for teachers conducted at the DST. In the case of mathematics, there are several ongoing communities sustained by faculty members. The common feature of these PLCs is their work around an overarching unifying theme, which encompasses many central aspects of mathematics education, such as curriculum issues, formative assessment, student learning, reflection on practice, and more. In the following, two of these PLCs are briefly described; they are covered in more detail in other chapters of this book.

A large body of theoretical foundations (the detailed literature review can be found in Koichu & Pinto, 2018) inspired the TRAIL community (Teacher-Researcher Alliance for Investigating Learning). TRAIL aims to actively involve teachers in the various stages of research, not to convert them into researchers, but rather to develop their abilities of inquiry, noticing, and reflection as an integral part of the daily teaching practice. Teachers are actively involved in formulating questions to which research can provide useful answers for practical purposes. Teachers learn how research operates and what researchable questions might be useful to answer, and they become research assistants rather than being the research 'subjects.' The communitarian aspect of this project is manifested by the cooperation among the possible roles taken by different individuals: contributing to the formulation of the research questions, collecting and shaping the dataset, participating in the analysis, creating summaries in writing, and more. For details and examples, please see Koichu and Pinto (2018). Initial results on the benefits and challenges of running TRAIL communities show that teachers enjoy taking part in producing new knowledge, discovering and noticing something 'new' for their personal benefit and for sharing with others, and reflecting on issues of practice with hindsight (Koichu et al., 2020).

The VIDEO-LM project (Viewing, Investigating and Discussing Environments of Learning Mathematics) was designed to support and enhance teachers' mathematical content and pedagogical knowledge, as well as to engage them in deep reflection on their practice by means of an ad hoc created framework for viewing and discussing authentic videotaped mathematics lessons (see Karsenty & Arcavi, this volume). The success of the project in terms of enhancing teacher reflection and knowledge led us to design a follow-up project titled Math-VALUE (Video Analysis and Lesson-Study to Upgrade Expertise). In this PLC, 'graduates' of VIDEO-LM apply the learned reflective capabilities to in-school communities of peers who, together, design authentic lessons, test them, and redesign them following the Japanese model of Lesson Study. This project is in its infancy, and preliminary informal impressions from the facilitators' preparative course are very promising.

5 Post Hoc Reflections

With more than 50 years of hindsight, the present panoramic retrospective of the work of the DST in the field of professional development of mathematics and science teachers shows interesting developmental trends and important morals. It all started with the motivation to improve science and mathematics education from an academic perspective, making use of academic tools such as reflection, theory, re-search, and lifelong learning. From the very beginning, there was a clear understanding that the quality and outcome of education is highly contingent upon of the role of teachers and teaching, long before this was 'universally' sanctioned as "The quality of an educational system cannot exceed the quality of its teachers" by Barber & Mourshed (2007, also known as the McKinsey Report). Thus, the professional development of mathematics and science teachers has been a main component of the activities of the DST throughout the half century of its existence.

Following the recognition of the centrality of teachers and teaching, an awareness of the need for continuous professional development as a lifelong endeavor emerged. Through the decades, the approaches to professional development have gone through several stages, each of them feeding on both the successes and challenges revealed by its predecessor and on advances in theory and research. Alongside the development of the different approaches, a conception of the teaching profession evolved: from the teacher as a mere "client" of academic-driven projects to an autonomous and respected professional with lifelong learning needs, who can establish sound and durable partnerships with academia. Accordingly, not only the spaces, scope, and essence of the professional development activities evolved, but also the ways in which teacher learning was promoted and supported:

- as an active participant in all activities,
- from a lone individual to a participant in a working community,
- from an implementer of curricula to a professional who bases teaching on students' capabilities and challenges,
- from learning about students to reflection on practices,
- from a listener of research findings to a scaffolded inquirer.

The account of the development of professional development approaches in the DST also underlines the role of academia, the natural home for advancing theory, reflection, creation, and research as inspiring and driving the practice of science education. The aim of academia is to advance knowledge in all of its forms, and it is therefore capable of building upon previous approaches and paradigms by accumulating experiences, benefiting from and feeding on successes, and recognizing and facing emerging limitations and challenges in systematic ways.

Finally, any historical account would be incomplete without a glimpse at the future, delineating present trends on the basis of what has been achieved to date, without any pretense of making definite predictions.

Since it is agreed that professional development is a lifelong enterprise for teachers, it will continue to be a lifelong line of work at the DST. The PLC seems to be a promising model, given the protagonism bestowed upon teachers, and the initial indications of successes across the board. It remains to be seen whether this model will be sustainable when the intensive academic involvement starts to fade and/or when the current, official policies change for bureaucratic or other reasons.

The present worldwide COVID-19 pandemic may have a considerable influence on the approaches to professional development, both in the ways in which it will function and the contents that will be chosen. Virtual reality may also have an impact on teachers and teaching, as may artificial intelligence (AI) and big data. It is the belief of this author that teachers will never be replaced by machines. Yet AI may become a useful resource for teachers, for example, by providing them with an 'AI teaching assistant' or by supporting "timely, smarter, teacher professional development" (for these and other possible roles, see Luckin et al., 2016). Only time will tell if research and development in AI, machine learning, or big data will indeed yield breakthroughs in fulfilling the promise of becoming a powerful resource for teachers and teaching, and how professional development will make use of them if at all.

These and many other challenges (i.e., customized professional development, or any other emerging but as yet unforeseen or unimaginable avenues) will certainly keep academia busy for another 50 years – with the main goal of ongoing improvements in science and mathematics education for all.

The author of this chapter would very much like to live for another 50 years to both accompany the developments as he has done for the last 40 years of his professional life, and witness the sequel to this historical account.

Note

1 See http://content.time.com/time/magazine/article/0,9171,991230,00.html

References

Adler, A. (2012). Knowledge resources in and for school mathematics teaching. In G. Geudet, B. Pepin, & L. Trouche (Eds.), *From text to 'lived' resources. Mathematics curriculum materials and teacher development* (pp. 3–22). Springer.

Arcavi, A. (1985). *History of mathematics as a component of mathematics teachers background* [Unpublished doctoral dissertation]. Weizmann Institute of Science. http://www.weizmann.ac.il/ScienceTeaching/Arcavi/sites/ScienceTeaching.Arcavi/files/uploads/Phd%20 Dissertation%20 Arcavi.pdf

Arcavi, A. (2020). From tools to resources in the professional development of mathematics teachers: General perspectives and crosscutting issues. In O. Chapman & S. Llinares (Eds.), *The international handbook of mathematics teacher education: Volume 2 – Tools and processes in mathematics teacher education* (2nd ed., pp. 421–437). Sense Publishers. http://dx.doi.org/10.1163/9789004418967_016

Arcavi, A., Hadas, N., & Dreyfus, T. (1994). Engineering curriculum tasks on the basis of theoretical and empirical findings. In J. P. da Ponte & J. F. Matos (Eds.), *Proceedings of the 18th International Conference on the Psychology of Mathematics (PME 18), Vol. II* (pp. 280–287). University of Lisbon.

Arcavi, A., & Karsenty, R. (2018). Enhancing mathematics teachers' knowledge and reflection through peer-discussions of videotaped lessons: A pioneer program in Israel. In N. Movshovitz-Hadar (Ed.), *K-12 mathematics education in Israel: Issues and innovations* (pp. 303–310). World Scientific Press. http://dx.doi.org/10.1142/9789813231191_0033

Barber, M., & Mourshed, M. (2007). *How the world's best-performing school systems come out on top*. https://www.mckinsey.com/~/media/McKinsey/Industries/Public%20and%20Social%20Sector/Our%20Insights/How%20the%20worlds%20best%20performing%20school%20systems%20come%20 out%20on%20top/How_the_world_s_best-performing_school_systems_come_out_on_top.pdf

Bar-Joseph, I. (2017). Main insights regarding the implementation of reforms. In N. Strauss (Ed.), *Insights from past initiatives to promote science education in Israel – Learning from selected issues*. The Initiative of Applied Educational Research. The Israeli Academy of Sciences and Humanities. http://education.academy.ac.il/SystemFiles/23191.pdf

Bruckheimer, M. (1979). Creative implementation. In P. Tamir, A. Blum, A. Hofstein, & N. Sabar (Eds.), *Proceedings of the Bat-Sheva Seminar on curriculum implementation and its relationships to curriculum development in science* (pp. 43–49). The Weizmann Institute of Science.

Bruckheimer, M., & Hershkowitz, R. (1983). In-service teacher training: The patient, diagnosis, treatment and cure. In P. Tamir, A. Hofstein, & M. Ben-Peretz (Eds.), *Preservice and in-service training of science teachers*. Balaban International Science Services.

De-Shalit, A. (1968). *Department of Science Education. A proposal submitted to the executive council of the Weizmann Institute of Science* [Unpublished document]. https://stwww1.weizmann.ac.il/en/wp-content/uploads/sites/26/2016/10/de-Shalit_creation_of_SciTeachDept.pdf

Dufour, R., & Eaker, R. (1998). *Professional learning communities at work: Best practices for enhancing student achievement*. Solution Tree Press.

Even, R. (1999). The development of teacher leaders and in-service teacher educators. *Journal of Mathematics Teacher Education*, 2, 3–24. http://dx.doi.org/10.1023/a:1009994819749

Even, R. (2005). Integrating knowledge and practice at Manor in the development of providers of professional development for teachers. *Journal of Mathematics Teacher Education, 8*, 343–357. http://dx.doi.org/10.1007/s10857-005-0855-3

Eylon, B., Berger, H., & Bagno, E. (2008). An evidence-based continuous professional development programme on knowledge integration in physics: A study of teachers' collective discourse. *International Journal of Science Education, 30*, 619–641. http://dx.doi.org/10.1080/09500690701854857

Fernandez, C., & Yoshida, M. (2011). *Lesson study: A Japanese approach to improving mathematics teaching and learning*. Routledge.

Feynman, R. P. (1965). New textbooks for the "new" mathematics. *Engineering and Science, 28*(6), 9–15.

Freudenthal, H. (1973). *Mathematics as an educational task*. D. Reidel Publishing Co. http://dx.doi.org/10.1007/978-94-010-2903-2_10

Fullan, M., & Pomfret, A. (1977). Research on curriculum and instruction implementation. *Review of Educational Research, 47*(1), 335–397. http://dx.doi.org/10.3102/00346543047002335

Harari, H. (1964–1965). *A course for teachers of natural sciences* [Unpublished manuscript] (in Hebrew). https://www.weizmann.ac.il/particle/harari/sites/particle.harari/files/uploads/teachers_course_in_physics_1964-65_-_haim_harari.pdf

Hershkowitz, R., & Israeli, R. (1981). *Who is the mathematics teacher in grades 7, 8, 9*? Internal report in Hebrew. The Department of Science Teaching, Weizmann Institute of Science.

Karsenty, R., & Arcavi, A. (2017). Mathematics, lenses and videotapes: A framework and a language for developing reflective practices of teaching. *Journal of Mathematics Teacher Education, 20*, 433–455. http://dx.doi.org/10.1007/s10857-017-9379-x

Karsenty, R., Arcavi, A., & Hadas, N. (2007). Exploring informal mathematical products of low achievers at the secondary school level. *Journal of Mathematical Behavior, 16*, 156–177. http://dx.doi.org/10.1016/j.jmathb.2007.05.003

Kline, M. (1973). *Why Johnny can't add: The failure of the new math*. St. Martin's Press. http://dx.doi.org/10.1177/019263657405837820

Koichu, B., & Pinto, A. (2018). Developing education research competencies in mathematics teachers through TRAIL: Teacher-Researcher Alliance for Investigating Learning. *Canadian Journal of Science, Mathematics and Technology Education, 18*, 68–85. http://dx.doi.org/10.1007/s42330-018-0006-3

Koichu, B., Zaks, R., & Farber, M. (2020). Teachers' voices from two communities of inquiry engaged in practices of mathematics education research. In H. Borko & P. Despina (Eds.), *Teachers of mathematics working and learning in collaborative groups. Proceedings of the twenty-fifth ICMI study* (pp. 364–371). University of Lisbon. https://www.mathunion.org/fileadmin/ICMI/ICMI%20studies/ICMI%20Study%2025/BaseProceedings4.24.2020_PageNumbers_FINAL.pdf

Lampert, M. (2001). *Teaching problems and the problems of teaching*. Yale University Press.

Luckin, R., Holmes, W., Griffiths, M., & Forcier, L. B. (2016). *Intelligence unleashed. An argument for AI in education*. Pearson. https://www.pearson.com/content/dam/corporate/global/pearson-dot-com/files/innovation/Intelligence-Unleashed-Publication.pdf

Maass, K., Cobb, P., Krainer, K., & Potari, D. (2019). Different ways to implement innovative teaching approaches at scale. *Educational Studies in Mathematics, 102*, 303–318. http://dx.doi.org/10.1007/s10649-019-09920-8

Magidson, S. (2004). *Learning on the job: Instructional design as professional development* [Unpublished report] (available from the author of this chapter).

Markovits, Z., Eylon, B., & Bruckheimer, M. (1986). Functions today and yesterday. *For the Learning of Mathematics, 6*(2), 18–24, 28.

National Research Council. (2012). *Discipline-based education research: Understanding and improving learning in undergraduate science and engineering*. The National Academies Press. https://www.nap.edu/catalog/13362/discipline-based-education-research-understanding-and-improving-learning-in-undergraduate

NDEA. (1958). *National Defense Education Act*. https://www.govinfo.gov/content/pkg/STATUTE-72/pdf/STATUTE-72-Pg1580.pdf

Owens, S. A. (2013). We teach how we've been taught: Expeditionary learning unshackling sustainability education in U.S. public schools. *Journal of Sustainability Education, 5*. http://www.jsedimensions.org/wordpress/content/we-teach-how-weve-been-taught-expeditionary-learning-unshackling-sustainability-education-in-u-s-public-schools_2013_06/

Prytula, M., & Weiman, K. (2012). Collaborative professional development: An examination of changes in teacher identity through the professional learning community model. *Journal of Case Studies in Education, 3*. https://files.eric.ed.gov/fulltext/EJ1109722.pdf

Robinson, N., & Taizi, N. (2000). Learning mathematics – From theory to practice (in Hebrew). The Department of Science Teaching, The Weizmann Institute of Science. https://stwww1.weizmann.ac.il/?page_id=940

Shulman, L. S. (1986). Those who understand: Knowledge growth in teaching. *Educational Researcher, 15*(2), 4–14. http://dx.doi.org/10.3102/0013189x015002004

Tabach, M., Hershkowitz, R., Arcavi, A., & Dreyfus, T. (2008). Computerized environments in mathematics classrooms: A research-design view. In L. D. English, M. B. Bussi, G. A. Jones, R. A. Lesh, B. Sriraman, & D. Tirosh (Eds.), *Handbook of international research in mathematics education* (2nd ed., pp. 784–805). Routledge. http://dx.doi.org/10.4324/9780203930236.ch29

Thompson, D. R., & Usiskin, Z. (2014). *Enacted mathematics curriculum*. Information Age Publishing.

Tomorrow 98. (1992). *A report for the Superior Committee for Science and Technology Education*. Submitted to the Ministry of Education (in Hebrew). http://www.weizmann.ac.il/particle/harari/sites/particle.harari/files/uploads/tomorrow-98.pdf

Wissehr, C., Barrow, L. H., & Concannon, J. (2011). Looking back at the Sputnik era and its impact on science education. *School Science and Mathematics, 111*, 368–375. http://dx.doi.org/10.1111/j.1949-8594.2011.00099.x

CHAPTER 11

Integrating Experimental Research Practices

Teachers' Professional Development in Significantly Different Educational Settings

Smadar Levy, Dorothy Langley and Edit Yerushalmi

Abstract

Ongoing calls to better represent experimental research practices in science instruction conflict with the structural constraints of high-stakes exams and limited resources of the instructional laboratory. These constraints favor closely prescribed tasks over open-ended ones involving iterative inquiry processes. Moreover, the teachers themselves need to undergo a process of change, as their practice is often shaped in the traditional laboratory. This chapter aims to inform educators and policymakers who are interested in creating professional development opportunities that encourage an inquiry culture in high-school physics, based on findings from three studies. First, we examined teachers' dispositions toward the integration of experimental research practices in the instructional laboratory. Then we examined the challenges faced by teachers, and their responses to them, in two long-term professional development programs in significantly different settings: (a) professional learning communities of physics teachers, incorporating Restricted Inquiry Laboratories adapted to the constraints of the national matriculation advanced-level physics laboratory exam; (b) the Research Physics Certification Program, serving teachers that mentor student teams carrying out long-term research projects leading to an additional matriculation credit. We compare the teachers' change processes in these two settings, and draw conclusions regarding achievable goals and pedagogical means to meet them.

Keywords

high-school physics – inquiry projects – laboratory – scientific practices – professional development – professional learning communities

DOI: 10.1163/9789004503625_011

1 Introduction

Calls to better represent the scientific process in science instruction are over a century old, starting with Dewey's critique on the manner in which school science is taught: "Science teaching has suffered because science has been so frequently presented just as so much ready-made knowledge, so much subject-matter of fact and law, rather than as the effective method of inquiry into any subject-matter" (Dewey, 1910, p. 124), and continuing to current position statements (Kozminski et al., 2014; National Research Council, 2013), which specify key scientific practices – behaviors that scientists engage in as they investigate and build models and theories about the natural world – that science instruction should strengthen. In particular, scientists identify the absence of experimental research practices in students' experimental experience, as portrayed in the cognitive task analysis of Nobel laureate Carl E. Wieman, which compared the experimental scientist's work to students' work in the instructional laboratory and revealed a disturbing mismatch that drives students to experience laboratory activities as closely prescribed (Wieman, 2015). Moreover, educators point to the iterative nature of the experimental physicist's work – the ability to construct, use, and revise models – as rarely manifested, even in upper-level university laboratories (Dounas-Frazer & Lewandowski, 2018).

In physics instruction, experimental research practices are integrated in course settings that differ in their structural features (e.g., designated hours, available equipment, credit) and as a result, in the scope and depth of the experimental research practices experienced by the students (Holmes & Wieman, 2016). At one end are inquiry-oriented instructional laboratories accompanying Introductory Physics courses (Doucette et al., 2019; Etkina et al., 2006; Gandhi et al., 2016; Kapach, 2014; Langley, 2001). These laboratories are limited in terms of resources, such as equipment and instructional time, thus restricting the scope and depth of the inquiry experience. At the other end are supplementary frameworks for capable and talented students, such as high-school research projects (Kapon, 2016; Perl Treves & Yerushalmi, 2018) and research apprenticeship programs (Sadler et al., 2010), allowing a prolonged, wider and deeper research experience.

In all of these settings, it is the teachers' responsibility to establish the norms and practices defining an inquiry-friendly classroom culture. However, the teachers themselves may need to engage in a significant learning process, as their habits and expectations are constructed within former experiences that are often shaped by the traditional, closely prescribed instructional laboratory. Such a process can be supported by professional development (PD) programs that are situated in teachers' practice (Penuel et al., 2007; Putnam & Borko, 2000) and scaffold participants along guidelines of the cognitive apprenticeship paradigm (Collins et al., 1991; Yerushalmi & Eylon, 2013). Scaffolding involves structuring collaborative reflection on classroom practice and problematizing challenging aspects in teachers' work (Reiser, 2004).

This paper describes and compares two PD programs for high-school physics teachers, both of which aim to support teachers introducing experimental research practices to their students, yet anchored in settings with significantly different structural features. One program took place within the national network of professional learning communities (PLCs) for advanced-level high-school physics teachers. The program consisted of a teacher leaders' PLC (N = 24) and 11 regional PLCs (N = 225). During the 2019 school year, one of the focal topics for the PLCs was Restricted Inquiry Laboratories (RILs), which were designed to structure and problematize the aspect of experimental design, while maintaining many features of the prescribed instructional laboratories to comply with the laboratory norms to which the teachers are accustomed. They first experienced the RILs as learners in four PLC meetings, then, if they were interested, tried them out in their classrooms, and finally, reflected upon their experience in a subsequent PLC meeting. The second program that we studied was the Research Physics Professional Development program (RP-PD) – an accelerated national certification program aimed at preparing teachers as research advisors (RAs) for students carrying out projects, as part of a national initiative to introduce a new school subject titled "Research Physics Project" (RP), which targets an elite group of capable and interested students (Arica, 2015). Successful completion of an 18-month-long research study grants students an extra matriculation credit, in addition to the advanced level physics credit. Table 11.1 summarizes the differences between the two PD programs.

Both PD programs are operated by the Physics Education Group in the Department of Science Teaching at the Weizmann Institute of Science, and are both supported by the Ministry of Education. Both programs are long-term and scaled up. Their design considered the three dimensions of the Model of Educational Reconstruction (MER) (Duit et al., 2005): (1) analysis of content structure – clarifying the scientific experimental practices; (2) construction of the intervention – the implementation of structuring and problematizing to scaffold the relevant pedagogical content knowledge (Shulman, 1987); (3) empirical investigations – the study of participants' conceptions, practices, achievements and learning processes in the context of the PD program.

The programs differ in several aspects. The RP-PD participants had chosen a-priori to participate in a PD program aimed at increasing students' autonomy in performing experimental research, and in collaborative reflection related to

TABLE 11.1 A comparison between the two PD programs

Dimension		RILs in the PLCs	RP-PD
School setting	Target audience	All advanced-level high-school physics students	Capable & interested students majoring in advanced-level high-school physics
	School laboratory setting	Standard high-school instructional laboratories	Regional, well-equipped laboratory in a community outreach arm of a research institution
	Research scope	Four RILs, 2–4 hours each	Research project, 18 months
	Assessment & credit	National laboratory exam, 15% of the advanced-level high-school physics matriculation grade	Personalized exam focused on students' project, 100% of the Research Physics Project matriculation grade
PD setting		National, one of the annual PLC topics, ~ 4 meetings	National, certifying RAs, 240 hours
Classroom experience		PLC participants could choose to implement RILs	RP-PD participants serve as RAs on a RP project

their prolonged interaction with one pair of students. The teachers experiencing RILs were not aware in advance that the PLCs would focus on experimental practices. In addition, they reflected upon a classroom experience involving a shorter interaction (2–3 lessons) with a larger group of students (10–20 pairs). Another difference is that the RILs afforded the teacher and students alike a narrow window for possible manipulations of an existing experimental system, whereas the RP-PD program granted autonomy in many experimental aspects, from the selection of a phenomenon to study, to the construction of an experimental system, and ultimately, to the presentation of the results for peer evaluation.

In the following sections, we first present study 1, examining initial dispositions with respect to experimental research practices in the large population of teachers participating in the PLCs: To what extent do they value various experimental research practices as learning goals for the instructional laboratory? Are they satisfied with their manifestation in the national physics laboratory exam? Do they perceive these practices as characterizing students' experience in the instructional laboratory vs. physicists' experience in a research laboratory?

We then present two studies that examine the PD of teachers in the two programs. Study 2 focused on the PLCs (involving 225 teachers), taking a survey approach to examine participants' PD with respect to the implementation of RILs: the extent to which participants implemented the RILs; the manner in which they operationalized student autonomy; the challenges they faced and how they coped with them.

Study 3 focused on the RP-PD program involving about 20 RAs, taking a case study approach. It looked in depth at four RAs and through them, portrayed central RAs' PD profiles within the certification program, with respect to their conceived roles in the context of mentoring student RP projects.

We conclude with a discussion of the commonalities and differences in teachers' initial operationalization of student autonomy, and the changes they underwent during collaborative reflection in the community of peers about their encounter with their students.

2 Study 1: Teachers' Dispositions toward Experimental Research Practices

The first study aimed to explore teachers' dispositions toward the experimental research practices outlined in key position papers. In particular, we focused on the following research questions:
- To what extent do teachers value various experimental research practices as learning goals for the instructional laboratory, and to what extent are they satisfied with the manifestation of these goals in the national physics laboratory exams?
- To what extent do teachers perceive various experimental research practices as characterizing students' experience in the instructional laboratory vs. physicists' experience in a research laboratory?

2.1 *Research Design*

2.1.1 Participants

The participants were teachers taking part in a national network of PLCs of high-school physics teachers. The study was carried out in 11 regional PLCs representing about a quarter of the national workforce of physics teachers, operating in the high-stakes setting of the advanced-level physics national matriculation exam. The study sample (N = 172) was based on teachers' attendance at the first PLC meeting of the 2019 school year. The participants represented diverse profiles, teaching at schools across a broad range of socio-economic levels. More than half (54%) were second-career teachers, who had transferred to physics teaching following an engineering career. The gender distribution was 37% females, 63% males; sector distribution was 74% Jews, 26% Arabs. The teachers had a wide range of teaching experience (1–49 years, Md = 7), and experience in preparing students for the national matriculation laboratory exam (0–30 years, Md = 5).

2.1.2 Data Collection and Analysis Tools

A questionnaire was administered during the first meeting of the 2019 school year in all 11 regional PLCs. In the first part, teachers were given a list of 11 experimental research practices selected from practices outlined in national and international key position papers (Kozminski et al., 2014; Ministry of Education, 2008; National Research Council, 2013):

1. Establishing the goals of the experiment and formulating measurable questions
2. Designing and improving an experiment in accordance with the difficulties encountered in execution
3. Using standard data analysis and representation tools
4. Using physical principles to predict phenomena studied in the experiments
5. Formulating a scientific argument linking the results of the experiment to the theory
6. Writing a report summarizing the results of the experiment and its conclusions
7. Taking responsibility and self-regulation while dealing with an open task
8. Teamwork
9. Proficiency in performing mandatory experiments in the national laboratory exam
10. Technical skills in using a variety of measuring tools
11. Deepening students' scientific knowledge and understanding

For each of these 11 practices, the teachers were asked to rate its importance and their satisfaction with its manifestation in the national laboratory exam on a 5-point Likert scale (5 – very important/very satisfied to 1 – not important at all/not satisfied at all). Cronbach's alpha reliability coefficient for this part of the questionnaire was 0.83 for the importance aspect and 0.91 for the satisfaction aspect.

The second part of the questionnaire was a modification of the E-CLASS survey (Wilcox & Lewandowski, 2016), in which students are presented with

30 statements representing strategies, habits of mind, and attitudes related to central laboratory practices, and are asked to rate their extent of agreement from both their personal perspective and that of a hypothetical experimental physicist. The modified version was composed of 21 selected translated statements pertinent to the national high-school laboratory context. The teachers were asked to rate the extent of their agreement with each statement on a Likert scale (5 – strongly agree; 1 – strongly disagree) from the perspective of an average student in their class working in a high-school instructional laboratory, and that of a hypothetical physicist in a research laboratory. Cronbach's alpha reliability coefficient for the second part of the questionnaire was 0.81 for the student's perspective and 0.77 for the physicist's perspective.

Both parts of the questionnaire were content-validated by six experts from the Weizmann Institute's Physics Education Research (PER) Group, as well as by the 24 teacher leaders.

2.2 *Analysis and Findings*

All 11 experimental research practices were highly valued by the teachers (M = 4.34, SD = 0.403), suggesting that teachers value the practices recommended in key position papers. Teachers' satisfaction with the manifestation of these experimental research practices on the national laboratory exam was lower (M = 3.74, SD = 0.658). Teachers' profile variables (see Participants section) did not affect the results.

There were significant disparities between the importance attributed to the practices and satisfaction with their manifestation in the national laboratory exam ($p < .0001$, paired t-test). These gaps might serve as an opportunity for professional development.

The disparity was particularly evident for practice 2 (importance M = 4.34, SD = 0.642; satisfaction M = 3.42, SD = 0.967), related to experimental design: "Designing and improving an experiment according to the difficulties encountered in execution," as revealed in repeated measures ANOVA. The disparity for practice 2 was the largest and was identified as a significantly separate group ($p < .0001$, Duncan's Multiple Comparisons test). Accordingly, teachers' satisfaction with the manifestation of practice 2 was identified (using repeated measures ANOVA) as significantly lower than all the other practices ($p < .0001$, Duncan's Multiple Comparisons test).

This disparity was echoed in teachers' perception of the experimental design practice as experienced by students in the instructional laboratory vs. physicists in a research laboratory. The deliberate nature of this practice was manifested most clearly in three statements in the survey: (1) "When doing an experiment, I try to understand how the experimental setup works"; (16) "A common approach for fixing a problem with an experiment is to randomly

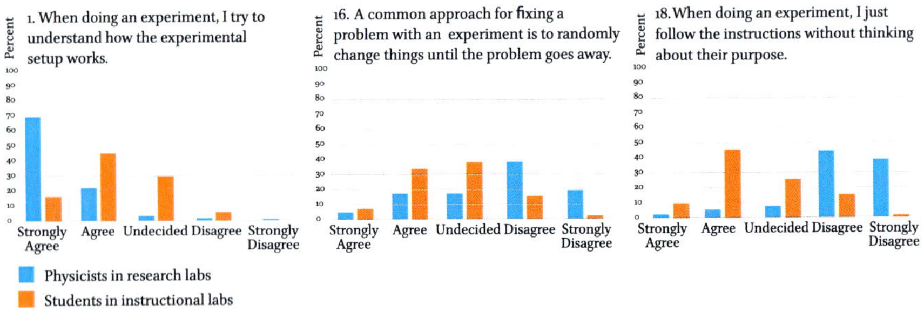

FIGURE 11.1 Teachers' views of strategies and habits of mind related to the practice of experimental design by physicists in research laboratories and students in the instructional laboratory. Frequency distribution

change things until the problem goes away"; (18) "When doing an experiment, I just follow the instructions without thinking about their purpose." Statement 1 is positive in terms of the desired laboratory practice of experimental design, whereas statements 16 and 18 are negative. With respect to all three statements, the teachers acknowledged a significant gap ($p < .0001$, paired t-test) between strategies and habits of mind from the perspective of students in the instructional laboratory and that of physicists in a research laboratory (Figure 11.1).

Teachers strongly agreed that physicists try to understand how an experimental setup works, students less so (Figure 11.1a). The practice of fixing a problem by randomly changing things (Figure 11.1b) was perceived by teachers as more typical of students and rare for physicists. They agreed that students, unlike physicists, follow instructions without thinking about their purpose (Figure 11.1c).

3 Study 2: PD of the PLC Teachers with Regard to the Integration of RILs

Study 2 focused on the PD of teachers in the national PLC network of high-school physics teachers, with regard to their experience with RILs. We first describe the intervention: the PLCs' mode of operation and the introduction of the RILs. Then we present the study of teachers' PD in this context.

3.1 *The PLC Context*

The national network of PLCs for high-school physics teachers served as the context to promote reform in the high-school physics instructional laboratory. The PLCs network operates in a "Fan Model" (Figure 11.2): 24 teacher leaders, all practicing high-school physics teachers, participate in a PLC operated by the PER group at the Weizmann Institute of Science. Simultaneously, they lead 11 nationwide regional PLCs of physics teachers (N = 225, teaching ~15,000

FIGURE 11.2 The "Fan Model" used in the PLCs program

high-school physics students). The teacher leaders' PLC and the regional PLCs meet alternately, twice a month, during the school year (for a total of 60 h).

The program was designed following research on PLCs that showed them to be an effective PD framework (Vescio et al., 2008), providing opportunities for teachers to collaboratively examine their teaching, as well as their students' learning (Borko et al., 2010), and to learn from one another (Grossman et al., 2001). The teachers' learning is situated in their practice, and is based on their active experiences in both the PLC meetings and their classes. The teacher leaders first experience each new instructional activity as learners in the teacher leaders' PLC, try it out with their students, and reflect collaboratively on their experiences in the next teacher leaders' meeting. They then implement the new activity in their regional PLC in a similar process (Levy et al., 2018).

The contents of the program are renewed every year, to serve a large majority of the PLC teachers that participate in the program for several years. There are two to four annual focal topics, each spanning three or four PLC meetings (Levy et al., 2020). To encourage implementation by so many teachers in diverse classrooms, the offered activities include a variety of examples in different subjects of the curriculum, for each of the high-school grade levels, and in accordance with the period during the school year.

3.2 *Representing Experimental Research Practices in the Instructional Laboratory: The RILs*

One of the topics chosen as the focus of the PLC meetings during the 2019 school year was the representation of experimental research practices in the instructional laboratory, toward shifting laboratory instruction away from closely prescribed laboratory norms. In particular, the emphasis was on experimental design, addressing the results of Study 1, namely, the large disparity between valued and implemented practices that teachers acknowledged with regard.

The physics teachers in the PLCs operate in a tightly constrained, test-driven context. The advanced-level high-school national laboratory exam requires students to master seven highly structured standard experiments. The laboratory equipment is intended to serve the mandatory laboratories and in many schools, there is a lack of the additional equipment needed for more open inquiry. Furthermore, there is a shortage of laboratory technicians, so many teachers have to prepare equipment and tackle problems with the experimental systems on their own. To address the structural constraints faced by most teachers in this large-scale program, a series of RILs was developed involving a modest restructuring of traditional laboratories. The RILs related to existing manuals of standard laboratory experiments. They encompassed experiments in Mechanics, Electromagnetism and Optics, transforming the manuals to encourage students to reflect on the considerations underlying their experimental design. The RILs were designed to accommodate the goal of providing more autonomy to students, within the structural constraints (e.g., time allotted for the activities, equipment available in schools, relevance to the national laboratory exam). Hence, students were not asked to design a complete experimental setup on their own. Instead, they were asked to either explicate the considerations underpinning one or more experimental setups, or design limited aspects of an experimental setup.

For example, one of the RILs presented students with five standard, ready-to-use experimental systems (Figure 11.3). Group work focused on discussing the considerations underlying the design of each of the experimental setups. One of these experimental systems was the Tangent Galvanometer, in which

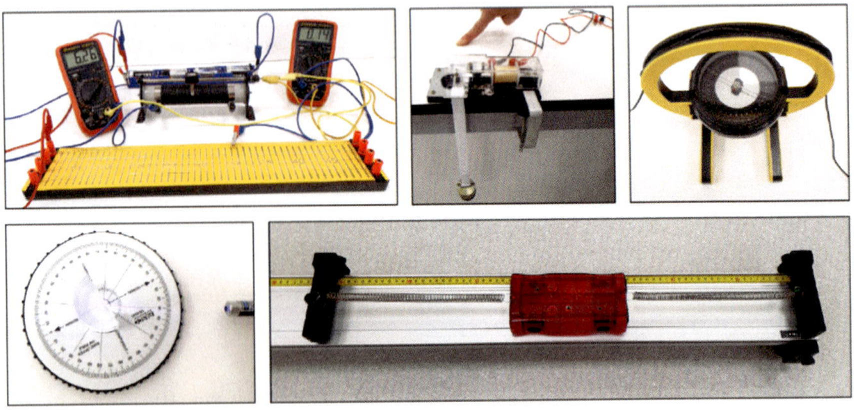

FIGURE 11.3 Experimental setups used in a sample RIL

the students discuss how to position the apparatus to take accurate measurements and why it is preferable to adjust the current in the loop and measure the angle obtained in the compass, rather than the other way around.

Another RIL involved a more substantial change in the experimental design of Newton's Second Law laboratory (relating force and acceleration): the students were given a vertical experimental system instead of the traditional horizontal set and were required to design how to control the experimental variables.

The PD activities followed the cognitive apprenticeship guidelines (Collins et al., 1991), in that they were situated in a complex and authentic pedagogical dilemma: introducing changes into the highly constrained setting of the school laboratory, and providing opportunities to externalize and reflect on the considerations underlying the experimental design, as well as on the nature of laboratory instruction. The teachers, and the teacher leaders, first experienced each RIL as learners; they collaboratively reflected on the strengths and weaknesses that they identified, and explicated the goals that the RILs could promote, as well as the challenges they expected to face in carrying out these activities in their classrooms. They were encouraged to try out RILs in their laboratory lessons and subsequently reflected collaboratively on classroom enactments of the restructured laboratories. The teacher leaders experienced this PD process before leading their regional PLCs in a similar PD process.

3.3 *Research Design*

The study examined the following research questions:
- To what extent did teachers implement the RILs? In particular, how did they operationalize student autonomy?
- What challenges did teachers face when implementing RILs, and how did they perceive their students' ability to cope with the changes?
- How did the teachers cope with the challenges they encountered?

3.3.1 Participants

The research participants were the physics teachers in all 11 regional PLCs that experienced the RILs (N = 225). The diverse profiles of the PLC teachers were as described for Study 1.

3.3.2 Data Collection and Analysis Tools

A post-questionnaire was administered at the last PLC meeting, toward the end of the school year. The questionnaire consisted of open-ended questions in which the teachers were asked whether they had implemented the RILs, what other changes they had made in their laboratory lessons, how their students coped with these changes, which challenges they faced as teachers, and how they addressed those challenges. The post-questionnaire was content-validated by the six PER experts, as well as by the 24 teacher leaders. Teachers' responses (N = 119) were analyzed qualitatively using the grounded theory approach (Glaser & Strauss, 1967). The categories were validated in an iterative process involving the coding of 70% of teachers' statements, and comparison and discussion by the first and third author until full agreement was reached.

3.4 *Analysis and Findings*

Despite the severe constraints within which the teachers operate, half (N = 61) implemented at least one RIL in their laboratory lessons, or alternatively, reported that they changed laboratory norms to give more autonomy to their students. The only significant difference found regarding background variables between teachers who did and those who did not implement RILs was experience in preparing students for the national laboratory exam (M = 8.2 years for those who implemented RILs vs. M = 5.0 years for those who did not, $p < .05$). This finding could be explained by the increased confidence to try changes that comes with more experience in instructional laboratory work.

In the following, we describe the findings of the qualitative analysis of the responses of the 61 teachers who implemented RILs in their laboratory lessons. In particular, we focus on three themes: (1) operationalization of student autonomy; (2) challenges in implementing the activities, in particular, how teachers perceived their students' ability to cope with the changing roles; (3) approaches to coping with the challenges.

3.4.1 Teachers' Operationalization of Student Autonomy

The RILs are designed to give some autonomy to students in various aspects of experimental design. The level of autonomy that teachers gave their students, as expressed in teachers' responses, spanned a wide range. Most of the teachers (87%) increased their students' autonomy by omitting some of the instructions in the traditional laboratory manual (64%) or by not using a laboratory manual at all (23%). Many teachers (39%) reported that they gave their students autonomy in designing many aspects of the experiments, e.g., "I let the students design the experiment on their own," whereas others focused on specific aspects. A third of the teachers asked students to plan how to control variables in the experimental system, e.g., "The students had to select the appropriate variables and decide how to control them." A few (16%) devoted more time to a preliminary discussion with their students about the goals and design of the experiments, and the rest (12%) referred to the analysis and interpretation of the results.

The variance in teachers' responses is not surprising, because both teachers and students are used to the traditional step-by-step laboratory manuals, and transferring more autonomy to students is a long and gradual process.

3.4.2 Implementation Challenges and Students Ability to Cope with the Changes

Teachers' responses were categorized into two main aspects of students' experiences while coping with the RILs: (1) students' engagement; (2) students' difficulties and frustration.

Students' engagement: Most of the teachers (85%) referred to students' engagement, e.g., "The students had to cope with the missing instructions, and think alone what to do"; "I really liked to hear their lively discussions, coping with the challenge together"; "The students were enthusiastic about being able to express their ideas"; "The students felt ownership and improved understanding of the experiment"; "The weaker students were excited by the chance to express their ideas."

Students' difficulties and frustration: More than half of the teachers (56%) were concerned about their students' difficulty coping with the challenge presented by the increased autonomy, e.g., "Some students failed to carry out the experiment, and some gave up"; "They had problems designing the experimental system on their own"; "Sometimes the students got stuck and needed guidance."

A third of the teachers were concerned about students' frustration when trying to cope with the changes, e.g., "The students did not understand what was required of them"; "The weak students felt even more abandoned than usual"; "There were crisis points for students who were less creative or less proficient in the subject."

Almost half of the teachers (41%) referred to their own class-management challenges while implementing the RILs, due to the differences between the students, e.g., "I had a hard time not knowing how the lesson would progress"; "I didn't know when and how to help the students"; "I tried to work without accurate instructions. Initially it created chaos and resentment, but in the end it paid off."

A third of the teachers referred to facing structural constraints, mainly shortage of equipment, e.g., "We do not have enough equipment for experiments other than those which are part of the mandatory curriculum"; "We have to be careful with the equipment, so it is important to tell students exactly what to do," and lack of time, e.g., " It took much more time, so we didn't finish. It was necessary to continue during the next lesson and set up the experimental system again"; "Much more time is needed to get a real sense of inquiry, time that we don't have."

3.4.3 Teachers' Approaches to Coping with the Challenges

Despite the challenges, almost half of the teachers (44%) reported that as a result of their experiences during the year, they intended to keep using RILS, and to give even more autonomy to their students in the future, e.g., "I plan to give the students less guidance next year, and to increase the 'degrees of freedom' in higher grades"; "I will continue to apply these ways of working in the lab, now that I have more confidence in how to go about it"; "I was surprised to find out how challenging it was for the students not to receive an immediate answer from the teacher on how and what to do."

On the other hand, about a third of the teachers were concerned about the challenges that they faced. About half of those stated that they planned to curtail the freedom they gave students somewhat, mainly because of students' difficulties and frustration, or time constraints, e.g., "I think it is important, but when you change a lab, even at a basic level and give students the opportunity to think about things themselves or design things, it takes much more time, and we don't have that time." The other half stated that they were planning various scaffolds to help students cope with the challenges, e.g., more explanations before the activity, hints during the activity, or different levels of autonomy to address students' heterogeneity. Almost a third of the teachers (28%) discussed the need to change their instructional priorities in the future to promote laboratory practices and integrate more RILS, e.g., "I have to think how to integrate these activities into the lab reports, which always have the same format. On the other hand, it is time that the lab report focus more on lab practices and less on the theory." Teachers also highlighted the demands of the new approach, as compared to those of the national matriculation laboratory exam, and raised the need to negotiate national assessment policies to enable implementation of the RILS.

4 Study 3: RAS' PD Profiles within the RP-PD Course

Study 3 corresponds to the research goal concerning the RAS' PD profiles within the certification program regarding their conceived roles in the context of mentoring RP student research projects. We first present the RP-PD context and describe how it was designed to reinforce specific conceived roles. Then, we present the study of teachers' PD in this context.

4.1 *The RA Certification (RP-PD) Course Context*

The RP-PD program is anchored in the context of the high-school RP project subject, launched in Israel by the National Physics Education Authority in 2016–17 as a system-wide educational initiative with a dual vision focusing on new opportunities for high-school students and teachers alike. It aims to allow capable and motivated high-school physics students to experience open-ended projects, developing their autonomy and ownership and providing a channel for scientific creativity (Stepanek, 1999). In contrast to research apprenticeships (Burgin et al., 2012), in which a single student acts as a novice apprentice (with very restricted opportunities for autonomy and ownership) in ongoing research in a scientist's laboratory away from school, RP is intended to take place in two-student research teams advised by a trained high-school teacher, within well-equipped high-school physics laboratories.

This study relates to the second cycle of a regional RP class which was run at the Davidson Institute – an outreach center at the Weizmann Institute of Science. A total of 34 high-school students were selected out of ~80 students who had participated in the preparatory 10th-grade stage. They met for weekly afternoon sessions over a period of 2 school years (11th and 12th grades). In the first semester of grade 11, they studied VPython programming and computational methods. Then, they were grouped into 17 research teams, and guided by RAs, they performed an 18-month-long research project. The RAs were supported by an academic and a pedagogical coordinator. At the end of grade 12, the projects were evaluated by an official external examiner and students were granted the RP matriculation credit.

Equally important, RP provides a PD avenue for physics educators seeking more relevance to 21st century real-world goals in their work, and in particular, establishes an arena in which the increasing number of recruits from various engineering domains can express their strengths and interests.

One of the main challenges of system-wide RP implementation was the need for the accelerated certification of RAs (namely, physics teachers who also serve as mentors for the students' research teams). A 240-hour, 2-year course was launched by the Science Teaching Department of the Weizmann Institute in August 2017, as one of two leading national certification frameworks. The course had two main components: (1) three concentrated courses during the summer vacation (90 hours), dedicated to experience, as students, of important aspects of physics research: small-scale research experiences, computational modeling methods, and advanced physics theory issues; (2) three extended courses, during the school year, dedicated to reflecting on experience as RAs for inquiry activities and research project work: an introductory unit (30 hours, August–October 2017) reflecting on the differences between traditional laboratory experiments and inquiry activities through workshop activities; a practical mentoring experience – acting as RAs to pairs of 11th-grade high-school students participating in the regional RP class, one team per RA; in parallel to the practical mentoring experience, the RAs participated for 2 years in a Research Advisors Community (120 hours, 2017–19) consisting of a series of activities that required them to deal with crucial issues involved in advising students who are carrying out RP projects. Each step in the practical mentoring process was conducted in tandem with the Research Advisors Community activities that accompanied the particular step prior to and during its performance, and following its completion.

Five milestones formed the overarching structure of the RP-PD course design and defined the RAs' expected roles: Research topic presentation and selection, Research proposal (intention declaration), Interim-stage (end of 11th grade) and final-stage (toward the end of 12th grade) presentations followed by feedback from a subgroup of advisors and student peers, and Summative evaluation. Each milestone involved work by the students and by the RAs, and interactions between them. This "formula" placed the RA in the role of "coach" who subdivides the "big project" into a sequence of steps, constructing, with the students, an action plan (often accompanied by a form) listing the details of the current step in the plan to be carried out autonomously, examines the students' products, and provides constructive feedback based on explicit quality criteria, upon which the students can base their revised products. This sequence ensures that the students are given and accept responsibility for progressing along the project's process, including backtracking when necessary, while the RA carries the burden of steering/monitoring the students between given stations along the path, and supporting compliance with timetables and the required product standards. To carry out his or her responsibility, the RA may need to consult with peers and coordinators about project alternatives and, given the time and resource constraints, study advanced content and experimental research practices.

Thus, learning to become RAs for high-school research projects entailed a major transformation for the teachers in three aspects: conceived role, scientific and experimental content knowledge, and research-management skills. The scaffolding of this complex transformation followed design principles derived from cognitive apprenticeship (Collins et al., 1991) – a combination of structuring and problematizing (Reiser, 2004). Structuring was accomplished by decomposing the complex task of research project mentoring and management into a specified sequence of milestones, with specific activities focusing effort and involving collaborative reflection and expert feedback in a community of peers led by academic and pedagogical leaders. The activities also served as tools for problematizing the aspect of "conceived roles," on which this study focuses.

To illustrate the RP-PD design and its expected impact on conceived roles, we focus on one of the PD goals: supporting teachers in presenting research project topics (Table 11.2).

TABLE 11.2 RP-PD design example: supporting teachers in presenting research project topics

Subgoals: Issues to be considered by RAs	PD design
Identifying general challenges involved in selecting research topics for RP projects	Problematizing: Small group discussion followed by plenum summary; eliciting RA expectations and coordinating with those of PD leaders.
Exposure to acceptable research project topics	Structuring: PD leader illustrates examples of past project topics that he or she mentored and identifies several research topic clusters (e.g., vibrations and coupling in springs and pendulums), and examples compatible with students' expected prior knowledge and knowledge extension potential.
Explication of specific challenges related to the suggested research topics	Structuring & Problematizing: Participants analyze the presented topics according to a given list of criteria e.g., theoretical, experimental and mentoring challenges.
Preparing the presentation of project topics	Structuring & Problematizing: Small groups, according to teachers' research topic preference, create a presentation of the research topic, receive feedback in the plenum and then, in the next session, display to student teams.

This sequence explicated, as evidenced in both the PD presentations and the RAs' reflections, some aspects of shaping RAs' conceived roles:

a. The RA is responsible for suggesting a variety of feasible broad topics (regarding physics content, equipment, available time) to student teams, rather than allowing free selection.
b. The RA is responsible for consulting with the student team to decide on a mutually acceptable research focus within the broad topic.
c. In exceptional cases, RAs can consider "risky" topics, but will need to monitor the students' progress closely, to safeguard the eventual outcome.

4.2 *Research Design*

The study examines the following research questions:

1. What were the teachers' initial conceived roles?
2. How did the teachers adapt their conceived roles in response to the interaction with student teams, peers and RP-PD leaders?

4.2.1 Participants

The RP-PD course included 14 participants whose backgrounds and concurrent occupations spanned a wide range, involving engineering and physics education in high school or college. Some of the participants were planning to offer RP as an additional elective credit to students at their home school, and their motivation was to receive the accreditation that would entitle them to run the program at their schools and receive the related benefits, as well as to collect experience and resources for implementing the RP program.

The current study focuses on participants who mentored research projects of students in the regional RP class in their second year of the course (November 2018–June 2019). We selected four RAs, aged 45 to 60 years, representing a variety of backgrounds and abilities, which can be considered four case studies and will be referred to by the pseudonyms Yulia, Izzac, Solomon and Matan. Table 11.3 presents the student teams and research topics that the teachers mentored.

Yulia was a graduate of the Rothschild–Weizmann MSc program without a thesis for excelling science teachers, a high-school physics teacher with over 20 years of teaching experience, with no engineering or research background. Izzac had an academic background in mechanical engineering and taught physics in an engineering college, in addition to his work as head physics teacher in a regional high school. Solomon was a retired engineer who decided

TABLE 11.3 Student teams and research topics mentored by the selected participants

RA	Student team	Research topic
Yulia	Two boys who were the mentor's students at school. One of the students developed learning difficulties in physics.	Elastic objects (spring, elastic band, Slinky spring): force vs. extension, oscillations, dynamics
Izzac	Two girls: a gifted student from a prestigious central school; a relatively new immigrant from an outlying boarding school.	One-dimensional horizontal oscillations of coupled carts connected to springs, vibration modes, resonance
Solomon	Two boys, school friends from an outlying boarding school. One student was visually impaired.	Water waves in an aquarium, the dispersion coefficient
Matan	Two boys, school friends from a central urban school.	Wilberforce pendulum, parametric oscillations

to launch a second career in physics education after a long career in the army and hi-tech industry. Matan was a hi-tech engineer and entrepreneur, with a physics degree, who had retrained as a physics teacher a few years back and hoped to implement his educational ideals as a high-school research project mentor.

4.2.2 Data Collection and Analysis Tools

Evidence was collected from several sources: observation summaries of weekly sessions between November 2018 and June 2019; RP-PD course assignments submitted during the 2018–2019 period; interviews following the final external examination (June 2019). Selected evidence from the data resources will be presented to show the PD process that the teachers underwent. The analysis attempts to present information regarding the initial state and evolving conceived roles along the research project's prescribed milestones within the context of the particular research project and student team.

4.3 *Analysis and Findings*

The RAs interacted with the student teams and dealt with the research-project management in ways that reflected their conceived roles.

4.3.1 What Were the Teachers' Initial Conceived Roles?

Case Study 1

Yulia was a novice mentor and a novice researcher: "I am experienced in preparing my students for the physics matriculation exams, I never had experience as a research project mentor."

Yulia hoped to develop professionally and raise her school's prestige by importing the RP subject. Her initial frame of reference was being a student in the course: "In the beginning, I was like a student myself… I brought lots of ideas… I felt that the responsibility was mainly on me." Since Yulia framed her position as " student," it followed that she first interpreted her role as "principal investigator" responsible for showing her abilities to the PD leaders. After a while, she realized that she had failed to engage the students: "In the beginning, I was a totally inexperienced mentor, and I believed that this was really my project… At a certain stage I realized that I was more interested in the project than they [the students] were."

Case Study 2

Izzac's statements and observed behavior placed him in the role of "accountable teacher." This belief guided Izzac's decisions regarding the content and scope of the research project he mentored:

> I am not here to discover new things in physics, with the danger of running into complications, and risking the failure of my students… The teacher's main task is to guide the students toward a successful completion of the course and achieving a high grade in the external exam… It is vital to consider the research topics offered to high-school students carefully, from the point of view of the content complexity.

Case Study 3

Solomon had some prior experience in guiding student research projects at his school. He was aware of the dilemma regarding the level of teacher involvement:

> Initially I was uncertain: To what extent should I lead? Tell them what to do?… Motivating students – for me, that is the most significant aspect of mentorship. I needed to create a situation in which the students felt they were leading the project, while in fact I significantly influenced the decision making… I started by presenting myself as one of the team.

Case Study 4

Matan's initial conceived role was "enabler" – providing total autonomy and expecting the students to respond accordingly. He entered the certification program with very strong views about learning management:

> My personal experience has led me to believe strongly in self-motivated and self-managed learning, driven by curiosity and the desire to understand the real world. My aim as a teacher is to provide students with opportunities for such learning.

4.3.2 How Did the Teachers Adapt Their Conceived Roles in Response to the Interaction with Student Teams, Peers and PD Leaders?

Case Study 1

Phase 1: Yulia mentored 2 students from her own physics class, so she knew what to expect regarding their background knowledge and abilities. She describes her attempt to balance authentic learning with RA support:

> They decided to handle the material independently, but they told me that they didn't understand it fully. In the next session, I explained the material, derived and explained the formulas.

Phase 2: After Yulia realized that the students had not fully engaged in the research process, she tried to correct the situation by drastically shifting the responsibility onto the students:

> I started learning how to give more responsibility to the students. If the students rejected ideas that I presented, I told them to bring their own ideas; 1–2 weeks passed and they did not deliver any ideas.

Yulia assumed the role of "enabler–advisor," without due regard for her students' lack of ability to take on the responsibility she had delegated to them. As a novice RA, Yulia lacked the skills and knowledge to construct a "ladder" which would lead and support the students in developing ownership of their project.

Case Study 2
Izzac's conceived role as "accountable teacher" manifested itself in the mentoring procedures he carried out with his two-girl team in the areas with which he was familiar and considered himself an expert:

> For material they could handle independently, I gave little support. Where they had no background (such as dealing with differential equations), I used a college textbook and gave them 3 or 4 lessons…

In areas in which Izzac lacked expertise, such as computational modeling, he "allowed" the students' autonomy:

> They proposed the idea of writing a VPython simulation to provide answers for coupled vibrations with arbitrary initial conditions.

Izzac's students' reflective summary provides additional evidence of his mentoring approach. The very capable two-girl team stated that they would have preferred greater freedom to explore.

Case Study 3
Solomon declared in the final interview:

> In every session, I included myself on the "to do" list. This is an example of "following the commander." The commander is not necessarily the one who knows what to do. He is the one who assumes responsibility for the process. Decisions are taken by the whole team.

Solomon's role metaphor of a commander entailed presenting a personal example of the expected team-member behavior, as well as stepping back a little to allow the team members to perform their tasks, under his "distant" supervision. He remained in command of the situation at all times, and did his share of the work, investing extraordinary amounts of time and taking advanced academic courses to complete his theoretical knowledge. Solomon's very ambitious students joined him in the advanced academic courses. One of them insisted on coding an advanced computational model of water waves. The reflective summary in the final project report provides evidence of their view of Solomon's mentoring approach:

> The project allowed us to carry out independent research and expand it as we wished. The freedom to explore was very significant for our learning.

Case Study 4
Matan's conceived role underwent a transformation following the students' inability to embrace the autonomy he provided, and his realization of the cognitive/emotional dissonance between his expectations and his project team's response:

> I needed to support them psychologically. This was a new experience for them. You need to generate trust. To create a feeling that you are their partner, rather than the teacher who will judge them.

In the final interview Matan admitted:

> Today I am less naïve than in the past. I used to believe that all that was needed was to enable, and the students would embrace the intellectual opportunity. That was an illusion.

Matan's conclusion was that while his basic approach may be valid, it cannot thrive in the educational climate that traditionally exists at school: "… this can become a frustrating experience, undermining the students' self-confidence and their directedness to future learning."

4.4 *Summary*

Conceived roles emerged as multifaceted personal constructs that were shaped by previous experience, designated RP-PD activities and modeling by course leaders, and interactions with students and peers in the course of acting as RAs of a particular student team performing a particular research project. Izzac and Solomon could proceed with their initial conceived roles because Izzac tailored the scope of the project to his abilities, while Solomon was willing to make a great effort to take the project beyond the scope of his initial theoretical and experimental knowledge, and the students were willing and able to follow. Yulia was forced to change her initial conceived role because the students experienced difficulties and could not engage in the research, and Matan realized that his initial belief about his students' abilities to function in the new learning culture he provided was mistaken, and that increased practical and psychological support was essential.

5 Discussion

We presented three studies. First, we studied the extent to which teachers are interested in better representing experimental research practices in students' laboratory experiences. We found that teachers' views regarding the instructional laboratory learning outcomes were aligned with the recommendations of the key position papers (Kozminski et al., 2014, National Research Council, 2013). However, the teachers acknowledged the disparities between the scientific practices in which students engage during the instructional laboratory and the practices of physicists in research laboratories, in particular with respect to experimental design. Thus, one would expect that regarding experimental design, teachers would be most receptive to making laboratory instruction more "science process-oriented" (Etkina et al., 2006).

We followed with two studies of the teachers' PD in different contexts: the introduction of RILs in a network of PLCs, targeting teachers who are accustomed to operating in the closely prescribed setting of instructional laboratories; and an accelerated certification program, aimed at advancing teachers as research project mentors of students in the novel RP school subject.

In the light of plausible initial predictions, we now look at the commonalities and differences between teachers' PD in these two contexts: their initial conceived roles, and the changes they underwent following the encounter with their students and the collaborative reflection in the community of peers.

Given that RP-PD participants had a-priori chosen to work in a relatively open context, as compared to the PLC teachers who were not aware in advance of the RIL component, a difference in the operationalization of student autonomy was expected between teachers participating in the two PD frameworks. On a "student-autonomy scale," this would have placed all of the RP-PD teachers at the high end of the scale, while the RIL teachers could be expected to be scattered along the entire scale (Brown et al., 2006).

Indeed, we found that despite the constraints in which the PLC teachers were operating, half of the participants implemented RILs in their laboratory lessons. The RIL teachers' reports on their classroom experiences indicated dispersion across the "student-autonomy scale": from the requirement of very little autonomy, merely involving students in a preliminary discussion on the design of the experiment to meet the experimental goals, to a higher level of autonomy, involving students in the independent design of the experiment.

Contrary to our expectations, however, was the variability in the initial approach to student autonomy held by the small RP-PD teacher sample. Yulia started by assuming the role of "chief investigator," leaving little space for student autonomy. Izzac dictated the topic, related theory, experimental setup, and scope and depth of the students' research from the start. The team's "autonomy" was expressed in their performance of the technical work. Solomon was prepared to grant his student team the level of autonomy that they demonstrated the ability to handle, in all aspects of the research. Matan started by granting his students total autonomy for the experimental design, but retained responsibility for the theoretical aspects.

Both PD frameworks covered year-long processes and included strong support by a community of peers. However, the experience of the teachers with their students differed significantly. The RP-PD teachers interacted with one pair of students on a scale of tens of meetings, whereas the RIL teachers interacted with a full classroom of their students (10–20 pairs) over two or three lessons. Thus, one might expect the awareness of the possible range of student reactions to be more noticeable amongst the RIL teachers.

We found that almost all of the PLC teachers were satisfied with their students' engagement when carrying out the RILs. However, they were concerned with students' difficulties and frustration when trying to cope with the changes: some students failed to complete the experiments, others asked for guidance, and some gave up. Almost half of the teachers faced class-management challenges, e.g., not knowing when and how to help students who differed in their ability to cope with the autonomy granted to them. Teachers were worried about the RILs taking more time than the traditional experiments, and it was unclear to them how the laboratory lesson should progress. As a result, while almost half of the RIL teachers stated that they intend to continue using RILs, and to give even more autonomy to their students in the future, about 20% stated that they plan to somewhat reduce the students' autonomy. About the same percentage stated that they would plan various scaffolds to help students cope with the challenges, such as more explanations before the activity, or hints during the activity. They also raised the need to negotiate national assessment policies to enable implementation of the RILs.

Regarding the RP-PD sample, the eventual PD process of two of the teachers depended largely on the particular student team they mentored, i.e., their ability and willingness to respond to the teacher's guidance. Yulia mentored two students; the functioning of one of these students had declined in the regular physics class. As an outcome, the team's ability and drive to cope with their project work was impaired. Accordingly, Yulia took upon herself the task of closely directing her students. Several months later, when she realized her students were not actively engaged in the research, she tried to shift the responsibility onto them, assuming the role of "coach/enabler." Matan's initial conception of his role was as "enabler," believing that he would be providing his students with the freedom to explore, which they wanted. After several months, Matan realized that his students were not able to cope with the lack of structure, and he needed to become "a coach." On the other hand, two teacher-mentors maintained their initial approach. Izzac, who mentored a team of two girls (one of whom had exceptional abilities and drive), remained the "teacher" throughout the process, seeing his main responsibility as ensuring thc students' success within the scope of his ability to guide them. Solomon assumed the role of "commander," leading his team in a daring mission beyond their boundaries of knowledge, demanding of himself no less than he demanded of his students, and providing inspiration, guidance and material equipment throughout the different stages of the project.

This comparison indicates that regardless of the inquiry context being studied – whether we are attempting a minor shift from the existing culture or a major shift to a context in which the instructional laboratory culture is seemingly irrelevant – the central challenge facing teachers is the change in classroom culture, i.e., the norms of the allocation of responsibility between the teacher and students. Shifting the responsibility for enhanced experimental practices to the students, as recommended by many prominent position papers, was supported in both discussed settings by reflection within a community of peers on the challenges of change and ways of responding to them. This reflection assisted the teachers in externalizing (for themselves) the components of the required cultural change, and extending the range of approaches to deal with them – depending on the teacher's readiness to undergo change.

While we gave examples of teachers' ability to adopt the less structured instructional path and the support that it requires, the challenge of the cultural change never ends, because different students present different challenges. Thus, sustaining the required cultural change necessitates continued maintenance by circles of support – beginning with the close community of peers, but equally important, the norms of the broader educational community by means of constant discourse concerning assessment policies (Abrahams et al., 2013) between the individual and institutional stakeholders (Hofstein & Lunetta,

2004). Such discourse was established in the described contexts via different methods. Within the RP-PD context, the discourse was constructed amongst the different stakeholders, with the academic backing of the Weizmann Institute facilitating the conceptualization and explication of the required evaluation components. In the PLCs context, a negotiation process between the PLC development team (giving the teachers a voice following their RIL experience) and the national Physics Education Committee resulted in the decision to establish a committee to reassess the physics laboratory curriculum.

It is important to emphasize that a close circle of peers is not sufficient to sustain change. Any change has to be justified by ensuring the critical element of the "teacher–student contract": success in the high-stakes examinations.

Acknowledgments

We would like to thank Zvi Arica, Esther Bagno, Hana Berger, Bat-Sheva Eylon, Zehorit Kapah, Zeev Krakover, Esther Magen, and David Perl Nussbaum for their contribution to the establishment, development and leading of the PD programs studied in this paper, and to the physics teachers and teacher leaders for their devotion to continuing PD.

References

Abrahams, I., Reiss, M. J., & Sharpe, R. M. (2013). The assessment of practical work in school science. *Studies in Science Education, 49*, 209–251. http://dx.doi.org/10.1080/03057267.2013.858496

Arica, Z. (2015). *Inquiry Physics Project – Questionnaire 03588*. Talk presented at "Paths to Inquiry," Annual Physics Teachers' Conference, at the Davidson Institute for Science Education, Rehovot, Israel (in Hebrew).

Borko, H., Jacobs, J., & Koellner, K. (2010). Contemporary approaches to teacher professional development. In E. Baker, B. McGaw, & P. Peterson (Eds.), *International encyclopedia of education* – part 7 (3rd ed., pp. 548–555). Elsevier. http://dx.doi.org/10.1016/b978-0-08-044894-7.00654-0

Brown, P. L., Abell, S. K., Demir, A., & Schmidt, F. J. (2006). College science teachers' views of classroom inquiry. *Science Education, 90*, 784–802. http://dx.doi.org/10.1002/sce.20151

Burgin, S. R., Sadler, T. D., & Koroly, M. J. (2012). High school student participation in scientific research apprenticeships: Variation in and relationships among student experiences and outcomes. *Research in Science Education, 42*, 439–467. http://dx.doi.org/10.1002/sce.20151

Collins, A., Brown, J. S., & Holum, A. (1991). Cognitive apprenticeship: Making thinking visible. *American Educator, 15*(3), 6–11.

Dewey, J. (1910). Science as subject-matter and as method. *Science, 31*(787), 121–127. http://dx.doi.org/10.1126/science.31.787.121

Doucette, D., Clark, R., & Singh, C. (2019). What's happening in traditional and inquiry-based introductory labs? An integrative analysis at a large research university. *arXiv preprint*, arXiv:1911.01362. http://dx.doi.org/10.1119/perc.2018.pr.doucette

Dounas-Frazer, D. R., & Lewandowski, H. J. (2018). The modelling framework for experimental physics: Description, development, and applications. *European Journal of Physics, 39*(6), 064005. http://dx.doi.org/10.1088/1361-6404/aae3ce

Duit, R., Gropengießer, H., & Kattmann, U. (2005). Towards science education research that is relevant for improving practice: The model of educational reconstruction. In H. E. Fischer (Ed.), *Developing standards in research on science education* (pp. 1–9). Taylor & Francis.

Etkina, E., Murthy, S., & Zou, X. (2006). Using introductory labs to engage students in experimental design. *American Journal of Physics, 74*, 979–986. http://dx.doi.org/10.1119/1.2238885

Gandhi, P. R., Livezey, J. A., Zaniewski, A. M., Reinholz, D. L., & Dounas-Frazer, D. R. (2016). Attending to experimental physics practices and lifelong learning skills in an introductory laboratory course. *American Journal of Physics, 84*, 696–703. http://dx.doi.org/10.1119/1.4955147

Glaser, B. G., & Strauss, A. L. (1967). *The discovery of grounded theory: Strategies for qualitative research.* Aldine de Gruyter.

Grossman, P., Wineburg, S., & Woolworth, S. (2001). Toward a theory of teacher community. *The Teachers College Record, 103*, 942–1012. http://dx.doi.org/10.1111/0161-4681.00140

Hofstein, A., & Lunetta, V. N. (2004). The laboratory in science education: Foundations for the twenty-first century. *Science Education, 88*, 28–54. http://dx.doi.org/10.1002/sce.10106

Holmes, N. G., & Wieman, C. E. (2016). Examining and contrasting the cognitive activities engaged in undergraduate research experiences and lab courses. *Physical Review Physics Education Research, 12*(2), 020103. http://dx.doi.org/10.1103/physrevphyseducres.12.020103

Kapach, Z. (2014). *From traditional laboratory to inquiry-based laboratory in high-school physics instruction: Professional development of teachers* [Unpublished doctoral dissertation]. The Weizmann Institute of Science.

Kapon, S. (2016). Doing research in school: Physics inquiry in the zone of proximal development. *Journal of Research in Science Teaching, 53*, 1172–1197. http://dx.doi.org/10.1002/tea.21325

Kozminski, J., Lewandowski, H., Beverly, N., Lindaas, S., Deardorff, D., Reagan, A., Dietz, R., Tagg, R., Eblen-Zayas, M., Williams, J., Hobbs, R., & Zwickl, B. (2014). *AAPT recommendations for the undergraduate physics laboratory curriculum.* AAPT. https://www.aapt.org/resources/upload/labguidlinesdocument_ebendorsed_nov10.pdf

Langley, D. (2001). *Integrating inquiry activities into physics instruction in a computer-based information technology environment* [Unpublished doctoral dissertation]. Weizmann Institute of Science.

Levy, S., Bagno, E., Berger, H., & Eylon, B. S. (2018). Physics teacher-leaders' learning in a national program of regional professional learning communities. In A. Traxler, Y. Cao, & S. Wolf (Eds.), *Physics education research conference proceedings.* Washington, DC. http://dx.doi.org/10.1119/perc.2018.pr.levy

Levy, S., Bagno, E., Berger, H., & Eylon, B. S. (2020). Motivators, contributors, and inhibitors to physics teacher-leaders' professional development in a program of professional learning communities: The case of a collaborative reading assignment. In Y. B. D. Kolikant, D. Martinovic, & M. Milner-Bolotin (Eds.), *STEM teachers and teaching in the digital era – Professional expectations and advancement in 21st century schools* (pp. 159–184). Springer. http://dx.doi.org/10.1007/978-3-030-29396-3_9

Ministry of Education. (2008). *Physics high-school curriculum.* Division of Curriculum Development, Israel Ministry of Education, Jerusalem, Israel.

National Research Council. (2013). *Next Generation Science Standards: For states, by states.* National Academies Press. http://dx.doi.org/10.17226/18290

Penuel, W. R., Fishman, B. J., Yamaguchi, R., & Gallagher, L. P. (2007). What makes professional development effective? Strategies that foster curriculum implementation. *American Educational Research Journal, 44,* 921–958. http://dx.doi.org/10.3102/0002831207308221

Perl Treves, D., & Yerushalmi, E. (2018). Preparing students for long-term open inquiry projects – Students' perspective [Poster presentation]. *Physics Education Research Conference,* Washington DC, August 1–2.

Putnam, R. T., & Borko, H. (2000). What do new views of knowledge and thinking have to say about research on teacher learning? *Educational Researcher, 29*(1), 4–15. http://dx.doi.org/10.3102/0013189x029001004

Reiser, B. J. (2004). Scaffolding complex learning: The mechanisms of structuring and problematizing student work. *Journal of the Learning Sciences, 13,* 273–304. http://dx.doi.org/10.4324/9780203764411-2

Sadler, T. D., Burgin, S., McKinney, L., & Ponjuan, L. (2010). Learning science through research apprenticeships: A critical review of the literature. *Journal of Research in Science Teaching, 47,* 235–256. http://dx.doi.org/10.1002/tea.20326

Shulman, L. (1987). Knowledge and teaching: Foundations of the new reform. *Harvard Educational Review, 57*(1), 1–23. http://dx.doi.org/10.17763/haer.57.1.j463w79r56455411

Stepanek, J. (1999). *Meeting the needs of gifted students: Differentiating mathematics and science instruction.* Northwest Regional Educational Laboratory.

Vescio, V., Ross, D., & Adams, A. (2008). A review of research on the impact of professional learning communities on teaching practice and student learning. *Teaching and Teacher Education, 24*, 80–91. http://dx.doi.org/10.1016/j.tate.2007.01.004

Wieman, C. (2015). Comparative cognitive task analyses of experimental science and instructional laboratory courses. *The Physics Teacher, 53*, 349–351. http://dx.doi.org/10.1119/1.4928349

Wilcox, B. R., & Lewandowski, H. J. (2016). Students' epistemologies about experimental physics: Validating the Colorado Learning Attitudes about Science Survey for experimental physics. *Physical Review Physics Education Research, 12*(1), 010123. https://doi.org/10.1103/PhysRevPhysEducRes.12.010123; http://dx.doi.org/10.1103/physrevphyseducres.12.010123

Yerushalmi, E., & Eylon, B. S. (2013). Supporting teachers who introduce curricular innovations into their classrooms: A problem-solving perspective. *Physical Review Special Topics – Physics Education Research, 9*(1), 010121. https://doi.org/10.1103/PhysRevSTPER.9.010121

CHAPTER 12

Models of Professional Development for High-School Chemistry Teachers in Israel

Rachel Mamlok-Naaman and Avi Hofstein

Abstract

Teachers are key to any sustainable reform or innovation in educational practices in general, and in chemistry teaching and learning in particular. The National Science Education Standards present a vision of learning and teaching science in which all students have the opportunity to become scientifically literate. The standards provide criteria for judging the quality of the professional development opportunities that teachers of science will need to implement. Professional development for teachers should be analogous to professional development for other professionals. Each teacher will encounter a large number of students during their years of work in the educational system, and they will therefore have a major impact on Science and Technology education at all levels. To meet the challenges of reforms in science education, we need to help schools and other educational institutions that are involved in these reforms meet the challenges of the times. One way to attain these goals is to treat teachers as equal partners in decision-making. In other words, teachers have to play a greater role in providing key leadership at all levels of the educational system, by attending long-term continuous professional development workshops.

Keywords

continuous professional development of chemistry teachers (CPD models of professional development) – action research – leadership – evidence-based professional development – teachers as curriculum developers – professional learning communities

1 Theoretical Background

In the theoretical background we will refer to: (1) teachers' role in achieving the goals in science education, (2) teachers as key for any sustainable innovation in educational practices, (3) long-term and continuous professional

 | DOI: 10.1163/9789004503625_012

development (CPD) to enable teachers to gain pedagogical content knowledge (PCK).

The critical role of teachers in attaining the goal of quality education in the sciences is highlighted in the research literature on education. An international policy document written by Osborne and Dillon (2008, p. 25) reflects a consensus on the importance of good quality teachers:

> Good quality teachers with up-to-date knowledge and skills are the foundation of any system of formal science education. Systems to ensure the recruitment, retention, and continuous professional training of those individuals must be a policy priority in Europe.

Teachers have repeatedly been described as being key for any sustainable innovation in educational practices (Eilks et al., 2006). There are a variety of professional development models and courses for teachers. Some of them are single-contact courses and traditional top-down models of in-service teacher training. The single-contact courses have been viewed critically by a few science educators and researchers (e.g. Smith & Neale, 1989; Tobin & Dawson, 1992). That is why long-term, extensive and dynamic professional development of science teachers was recommended in the framework of reform in science education (Loucks-Horsley & Matsumoto, 1999; National Research Council, 1996), which would allow teachers' sustainable learning (Anderson & Helms, 2001). Within such a framework, teachers receive guidance and support throughout the various stages of change implementation in the curriculum or in their teaching methods (Harrison & Globman, 1988). Any change of substantial character in science education should consist of long-term professional development programs (Huberman, 1993). Under these circumstances, it has been noted that in general, teachers are excellent learners, and are interested in trying to teach new curricula, as well as to improve and enrich their teaching methods (Joyce & Showers, 1983).

Teachers need to familiarize themselves with new ideas, and to understand the implications for themselves as teachers and for their students in the classroom before they adopt and adapt them. Previous research has highlighted important features that characterize effective CPD programs (Loucks-Horsley et al., 1998), such as: (1) engaging teachers in collaborative long-term professional development activities on teaching practice and student learning; (2) introducing teachers to the approach of real classroom contexts, through reflections and discussions of each other's teaching; (3) focusing on the specific content or curriculum that the teachers will be implementing.

Science has a rapidly changing knowledge base and long-term CPD is essential for school science teaching to become more meaningful, more inquiry-based, more educationally effective, and better aligned with 21st century science and its related socio-scientific issues. Thus, accomplished teaching of science can be defined in terms of the content knowledge (CK), pedagogical knowledge (PK), and PCK that teachers use in their teaching (Shulman, 1987). Teachers who feel confident in their PCK will also be able to develop a sense of ownership toward their educational profession (Mamlok-Naaman et al., 2007).

2 Models of Professional Development Programs for Chemistry Teachers Developed in Israel

The implementation of new content and pedagogical standards in science education in Israel, as in other countries, necessitates intensive, life-long professional development of science teachers. In Israel, in 1992, the Ministry of Education initiated a reform in science education (Tomorrow 98, 1992). The Tomorrow 98 report, which refers to the reform, includes 43 educational and structural recommendations for special projects, changes, and improvements in the areas of curriculum development and implementation, pedagogy of science and mathematics, and directions and actions to be taken in the professional development of science and mathematics teachers. More specifically, the report recommends:

- Providing science teachers with the opportunity to engage in life-long-learning.
- Creating an environment of collegiality and collaboration among teachers who teach the same or related subjects, an environment that encourages reflection on their work in the classroom.
- Incorporating the process of change into professional development (support for these goals can be found in Loucks-Horsley et al., 1998).

To attain these goals, regional centers for the professional development of science and mathematics teachers were established (for more details, see Hofstein & Even, 2001), and later – national centers. The National Center for Chemistry Teachers in Israel, for example, was established at the Weizmann Institute of Science in 2000. These national centers specialize in the CPD of science teachers. The centers are directed by experienced staff scientists of the departments of science teaching, and act as centrally located academic and practical home bases (hosting, for example, national conferences). The centers support and provide counseling for regional professional development programs, develop and provide resource materials, and evaluate the outcomes.

The underlying principles of the Israeli National Center for Chemistry Teachers derive from the notion that professional development programs conducted in the 21st century need to build on conclusions from the 'golden age' of science curriculum development and implementation and the first generation of National Science Education Standards (National Research Council, 1996). Thus, to make the learning of science more relevant to students, teachers should be involved in the content and pedagogy of the teaching and learning, and more recently, in the United States, in the design of the Next Generation Science Standards (National Research Council, 2013). The start of the 21st century saw the use of a more "bottom-up" approach for teachers' professional development, in which many of the decisions made regarding content and pedagogy of chemistry teaching involve teachers who have undergone long-term, leadership-type, professional experiences (National Research Council, 2013).

The model, which was used in designing the activities of the National Center for Chemistry Teachers, was based on chemistry leadership programs conducted from 1995 at the Weizmann Institute of Science (Hofstein et al., 2003), due to their success in the development of: (1) teachers' personal beliefs about themselves (their self-efficacy), about teaching chemistry, and about becoming leaders, (2) teachers' professional behavior and activities in their chemistry classroom, focusing primarily on the development of their PCK, and (3) leadership skills, ownership, and activities involving other chemistry teachers in and outside their schools (teachers' social development).

2.1 *Developing Leadership among Chemistry Teachers*

Leadership in the context of science education should be regarded as a person's ability to bring about changes among teachers and teaching. An innovative program, whose aim is to improve the pedagogy of chemistry education in the Israeli educational system, was developed at the Weizmann Institute's National Center for Chemistry Teachers. It focuses on a model aimed at the professional development of chemistry teacher leaders. Israel has a centralized education system. The syllabi and curricula are regulated by the Ministry of Education. Since the 1960s, the Ministry of Education has provided for the long-term and dynamic development of science curricula and their implementation. These initiatives are usually accompanied by short courses (summer schools) for science teachers in general, chemistry teachers in particular, intended to introduce them to the new approach and its related scientific background.

The program was planned with the assumption that the participants (chemistry teachers) are thoughtful learners; that they are prepared to be professional teacher leaders; that after completion of the program, the teachers would develop creative strategies for initiating reform in the way chemistry is taught, and in professionalizing other chemistry teachers. Consequently, it was decided to design the program around the following three components:

- Developing teachers' understanding of the current trends in chemistry teaching and learning to include both the content and pedagogy of chem-

istry learning and teaching; for example, with the current trend to make chemistry more relevant, it was suggested that new programs in chemistry should also include its societal and personal applications, technological manifestations, and those components that can be characterized as historical and relating to the nature of chemistry, in addition to the conceptual approach and the process of chemistry (Kempa, 1983).
- Providing teachers with opportunities to develop *personally, professionally,* and *socially* (Bell & Gilbert, 1994).
- Developing leadership among these teachers and enhancing their ability to work with other chemistry teachers.

The professional development program consisted of four partially overlapping steps: the teacher as learner, the teacher as teacher, the teacher as reflective practitioner and finally, for some of the teachers who were responsible for developing a high-level sense of ownership, the teacher as leader. The program extended over a period of two academic years, totaling 450 hours, conducted one day a week, in an effort to allow for the gradual development and growth of the participants' conceptions, beliefs, and changes in behavior – in other words, to allow enough time for the development of teachers personally, professionally, and socially. The first year of the program was mainly devoted to the development of the teachers' CK in various topics in chemistry that were characterized as relevant to the learners, have a historical background, and also have technological ramifications and applications. Among these topics were: forensic chemistry, solid-state chemistry, the chemistry of nutrition, and selected topics in the area of interactions between radiation and matter. In addition, a large segment of this first year was devoted to the development of the chemistry teachers' PCK. The second year was mainly devoted to the development of skills in the area of leadership.

The program for chemistry teacher leaders was designed to include all of the necessary components that comprise life-long professional development of science teachers, as well as components that are unique to the development of leadership among chemistry teachers. In the following sections, we provide examples of CPD models for chemistry teachers – models which were developed and implemented in the framework of the National Center for Chemistry Teachers (Mamlok-Naaman & Taitelbaum, 2019).

2.2 *Action Research*

Accomplished teaching should always occur simultaneously with reflection, to improve the teaching strategy. It should be followed by protocols assembled in a portfolio, which can be used to demonstrate evidence-based accomplished practice in science teaching, in an effort to achieve more effective teaching. The portfolio should document the activities, interactions, and behavior in the chemistry laboratory where inquiry-type experiments are implemented. It can be viewed as a systematic and organized collection of evidence used to monitor the growth of a learner's knowledge, skills, and attitudes in a specific content area.

One set of medium- to long-term strategies to connect research and practice, and researchers and practitioners, is the wide variety of action research methods (e.g., Bencze & Hodson, 1999; Eilks & Ralle, 2002; Feldman, 1996; Parke & Coble, 1997), or related strategies such as content-focused coaching (Staub et al., 2003), teachers' learning communities (Putnam & Borko, 2000), and knowledge-creating schools (McIntyre, 2005). These models have different foci and different strategies. However, they all include strong bottom-up and teacher-centered components. The differentiation among these strategies often lies in (1) the researcher–practitioner relationship and (2) (the degree to which OR whether) the approach is thought to implement a pre-thought concept efficiently vs. helping practitioners ask their own questions and develop their practice according to their own needs (see, e.g., Eilks, 2003; Eilks & Ralle, 2002; Eilks et al., 2010). In this context, action research is thought to be an inquiry by the teachers regarding their work and their students' learning in the classroom oriented to the needs of the practitioners (Feldman & Minstrel, 2000), or the development of new teaching strategies oriented to the deficits or interests of the teachers and their students (Eilks & Ralle, 2002). According to Feldman (1996), the primary goal of action research is not to generate new knowledge, whether more local or universal, but to change and improve classroom practices. Nevertheless, this point can be viewed differently depending on the action research mode chosen and the objectives negotiated within the group where the development of the individual practice and the generation of results of general interest can be seen as two sides of the same coin, holding equal importance (Eilks & Ralle, 2002).

Following the large number of examples in science education and beyond, action research is becoming a more and more widely accepted tool for the professional development of teachers in all stages of their career, including their pre-service preparation (e.g., Gipe & Richards, 1992; Gore & Zeichner, 1991; Korthagen, 1985). Loucks-Horsley et al. (1998) claimed that the strength of action research as a professional development strategy is that teachers either define the research questions or contribute to defining them in a meaningful way, and are actively involved in the research process (Parke & Coble, 1997). The use of action research as a strategy for professional development is based on the following assumptions (Loucks-Horsley et al., 1998, p. 97):

> Teachers are intelligent, inquiring individuals with important expertise and experiences that are central to the improvement of education practice. By contributing to or formulating their own questions and by collecting data to answer these questions, teachers grow professionally. Teachers are motivated to use more effective practices when they are continuously investigating the results of their action in the classroom.

For action research to be an effective means of helping teachers reflect on their practice, we must provide them with opportunities to engage in life-long professional development. A workshop can serve as an action research model of professional development. Such a project (e.g., Dass et al., 2008) focused mainly on allowing teachers to develop their own individual practices by enabling them to conduct small-scale action research studies in their schools. Therefore, a workshop structure was established to build the teachers' confidence in the area of conducting action research as part of their professional development. The course developed for this purpose was part of a wider educational program for chemistry teachers. Action research was selected as a topic within this program to (1) provide teachers with a powerful tool for enhancing their professional expertise by performing small-scale research projects in their local environments, (2) improve opportunities to practice the technique in the teachers' schools, and (3) create a professional community of connected, collaborating chemistry teachers. In planning the program, it was assumed that the teachers needed to improve their CK, PCK, and leadership skills to become professionals. Action research was assumed to offer potential solutions for all of these goals using a joint approach. The action research segment of the program was structured around a series of workshops teaching the methodology and research tools necessary for data collection and evaluation. This was carried out by coupling workshop phases with action research activities performed directly in the teachers' regular school environments. In between workshops, the teachers were asked to both discuss the content of the workshop with their school colleagues and apply the learned strategies and methods to several aspects of their own practice, including specific research questions involving different domains: pedagogical, affective, behavioral, and cognitive.

The action research meetings dealt specifically with the following topics and activities: (1) action research principles, (2) the qualitative research approach, (3) methodology (the rationale for choosing a subject for research, defining good research questions, types of research tools and data collection, methods of data analysis), (4) self-reflection during each of these stages, and (5) the presentation of reports. During the first four meetings, the workshop leaders

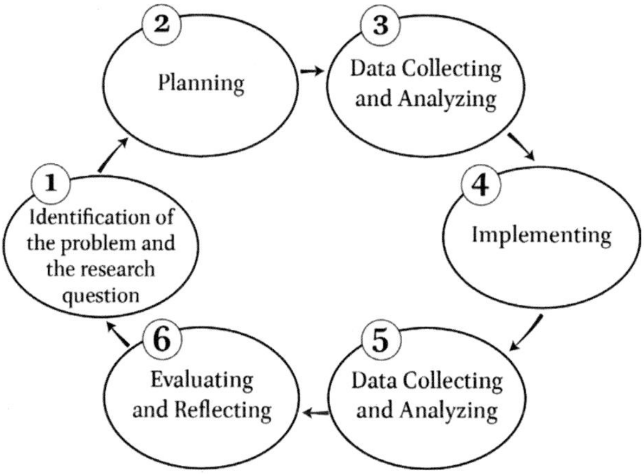

FIGURE 12.1
The various stages of action research

would present the theoretical framework and issues. The meetings that followed were then devoted to discussing the various stages of classroom-based action research: (1) identifying general problems and teachers' own research question; (2) planning the research, including the development of research tools; (3) data collection and analysis; (4) implementation; (5) further data collection and analysis; and (6) evaluating and reflecting on the results (Figure 12.1).

After each meeting, the participants were asked to meet with their colleagues at school and share with them the topics and subjects discussed in the workshops. In this way, the teachers involved their school's entire chemistry staff in the action research process. During the course meetings, participants reported on their work, discussed the difficulties that had arisen during their teamwork, and received comments, clarification, and support from other participants and the facilitators. The participants were advised to choose research questions that were relevant to their work in the school and in their classrooms.

The effects of the workshop were studied (Mamlok-Naaman et al., 2004, 2005). The main goal of the study was to discover how the action research workshop influenced the professional development of the participants. Ten female teachers were chosen to participate in this study. All of them taught chemistry in schools that were located in the central part of Israel and were attended mainly by middle-class students. Three sources of data were used for evaluation: (1) an opinion questionnaire administered after the course, (2) follow-up interviews (30 minutes each) employing open-ended questions given 1 year later, and (3) self-reported stories provided by the participating teachers (Lawrenz, 2001). The attitude questionnaire used the Likert format and was administered to the 10 teachers after completion of the workshop. The Likert items used a scale of 1–4 (4 – "fully agree" to 1 – "do not agree"). They included

TABLE 12.1 Teachers' attitudes regarding how the action research workshop contributed to their work (n = 10)

Statements related to the action research workshop	X	SD
It increased my interest in integrating action research into my own class	3.80	0.42
It encouraged me to strengthen my relationship with science-teaching experts	3.70	0.48
It improved my teaching strategies	2.80	0.92
It improved my ability to reflect on my work	3.70	0.48
I became part of a community of practice	3.80	0.42
I would be happy to participate in a continuing workshop on action research	3.60	0.52
I would recommend that my friends participate in a similar workshop	3.90	0.32

seven items assessing the teachers' opinions regarding the extent to which the workshop had contributed to both their professional development and their ability to continue using action research methods in their teaching practice. Table 12.1 summarizes the questionnaire and presents the participants' answers showing that the action research workshop contributed positively to their work (Mamlok-Naaman & Eilks, 2012).

According to the questionnaire, most of the teachers expressed satisfaction with the workshop. This was particularly true with respect to their personal interest in conducting action research in their own classrooms and in becoming part of a community of practice. Some participants did not feel that the workshop had broadened their teaching strategies. However, since our candidates were all experienced teachers, we assume that most of them already possessed a large repertoire of teaching strategies. From the interviews, three categories emerged by applying grounded theory (Glaser & Strauss, 1967): (1) enactment followed by reflection, (2) membership in a community of practice, and (3) contact with science-teaching experts. In the analysis, 7 of the 10 participants interviewed stressed the fact that they had learned the importance of reflecting upon their work using the methods taught during the action research process.

Some of them continued conducting interviews with their students, stating that their pupils raised very good points that contributed to their work. Almost all of the teachers claimed that they felt like members of a team during the workshop meetings, and that they continued to exchange ideas over a year later. During the action research workshop, the teachers established closer contact with the academic staff on a professional basis and could consult with the experts whenever they needed to.

We can conclude that the program presented here fulfilled its objectives. By integrating action research into their work, teachers can learn to better understand their students and how they think and learn. They can also increase their professional esteem and directly share their experiences with their colleagues. Both action research-based critical reflection upon one's own experiences and exchanges between trusted colleagues provide a promising environment for strengthening teachers' professional repertoire.

2.3 *Evidence-Based Professional Development for Chemistry Teachers*

In Israel, the inquiry laboratory was integrated into the teaching and learning of high school chemistry (Hofstein et al., 2005), and an evidence-based model for the CPD of chemistry teachers was developed and implemented (Taitelbaum et al., 2008). Use of the CPD model enabled teachers to gain the unique PCK needed to be good guides for their students. The inquiry approach entails that teachers try to recognize the way in which students think to help them construct their understanding and create rich and meaningful interactions in the classroom during the learning process. However, to use the inquiry approach, teachers need to undergo an intensive process of professional development, so that they will experience the same skills, knowledge, experience, and thinking habits as their own students (Windschitl, 2003). To be effective guides for their students, teachers must gain such skills as the ability to organize collaborative teamwork and promote students' questioning skills, keeping the classroom-laboratory workplace safe, and properly assessing students' work.

The model was developed during an evidence-based CPD program, which was part of a more comprehensive project (between Kings' College, London and the Weizmann Institute of Science) (Hofstein & Mamlok-Naaman, 2004) conducted at the Weizmann Institute's National Center for Chemistry Teachers. The main goal of the project was to develop, through collaborative research with teachers, a CPD program that focuses on a set of characteristics and protocols assembled in a portfolio be used to demonstrate evidence-based practice in teaching chemistry in the classroom laboratory using inquiry-type experiments, e.g., asking questions, defining research questions, drawing conclusions, participating in discussions, and writing laboratory reports (Taitelbaum et al., 2008). The key objective of the CPD program was to develop teachers' knowledge and pedagogy, through a design-based approach, so that they would be able to scaffold their students' acquisition of inquiry skills (Fortus et al., 2004). The CPD program was designed and implemented throughout a period of 3 years with 10 teachers. The first year focused mainly on developing a teacher's guide and planning a summer induction course. The program was implemented in the second and third years, with modifications between the second and third year. Ten high-school chemistry teachers participated in this program in each of the three years. They were novices in teaching the inquiry approach in chemistry laboratories, but most of them had several years of experience in teaching chemistry. The model consisted of three phases: (1) development of the CPD components, (2) summer induction course, and (3) a workshop, which included preparation of an evidence-based portfolio and videotaped observations and discussions. The workshop was accompanied by a study which demonstrated the changes undergone by the 10 teachers who participated in the workshop in terms of their professional behavior related to the inquiry program (Taitelbaum et al., 2008).

Based on the study findings and observations, Taitelbaum et al. (2008) suggested that teachers who teach chemistry according to the inquiry approach should develop a novel approach regarding their CK and PK. To provide students with guidance and support, the teachers themselves need to develop many of the earlier mentioned inquiry skills. A CPD model was developed to achieve these objectives. The model that was developed and implemented in this study was time-consuming and very intensive. We presented a model in which the teachers developed some of the needed skills. We also presented a few examples of how they developed a new pedagogical approach. The change in the method used in grouping the students, the change in managing the laboratories' lessons (for example, student-centered rather than teacher-centered), and the change in phrasing and posing an inquiry question, serve as examples of teachers' changes. The study was aimed at understanding some of the unique teaching strategies that teachers have to adopt when teaching the inquiry approach in their classes, and how these are developed and enriched throughout their various experiences. The study was based on teachers' points of view, for example, the different opportunities for reflection, and was supported by looking into their practice, e.g., observations. Although we observed various teaching strategies in the classroom laboratory, we decided to focus on group work because the literature points to its importance in achieving the teaching and learning goals (Shachar & Sharan, 1994; Sharan & Sharan, 1992; Slavin, 1990). Results of the study indicated that even a minor change in pedagogy, such as the grouping of students, can influence teachers' self-confidence. Reflecting upon the preparations and enactment of the inquiry activity helped them understand their professional improvement and progress (Taitelbaum et al., 2008).

The results also indicated that a change in CK, such as the phrasing of inquiry questions, is not immediate, and participating in a summer induction course is not enough for this change to occur. It was suggested that involving teachers in a reflective-type process accompanied by continuous support and scaffolding can promote the necessary professional development to include both CK and PK. In addition, once teachers had acquired this knowledge, they could use it explicitly as they guided and supported their students, thus making their guidance effective and meaningful.

It was suggested that during the CPD initiative, teachers had gained more self-confidence in critiquing their own work, understanding their teaching strategies in leading and tutoring students who work in small collaborative groups, and developing the investigative skills of students, e.g., discussing the types of questions posed, the nature of the hypotheses raised, the questions selected for further investigation, and the process of planning more experiments (Davis & Honan, 1998). For more details, please see chapter 7 in Mamlok-Naaman et al. (2018).

As already noted, teachers need to receive guidance and support throughout the various stages of their career (Harrison & Globman, 1988), and especially during their first years of teaching (Feiman-Nemser et al., 2000). Novice teachers should participate in long-term workshops and experience different models of CPD to become professionals as quickly as possible. The model described below exemplifies a professional development course in which experienced teachers participated with novice teachers with the aim of supporting the latter. The first working years of novice teachers are a critical stage in their success and long-term survival in the system (Feiman-Nemser et al., 2000). Supporting novice teachers is key in the professional development of both novice and experienced teachers (Elliott & Calderhead, 1995; Kajs, 2002). For the experienced teachers, the course empowered them and formed a significant stage in their professional development. They received recognition from the course coordinators for their ability to mentor a new generation of teachers. The novice teachers who participated in this type of course received support in the areas of CK, PK, and PCK, as well as in the affective aspects (Taitelbaum et al., 2008).

In summary, continuous support of teachers (novice and experienced) has the potential to enhance teachers' professional practice in an attempt to reach newer and higher pedagogical standards.

2.4 *Science Teachers as Curriculum Developers*

In the framework of reform in science education, there should be extensive, dynamic, and long-term professional development of science teachers (Loucks-Horsley & Matsumoto, 1999; National Research Council, 1996). Teachers need to receive guidance and support throughout the various teaching and implementation stages involved in changes in the curriculum (Harrison & Globman, 1988; Loucks-Horsley & Matsumoto, 1999). On the one hand, although teachers are excellent learners, and are interested in trying to adopt new curricula, as well as in improving and enriching their teaching methods, it is not easy for them to undergo modifications that include changes in content and in the ways they teach (Joyce & Showers, 1983). An interdisciplinary science curriculum differs from a subject-oriented one. Science teachers usually receive good preparation in teaching the traditional science curriculum – i.e., one or two science disciplines – but not integrated science. However, they need to learn the knowledge, skills, attitudes, and teaching skills to teach interdisciplinary topics (Bybee & Loucks-Horsley, 2000). They should be encouraged to expand their repertoire of student-assessment strategies to include techniques such as observation checklists, portfolios, and rubrics (Wiggins & McTighe, 1998).

For example, one of the ways to overcome teachers' anxiety regarding reforms such as Science, Technology and Society (STS), consists of their active involvement in the development of learning materials, instructional techniques, and related assessment tools (Loucks-Horsley et al., 1998; Parke & Coble, 1997). Similarly, Sabar and Shafriri (1982) claimed that "Participation in curriculum development, which is a protracted process, is likely to take the teacher from a conscious phase to one of greater autonomy and internalization phase" (p. 310). It is generally believed that involving teachers in the process of curriculum development leads to a wide variety of pedagogical ideas regarding instructional techniques and their related tools (Connelly & Ben-Peretz, 1980).

Based on this rationale, we designed a workshop for science teachers to implement learning materials and to develop assessment tools for a "Science for All" program (Mamlok-Naaman et al., 2007), described in the following. The workshop was accompanied by evaluation procedures, to determine whether the objectives of the STS were being accomplished. The workshop participants met eight times for 4 hours every other week. Two science education researchers conducted the STS workshop and the research associated with it. They were experts in curriculum development and in the professional development of teachers. The workshop was initiated to address the teachers' questions: "what strategies should we use in teaching STS-type modules, and how should we assess the students who are studying such modules?"

The workshop participants consisted of 10 science teachers from 10 different high schools in Israel. Each taught the Science for All program in one class and had at least 10 years of high-school science-teaching experience, mainly in grades 10–12. All of them had already participated in several in-service professional development workshops. Their scientific backgrounds differed, including areas such as chemistry, biology, agriculture, nutrition, technology, and physics. The teachers had already taught the Science for All modules but had difficulty using a variety of teaching strategies in general, and in grading and assessing their students in particular. Each of the teachers who participated in the workshop had taught at least one of the Science for All modules in one class consisting of about 30 students. The workshop coordinators focused on guiding the participating teachers in using a variety of teaching strategies, and in the development of auxiliary assignments used in this workshop, consisting of detailed checklists (rubrics) and rating scales.

In the first three meetings, the participating teachers were exposed to lectures and activities related to alternative assessment tools and methods, and especially to how they should get used to working with rubrics. Each teacher prepared the assignments for his or her students, followed by assessment tools. The assessment tools included tests, quizzes, assessment guides for carrying out mini-projects, essay writing and critical reading of scientific articles. All of the assignments were developed in stages, each of which required consideration and an analysis of assessment criteria, as well as scoring. These assignments were administered stage-by-stage at school. Students were involved in the assessment methods and their respective weights. The students learned how to be aware of the alternative assessment method, the weight percentage for each of the assessment components, and the final grade. This continuous assessment provided them with more control over their achievements. At each stage, students would submit their papers to the teacher for comments, clarification, and assessment. They would meet the teachers before and after school for extra instruction and consultation. The detailed checklist given to each student after each assignment compelled them to address the comments with the utmost seriousness if, of course, they wanted to improve their grade.

The students reflected on their work and ideas at each stage, and followed their teacher's comments on a detailed checklist and corrected them accordingly. Thus, they were able to improve their grades. The teachers revised the rubrics related to the assignments at each stage. Samples of the student assignments were brought to the workshop for further analysis and the process involved both the coordinators and their colleagues – the participating teachers. The group discussed the revision of the rubrics, and agreed on the percentage (weight) allocated to each of the assignment components. They also agreed on the criteria for performance levels, to grade the students as objectively as possible. The different components of the workshop were (1) discussions of the teaching methods, (2) preparation of learning and auxiliary materials and assessment tools, (3) development of rubrics – criteria for the assessment of the assignments, (4) analysis of samples of student assignments, and (5) improvement and revision of the rubrics according to samples of the student assignments. At the end of the year, the students in each class presented their assignments to an audience of their peers from parallel classes, their parents, science teachers, and the school principal.

The goal of the study, which followed the workshop, was to find out whether the objectives of the workshop had been attained. The researchers used teachers' self-report questionnaires and interviews (Mamlok-Naaman et al., 2007). This decision was based on the literature (Lawrenz, 2001) claiming that such instruments can be regarded as valid and reliable if they are administered and the data are collected when a person's almost immediate response can be obtained.

Regarding the students, the researchers focused on the affective aspects of learning and not on the cognitive ones, since one of the main objectives of the reform in Israel is to make science an integral part of all citizens' education (Tomorrow 98, 1992). Thus, changing the attitudes of non-science-oriented students to science is one of the main objectives of the reform in Israel. Five sources of data were used: (1) an attitude questionnaire administered to participating teachers, (2) semi-structured interviews with the teachers, (3) minutes of the meetings, (4) an attitude questionnaire administered to the students, and (5) structured interviews with the students. The interviews and minutes were analyzed using basic methods of qualitative data analysis (Glaser & Strauss, 1967; Tobin, 1995).

The findings of the study (Mamlok-Naaman et al., 2007) revealed that the teachers who participated in the workshop had gained self-confidence in the teaching and assessment methods of this new interdisciplinary curriculum and were motivated to try new content and teaching strategies. Moreover, they could better understand the advantages of the alternative assessment methods and were better prepared to use them. They were satisfied with their accomplishments and felt pride in their work.

Teachers' knowledge of science is based on previous experiences (von Glaserfeld, 1989), and on doing and experiencing (Gilmer et al., 1996). Moreover, it has been shown that personal involvement helps in reducing the anxiety involved in teaching an unfamiliar subject (Joyce & Showers, 1983). Therefore, teachers who actually develop the teaching strategies and assessment materials get a better understanding of how it should be taught and experience some kind of self involvement: they are part of the curricular process (Parke & Coble, 1997), feel pride in their work, and become producers rather than consumers (Sabar & Shafriri, 1982). The new curriculum materials also appeared to be effective vehicles for teachers' learning (Bybee & Loucks-Horsley, 2000). They were involved in the development of learning materials as well as the teaching strategies and assessment tools, which must be tailored adequately to the students' cognitive and affective characteristics, as mentioned by Ben-Peretz (1990).

The teachers who participated in the workshop were aware of the difficulties that could arise regarding the validity and reliability of the assessment tools. Thus, they made great efforts to improve and revise the assignments and rubrics according to the students' assignments. In fact, their anxiety about the alternative assessment methods gradually declined when they realized that the continuous assessment of students' progress and achievements, consisting of detailed and clear assessment instructions, could present a broad, valid, and reliable picture of their students' knowledge and abilities. To attain a wide range of assessment models, clearly, time is needed to construct a supporting framework for science teachers (Westerlund et al., 2002). Indeed, the teachers in the workshop were continuously supported and assisted by the workshop coordinators.

Three European projects in which the Chemistry Group in the Weizmann Institute's Department of Science Teaching is involved may serve as additional examples of the model:

- Popularity and Relevance in Science Education and Literacy (PARSEL), a project promoting relevance and interest in science education for scientific literacy, to initiate learning through everyday language and to guide the students to recognize their lack of conceptual science learning for considering everyday issues or concerns (Blonder et al., 2008).
- Professional Reflection-Oriented Focus on Inquiry-Based Learning and Education through Science (PROFILES), a project aimed at disseminating inquiry-based science education (IBSE). To achieve this, the PROFILES partners use and conduct innovative learning environments and programs for the enhancement of teachers' CPD. All participants involved in the PROFILES project are supported by stakeholders from different areas of society (Hofstein et al., 2012).
- Teaching Enquiry with Mysteries Incorporated (TEMI) – a project aimed to help teachers transform science and mathematics teaching practice across Europe by giving them new skills to engage with their students, exciting new resources, and the extended support needed to effectively introduce inquiry-based learning into their classrooms (Peleg et al., 2017).

In summary, teachers who implement a new curriculum should receive sustained support to gain knowledge of different teaching strategies and assessment skills. This can be done by attending professional development workshops that deal with those topics, which will consequently stimulate their creativity and diversify their instructional strategies in the classroom. Such skills should improve their ability to teach and understand their students' learning difficulties. Since they will better understand the goals, strategies, and rationale of the curriculum, they will feel more qualified to modify it as needed. We believe that such workshops help more teachers become producers rather than just consumers, and to gain a sense of ownership (Hofstein et al., 2012). Such efforts and reform in the way students are assessed (school-based assessment) necessitate approval and support from other people who are not directly connected to the program, namely school principals, science coordinators, and regional government consultants (Krajcik et al., 2001).

2.5 *The Development of Professional Learning Communities* (PLCs)

Creating PLCs for teachers is an effective bottom-up method of bringing innovation into the science curriculum through professional development. The PLC models are based on principles of learning that emphasize the co-construction of knowledge by learners, who in this case are the teachers themselves. Teachers in a PLC meet regularly to explore their practices and their students' learning outcomes, analyze their teaching and their students' learning processes, draw conclusions, and make changes to improve their teaching and their students' learning (Tschannen-Moran, 2014). The concept of PLC arose in the field of education in the context of workplace-based studies conducted in the 1980s that addressed teachers whose professional relations were characterized by continuous striving for improvement, focused on student learning, and who collaborated and explored their work. Such relationships differ from the norms used in the teaching of a more individualistic culture, which typically characterizes schools as a place of work (Lortie & Clement, 1975).

In 1982, Little conducted an anthropological study of six primary and secondary schools in four counties in the western United States. She found that schools with norms of collaboration, collegiality, and research responded better to the pressures of external changes and education initiatives (Little, 1982). This finding was reinforced by Rosenholtz (1989), who combined surveys and interviews with 78 primary schools. She distinguished "rich" and "poor" schools with respect to learning. The learning-rich schools were more likely to establish norms of cooperation and continuous improvement.

Newmann (1996) argued that a professional community of teachers offers a supportive environment in which teacher learning can occur. For example, the Center for Organizing and Building in Schools at the University of Wisconsin conducted systematic research on 24 primary, junior high, and high schools in which structural and organizational changes had been carried out, with an emphasis on the quality of instruction in mathematics and social sciences. It was found that aspects of a school's professional community that include common norms and values, a focus on student learning, reflective dialogue, transformation of teachers' practice in public classes, and a focus on collaboration, are linked to robust teaching and support for teacher learning.

Shulman (1997), in his lecture at the Mandel Institute in Israel, spoke enthusiastically about the idea of both teacher communities and student communities. He argued that since a single teacher can never possess perfect knowledge of pedagogical content, we must continue to create conditions in which a teacher can collaborate with other teachers and be part of a community of teachers facing difficult teaching challenges. In other fields, no one expects a single professional working alone to solve an important problem, because complex, real-world problems require "distributed expertise" – the sharing of highly specialized professionals in dealing with common challenges.

Bryk et al. (2010) identified professional communities, along with a work-oriented culture (Markic et al., 2016), toward improvement and access to professional development, with elements of "professional capacity" associated with improvements measured in primary school achievement in Chicago over a period of 6 years in the 1990s. A recent study by Kraft and Papay (2014) reinforced this important insight. These researchers used a measure for professional environment that was composed of teachers' responses to a survey in North Carolina combined with a national test in mathematics and elementary school reading. They found that teachers who work in a supportive environment, compared to those who work in a less supportive one, have increased effectiveness over time.

In Israel, at the Weizmann Institute of Science, PLC workshops for chemistry teachers were initiated in 2016, supported by the Ministry of Education and sponsored by the Trump Foundation, the Weizmann Institute of Science, and the National Center for Chemistry Teachers at the Weizmann Institute. The workshop operates on a cascade model: a leading team of researchers guides a group of teachers, who will then lead communities of teachers in regional communities – "professional learning communities close to home" (see Figure 12.2).

To date, the chemistry teachers who have participated in the PLC workshops have claimed that the professional community environment improved their self-efficacy and enhanced their ability to share teaching difficulties with their colleagues. The teaching culture was improved, as the community increased the degree of cooperation among teachers, including trust, ownership and friendship (Tschannen-Moran, 2014). They said that during the meetings, a feeling of trust was developed among the participants, which enabled them to discuss and analyze their students' cognitive and affective problems, misconceptions, and learning outcomes. In addition, the fact that they could share

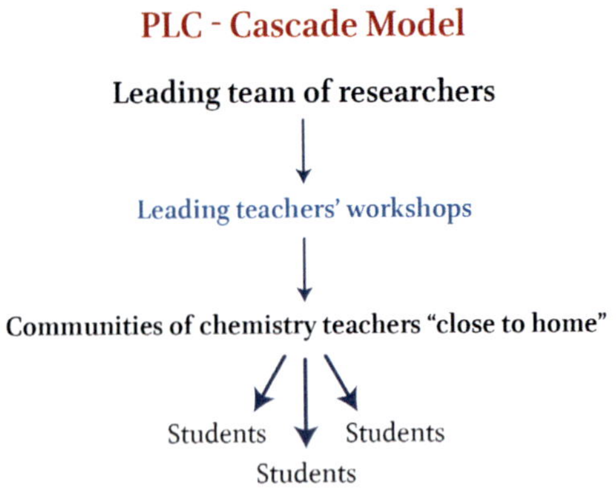

FIGURE 12.2
PLC cascade model (from Mamlok-Naaman et al., 2018)

ideas, lesson plans and interesting experiments was an asset in itself. They were encouraged to develop ownership of innovations in education, becoming more student-centered (Mamlok-Naaman et al., 2018).

The PLC has an impact on teaching practices, and serves as a perfect environment for preparing and encouraging teachers to conduct changes – toward gaining PCK in conveying important issues in education, and preparing the future citizen in a mixed cultural society, focusing on the processes of learning rather than the accumulation of knowledge, with the aim of enabling students to be innovative, creative, and critical.

3 Summary

The education system in Israel is centralized. The syllabi and students' final examinations (matriculation) in the sciences are controlled by the Ministry of Education. However, the way in which science is taught – its contents and pedagogy, is often controlled by science education centers, such as departments of science teaching and national centers for science teachers. Over the last decade, in these institutions, science teachers have been involved in many CPD initiatives, aligning the teaching to students' various needs and abilities, as well as to the teachers' professional and social development. However, Israel is a multicultural state, and in some cultures, lecturing is the prevalent teaching method: the students are passive receivers of knowledge, and construction or transformation of that knowledge is not an essential part of their learning (Dkeidek et al., 2011). In this chapter, we chose to describe five models of professional development that, over the years, have been implemented in the National Center for Chemistry Teachers. Each of the models is unique, has its own educational goals, and addresses different types of teacher populations.

The first model (leadership workshops for teachers) is aimed explicitly for future teacher leaders in science education. It consists of four phases: the teacher as learner (getting acquainted with the CK); the teacher as teacher (experiencing new pedagogies and teaching strategies); the teacher as reflective practitioner (getting used to structured self-reflections); the teacher as leader (leading innovations and changes in the educational system).

The other four models (action research, evidence-based professional development, teachers as curriculum developers, and PLCs) present long-term strategies to connect research and practice, as well as researchers and practitioners (Mamlok-Naaman & Eilks, 2012). They include bottom-up initiatives (e.g., teachers who develop their own learning materials and assessment tools), reflection strategies, and inquiry skills, among others. By attending these professional development workshops, teachers felt that they had gradually become part of a community of practice, developing a sense of ownership toward the projects that they were a part of. Some of these teachers developed a strong sense of ownership, and became teacher leaders, namely providing leadership for future CPD initiatives. It should be noted that one of the difficulties regarding implementation of new learning materials, modules or pedagogies is the need to provide teachers with continuous support. These teacher leaders are expected to help in these initiatives.

To sum up, during professional development programs, teachers develop socially; they learn how to collaborate with their colleagues in new ways, and how to receive support and feedback from them (Bell & Gilbert, 1994; Mamlok-Naaman et al., 2013). There are various models of professional development, and teachers may choose the ones that match their needs at a certain stage in their career and in alignment with the educational system's demands.

References

Anderson, R., & Helms, J. (2001). The ideal of standards and the reality of schools: Needed research. *Journal of Research in Science Teaching, 38*, 3–16. http://dx.doi.org/10.1002/1098-2736(200101)38:1<3::aid-tea2>3.0.co;2-v

Bell, B., & Gilbert, J. (1994). Teacher development as personal, professional, and social development. *Teaching and Teacher Education, 10*, 483–497. http://dx.doi.org/10.1016/0742-051x(94)90002-7

Bencze, L., & Hodson, D. (1999). Changing practice by changing practice: Toward more authentic science and science curriculum development. *Journal of Research in Science Teaching, 36*, 521–539. http://dx.doi.org/10.1002/(sici)1098-2736(199905)36:5<521::aid-tea2>3.0.co;2-6

Ben-Peretz, M. (1990). Teachers as curriculum makers. In T. Husen & N. T. Postlethwaite (Eds.), *The international encyclopedia of education* (2nd ed., pp. 6089–6092). Pergamon Press.

Blonder, R., Mamlok-Naaman, R., & Hofstein, A. (2008). Analyzing inquiry questions of high-school students in a gas chromatography open-ended laboratory experiment. *Chemistry Education: Research and Practice in Europe*, 9, 250–258. http://dx.doi.org/10.1039/b812414k

Bryk, A. S., Gomez, L. M., & Grunow, A. (2010). *Getting ideas into action: Building networked improvement communities in education.* Carnegie Foundation for the Advancement of Teaching. http://dx.doi.org/10.1007/978-94-007-1576-9_7

Bybee, R. W., & Loucks-Horsley, S. (2000). Supporting change through professional development. In B. Resh (Ed.), *Making sense of integrated science: A guide for high schools* (pp. 41–48). BSCS Science Learning.

Connelly, F. M., & Ben-Peretz, M. (1980). Teachers' role in the using and doing research and curriculum development. *Journal of Curriculum Studies*, 12, 95–107. http://dx.doi.org/10.1080/0022027800120202

Dass, P., Hofstein, A., Mamlok, R., Dawkins, K., & Pennick, J. (2008). Action research as professional development of science teachers. In I. V. Erickson (Ed.), *Science education in the 21st century* (pp. 205–240). Nova.

Davis, C. L., & Honan, E. (1998). Reflections on the use of teams to support the portfolio process. In N. Lyons (Ed.), *With portfolio in hand: Validating the new professionalism* (pp. 90–102). Teachers College Press.

Dkeidek, I., Mamlok-Naaman, R., & Hofstein, A. (2011). Effect of culture on high-school students' question-asking ability resulting from an inquiry-oriented chemistry laboratory. *International Journal of Science and Mathematics Education, 9*, 1305–1331. http://dx.doi.org/10.1007/s10763-010-9261-0

Eilks, I. (2003). Co-operative curriculum development in a project of participatory action research within chemical education: Teachers' reflections. *Science Education International*, 14(4), 41–49.

Eilks, I., & Ralle, B. (2002). Participatory action research in chemical education. In B. Ralle & I. Eilks (Eds.), *Research in chemical education – What does this mean?* (pp. 87–98). Shaker.

Eilks, I., Ralle, B., Markic, S., Pilot, A., & Valanides, N. (2006). Ways towards research-based science teacher education. In I. Eilks & B. Ralle (Eds.), *Towards research-based science teacher education* (pp. 179–184). Shaker.

Eilks, I., Markic, S., & Witteck, T. (2010). Collaborative innovation of the science classroom by participatory action research – Theory and practice in a project of implementing cooperative learning methods in chemistry education. In M. Valenčič Zuljan & J. Vogrinc (Eds.), *With the teacher's innovation and research to student's quality knowledge*. University of Ljubljana.

Elliott, B., & Calderhead, J. (1995). Mentoring for teacher development: Possibilities and caveats. In T. Kerry & A. S. Mayes (Eds.), *Issues in mentoring* (pp. 35–58). Routledge.

Feiman-Nemser, S., Carver, C., Schwille, S., & Yusko, B. (2000). Beyond support: Taking new teachers seriously as learners. In M. Scherer (Ed.), *A better beginning – Supporting and mentoring new teachers* (pp. 3–13). Association for Supervision and Curriculum Development.

Feldman, A. (1996). Enhancing the practice of physics teachers: Mechanisms for the generation and sharing of knowledge and understanding in collaborative action research. *Journal of Research in Science Teaching, 33*, 513–540. http://dx.doi.org/10.1002/(sici)1098-2736(199605)33:5<513::aid-tea4>3.0.co;2-u

Feldman, A., & Minstrel, J. (2000). Action research as a research methodology for study of teaching and learning science. In A. E. Kelly & R. A. Lesh (Eds.), *Handbook of research design in mathematics and science education* (pp. 429–455). Lawrence Erlbaum Associates.

Fortus, D., Dershimer, R. C., Krajcik, J., Marx, R. W., & Mamlok-Naaman, R. (2004). Design-Based Science (DBS) and student learning. *Journal of Research in Science Teaching, 41*, 1081–1110. http://dx.doi.org/10.1002/tea.20040

Gilmer, P. J., Grogan, A., & Siegel, S. (1996). Contextual learning for premedical students. In J. A. Chambers (Ed.), *Selected papers from the 7th National Conference on College Teaching and Learning* (pp. 79–89). Florida Community College at Jacksonville.

Gipe, J. P., & Richards, J. (1992). Reflective thinking and growth novices' teaching abilities. *The Journal of Educational Research, 86*, 52–54. http://dx.doi.org/10.1080/00220671.1992.9941827

Glaser, B. G., & Strauss, A. L. (1967). *The discovery of grounded theory: Strategies for qualitative research.* Aldine.

Gore, J., & Zeichner, K. (1991). Action research and reflective teaching in preservice teacher education: A case study from the United States. *Teaching and Teacher Education, 7*, 119–136. http://dx.doi.org/10.1016/0742-051x(91)90022-h

Harrison, C., Hofstein, A., Eylon, B., & Simon, S. (2008). Evidence-based professional development of science teachers in two countries. *International Journal of Science Education, 30*, 577–591. http://dx.doi.org/10.1080/09500690701854832

Harrison, J., & Globman, R. (1988). *Assessment of training teachers in active learning: A research report.* Bar-Ilan University (in Hebrew).

Hofstein, A., Carmi, M., & Ben-Zvi, R. (2003). The development of leadership among chemistry teachers in Israel. *International Journal of Science and Mathematics Education, 1*, 39–65. http://dx.doi.org/10.1023/a:1026139209837

Hofstein, A., & Even, R. (2001). *Developing chemistry and mathematics teacher leaders in Israel.* ERIC Clearinghouse for Science, Mathematics, and Environmental Education.

Hofstein, A., & Mamlok-Naaman, R. (2004). *Chemistry inquiry lessons* [Presented paper]. Meeting of the American Educational Research Association, April, San Diego, CA, USA.

Hofstein, A., Navon, O., Kipnis, M., & Mamlok-Naaman, R. (2005). Developing students' ability to ask more and better questions resulting from inquiry-type chemistry laboratories. *Journal of Research in Science Teaching, 42*, 791–806. http://dx.doi.org/10.1002/tea.20072

Hofstein, A., Katchevich, D., & Mamlok-Naaman, R. (2012). Teachers' ownership: What is it and how is it developed? In C. Bolte, J. Holbrook, & F. Rauch (Eds.), *Inquiry-based science education in Europe: Reflections from the PROFILES Project* (pp. 55–58). Alpen-Adria-Universität Klagenfurt.

Huberman, M. (1993). Linking the practitioner and researcher communities for school improvement. *School Effectiveness and School Improvements, 4*, 1–16. http://dx.doi.org/10.1080/0924345930040101

Joyce, B., & Showers, B. (1983). *Power and staff development through research on training*. Association for Supervision and Curriculum Development.

Kajs, L. T. (2002). Framework for designing a mentoring program for novice teachers. *Mentoring and Tutoring, 10*, 57–69. http://dx.doi.org/10.1080/1361126022013315З

Kempa, R. F. (1983). Developing new perspectives in chemical education. In *Proceedings of the 7th International Conference in Chemistry, Education, and Society* (pp. 34–42). Montpellier, France.

Korthagen, F. A. J. (1985). Reflective teaching and preservice teacher education in the Netherlands. *Journal of Teacher Education, 36*(5), 11–15. http://dx.doi.org/10.1177/002248718503600502

Kraft, M. A., & Papay, J. P. (2014). Can professional environments in schools promote teacher development? Explaining heterogeneity in returns to teaching experience. *Educational Effectiveness and Policy Analysis, 36*, 476–500.

Krajcik, J. S., Mamlok, R., & Hug, B. (2001). Modern content and the enterprise of science: Science education in the 20th century. In L. Corno (Ed.), *Education across a century: The centennial volume* (pp. 205–238). National Society for the Study of Education.

Lawrenz, F. (2001). Evaluation of teacher leader professional development. In C. R. Nesbit., J. D. Wallace., D. K. Pugalee, A.-C. Miller, & W. J. DiBiase (Eds.), *Developing teacher-leaders: Professional development in science and mathematics*. ERIC Clearinghouse for Science, Mathematics, and Environmental Education.

Little, J. (1982). Norms of collegiality and experimentation: Workplace conditions of school success. *American Educational Research Journal, 19*, 325–340. http://dx.doi.org/10.3102/00028312019003325

Lortie, D. C., & Clement, D. (1975). *Schoolteacher: A sociological study*. University of Chicago. http://dx.doi.org/10.1177/019263657505939422

Loucks-Horsley, S., Hewson, P. W., Love, N., & Stiles, K. E. (1998). *Designing professional development for teachers of science and mathematics.* Corwin Press.

Loucks-Horsley, S., & Matsumoto, C. (1999). Research on professional development for teachers of mathematics and science: The state of the scene. *School Science and Mathematics, 99*, 258–271. http://dx.doi.org/10.1111/j.1949-8594.1999.tb17484.x

Mamlok-Naaman, R., & Eilks, I. (2012). Different types of action research to promote chemistry teachers' professional development – A joint theoretical reflection on two cases from Israel and Germany. *International Journal of Science and Mathematics Education, 10*, 581–610. http://dx.doi.org/10.1007/s10763-011-9306-z

Mamlok-Naaman, R., Eilks, I., Bodner, A., & Hofstein, A. (2018). *Professional development of chemistry teachers* (pp. 76–80). RSC Publications. http://dx.doi.org/10.1007/s10337-018-3634-x

Mamlok-Naaman, R., Hofstein, A., & Penick, J. (2007). Involving teachers in the STS curricular process: A long-term intensive support framework for science teachers *Journal of Science Teacher Education, 18*, 497–524. http://dx.doi.org/10.1007/s10972-007-9046-7

Mamlok-Naaman, R., Navon, O., Carmeli, R., & Hofstein, A. (2004). A follow-up study of an action research workshop. In B. Ralle & I. Eilks (Eds.), *Quality in practice oriented research in science education* (pp. 63–72). Shaker.

Mamlok-Naaman, R., Navon, O., Carmeli, M., & Hofstein, A. (2005). Chemistry teachers research their own work two case studies. In K. M. Boersma, O. De Jong, & H. Eijkelhof (Eds.), *Research and the quality of science education* (pp. 141–156). Springer. http://dx.doi.org/10.1007/1-4020-3673-6_12

Mamlok-Naaman, R., Rauch, F., Markic, S., & Fernandez, C. (2013). How to keep myself being a professional chemistry teacher? In I. Eilks & A. Hofstein (Eds.), *Teaching chemistry – A studybook: A practical guide and textbook for student teachers, teacher trainees and teachers* (pp. 269–298). Sense Publishers. http://dx.doi.org/10.1007/978-94-6209-140-5_10

Mamlok-Naaman, R., & Taitelbaum, D. (2019). The influences of global trends in teaching and learning chemistry on the chemistry curriculum in Israel. *Israel Journal of Chemistry, 59*, 1–11. http://dx.doi.org/10.1002/ijch.201800088

Markic, S., Mamlok-Naaman, R., Hugerat, M., Hofstein, A., Dkeidek, I., Kortam, N., & Eilks, I. (2016). One country, two cultures – A multi-perspective view on Israeli chemistry teachers' beliefs about teaching and learning. *Teachers and Teaching: Theory and Practice, 22*, 131–147. http://dx.doi.org/10.1080/13540602.2015.1055423

McIntyre, D. (2005). Bridging the gap between research and practice. *Cambridge Journal of Education, 35*, 357–382. http://dx.doi.org/10.1080/03057640500319065

National Research Council. (1996). *National science education standards.* National Academy Press. http://dx.doi.org/10.17226/4962

National Research Council. (2013). *Next Generation Science Standards: For states, by states.* National Academies Press.

Newmann, F. M. (1996). *Authentic achievement: Restructuring schools for intellectual quality.* Jossey-Bass. http://dx.doi.org/10.17226/18290

Osborne, J., & Dillon, J. (2008). *Science education in Europe: Critical reflections.* A report to the Nuffield foundation. https://mkonuffieldfounpg9ee.kinstacdn.com/wp-content/uploads/2019/12/Sci_Ed_in_Europe_Report_Final1.pdf

Parke, H. M., & Coble, C. R. (1997). Teachers designing curriculum as professional development: A model for transformational science teaching. *Journal of Research in Science Teaching, 34,* 773–789. http://dx.doi.org/10.1002/(sici)1098-2736(199710)34:8<773::aid-tea2>3.0.co;2-s

Peleg, R., Yayon, M., Katchevich, D., Mamlok-Naaman, R., Fortus, D., Eilks, I., & Hofstein, A. (2017). Teachers' views on implementing storytelling as a way to motivate inquiry learning in high-school chemistry teaching. *Chemistry Education Research and Practice, 18,* 304–309. http://dx.doi.org/10.1039/c6rp00215c

Putnam, R. T., & Borko, H. (2000). What do new views of knowledge and thinking have to say about research on teacher learning? *Educational Researcher, 29,* 4–15. http://dx.doi.org/10.3102/0013189x029001004

Rosenholtz, S. J. (1989). *Teachers' workplace: The social organization of schools.* Addison-Wesley Longman Ltd.

Sabar, N., & Shafriri, N. (1982). On the need for teacher training in curriculum development. *Studies in Educational Assessment, 7,* 307–315. http://dx.doi.org/10.1016/0191-491x(81)90008-0

Shachar, H., & Sharan, S. (1994). Talking, relating and achieving: Effects of cooperative learning and whole-class instruction. *Cognition and Instruction, 12,* 313–353. http://dx.doi.org/10.1207/s1532690xci1204_2

Sharan, Y., & Sharan, S. (1992). *Expanding cooperative learning through group investigation.* Teachers College Press.

Shulman, L. S. (1987). Knowledge and teaching: Foundations of the new reform. *Harvard Educational Review, 57*(1), 1–23. http://dx.doi.org/10.17763/haer.57.1.j463w79r56455411

Shulman, L. S. (1997). *Communities of learners & communities of teachers.* Mandel Institute.

Slavin, R. (1990). *Cooperative learning: Theory, research and practice.* Prentice Hall.

Smith, D. C., & Neale, D. C. (1989). The construction of subject matter knowledge in primary science teaching. *Teaching and Teacher Education, 5,* 1–20. http://dx.doi.org/10.1016/0742-051x(89)90015-2

Staub, F. C., West, L., & Bickel, D. D. (2003). What is content-focused coaching? In L. West & F. C. Staub (Eds.), *Content-focused coaching. Transforming mathematics lessons* (pp. 1–17). Heinemann.

Taitelbaum, D., Mamlok-Naaman, R., Carmeli, M., & Hofstein, A. (2008). Evidence-based Continuous Professional Development (CPD) in the Inquiry Chemistry Laboratory (ICL). *International Journal of Science Education, 30*(5), 593–617.

Tschannen-Moran, M. (2014). *Trust matters: Leadership for successful schools.* John Wiley & Sons. http://dx.doi.org/10.1080/09500690701854840

Tobin, K. (1990). Research on science laboratory activities: In pursuit of better questions and answers to improve learning. *School Science and Mathematics, 90,* 403–418. http://dx.doi.org/10.1111/j.1949-8594.1990.tb17229.x

Tobin, K. (1995, April). *Issues of commensurability in the use of qualitative and quantitative measures* [Presented paper]. Annual Meeting of the National Association for Research in Science Teaching, San Francisco, CA.

Tobin, K. G., & Dawson, G. (1992). Constraints to curriculum reform: Teachers and the myths of schooling. *Educational Technology Research and Development, 40*(1), 81–92. http://dx.doi.org/10.1007/bf02296708

Tomorrow 98. (1992). *Report of the superior committee on science mathematics and technology in Israel.* Ministry of Education and Culture (English Edition: 1994).

von Glaserfeld, E. (1989). Cognition, construction of knowledge, and teaching. *Synthese, 80,* 121–140. http://dx.doi.org/10.1007/bf00869951

Westerlund, J. F., Garcia, D. M., Koke, J. R., Taylor, A. T., & Mason, D. S. (2002). Summer scientific research for teachers: The experience and its effects. *Journal of Science Teacher Education, 13,* 63–83. http://dx.doi.org/10.1023/a:1015133926799

Wiggins, G., & McTighe, J. (1998). *Understanding by design.* Merrill Prentice Hall.

Windschitl, M. (2003). Inquiry project in science teacher education: What can investigative experiences reveal about teacher thinking and eventual classroom practice? *Science Education, 87,* 112–143. http://dx.doi.org/10.1002/sce.10044

CHAPTER 13

Professional Learning Communities for Science and Technology Teachers

Models and Modeling

Zahava Scherz, Bat-Sheva Eylon and Anat Yarden

Abstract

This chapter describes an evolving professional learning community (PLC) project for science and technology (S&T) teachers in Junior High Schools across Israel. The 5-year (2015–2020) S&T teacher PLC project started with one national leading teachers' PLC and grew to 22 regional PLCs around Israel. The PLC characteristics were: shared setup and structured process; relations of trust and norms of collaboration; targeted focus on student learning; assessment-based learning and decision-making; and reflective dialogues and inquiry. Two PLC models evolved during the 5 years of this research-based project: a multilevel Collaboration Model of community skills enhancement; and a Network Model of knowledge transmission among S&T PLC participants. Data from questionnaires, interviews, and various meetings indicate that PLC members developed professional profiles that combined aspects such as S&T education proficiencies, a sense of mission, a desire for excellence, passion, commitment, and the motivation to have an impact.

Keywords

professional learning community – teacher professional development – middle school science – STEM – science and technology – professional development models

1 Introduction

Teaching science and technology in Junior High School (JHS) presents significant challenges as well as enormous opportunities. Science and technology are among the most important resources of modern society and for this reason, "Science and Technology (S&T)" education for every child should be an important mission for the Israeli education system (Tomorrow 98, 1992). According

 | DOI: 10.1163/9789004503625_013

to the present regulations of the national curriculum in Israel, science is not compulsory after JHS (grades 7–9) and therefore, JHS may be the last opportunity for Israeli children to acquire a basic S&T education and develop positive attitudes toward S&T subjects. The methods and pedagogies used for S&T subjects that are taught at this stage, to a great extent, determine whether and how many students will continue studying S&T subjects in high school. Therefore, teachers need to continuously develop their disciplinary knowledge, pedagogical content knowledge, and ability to integrate 21st century skills into their S&T teaching.

In the last few years, many educational professional development programs in Israel have adopted the format and philosophy of the professional learning community (PLC). Some PLCs target professional teachers from specific school disciplines. We advocate for the embedding of these PLCs' pedagogical considerations and community-building activities in the disciplines' contents and capabilities, in order to create a unique professional development environment (Borko et al., 2010; DuFour, 2004). Here, we elaborate on a 5-year S&T PLC (2015–2020) project that started with 1 PLC and grew to 22 regional PLCs around Israel. We describe the conceptual structure and main characteristics of the S&T PLC project and refer, in particular, to two models that evolved during the 5 years of research, development, and implementation: a four-level model for developing *collaboration skills* of PLC members and a *network model* of knowledge transmission among S&T PLC participants.

2 The S&T PLC Program

2.1 *Characteristics*

There is no consensus in the literature regarding the definition of PLCs. A consideration of characteristics that are highlighted in many studies (Bolam et al., 2005; DuFour, 2004; Grossman et al., 2001; Koellner et al., 2011; Little, 2012; Vescio et al., 2008) and our own experience in running research-based continuing professional development programs with science educators, led us to the following characterization: PLCs provide a framework for a group of educators to meet regularly and develop norms of trust and sharing. The educators actively investigate their teaching, collect evidence from their practice and their students' learning, reflect collaboratively on their practice, and learn from one another. The last decade has seen the fruit of an initiative that promoted the enacting of national, regional and in-school teacher PLCs in Israel, carried out in various disciplines (e.g., mathematics, language, science). In particular, there has been a major effort to distinguish PLCs from

TABLE 13.1 Characteristics of teachers' PLCs

Characteristics	Description
Relations of trust and norms of sharing	Relations of trust and mutual respect create a safe environment that enables teachers to learn and develop professionally. The PLC serves as a responsive and proficient "safety net" in the event of challenging experiences.
Regular meetings and mechanisms, structured processes	Optimal learning processes require a well-maintained setup: regular meetings with schedules, meeting times, pleasant physical conditions, and more.
Focus on student learning, and the connections between teaching and learning	Pedagogical discourse in PLCs focuses on student learning and its relationship to teaching.
Decision-making based on data collection and evaluation	To achieve better learning and teaching, alternative assessment methods are discussed (e.g., systematic analysis of student assignments, classroom observations, interviews) while collecting, understanding, and interpreting classroom data.
Reflective dialogues, inquiry, and reflection	Effective professional learning involves collective reflection on practice, examining teaching methods, and continuous self-examination, including structured processes for "learning from successes and failures."

SOURCE: DUFOUR (2004) AND BENAYA ET AL. (2013)

other professional development programs for teachers. Based on professional research & development reports (Benaya et al., 2013; DuFour, 2004), we agreed upon major characteristics of PLCs (see Table 13.1) and tailored them to our middle-school S&T teachers' PLCs. The characteristics were also negotiated with the relevant stakeholders, including policymakers from the Ministry of Education, as well as regional authorities and PLC providers. Views of practitioners such as teacher leaders and teachers, as well as in-situ observations, provided input to this process.

Toward the beginning of the 2015–2016 school year, the Weizmann Institute of Science's Department of Science Teaching launched a 5-year program to develop PLCs for middle-school S&T teachers, with funding from the Trump Foundation and with the cooperation of Israel's Ministry of Education. We

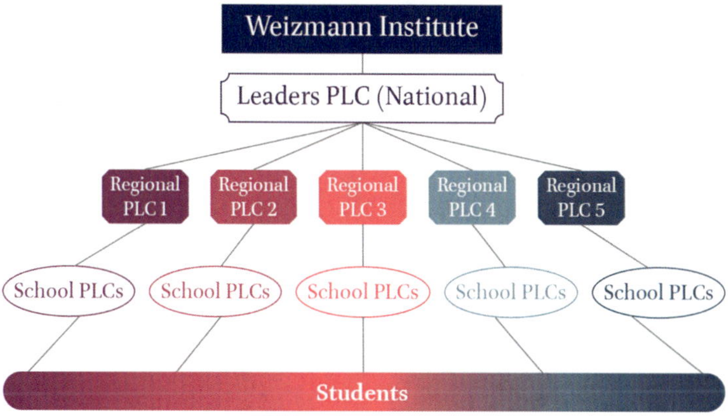

FIGURE 13.1 The initial hierarchical model of the S&T PLC program

tailored our PLC program to the unique professional needs and diverse profiles of middle-school S&T leading teachers, teachers and students.

The target structure of our S&T PLC program was based on teachers' leadership models (Darling-Hammond & Richardson, 2009; Little, 2012; Shulman 1997, 1998, 2011; Timperley et al., 2008) and was derived from our department's long experience and expertise accumulated over more than two decades of running national teacher centers and long-term courses for teacher leaders in science and mathematics (Eylon et al., 2008; Scherz et al., 2008).

Targeting a hierarchical structure for the PLC project, we established an academic leading team which sought to: (1) create and monitor a national PLC of leading S&T teachers (teacher leaders' PLC); (2) establish regional PLCs of S&T coordinators and teachers; (3) enhance school-based learning communities for S&T teachers' teams that promote meaningful, high-quality, and challenging teaching in S&T classrooms; (4) provide students with meaningful learning, positive attitudes, and eventually, increase their motivation to continue studying S&T in high school (see Figure 13.1).

2.2 *PLC Participants*

Following this hierarchical structure, the overall number of S&T PLCs increased gradually from 1 national PLC to 63 PLCs during the 5 years of implementing the PLC program (Table 13.2). The overall turnover of participants between years was low, and many participants are still members of the PLCs. We estimate that the 1021 participants during this 5-year period have taught 3363 classes and 67,000 students.

In the program's first year (2015–2016), the national teacher leaders' PLC consisted of 9 S&T instructors and coordinators, and 10 members of the Department of Science Teaching (3 faculty members directing the program,

TABLE 13.2 Learning communities for middle-school S&T teachers

Years	No. of PLCs	No. of PLC leaders	No. of PLC participants
2015–2016	1 national teacher leader PLC	3	9
2016–2017	2 teacher leader PLCs	4	105
	5 regional PLCs	10	
2017–2018	2 teacher leader PLCs	4	210
	12 regional PLCs	24	
2018–2019	2 teacher leader PLCs	4	323
	17 regional PLCs	34	
2019–2020	2 teacher leader PLCs	4	374
	20 regional PLCs	40	
Total	63	127	1021

other department members, a psycho-pedagogical advisor, Ph.D. students and postdoctoral fellows). Interviews and concluding discussions toward the end of the first year reflected the strong sense that the initial group members had become a PLC of leaders. The results indicated that the group performed as a PLC in terms of most of the above mentioned characteristics (see Table 13.1).

From the 2nd year on, we operated two national PLCs for teacher leaders and several new regional PLCs yearly. All of the PLCs ran continuously from their establishment. The national PLC members were carefully selected to include qualified leading teachers, recommended by the national S&T superintendent. The regional PLCs were comprised of heads of S&T school departments. During these years, all of the regional PLCs continued their activities under our academic auspice and guidance, following the PLC's rationale and basic characteristics. The leading teams of the PLCs were mentored by the project team.

2.3 *PLC Setup*

Each PLC included a minimum of 15 participants. The meetings were 4 hours each – for a total of 45 hours of face-to-face meetings per year and 15 hours for personal and/or group work. All face-to-face meetings in the teacher leaders' PLCs had a *recurring structure* consisting of the sessions shown in Table 13.3.

All of these sessions were carried out in the context of (1) S&T contents, and (2) a special emphasis on using online technology and applications. Each meeting also included a pleasant mealtime, and the participants were asked to fill out an online feedback questionnaire which was subsequently analyzed

TABLE 13.3 PLC meeting: Recurring structure

– *An opening session*, geared toward establishing a sense of connection
– *A content-knowledge session*, relating to S&T content knowledge and/or S&T pedagogical content knowledge
– *A building-PLC session*, pertaining to defining, developing, and collaborative learning, leadership strategies, psycho-pedagogy
– *A closing session*, aimed at summing up and reflection

and addressed. We explicitly encouraged the leaders' PLC participants to relate to our guidance and methods as a *model* and to consider ways to adapt them to their PLCs. The members of the leaders' PLC implemented the activities in meetings of their school-based S&T communities as well as in their S&T classrooms between meetings, and reflected back to the leaders' PLC. Throughout the year, the PLC leaders compiled an evolving online folder of all their PLC activities. A selection of exemplary activities was available to share with other PLC participants. Electronic mail served as the formal means of communication between meetings, while use of WhatsApp for spontaneous informal messages between PLC members became increasingly common. Each school year ended with a conference for all PLC members.

2.4 *PLC Models*

The program included components of formal and informal research and evaluation including feedback forms. One of our main objectives was to follow meaningful PLC processes that recurred during the project and formalize them. Here, we elaborate on two influential models that evolved and formalized through research observations during the 5 years of our PLC project: (1) the *Collaboration Model* which formalizes design and implementation of collaboration skills in PLCs, and (2) the *Network Model*, which emerged by following processes of knowledge transmission among the PLCs.

2.4.1 The Collaboration Model

"Collaboration" is considered a 21st century skill that relates to the potential for success in future professional careers (Evans, 2020). Collaboration skills reflect the individual's ability to perform complex tasks with a group. More specifically, collaborative problem solving is a critical and necessary skill used in education and in the workforce. Collaboration has been defined as a "coordinated, synchronous activity that is the result of a continued attempt to construct and maintain a shared conception of a problem" (Roschelle & Teasley,

TABLE 13.4 The 4-levels Collaboration Model

Levels	Explanation	Examples
Participation	Attendance, active presence, following PLC norms.	Arrive on time; "Full Attendance"; Active in PLC discourses.
Sharing	Sharing of ideas, experiences, class activities and PLC practice with other members.	Present best practice; Present challenges; Offer support.
Cooperation	Working together on project aspects, teamwork, sharing responsibilities.	Group development of learning activities; Group learning.
Partnership	An arrangement between two or more people to manage projects and share challenges, consequences and benefits.	Initiating, leading and executing an inter-PLC project on the environmental issue.

1995, p. 70). To prepare school students to perform successfully, it is important to develop their collaboration skills, in addition to learning and research skills, communication skills and information and communication technology (ICT) skills. Therefore, it is highly important that the teachers' toolbox contain a theoretical background and practical means to impart collaboration skills to their students. Within the PLC project, we defined a Collaboration Model that specifies four levels of collaboration skills that differ in the intensity of commitment and complexity required to perform them, as presented in Table 13.4.

The Collaboration Model was implemented in the teacher leaders' PLC. During the first 2 years of the project, we mainly applied the levels of Participation and Sharing. The Cooperation level was implemented toward the 3rd year. We plan to implement the Partnership level toward the 6th year. Evidence that we collected from PLC meetings (feedback forms, audiotapes and videos) clearly indicated that collaboration with colleagues is not a routine part of school teachers' work. For example, initially, the routine of "sharing of practice and challenges" was rare among our PLC participants and was even rejected by some of them. We developed strategies that gradually turned "collaboration" into a norm and even a routine in the PLC project. Moreover, those PLC members who rarely shared their experiences/problems with other PLC members were eventually looked upon as outsiders. The regional PLCs followed and implemented the Collaboration Model according to their PLC's average stage and maturity.

2.4.2 The Evolving Network Model

The research team conducted interviews and observations that were combined into a variety of "PLC stories," taken from various S&T PLC events. Regular follow-up and analysis of these stories helped us better understand how a PLC develops. We will present two of these stories and follow how they evolved to create a Network Model of knowledge transmission in a PLC.

The Escape Box story. Escape rooms (López-Pernas et al., 2019) have become a popular, positive, instructional, and challenging form of recreation for adolescents and adults alike. At the beginning of the 2017–2018 school year, a number of the instructors and coordinators from a regional PLC in Israel, initiated a similar idea aimed at increasing student curiosity and motivation to learn about S&T subjects. Because building an escape room requires financial resources, space, and time, they decided to adopt the principles of escape rooms to develop "escape boxes" connected to science topics of Material Sciences. The escape boxes consisted of the following items: (1) bags/boxes/containers; (2) different types of locks; and (3) a collection of stories and queries conveyed through texts/drawings/games. Among the Escape Box development group there were three members of the national leaders' PLC who reported and shared this initiative in the Leaders PLC meetings, along with discussions and a pedagogical discourse regarding means of adaptation and implementation in other regional communities, the school S&T teams and S&T classes. As a result, it spread to many classes in Israel, where teachers, as well as students created new boxes and exchanged them. Figure 13.2 traces this Escape Box

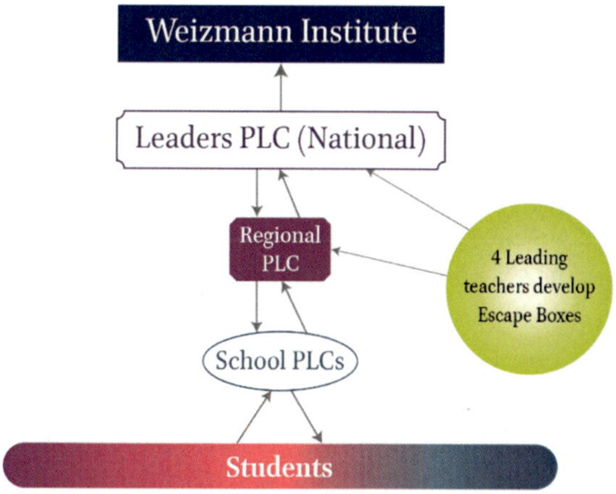

FIGURE 13.2
Graphical representation of the Escape Box story

FIGURE 13.3
The ice-water glass

story as a compound path of "knowledge transmission" that was initiated in a regional S&T PLC and spread via the national leaders' PLC to other PLCs, and from there to the students.

The Ice-Water Glass story. This is an example story taken from Material Sciences, which provides a taste of our S&T PLC meetings. It also sheds light on the learning processes inside a PLC and between PLCs, and how these relate to students' learning.

The Ice-Water Glass story relates to a diagnostic activity that was modeled in the teacher leaders' PLC. It involves observing a glass filled with ice and water; the participants are asked to draw the structure of all the materials inside the glass as "detected by a powerful magnifying apparatus," to share their drawings with others, and to explain them. The use of visual means forces the students to reveal their level of understanding (or misconceptions/lack of knowledge) of the microscopic structure of materials. Observing the drawings of various students initiated a pedagogical content-related discourse and a class discussion. The activity was also demonstrated on the S&T teachers' website and included a video and instructional materials.

Next, the teacher leaders' PLC members embedded the activity in the regional PLCs; from there it was introduced to the school-based communities and to their S&T classes. Relevant drawings, which were collected from the participating PLCs (teachers as well as students), were shared, analyzed, and discussed at PLC meetings. Teacher N, who belongs to a regional PLC, implemented the activity in her 8th-grade S&T class. Student A, who was shy and a loner, seemed to be unusually engaged in the activity, and teacher N asked him to share his drawings with the class. The students and the teacher were astounded when they realized how accurate his drawings were (see Figure 13.4). He correctly identified all three materials in the glass: water, ice, and air, and created an accurate drawing of their detailed molecular structures. Unlike

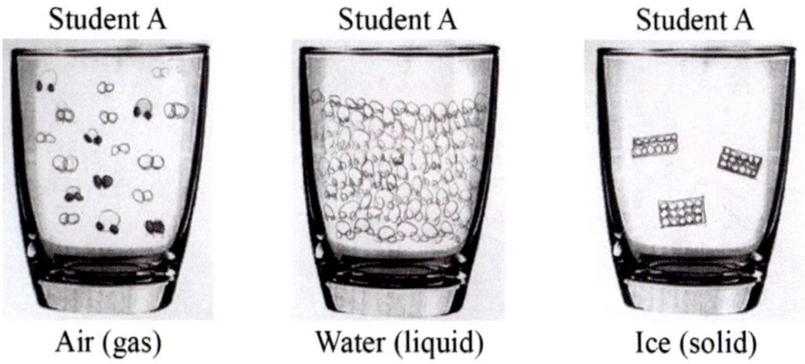

FIGURE 13.4 Student A's drawings: the microscopic structure of substances inside the ice-water glass

student A, some students did not mention the presence of air, and many drew incorrect microscopic structures.

The use of visual means encouraged Student A "to come out of his shell" and to show his drawings to the entire class. As a result, the other students' perception of him was totally altered, which in turn improved his self-image and social behavior.

Teacher N reported Student A's story to the regional PLC, where it was discussed, and from there it was referred back to the teacher leaders' PLC program at the Weizmann Institute of Science.

Teacher N, who is also an S&T coordinator at her school, shared the ice-water activity with her school-based PLC members, who, in turn, used the activity in their S&T classes. Teacher N also reported the story in the school newsletter. Figure 13.5 traces the compound "knowledge transmission" path of the Ice-Water Glass story to the Weizmann Institute, different PLCs, and students.

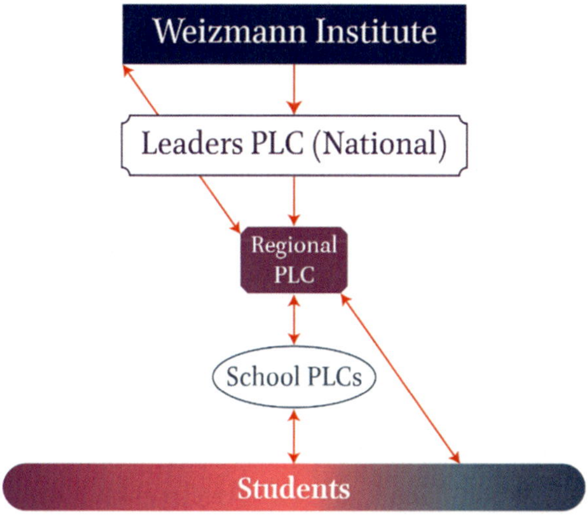

FIGURE 13.5 Graphic representation tracing the knowledge transmission path in the Ice-Water Glass story

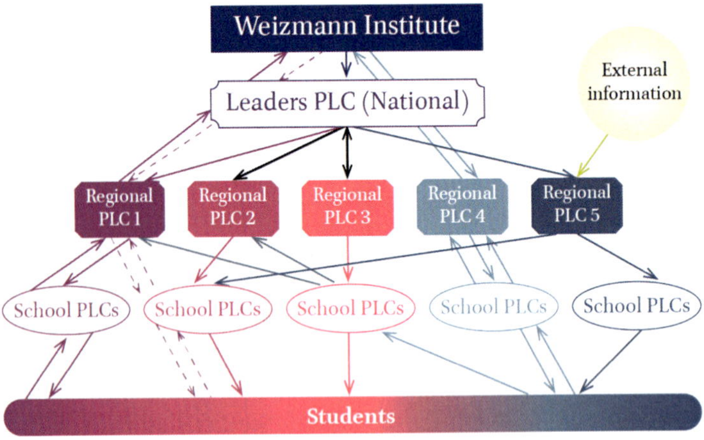

FIGURE 13.6 The Network Model: paths of knowledge transmission among S&T PLCs

From the stories to the Network Model. Additional stories were written, analyzed, and presented as various graphic paths of "knowledge transmission" and drawn as a combined illustration as shown in Figure 13.6. Each story is illustrated by connected set of arrows having the same color.

The Ice-Water Glass (Figure 13.4) and Escape Box (Figure 13.2) stories are also represented as paths on Figure 13.6, adjacent to other knowledge-transmission paths. The empirical research (observations, interviews, and more) indicated that the initial (hierarchical) model had been transformed into a Network Model (Figure 13.7).

It is clear that knowledge-transmission occurs among PLCs in many directions: from the teacher leaders' PLC to the regional PLCs and vice versa, and from there to other school-based communities, PLCs, and educational entities outside the PLC program.

The Network Model that emerged during the implementation of our PLC program brought about various knowledge-transmission processes, both within a single PLC and between PLCs. The Network Model demonstrates relationships between individuals who share the same views within a specific community, as well as direct and indirect relationships between regional and teacher leaders' PLCs. These relationships motivate and influence the PLC participants. Our findings may imply that important, relevant knowledge is conveyed in the PLC network, and improves and becomes more accurate over time, whereas knowledge that is inadequate (for teachers or students) diminishes and eventually disappears. The findings illustrated in the PLC stories indicate that the initial hierarchical PLC structure was gradually transformed into interactive and collaborative learning and sharing of responsibilities among PLC members. This led to a "change in roles" that enabled knowledge-transmission between the academic teams, the practitioners and the students.

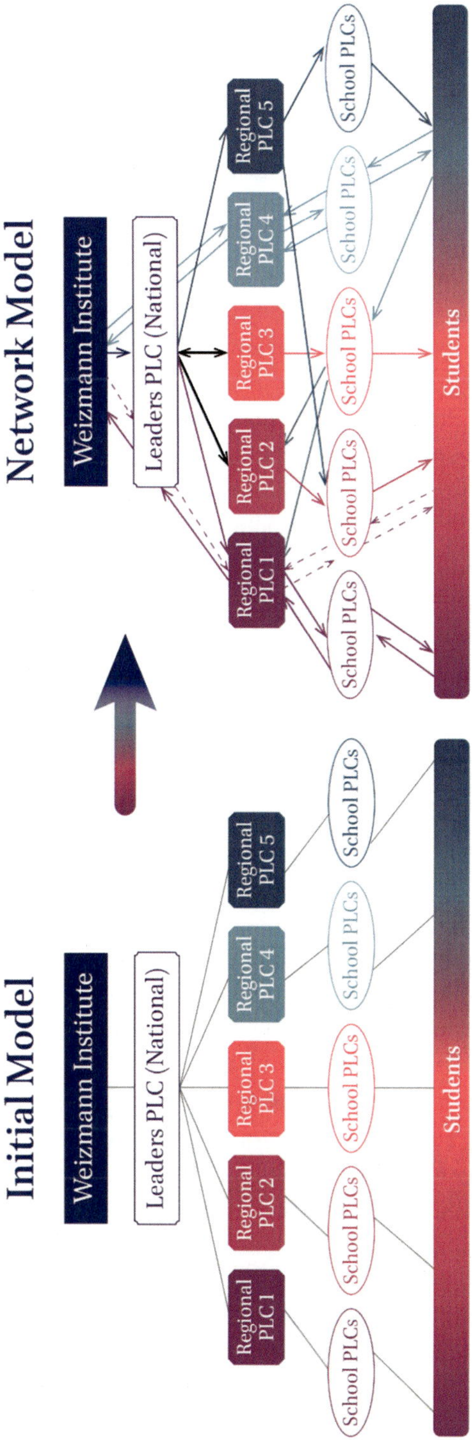

FIGURE 13.7 S&T PLCs' knowledge-transmission model: from Initial Model (see Figure 13.1) to a Network Model (see Figure 13.6)

3 Concluding Remarks

Our PLC program for middle-school S&T teachers involves complex, nonlinear professional development processes that had effective and sometimes unpredictable outcomes. These were formalized as two models: the 4-levels *Collaboration Model* and the *Network Model* that represents knowledge transmission processes among PLCs. The interweaving existence of the two models drive the progress of each PLC and create an assembly of PLCs that grow together, support and influence each other, and bring about a change in teachers professional development. For instance: Many of the PLCs developed a collective professional PLC *profile*, which comprises aspects such as S&T proficiencies, a sense of mission, a desire for excellence, passion, commitment, and a motivation to make a change. These inspired teacher leaders to implement similar PLC principles and processes in their regional PLCs. In addition, research indicated that belonging to a PLC enriches and updates teachers' S&T-based knowledge, as well as their pedagogical content knowledge. It also expands and deepens the members' pedagogical knowledge and their leadership skills, and encourages innovations and creativity (Eylon et al., 2020). Through the PLC network, activities that were developed within PLCs were used by a variety of S&T teachers and students with diverse interests and needs. We hope that this paved the way to improving students' performance and attitudes, and potentially encouraged them to choose a S&T subject in their future studies.

4 Epilogue

In the middle of the 5th year of our PLC project, the COVID-19 pandemic began to infiltrate our lives. By March 2020, many professional development program frameworks were transformed into distance learning and in the middle of March 2020, all schools shut down.

We decided to continue the S&T leaders' and regional PLC meetings using the online platform ZOOM, based on our deep belief that our support and modeling approach remained necessary. The guiding principles were to follow the yearly PLC design; to retain the original format, duration and regularities of the meetings; to continue with the interactive nature of the meetings, the group work sessions and discussion groups; and to implement a variety of online tools to pedagogically apply all of these. One important effort was to encourage the participants to use the PLCs to share their experiences, challenges and solutions toward continuing S&T learning and instruction in the changing reality. The leaders' PLC meetings served as models for best practices.

Participants' reflections at the end of the year revealed that our online transformation of the existing face-to-face PLCs had provided a solid framework of professional support that helped PLC teachers cope with their S&T teaching, even under the COVID-19 restrictions. Moreover, these online implementations highlighted the power of the already established face-to-face PLCs as support frameworks in challenging periods of uncertainty. The role played by the teachers' PLCs during the COVID-19 crisis provides authentic evidence of these communities being a suitable, up-to-date, innovative and robust means of supporting teachers' continual professional needs, which can be operated online as well as face-to-face, or via some hybrid of the two.

Acknowledgments

We would like to acknowledge our colleagues and students for their valuable contribution to the development of the Science & Technology PLC project along 2014–2019: Dr. T. Berglas-Shapiro, M. Oren, Dr. M. Frailich, Dr. Y. Harari, E. Ben-Elyahu, D. Pano-Einy and Dr. Y. Shwartz. We thank the teachers who participated in our leaders PLCs – for sharing their experience with us and for their devoted guidance of the regional PLCs. We thank the Trump Family Foundation for their generous support and helpful discussions during the first 5 years of the project and the Israel Ministry of Education for their support since 2018.

References

Benaya, Y., Yakobson, I., & Zadik, Y. (2013). *Professional learning community in school.* Avney Rosha Institute (in Hebrew).

Bolam, R., McMahon, A., Stoll, L., Thomas, S., & Wallace, M. (2005). *Creating and sustaining effective professional learning communities.* Research report RR637. https://dera.ioe.ac.uk/5622/1/RR637.pdf

Borko, H., Jacobs, J., & Koellner, K. (2010). Contemporary approaches to teacher professional development. In P. Peterson, E. Baker, & B. McGaw (Eds.), *International encyclopedia of education*, part 7 (3rd ed., pp. 548–555). Elsevier. http://dx.doi.org/10.1016/b978-0-08-044894-7.00654-0

Darling-Hammond, L., & Richardson, N. (2009). Research review/teacher learning: What matters? *Educational Leadership, 66*(5), 46–53.

DuFour, R. (2004). What is a "professional learning community"? *Educational Leadership, 61*(8), 6–11.

Evans, C. (2020). *Measuring student success skills: A review of the literature on collaboration*. National Center for the Improvement of Educational Assessment.

Eylon, B. S., Berger, H., & Bagno, E. (2008). An evidence based continuous professional development program on knowledge integration in physics: A study of teachers' collective discourse. *International Journal of Science Education, 30*(5), 619–641. http://dx.doi.org/10.1080/09500690701854857

Eylon, B. S., Scherz, Z., & Bagno, E. (2020). Professional learning communities of science teachers: Theoretical and practical perspectives. In Y. Ben-David Kolikant, D. Martinovic, & M. Milner-Bolotin (Eds.), *STEM teachers and teaching in the digital era* (pp. 65–89). Springer. http://dx.doi.org/10.1007/978-3-030-29396-3_5

Fishman, B. J., Penuel, W. R., Allen, A.-R., & Cheng, B. H. (2013). Design-based implementation research: Theories, methods, and exemplars. *National society for the study of education yearbook* (pp. 400–425). Teachers College Press.

Grossman, P., Wineburg, S., & Woolworth, S. (2001). Toward a theory of teacher community. *The Teachers College Record, 103*, 942–1012. http://dx.doi.org/10.1111/0161-4681.00140

Koellner, K., Jacobs, J., & Borko, H. (2011). Mathematics professional development: Critical features for developing leadership skills and building teachers' capacity. *Mathematics Teacher Education and Development, 13*, 115–136.

Little, J. W. (2012). Professional community and professional development in the learning-centered school. In M. Kooy & K. van Veen (Eds.), *Teacher learning that matters: International perspectives* (pp. 22–46). Routledge.

López-Pernas, S., Gordillo, A., Barra, E., & Quemada, J. (2019). Examining the use of an educational escape room for teaching programming in a higher education setting. *IEEE Access, 7*, 31723–31737. http://dx.doi.org/10.1109/access.2019.2902976

Roschelle, J., & Teasley, S. D. (1995). The construction of shared knowledge in collaborative problem-solving. In C. E. O'Malley (Ed.), *Computer-supported collaborative learning* (pp. 69–97) Springer-Verlag. http://dx.doi.org/10.1007/978-3-642-85098-1_5

Scherz, Z., Eylon, B., & Bialer, L. (2008). Professional development in learning Skills for Science (LSS): the use of evidence-based framework. *International Journal of Research in Science Education, 30*(5), 643–668. http://dx.doi.org/10.1080/09500690701854865

Scherz, Z., Eylon, B., & Yarden, A. (2020). *Science and technology professional learning communities project*. Report to the Trump Foundation, Weizmann Institute of Science, private communication (in Hebrew).

Shulman, L. S. (1997). *Communities of learners and communities of teachers*. Monographs of the Mandel Institute.

Shulman, L. S. (1998). Theory, practice, and the education of professionals. *The Elementary School Journal, 98*, 511–526. http://dx.doi.org/10.1086/461912

Shulman, L. S. (2011). Feature essays: The scholarship of teaching and learning: A personal account and reflection. *International Journal of the Scholarship of Teaching and Learning, 5*. https://doi.org/10.20429/ijsotl.2011.050130

Timperley, H., Wilson, A., Barrar, H., & Fung, I. (2008). *Teacher professional learning and development*. New Zealand Ministry of Education, Wellington, New Zealand.

Tomorrow 98. (1992). *Tomorrow 98, report of the Superior Committee on Science, Mathematics and Technology Education in Israel*. Israel Ministry of Education.

Vescio, V., Ross, D., & Adams, A. (2008). A review of research on the impact of professional learning communities on teaching practice and student learning. *Teaching and Teacher Education*, *24*, 80–91. http://dx.doi.org/10.1016/j.tate.2007.01.004

CHAPTER 14

"Life Trajectory" of a Professional Development Project

The Case of ***VIDEO-LM***

Ronnie Karsenty and Abraham Arcavi

Abstract

This chapter provides a bird's-eye view on the trajectory of VIDEO-LM, a video-based professional development (PD) project for secondary-school mathematics teachers. VIDEO-LM is aimed at enhancing mathematics teachers' reflection on their practice, and refining their mathematical knowledge for teaching. We describe the project's development, from its design phase, based on previous research and experimentation, through pilot implementation, to a wide upscaling process, and toward the next phase of upgrading the project to encompass broader aims. Studies following VIDEO-LM revealed changes in teachers' awareness of the complexities involved in the mathematics teaching practice, and crystallization of teachers' mathematical knowledge for teaching. First, we review this research. Then, we use the case of VIDEO-LM to explore core questions that lie at the heart of similar work carried out worldwide on PD projects for mathematics teachers: What characterizes a research-based design of a PD program? What is the role of frameworks in such design, and how may such frameworks be developed and adapted to changing situations? What kinds of challenges are involved in scaling up a PD program? We close with some concluding thoughts about what understanding the "life trajectory" of a PD project may mean and the importance of such an understanding.

Keywords

professional development – mathematics teachers – research-based PD design – upscale – project trajectory – conceptual frameworks

1 Introduction

It is not often that researchers have the motivation, time and energy to look retrospectively at their projects and inspect their trajectories from a mere idea

 | DOI: 10.1163/9789004503625_014

to a full-fledged enterprise. However, those who do so seem to find it rewarding. For example, Borko et al. (2015) wrote:

> Working on this book provided us an opportunity to reflect on the knowledge we have gained by designing, implementing and researching the PSC and MLP[1] models… We gained new insights… as we discussed the various sets of research findings. (p. xv)

Similarly, this chapter is an opportunity to reflect on an almost decade-long, and still ongoing, professional development (PD) project. We examine the project's design, its implementation, challenges faced along the way and the research around it. Then, we attempt to look at this project as one case in the growing field of professional development for mathematics teachers, and explore what may be learned from this case toward a better understanding of this field.

2 VIDEO-LM: Overview of a Project's Research-Based Trajectory

VIDEO-LM (Viewing, Investigating and Discussing Environments of Learning Mathematics) is a PD project designed for secondary mathematics teachers. It is aimed at the elaboration and use of tools for reflection on the mathematics teaching practice, through the development of a language that supports peer conversations on core issues related to mathematics teaching and learning (Arcavi & Karsenty, 2018). It is also intended to promote the development and enrichment of mathematics knowledge for teaching (Ball et al., 2008). In the following, we describe the different stages that the VIDEO-LM project went through since 2012: design, pilot implementation, upscale, and the emergence of a revisited PD model (see timeline in Figure 14.1).

Despite various forms of communication and collaboration among teachers, teaching remains a lonely profession. Once they close the classroom door, teachers are on their own, and rarely get the chance to watch their peers in action. This is not merely a social deficit, but also a barrier to professional progress enabled by peer learning *in situ*.

VIDEO-LM was designed to generate opportunities for teachers to watch and discuss lessons given by other teachers, by creating a large database of authentic videotaped lessons to serve as learning artifacts and sources for peer reflection. Teachers watch recorded lessons of peers that are unknown to them, such that these become "vicarious experiences" allowing for indirect

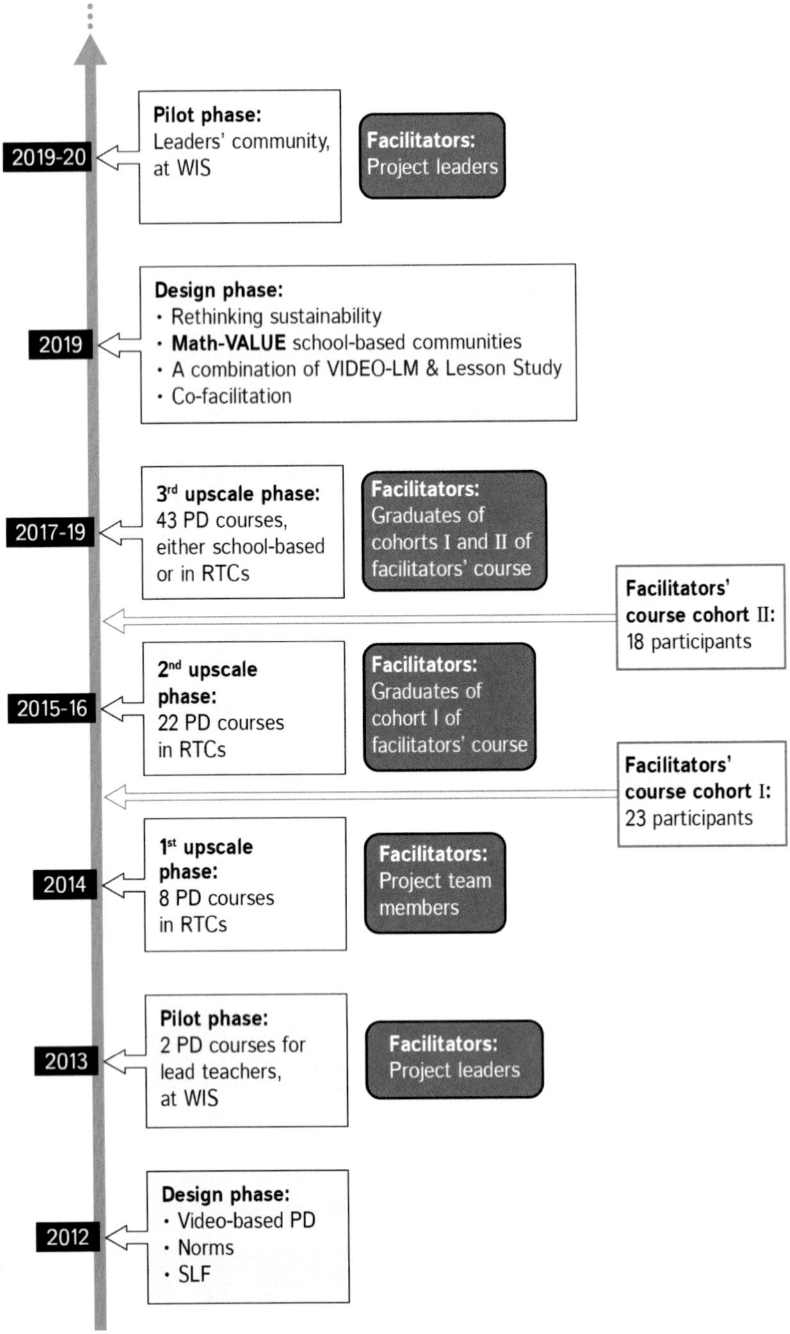

FIGURE 14.1 The development of VIDEO-LM over time
Abbreviations: PD = professional development; SLF = six-lens framework; WIS = Weizmann Institute of Science; RTC = Regional Teacher Center

exploration of one's own perceptions on the practice of mathematics teaching, through the observation of "remote" teaching events (Karsenty & Arcavi, 2017).

The design was rooted in two theories: *Teaching in Context* (Schoenfeld, 1998, 2010), and *Mathematical Knowledge for Teaching* (MKT; Ball et al., 2008). According to Schoenfeld, teaching is a goal-oriented profession; teachers strive to achieve various types of goals and are constantly modifying and changing their goals according to the reality of the classroom. The theory asserts that teachers have a body of knowledge resources that they can call upon, for both expected and unexpected situations, and that like everyone else, teachers have orientations, i.e., predispositions and beliefs, in this case about mathematics, students, and teaching. This triad of goals, resources and orientations drives teachers' decision-making processes and shape their actions.

MKT (Ball et al., 2008) describes a kind of specialized knowledge which includes acquaintance with students' ways of reasoning, competency in providing appropriate examples and tasks, connections to previous and future mathematical ideas, and more. The design of VIDEO-LM was also inspired by the Japanese model of Lesson Study (e.g., Fernandez & Yoshida, 2004) which centralizes teacher collaboration, reflection and learning around the planning and implementation of well-developed lessons.

These three sources guided us in the building of a learning environment in which teachers would be actively involved in reflection on, and analysis of, their own (and others') goals, resources, and orientations, the mathematical ideas they wish to bring to the fore, the tasks chosen for that endeavor, and the way classroom interactions shape the construction of mathematical knowledge (Arcavi & Karsenty, 2018; Karsenty, 2018a; Karsenty & Arcavi, 2017). Following preliminary experimentation (Arcavi & Schoenfeld, 2008), we designed a framework consisting of six analytical tools with which mathematics teachers can reflect on a videotaped lesson. We named these tools *lenses*, to emphasize their use as a means of *observation*, in the dual sense of watching an occurrence but also commenting on it. Viewing a lesson through a certain lens implies shedding light on a specific feature of the mathematics teaching practice (Karsenty, 2018a). Figure 14.2 presents this six-lens framework (henceforth: SLF), consisting of the following components: mathematical and meta-mathematical ideas; goals; tasks and activities; interactions; dilemmas and decision-making; and beliefs about mathematics teaching. Figure 14.2 outlines the focus of the observation activities around each of these lenses, and exemplifies the sort of questions that direct discussions with teachers.

The SLF was the first step in the VIDEO-LM design, followed by the establishment of a learning environment in which the lenses can be productively used. Discussing practices of fellow teachers, even when unknown, requires

Lenses for observing a videotaped mathematics lesson	What the lenses unpack
Mathematical and meta-mathematical ideas	The space of relevant ideas and concepts that underlie the topic of a mathematics lesson; meta-mathematical ideas (e.g., one counter example is sufficient to refute a conjecture) that are employed within the lesson.
Explicit and implicit teacher goals	Possible goals that may be attributed to the teacher, on the basis of actions or decisions observed in the lesson, as well as pros and cons of preferring certain goals over others.
Classroom tasks and activities	Features of the tasks and activities and how they are enacted in the lesson, including whether and when this process develops differently than expected ("a posteriori task analysis").
Teacher-student interactions	How the teacher poses further questions to those included in the task; listens to (or ignores) comments or difficulties raised by students; manages discussions; delegates responsibilities in the process of knowledge generation.
Teacher dilemmas and decision-making	Teacher decisions prior to and during the lesson; situations of dilemma (i.e., when there is no evident optimal course of action) that the teacher seems to be facing during the lesson, and possible pathways that can be offered to resolve these dilemmas, while considering consequent tradeoffs.
Teacher beliefs about mathematics teaching, how students learn and the teacher's role	Orientations, beliefs and values that may be attributed to the teacher; implicit messages that may be conveyed to students through the teacher's communications and actions.

FIGURE 14.2 Description of the six-lens framework (SLF)

a supportive and nonthreatening setting, where participants feel comfortable to elicit ideas and thoughts that provoke reflection. Therefore, we explicitly defined the use of SLF in PD sessions around certain discussion norms.

The first norm was that the peer discussion would not be judgmental or evaluative. It was important to clarify that the SLF was not designed to provide feedback. Rather, in line with the works of Jaworski (1990) and Coles (2013), a SLF-based discussion is one in which the facilitator attempts to redirect highly evaluative or judgmental comments into "issues to reflect about."

The second norm was that participants in the discussion agree on a basic working assumption: that *the filmed teacher is acting in the best interest of his/her students*. The teachers watching the video are required to "step into the shoes" of the filmed teacher in an attempt to understand the goals, decisions and beliefs that may be ascribed to him or her.

The third norm was that the discussion does not seek to identify or define "best practice"; that for different teachers there may be different best practices; and that these differences may be linked to personal, contextual and cultural settings (a certain practice can be appropriate for one situation and inappropriate for others).

We believe that the enactment of these norms has played a considerable role in achieving the project's goals (e.g., Karsenty et al., 2019). For a detailed account on the assumed mechanisms associated with these norms, and how they affect teachers' participation, see Karsenty (2017).

2.1 *Pilot Implementation*

In 2013, the two co-authors of this chapter conducted two 30-hour pilot PD courses for lead teachers. This pilot served, as in any development and research project in education, to guide the refining of the original design. It allowed us to make further decisions on how we wanted a VIDEO-LM PD course to look. The pilot was followed by research, to investigate possible teacher gains. In this section, we describe the decisions taken, and what we learned, during this phase.

Our first decision was not to base the discussion during the PD course on clips or short episodes edited from a lesson, which is the common practice in video-based PDs as reported in the literature (e.g., Sherin & van Es, 2009). Rather, we wanted the units of analysis for teachers' discussions to be whole lessons, so that observers are presented with a 'story' that unfolds within the lesson. Such a story has a beginning, development, and closure (Stevenson & Stigler, 1992). Accordingly, each PD session was quite long (usually around 3 hours), to allow enough time for both screening the lesson and talking about it. When we were not able to screen the whole lesson, we presented significant parts of it, while completing the picture with a "lesson graph" (a one-page written "map" of the sections of the lesson; see Borko et al., 2011; Seago, 2003).

The second decision was to use various models for watching and discussing a lesson (Karsenty & Arcavi, 2017). For example, a discussion might begin after screening the video, but it could also begin prior to screening, with the participants requested to elicit possible mathematical and meta-mathematical ideas that they could associate with the topic of the lesson to be screened. In another model, the video could be stopped once the filmed teacher had presented a task, and the participating teachers were requested to solve the task, discuss their solutions and predict those expected from the students. The lesson itself may be either screened in predetermined sections or paused at points of interest raised by participants. Using different models allowed us to adjust the PD session to features of the presented lesson and to the lenses worth emphasizing. Different watching modes also allowed for diverse organization of PD sessions, rather than all of them having the same pattern, thus teachers may be more engaged.

The research conducted around the pilot phase of VIDEO-LM showed that we were on the right track: by constructing a methodological tool termed "utterances map" to capture shifts in teachers' discussions about mathematical content after watching videos of lessons, we could point to teachers' gains in mathematical knowledge for teaching (Karsenty et al., 2015; Nurick, 2015). One of our favorite examples of such a gain is the following.

Prior to watching a heterogeneous 7th-grade class deal with the associative and commutative laws of arithmetic, teachers were asked to elicit mathematical ideas related to this topic. They suggested a fairly wide range of ideas, from the simple fact that addition and multiplication satisfy both laws, while subtraction and division do not, through various models that demonstrate the laws, to efficient applications of the laws to solve exercises. The lion's share of the discussion was dedicated to considering the general algebraic forms of these properties (e.g., $a + b = b + a$), and suggesting why and how they should be taught.

In the screened lesson, the teacher asked the class whether operations that satisfy the commutative law necessarily satisfy the associative law as well, and vice versa. The students' spontaneous collective answer was "yes." The teacher then introduced several 3×3 operation tables that served as counterexamples to this assertion, and led a discussion resulting in the conclusion that the properties are not interdependent. The screening of this episode was followed by a discussion guided by the use of the SLF lenses. The discussions before and after watching the video were coded by the MKT categories, using the utterances map. This analysis revealed that watching the lesson produced a substantial shift in the content of the utterances, which now included profound mathematical ideas and examples that were not previously considered. One such shift concerned examples in which one of the laws is satisfied but not the other (an issue not raised before the lesson was watched). Teachers created operations such as $a\Box b = (a+b)^2$ and $a\Diamond b = |a+b|$, defined on $\mathbb{R}$ and accessible to students, and showed that these operations are commutative but not associative, within an infinite field (rather than within finite operation tables as used in the lesson). This shift was acknowledged even within the session itself, with one of the teachers saying: "When we spoke [earlier] about what are the possibilities… none of us touched upon even the outskirts of the rich world that she [the filmed teacher] opened for us in this lesson" (for more details on enhancement of MKT see Karsenty, 2018a; Nurick, 2015).

Our aim of enhancing deep reflection about the practice of teaching mathematics also appeared to be achieved in this pilot phase. We witnessed such reflection occurring during the sessions (e.g., in utterances such as the following: "I as a teacher ask myself what are her [the filmed teacher's] goals and what price she is willing to pay to demonstrate a certain mathematical principle or not demonstrate it"). Moreover, participants reported a shift in how they view certain issues, and even a change in their own practice, for example: "regarding our first session, I was among those who opposed [to the task shown in the video], and in retrospect I was wrong. I tried it in my class and it was good, it opened the possibility to see my class from a different angle. I was wrong… not everything you feel at the beginning is right… I was sure they won't understand and won't connect and I was very much surprised."

Following these and other positive findings from the pilot, the time was ripe for a wider implementation, as described in the next section.

2.2 *Going to Scale: Challenges, Successes and Open Questions*

The upscale phase was spread over 5 years, and included three stages, each with its own challenges. Once we had a working frame for a 30-hour PD course, we contacted several Regional Teacher Centers (RTCs)[2] and offered the course. As a result, the first upscale included eight PD courses, given in 2014.[3] At this stage, all facilitators were either the project leaders themselves, or one of the project team members, or one of three lead teachers from the pilot phase who agreed to conduct a course in the local RTC close to where they lived. The RTCs and the VIDEO-LM team performed assessments (based on feedback questionnaires and observations of random sessions). Both sources showed that this stage was successful in terms of teacher satisfaction and self-evidence of learning, as demonstrated in the following representative citations:

- The course is characterized [by the participating teachers] as relevant, highly interesting, enriching, thought provoking and allowing for processes of reflection on their practice (source: an external assessment report conducted by one of the RTCs).
- We were exposed to different teaching styles and approaches. The discussions maintained in the PD are high level ones… Learning was rooted in deep observation of teachers while they teach… and there was shared thinking about teaching and classroom interactions (source: an external assessment report conducted by another RTC, citing teachers' comments).

– It was thrilling to watch different teachers and different, diversified teaching styles that often mirrored my own practice and sometimes were a source for inspiration and pondering. The symbiosis between the videotapes and the peer discussions was above expectations, very useful and fascinating, as well as educative and thought provoking (source: internal feedback questionnaire).

The challenge that we faced at the end of this year was how to manage the growing demand for VIDEO-LM courses, that came from diverse educational sectors in Israel (including the Arab, Druze and ultra-Orthodox sectors). It became clear that a cadre of facilitators was needed to conduct PD sessions. It is well-known that a critical component of a sustainable and scalable PD model is the ability to prepare PD facilitators who can adapt the model to various contexts while maintaining integrity with its original goals and agenda (Borko et al., 2014; Cobb & Jackson, 2011; Roesken-Winter et al., 2015; Zehetmeier, 2015). Moreover, the non-trivial shift from a lead teacher in mathematics to a successful facilitator of PD has been extensively studied in recent years (e.g., Borko et al., 2015, 2017; Even, 2005, 2008; Karsenty, 2016, 2018b; Kuzle & Biehler, 2015; Prediger & Pöhler, 2019; Roesken-Winter et al., 2015; Schwarts, 2020). Back in 2014, much of this literature did not exist yet, and we had to find our own way to prepare new facilitators for future VIDEO-LM courses. We did, however, consider relevant work published prior to 2014. We adopted Maaß and Doorman's (2013) longitudinal model for what they termed the "education of multipliers" (p. 894), which includes three phases: *learning-off-job*, i.e., gaining fundamental knowledge; *learning-by-job*, i.e., using the knowledge acquired in the first phase of planning and implementing a PD course, with close support and counseling by experts; and *learning-on-job*, which consists of further growth enhanced by experience, reflection and peer support. Following Even (2005), we assumed that the interrelation between knowledge and practice plays a significant role in the development of facilitators, thus certain progress would only be achieved *after* the preparation phase (learning-off-job) is over. These sources influenced our awareness of what could and could not be achieved within the initial facilitator preparation course, and what needed to be taken into account for the future stage when facilitators were already out in the field, in terms of designing a support system.

In 2015, we opened a preparation course for future VIDEO-LM facilitators, arranged as seven monthly meetings (30 hours in total). Twenty-three secondary mathematics teachers participated in the first cohort of the course, led by us as the project heads.

Four design principles guided this *learning-off-job* stage (Arcavi & Karsenty, 2016; Karsenty, 2016): (1) *relevance*: course activities were directly linked to realistic issues that VIDEO-LM facilitators deal with, as accumulated during the first upscale stage; (2) *feasibility of future facilitators' learning goals*: during this learning-off-job period, participants needed to learn from the experiences of others. We therefore saw it as our responsibility to supply them with vivid facilitation cases to examine, while assisting them with developing a set of tools to analyze these cases, yet at the same time recognizing that we were merely "sowing the seeds" for an understanding that would fully ripen only when the participants became actual facilitators; (3) *commitment to the* VIDEO-LM *agenda and norms*: in analyzing cases, explicit and recurring references were made to the SLF and to the desired norms stated above; (4) *modeling*: our conduct as leaders of the facilitator course was aligned with what we expected participants to do as course leaders in the future, e.g., maintain a supportive atmosphere, use diversified and engaging activities, etc.

To examine the facilitation cases, we developed the "meta-lenses framework" (MLF), which "lifts" the SLF from the classroom level to the PD level (Karsenty et al., in press; Prediger et al., 2019). While watching videotaped PD episodes, participants analyzed the facilitator's goals, tasks, interactions with teachers, dilemmas, beliefs and maintenance of the VIDEO-LM agenda, ideas and norms (see Figure 14.3).

In parallel to the preparation course, the VIDEO-LM website[4] was launched in July 2015, with about 35 subtitled complete videotaped lessons[5] and supplementary materials for teachers and facilitators (e.g., observer guides, facilitator guides, lesson graphs, mathematical problems presented in the lessons, enrichment materials, and more). This was an important and essential tool for the next upscale. Graduates of the first cohort of the facilitators' course were assigned to lead PD courses across Israel, and in 2015–16, VIDEO-LM had opened 22 new courses in various RTCs, which constituted the second stage of our upscale.

However, in parallel to these events, unexpected ones presented a new implementation challenge. Due to certain reforms in the secondary-school system, teachers were now required to take part in PD activities *within* their schools, during the day, and the Ministry of Education was encouraging PD projects to design school-based disciplinary PDs to meet the new requirement. It became clear that afternoon participation in PD courses offered by RTCs would decline. Therefore, we began preparing for our third and most complicated upscale stage. School-based mathematics PDs are very different from PDs in RTCs, in two central aspects: first, whereas RTCs organize courses

Meta-lenses for the facilitator level	What the lenses unpack
The PD agenda, ideas and norms	What ideas that stand at the core of the project's agenda appear in the PD session. For example: the kind of reflection that is supported; the use made of the six lenses; the degree to which non-judgemental norms of discussion are followed; the video representations used.
Explicit and implicit facilitator goals	Possible goals that may be attributed to the facilitator, on the basis of actions or decisions observed in the PD session, as well as pros and cons of preferring certain goals over others.
PD tasks and activities	Features of the tasks and activities and how they are enacted in the PD session, including whether and when this process develops differently than expected.
Facilitator-teacher interactions	How the facilitator poses questions and manages the discussion; what facilitator moves are being employed; how the facilitator listens to (or ignores) comments raised by teachers and handles challenging situations such as norm violation; the degree to which the facilitator supports teacher collaboration.
Facilitator dilemmas and decision-making	Facilitator decisions prior to and during the PD session; situations of dilemma that the facilitator seems to be facing during the session, and possible pathways that can be offered to resolve these dilemmas, while considering consequent tradeoffs.
Facilitator beliefs about mathematics teaching, how teachers learn and the facilitator's role	Orientations, beliefs and values that may be attributed to the facilitator; implicit messages that may be conveyed to teachers through the facilitator's communications and actions.

FIGURE 14.3 The meta-lenses framework (MLF)

around a mutual interest of mathematics teachers (e.g., teaching advanced mathematics, or teaching low-track students), school-based PDs need to cater for diverse and sometimes conflicting interests, since the school's mathematics department often consists of teachers with different backgrounds, who specialize in different grades and levels within the 6-year span of the secondary mathematics curriculum. Second, school-based PDs are expected to enhance peer-collaboration among members of the mathematics team, which will permeate into their day-to-day work, a goal which is irrelevant to RTC courses where teachers come from different schools.

To meet this challenge, we opened the second cohort of facilitators' course in 2016, this time focusing on school-based VIDEO-LM PDs. This cohort included 18 participants. Following this course, we entered the third upscale phase (2017–2019), which included 43 VIDEO-LM courses facilitated by graduates of both cohorts, most of them in schools and some in RTCs (interestingly, the demand for RTC courses in the Arab, Druze and ultra-Orthodox sectors remained the same). A personalized support system was designed for the new facilitators who conducted school-based PDs, such that each novice facilitator was individually supported by an experienced facilitator, and in addition, all facilitators met as a group several times a year.

This process was accompanied by two types of research. The first focused on looking at the upscale from the perspective of facilitation: data were collected through the documentation of PD courses, facilitators' periodic journals, questionnaires, and video-stimulated interviews with facilitators. We were interested in how the new facilitators developed, how they adapted their practices to different contexts, and what could be learned in terms of the emerging field of professionalization processes of mathematics PD facilitators.[6] This research is still ongoing; however, preliminary findings (Karsenty et al., in press; Schwarts, 2019, 2020) suggest the occurrence of some very interesting phenomena when novice facilitators gradually gain expertise through experience and support, and the usefulness of the construct of *professional identity* in explaining some of these phenomena.

The second type of research was aimed at looking at the upscale from the perspective of teacher learning. We wanted to go beyond the period of the PD course participation, and examine if and how teachers' reflective processes outlived the course and became a part of their teaching practice. To achieve that, we selected 11 teachers from different VIDEO-LM courses,[7] and followed them through the first year after their participation in the PD. We used teachers' weekly journals and individual video clip interviews based on lessons filmed in the teachers' classrooms. The analysis of these data is still ongoing as well. Preliminary findings (Nurick, 2019) have revealed, on the one hand, the rich span of reflections found among teachers, but on the other, the disappointing result that we were not able to find overt "traces" of the SLF reflective language in the post-course data, at least not to a substantial degree that would suggest a long-lasting impact of the course. These findings left us with an intriguing open question: If we do not have enough evidence for visible effects of VIDEO-LM PDs on the development of reflective practices, what needs to change in our model? This question drove our rethinking of the project, and resulted in suggesting a revised model, as we now detail.

2.3 *The Next Phase*

During 2019–20, we have dedicated much effort to the above question. As portrayed on the far right-hand side of Figure 14.1, we have entered a new design phase, which focuses on the aim of sustainability, and we suggest a revised PD model which is currently in its pilot phase. In the following, we briefly describe this ongoing process.

At the heart of the revised model is the idea of integrating the VIDEO-LM principles with the Japanese approach of Lesson Study (see below). We therefore named the model Math-VALUE (Video Analysis and Lesson-study to Upgrade Expertise). Math-VALUE functions as a professional learning community (PLC), a PD format that is already widespread and has been studied in many countries (e.g., Arcavi, 2019; Brodie & Borko, 2018; Robutti et al., 2016). In Israel, the Ministry of Education has published a list of desired characteristics of PLCs, among them: intentional joint reflection, collaborative culture, collective inquiry, and regularity (Ministry of Education, 2017). Math-VALUE communities aim not only to develop participants' reflective skills through the use of the SLF, but also to develop their ability to apply these skills in hands-on experiences. These experiences consist of the collective conceptualization and planning of lessons (including a-priori analysis of the mathematical ideas to be developed, the tasks to be used, students' potential difficulties, etc.), teaching those lessons, analyzing the videos of the lessons and, when necessary, redesigning a lesson and possibly rerunning it in another class by another teacher from the community. All of these hands-on activities constitute the core of the Japanese Lesson Study approach (e.g., Fernandez & Yoshida, 2004), which has been shown to be sustainable nationwide in Japan, and has spread internationally over the years (e.g., Lewis & Lee, 2017). The design of Math-VALUE assumes that integrating the Lesson Study approach with the SLF language over an extended period of time could contribute to the sustainability of the VIDEO-LM ideas, i.e., the achievement of long-term reflective teacher collaboration in which the SLF is applied in practice.

Math-VALUE is designed as a school-based multiyear disciplinary PLC for secondary mathematics teachers, with an innovative approach to facilitation. Israeli PLCs are usually co-facilitated by two leaders; in Math-VALUE, one of these leaders is an external experienced VIDEO-LM facilitator, while the other is a leader from within the school (e.g., head of the mathematics department or a senior teacher). Once the PLC is established and functioning, the external facilitation will gradually fade, while the local leader gains experience and eventually becomes a professional facilitator who can support sustained and long-term activity with school peers.

As of November 2019, we have established a PLC for Math-VALUE future leaders, to pilot the new ideas and prepare facilitators. This PLC, led by the project heads, includes 16 participants, i.e., 8 pairs preparing for leading Math-VALUE PLCs in 8 schools that have entered the pilot phase. The schools represent various sectors in Israeli society: Jewish and Arab, rural and urban, religious and secular. This is a new stage in the trajectory of VIDEO-LM. Time (and research) will tell if this was a worthwhile direction.

3 What Is VIDEO-LM a Case Of?

In this section, the case of VIDEO-LM is reflected upon to explore core questions in the research domain of mathematics teachers' professional development, a domain which has become wider than ever before. We relate to the following three questions: (1) What characterizes a research-based design and implementation of a PD program? (2) What is the role of frameworks in a research-based design, and how may such frameworks be developed and adapted to changing situations? (3) What kinds of challenges are involved in scaling up a PD program? These questions are not new, and we do not intend here to review the literature concerning the many attempts already made to address them; rather, our contribution is limited to demonstrating how the work in VIDEO-LM enabled us to reflect and gain some insights which were useful to us, and hopefully will be useful to others as well.

3.1 *VIDEO-LM as a Research-Based PD Program*

As other PD projects created in the Department of Science Teaching, the VIDEO-LM project could not have existed without research. This may sound trivial, but actually, it is not. Worldwide, many non-academic or para-academic educational institutions, as well as commercial organizations, offer PD programs for teachers that are neither based on research nor followed by research. Some of these endeavors may be considered successful, others less so (Brighouse & Moon, 2013). In addition, teachers take part in many PD activities that are informally organized by schools or districts, as noted in the recent TALIS Survey results (OECD [Organisation for Economic Co-operation and Development], 2019, 2020). Here again, no research is involved, yet teachers often report that they have learned a lot (OECD, 2019). Since PD programs that are research-based are not necessarily the common practice, the questions of what characterizes research-based programs and what is gained by rooting the PD in research, are valid and non-trivial.

For us, some of the answers can be summarized as follows:

- In the design phase of a PD program, theories and previous research serve, metaphorically speaking, as a lighthouse. They help to see where you are headed and direct you to a safe shore. In the design of VIDEO-LM, use of the two frameworks of Teaching in Context (Schoenfeld, 1998, 2010) and MKT (Ball et al., 2008) guided us to define our focus on informed and cognizant decision-making, enhanced reflection on practice and refinement of specialized mathematical knowledge. In addition, previous research helped us distill what we wanted to include in the SLF. Inspecting early experimentation conducted by Arcavi and Schoenfeld (2008) allowed us to extend our perspective and add the lenses of interactions, tasks and dilemmas to the framework directing teachers' reflection. Furthermore, the extensive research published on the affordances of video as an efficient tool in PD settings (e.g., Borko et al., 2011; Coles, 2010; Sherin & van Es, 2009) helped us learn from other programs, namely which features we wish to "borrow" and keep, and in what ways we differentiate ourselves. In that sense, basing the design on research serves at least three purposes: to avoid "reinventing the wheel"; to be inspired; and to clearly shape your own vision and singularize it. Later on, in the pilot phase, conducting research to follow the first PDs is essential for refining the design.
- In the upscale phase, research serves several other purposes. First, previous research highlights important features and conditions to be taken into account when scaling up a PD program that worked well on a small scale. For instance, *scalability factors* (e.g., high quality of the program; realistic expectations; reasonable amount of effort required; proximity of creators to implementers) suggested by Sternberg et al. (2006) and Coburn (2003), were a helpful resource for us, as were the insights of Cobb and Jackson (2011), McLaughlin and Mitra (2001), and others. Second, as already detailed, the upscale stage requires qualifying facilitators. Research on the development of facilitators from various angles (e.g., Borko et al., 2014; Maaß & Doorman, 2013; van Es et al., 2014) was inspiring at this stage. Third, conducting our own research was essential for gaining a better understanding of what happens in VIDEO-LM PDs within the upscale (e.g., Karsenty, 2018a; Karsenty & Arcavi, 2017; Karsenty et al., 2019; Schwarts & Karsenty, 2018, 2020), and for unpacking processes that VIDEO-LM facilitators undergo (e.g., Schwarts, 2020). Finally, research (e.g., Nurick, 2019) was crucial in discovering that some of the sustained impact that we were hoping for was not achieved, a realization that resulted in a new cycle of diving into the literature (this time to learn about sustainability), designing a revised model, piloting it, and preparing for implementation, as described in Section 2.3 above.

3.2 *VIDEO-LM as an Example of How PD Design Builds on Evolving Frameworks*

The role of frameworks in the design of PD programs is under-researched. A framework is essentially "a multi-component structure, where connections among the different elements shed light on the 'big picture' as a whole" (Karsenty et al., in press). At the same time, a framework forms the specific perspective used by the researcher to explore, interpret or explain events or behaviors (Imenda, 2014). Thus, frameworks may be both a tool for research and a result of research, or, as Ravitch and Riggan (2016) put it, a framework can be both a process and a product. This dual nature is perhaps one of the reasons why this term is so often presented in an idiosyncratic manner (Karsenty et al., in press). However, in the design of a research-based PD program, for either teachers or facilitators, a framework may be defined more narrowly, as "a set of constructs that unpack various aspects of the knowledge and practices that mathematics teachers and mathematics teacher educators develop within their work" (Karsenty et al., in press).

Konuk (2018) describes four main approaches to creating such frameworks: the standards-based approach, the practice-oriented approach, the inquiry-based approach, and finally, the method of extending or revising existing frameworks. Due to space limitations, we will not present here the characteristics of each of these approaches (which can be found in Konuk, 2018; see also a short summary in Karsenty et al., in press). Instead, we use the VIDEO-LM case to exemplify how the two latter approaches were used.

During the design phase of VIDEO-LM, we realized we need a conceptual framework to be used for directing teachers' attention to various aspects of the lessons they are observing. We asked ourselves, as designers, which elements were necessary for unpacking mathematics teachers' knowledge and practices as they may be manifested in a lesson. Thus, our framework, SLF, was formed first through an inquiry-based approach. However, as already detailed, we also drew on Schoenfeld's (1998, 2010) ROG framework (the triad of resources, orientations and goals), extending it with three more components ("lenses"), hence we were also using the method of extending or revising an existing framework. The result was a conceptual framework that assisted us in organizing teachers' discussions while watching videos, as well as our own understanding, as researchers, of the complexities of teacher knowledge and practices.

When scaling up the project, we found ourselves again in need of a framework to conceptualize the knowledge and practices of VIDEO-LM facilitators. We used once more an inquiry-based approach, asking ourselves which elements are necessary to identify such knowledge and practices. We went through a process of comparing the knowledge and practices of mathematics teachers, which constitute the SLF components, to the knowledge and practices needed for facilitators whose job is to use the SLF with teachers. The result of this process was the creation of MLF, detailed in Section 2.2. Thus, we were also using (again) the method of revising an existing framework, this time through the *lifting* and *nesting* strategies (Prediger et al., 2019), to adapt a framework from the teacher level to the facilitator level, obtaining a double-level framework. Figure 14.4 presents a visual illustration of the lifting of SLF and its nesting within MLF.

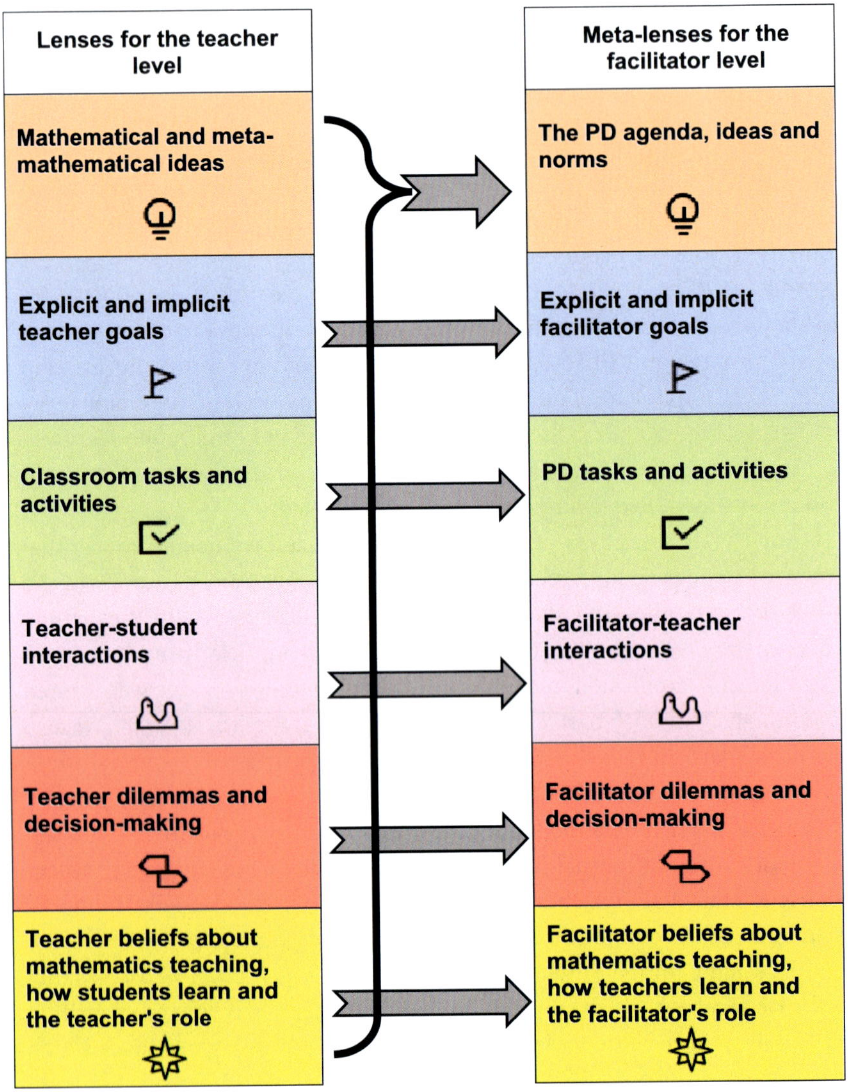

FIGURE 14.4 The six-lens framework (SLF) and the meta-lenses framework (MLF): a double-level framework (Karsenty et al., in press)

The construction of frameworks in the various design phases of VIDEO-LM therefore demonstrates (1) how frameworks can serve a PD program's research-based design, and (2) the dynamics of adapting frameworks to be useful, relevant and instructive in situations that evolve along the trajectory of the project.

3.3 *VIDEO-LM as a Case of a Successful Upscale Constantly Facing New Challenges*

It is well acknowledged that the process of upscaling any educational program is far from simple. In that regard, it is enlightening to read two of Richard Elmore's articles about scale, written 20 years apart from one another. Whereas the younger Elmore (1996) claims that the main challenge of scale is "understanding the conditions under which people working in schools seek new knowledge and actively use it" (p. 4), and moreover, presents some key principles for successful upscale, the older Elmore (2016) is much more skeptical, and regretfully sees his 1996 article as written "by someone – a person who now seems very unfamiliar to me – who believed in what seems to me now an irresponsibly simplistic and schematic view of human learning and development" (pp. 529–530). Indeed, in VIDEO-LM we also began with some naïveté regarding the diffusion of our promising idea and the prospects of its widespread dissemination. Eventually, we found ourselves facing various types of challenges, associated with policymakers' decisions, budget limitations, institutional constraints, the translation of schools' and teachers' motivations into a pragmatic frame of time and space dedicated to the PD, and more. Herein, we reflect on two of these challenges, and how the consideration of each of them eventually allowed us to reach more teachers and schools.

(1) The challenge of disseminating an educational viewpoint that does not centralize the notion of "best practice": As mentioned earlier, the focus of VIDEO-LM PDs is on discussing videotaped lessons insofar as they have potential to elicit significant issues of practice, rather than to portray models to imitate (or avoid). However, this perspective is not always accepted by funding agencies, policymakers, schools, or even some teachers. The following words by Elmore (2016) well exemplify this challenge:

> I routinely watch well-intentioned, highly motivated educators – teachers and administrators – talk obsessively about "best practice" as if it were a kind of super-hero jumpsuit you could slip on before you step into your formal role as "change agent." (Elmore, 2016, p. 530)

Sherin et al. (2009) differentiate between video-based PD programs that aim to show best practices, in order to "help teachers develop a vision of what is possible" (p. 215), and programs that use video to portray the problematics of teaching, in order to provide teachers with something to ponder about. In our view, these are two sides of the same coin, i.e., the message conveyed to teachers (even if only implicitly) is that they need to take the screened lesson as an example of practice that they should aim to implement, or be wary of, in their classrooms. Such messages are strengthened when teachers are required to watch their own videos with colleagues or instructors, using a pre-constructed rubric that hierarchizes for them which practices are better than others, such as the rubrics developed by Danielson (2013) or Hill et al. (2008).

We did not know how the VIDEO-LM approach would be received, when we moved from our pilot "boutique" courses, with selected lead teachers that already held similar views, to wide implementation. Our research has shown that VIDEO-LM facilitators constantly face the challenge of shifting the participating teachers from judgmental discussions to more issue-based conversations, which acknowledge complexities, nuances, and contextual factors. Yet, we found that over time, most PD participants gradually decreased their judgmental comments (e.g., "what should be done or avoided" or "what is best for students"), in favor of an approach that centralizes what can be learned from the screened lessons in terms of "issues of practice" (Karsenty & Arcavi, 2017; Karsenty et al., 2019). The following citations, taken from teachers' feedback during the upscale phase, demonstrate this change:

- At the beginning, I related to videos differently. I was inclined to criticize what I saw, and it was hard for me to abandon that approach. It took me time to understand what I can get from these videos.
- Theoretically, I know that there is an infinite variety of teachers that I can regard as "good teachers" and still they will be different from one another, and at various decision crossroads, they may take totally opposite decisions. However, each time I witness this it is a refreshing discovery, and I feel that slowly it is wearing down my inherent belief that there are absolute "rights" and "wrongs" in teaching too"

Moreover, we believe that our approach allowed many teachers to let go of their fear of being videotaped. Once they recognized that the PD course "does not put teachers in front of a firing squad," as one teacher put it, more and more teachers were willing, toward the end of the PD course, to bring their own videos to the group for peer analysis. Although this was not our original intention, we came to realize that this is an important step in enhancing the sustainability of VIDEO-LM ideas, and self-videotaping is now an integral part of the Math-VALUE design, as presented earlier.

(2) The challenge of adapting to changing situations: VIDEO-LM is an example of a project that had no choice but to adapt to new realities, if it was to

retain its impact. This, of course, is not unusual; in fact, it is typical of educational systems that are prone to frequent turnovers in governmental policy. Whereas in more stable systems, the main challenge in maintaining an upscale would be the preparation of qualified facilitators, in the constantly changing reality, the additional challenge is the need to stay flexible. We experienced this need at three points along the VIDEO-LM trajectory. The first was when we realized we should design school-based PDs and not only regional ones, as detailed in Section 2.2 above, due to reform-related requirements. The second was when we recognized that although the direction promoted by the Ministry of Education (at the time of our upscale phase), as well as by our funding agency, was to focus on teaching advanced students, the voices from the field pointed to the necessity of also relating to teaching mathematics in low-track classes. The result of this recognition was a new partnership that we formed along the way with a teacher education program focusing on teaching the lower tracks; this partnership yielded new videotaped lessons filmed in low-track mathematics classrooms, and a new PD course for teachers of these tracks. The third was when we realized that the Ministry of Education had shifted its focus regarding teachers' professional development, from courses to PLCs, with heavy emphasis on the insights and ideas developed through the constant and visible connections made by teachers between the PLC and the classroom. For us, this shift was aligned with the need to enhance the sustainability of VIDEO-LM, and resulted in revisiting our PD model and creating Math-VALUE communities.

4 Concluding Words: Understanding the "Life Trajectory" of a Project

A retrospective glimpse of the life and evolution of a decade-old project which aims at sustaining its impact and relevance provided us with two important insights. First, there were crucial decisions in the transition from one stage to the next which required adaptation, flexibility and ongoing monitoring. Accepting setbacks and analyzing them, being self-critical and at the same time open to the voices around us (from colleagues, teachers, policymakers, paper reviewers), were instrumental all along the way. Second, enacting the philosophy of the Department of Science Teaching which focuses on the interdependence of design, research, and implementation in a project, was a crucial mechanism that moved, and still moves the project forward.

Finally, no reflection on a project should leave out an inspection of the motivation driving its leaders. At the beginning, there is the a-priori belief that an idea is powerful and has the potential to have a positive impact and make desirable changes in the educational system, in this case by providing mathematics teachers with tools for bonding and reflecting. The creation of a workable "proof of existence" is then followed by an attempt to make ideas work at scale. Then, if short-term effects are satisfactory, the new "driver" is to aim for long-term wide-range impact by creating a follow-up project to address this need.

There are other levels of motivation as well. In our case, it was important to display examples in which the potency of academic tools could be fully harnessed to impact the field, in unique and powerful ways. In addition, and we should not deny this, there is the pleasure of creation and of facing intellectual challenges to solve, leaving out self-indulgence and exercising self-criticism. Lastly, we see values as a driving force, which is no less important than research opportunities, funding, or influence. In the work of VIDEO-LM, our guiding value was the empowerment of teachers as reflective practitioners, who do not merely adhere to the system's requested standards – according to which they are often evaluated and judged – but bring their knowledge, experience and own values to the forefront of the discussion about mathematics teaching and learning. We hope that this guiding value will continue to shape the way in which we conduct PD projects in the future.

Acknowledgments

We would like to deeply thank the Weizmann Institute of Science, and specifically the Department of Science Teaching, for their long-term support of VIDEO-LM. We are grateful to the many teachers and facilitators who joined us in different stages of the VIDEO-LM journey, enabling its growth. Special thanks to the VIDEO-LM team members Myriam Goor, Tzila Yarhi, Ahuva Gutman and Avital Elbaum-Cohen, and to our students Yael Nurick and Gil Schwarts, who advanced the research around VIDEO-LM. The design and implementation of VIDEO-LM were supported by the Israel Trump Foundation for Science and Mathematics Education, Grants #7/143. Research around VIDEO-LM was supported by the Israel Science Foundation, Grant #1539/15, and by the German-Israeli Foundation for Scientific Research and Development, Grant #1426.

Notes

1 PSC – Problem Solving Cycle; MLP – Mathematics Leadership Preparation (Borko et al., 2015).

2 RTCs are managed by the Israeli Ministry of Education and offer a variety of PD courses from which teachers can choose. Teachers enrolled in RTC courses pay a nominal fee and accrue credit points for promotion; however, enrollment is not obligatory.

3 Of these eight courses, five were held in RTCs, two at the Weizmann Institute, and one in a college of education (the latter being a special version for prospective teachers, whereas all others were for practicing teachers).

4 adasha.weizmann.ac.il

5 To date, the website includes more than 70 lessons.

6 Some of this research was conducted in collaboration with a German project that had gone through a similar process of preparing and supporting facilitators, with the support of the German–Israeli Foundation for Scientific Research and Development.

7 Teachers were selected on the basis of two criteria: (1) the recommendation of course facilitators, indicating those candidates who were likely to agree to take part in the research; and (2) a sampling table, to ensure as much diversity as possible in teacher age, background, gender and experience.

References

Arcavi, A. (2019). From tools to resources in the professional development of mathematics teachers: General perspectives and crosscutting issues. In S. Llinares (Ed.), *The international handbook of mathematics teacher education. Vol. 2: Tools and processes in mathematics teacher education* (2nd ed., pp. 421–440). Sense Publishers. http://dx.doi.org/10.1163/9789004418967_016

Arcavi, A., & Karsenty, R. (2016). *Students, teachers, teachers of teachers, teachers of teachers of teachers…: Reflections on the "learning-teaching pyramid"* [Lecture presentation]. 3rd Symposium on Video Resources for Mathematics Teacher Development, June, Weizmann Institute of Science.

Arcavi, A., & Karsenty, R. (2018). Enhancing mathematics teachers' reflection and knowledge through peer-discussions of videotaped lessons: A pioneer program in Israel. In N. Movshovitz-Hadar (Ed.), *K-12 mathematics education in Israel – Issues and challenges. Series on mathematics education, Vol. 13* (Chapter 33, pp. 303–310). World Scientific. http://dx.doi.org/10.1142/9789813231191_0033

Arcavi, A., & Schoenfeld, A. H. (2008). Using the unfamiliar to problematize the familiar: The case of mathematics teacher in-service education. *Canadian Journal of Science, Mathematics, and Technology Education, 8*, 280–295. http://dx.doi.org/10.1080/14926150802315122

Ball, D. L., Thames, M. H., & Phelps, G. (2008). Content knowledge for teaching: What makes it special. *Journal of Teacher Education, 59*(5), 389–407. http://dx.doi.org/10.1177/0022487108324554

Borko, H., Carlson, J., Mangram, C., Anderson, R., Fong, A., Million, S., Mozenter, S., & Villa, A. M. (2017). The role of video-based discussion in a model for preparing professional development leaders. *International Journal of STEM Education, 4*. https://doi.org/10.1186/s40594-017-0090-3

Borko, H., Jacobs, J., Koellner, K., & Swackhamer, L. E. (2015). *Mathematics professional development: Improving teaching using the problem-solving cycle and leadership preparation models*. Teachers College Press.

Borko, H., Koellner, K., & Jacobs, J. (2014). Examining novice teacher leaders' facilitation of professional development. *Journal of Mathematical Behavior, 33*, 149–167. http://dx.doi.org/10.1016/j.jmathb.2013.11.003

Borko, H., Koellner, K., Jacobs, J., & Seago, N. (2011). Using video representations of teaching in practice-based professional development programs. *ZDM – Mathematics Education, 43*, 175–187. http://dx.doi.org/10.1007/s11858-010-0302-5

Brighouse, T., & Moon, B. (2013). *Taking teacher development seriously: A proposal to establish a national teaching institute for teacher professional development in England*. The New Visions for Education Group.

Brodie, K., & Borko, H. (2018). *Professional learning communities in South African schools and teacher education programmes*. HSRC Press.

Cobb, P., & Jackson, K. (2011). Towards an empirically grounded theory of action for improving the quality of mathematics teaching at scale. *Mathematics Teacher Education and Development, 13*, 6–33.

Coburn, C. E. (2003). Rethinking scale: Moving beyond numbers to deep and lasting change. *Educational Researcher, 32*(6), 3–12. http://dx.doi.org/10.3102/0013189x032006003

Coles, A. (2010). Using video for professional development: A case study of effective practice in one secondary mathematics department in the UK. In M. Joubert (Ed.), *Proceedings of the British Society for Research into Learning Mathematics, 30*(2). https://bsrlm.org.uk/wp-content/uploads/2016/02/BSRLM-IP-30-2-01.pdf

Coles, A. (2013). Using video for professional development: The role of the discussion facilitator. *Journal of Mathematics Teacher Education, 16*, 165–184. http://dx.doi.org/10.1007/s10857-012-9225-0

Danielson, S. (2013). *The framework for teaching evaluation instrument* (2013 edition). The Danielson Group.

Elmore, R. F. (1996). Getting to scale with good educational practice. *Harvard Educational Review, 66*(1), 1–27. http://dx.doi.org/10.17763/haer.66.1.g73266758j348t33

Elmore, R. F. (2016). "Getting to scale…" It seemed like a good idea at the time. *Journal of Educational Change, 17*, 529–537. http://dx.doi.org/10.1007/s10833-016-9290-8

Even, R. (2005). Integrating knowledge and practice at MANOR in the development of providers of professional development for teachers. *Journal of Mathematics Teacher Education, 8*, 343–357. http://dx.doi.org/10.1007/s10857-005-0855-3

Even, R. (2008). Facing the challenge of educating educators to work with practicing mathematics teachers. In B. Jaworski & T. Wood (Eds.), *The international handbook of mathematics teacher education. Vol. 4: The mathematics teacher educator as a developing professional* (pp. 57–74). Sense Publishers. http://dx.doi.org/10.1163/9789087905521_005

Fernandez, C., & Yoshida, M. (2004). *Lesson study: A Japanese approach to improving mathematics teaching and learning*. Lawrence Erlbaum Associates.

Hill, H. C., Blunk, M., Charalambous, C., Lewis, J., Phelps, G. C., Sleep, L., & Ball, D. L. (2008). Mathematical knowledge for teaching and the mathematical quality of instruction: An exploratory study. *Cognition and Instruction, 26*, 430–511. http://dx.doi.org/10.1080/07370000802177235

Imenda, S. (2014). Is there a conceptual difference between theoretical and conceptual frameworks? *Journal of Social Sciences, 38*, 185–195. http://dx.doi.org/10.1080/09718923.2014.11893249

Jaworski, B. (1990). Video as a tool for teachers' professional development. *British Journal of In-Service Education, 16*, 60–65. http://dx.doi.org/10.1080/0305763900160112

Karsenty, R. (2016). *Preparing facilitators to conduct video-based professional development for mathematics teachers: Needs, experiences and challenges* [Paper presentation]. 2nd International Conference on Educating the Educators, November, Freiburg, Germany.

Karsenty, R. (2017). How do mathematics teachers learn from videotaped lessons of unknown peers? Exploring possible mechanisms that contribute to change in teachers' perspectives. In L. Gómez Chova, A. López Martínez, & I. Candel Torres (Eds.), *Proceedings of the 9th Annual International Conference on Education and New Learning Technologies* (pp. 1718–1728). IATED Academy. http://dx.doi.org/10.21125/edulearn.2017.1371

Karsenty, R. (2018a). Professional development of mathematics teachers: Through the lens of the camera. In G. Kaiser, H. Forgasz, M. Graven, A. Kuzniak, E. Simmt, & B. Xu (Eds.), *Invited lectures from the 13th International Congress on mathematical education* (pp. 269–288). Springer.

Karsenty, R. (2018b, June). *Talking about observed practices: Enhancing novice facilitators' proficiency to steer video-based discussions with mathematics teachers* [Paper presentation]. EARLI SIG-11 Conference on Teaching and Teacher Education, University of Agder, Kristiansand, Norway.

Karsenty, R. (2021). The role of frameworks in researching knowledge and practices of mathematics teachers and teacher educators. In S. Zehetmeier, D. Potari, & M. Ribeiro (Eds.), *Professional development and knowledge of mathematics teachers* (ERME book series: New perspectives on research in mathematics education, pp. 62–84). Routledge | Taylor & Francis. http://dx.doi.org/10.4324/9781003008460-5

Karsenty, R., & Arcavi, A. (2017). Mathematics, lenses and videotapes: A framework and a language for developing reflective practices of teaching. *Journal of Mathematics Teacher Education, 20*, 433–455. http://dx.doi.org/10.1007/s10857-017-9379-x

Karsenty, R., Arcavi, A., & Nurick, Y. (2015). Video-based peer discussions as sources for knowledge growth of secondary teachers. In K. Krainer & N. Vondrová (Eds.), *Proceedings of the 9th Congress of the European Society for Research in Mathematics Education* (pp. 2825–2832). European Research in Mathematics Education.

Karsenty, R., Peretz, Y., & Heyd-Metzuyanim, E. (2019). From judgmental evaluations to productive conversations: Mathematics teachers' shifts in communication within a video club. In U. T. Jankvist, M. van den Heuvel-Panhuizen, & M. Veldhuis (Eds.), *Proceedings of the Eleventh Congress of the European Society for Research in Mathematics Education* (pp. 3400–3407). Freudenthal Group & Freudenthal Institute, Utrecht University and European Research in Mathematics Education.

Karsenty, R., Pöhler, B., Schwarts, G., Prediger, S., & Arcavi, A. (in press). Processes of decision-making by mathematics PD facilitators: The role of resources, orientations, goals and identities. *Journal of Mathematics Teacher Education.*

Konuk, N. (2018). *Mathematics teacher educators' roles, talks, and knowledge in collaborative planning practice: Opportunities for professional development* [Unpublished doctoral dissertation]. Pennsylvania State University.

Kuzle, A., & Biehler, R. (2015). Examining mathematics mentor teachers' practices in professional development courses on teaching data analysis: Implications for mentor teachers' programs. *ZDM – Mathematics Education, 47*, 39–51. http://dx.doi.org/10.1007/s11858-014-0663-2

Lewis, C., & Lee, C. (2017). The global spread of lesson study: Contextualization and adaptations. In M. Akiba & G. K. Letendre (Eds.), *International handbook of teacher quality and policy* (pp. 185–203). Routledge. http://dx.doi.org/10.4324/9781315710068-13

Maaß, K., & Doorman, M. (2013). A model for a widespread implementation of inquiry based learning. *ZDM – Mathematics Education, 45*, 887–899. http://dx.doi.org/10.1007/s11858-013-0505-7

McLaughlin, M. W., & Mitra, D. (2001). Theory-based change and change-based theory: Going deeper, going broader. *Journal of Educational Change, 2*, 301–323. http://dx.doi.org/10.1023/a:1014616908334

Ministry of Education. (2017). *Characteristics of disciplinary professional learning communities in education.* Israel Ministry of Education (in Hebrew). http://kehilotmorim.macam.ac.il/kehilafeature

Nurick, Y. (2015). *The crystallization of mathematical knowledge for teaching of high school teachers in video-based peer discussions* [Unpublished master's thesis]. Weizmann Institute of Science (in Hebrew).

Nurick, Y. (2019). *Reflection on practice and opportunities for professional development of mathematics teachers in different settings.* Internal Report, Weizmann Institute of Science (in Hebrew).

OECD. (2019). *TALIS 2018 results (Vol. I): Teachers and school leaders as lifelong learners* (Summary). OECD Publishing. https://doi.org/10.1787/0d310598-en.

OECD. (2020). *TALIS 2018 results (Vol. II): Teachers and school leaders as valued professionals.* OECD Publishing. https://doi.org/10.1787/19cf08df-en.

Prediger, S., & Pöhler, B. (2019). Conducting PD discussions on language repertoires: A case study on facilitators' practices. In M. Graven, H. Venkat, A. Essien, & P. Vale (Eds.), *Proceedings of 43rd Annual Meeting of the International Group for the Psychology of Mathematics Education (PME 43), Vol. 3* (pp. 241–248). Psychology of Mathematics Education.

Prediger, S., Roesken-Winter, B., & Leuders, T. (2019). Which research can support PD facilitators? Strategies for content-related PD research in the Three-Tetrahedron Model. *Journal of Mathematics Teacher Education, 22*, 407–425. http://dx.doi.org/10.1007/s10857-019-09434-3

Ravitch, S. M., & Riggan, M. (2016). *Reason & rigor: How conceptual frameworks guide research.* Sage.

Robutti, O., Cusi, A., Clark-Wilson, A., Jaworski, B., Chapman, O., Esteley, C., Goos, M., Isoda, M., & Joubert, M. (2016). ICME international survey on teachers working and learning through collaboration: June 2016. *ZDM – Mathematics Education, 48*, 651–690. http://dx.doi.org/10.1007/s11858-016-0797-5

Roesken-Winter, B., Hoyles, C., & Blömeke, S. (2015). Evidence-based CPD: Scaling up sustainable interventions. *ZDM – Mathematics Education, 47*, 1–12. http://dx.doi.org/10.1007/s11858-015-0682-7

Schoenfeld, A. H. (1998). Toward a theory of teaching-in-context. *Issues in Education, 4*, 1–94. http://dx.doi.org/10.1016/s1080-9724(99)80076-7

Schoenfeld, A. H. (2010). *How we think: A theory of goal-oriented decision making and its educational applications.* Routledge. https://doi.org/10.4324/9780203843000

Schwarts, G. (2019). *Professionalization processes of facilitators in mathematics teachers' video-based professional development programs.* Internal Report, Weizmann Institute of Science.

Schwarts, G. (2020). Facilitating a collaborative professional development for the first time. In H. Borko & D. Potari (Eds.), *Teachers of mathematics working and learning in collaborative groups, Proceedings of the 25th ICMI study conference* (pp. 540–547). International Commission on Mathematical Instruction.

Schwarts, G., & Karsenty, R. (2018). A teacher's reflective process in a video-based professional development program. In E. Bergqvist, M. Österholm, C. Granberg, & L. Sumpter (Eds.), *Proceedings of the 42nd Conference of the International Group for the Psychology of Mathematics Education, Vol. 4* (pp. 123–130). Psychology of Mathematics Education.

Schwarts, G., & Karsenty, R. (2020). "Can this happen only in Japan?" Mathematics teachers reflect on a videotaped lesson in a cross-cultural context. *Journal of Mathematics Teacher Education, 23*, 527–554. http://dx.doi.org/10.1007/s10857-019-09438-z

Seago, N. (2003). Using video as an object of inquiry for mathematics teaching and learning. In J. Brophy (Ed.), *Using video in teacher education* (Advances in Research on Teaching Series, Vol. 10) (pp. 259–286). Emerald Group Publishing Limited. http://dx.doi.org/10.1016/s1479-3687(03)10010-7

Sherin, M. G., Linsenmeier, K. A., & van Es, E. A. (2009). Selecting video clips to promote mathematics teachers' discussion of student thinking. *Journal of Teacher Education, 60*(3), 213–230. http://dx.doi.org/10.1016/s1479-3687(03)10010-7

Sherin, M. G., & van Es, E. A. (2009). Effects of video participation on teachers' professional vision. *Journal of Teacher Education, 60*(1), 20–37. http://dx.doi.org/10.1177/0022487108328155

Sternberg, R. J., Birney, D., Kirlik, A., Stemler, S., Jarvin, L., & Grigorenko. E. L. (2006). From molehill to mountain: The process of scaling up educational interventions (firsthand experience upscaling the theory of successful intelligence). In M. A. Constas & R. J. Sternberg (Eds.), *Translating theory and research into educational practice* (pp. 205–222). Lawrence Erlbaum Associates. http://dx.doi.org/10.4324/9780203726556-21

Stevenson, H. W., & Stigler, J. W. (1992). *The learning gap*. Simon & Schuster.

van Es, E., Tunney, J., Goldsmith, L. T., & Seago, N. (2014). A framework for the facilitation of teachers' analysis of video. *Journal of Teacher Education, 65*(4), 340–356. http://dx.doi.org/10.1177/0022487114534266

Zehetmeier, S. (2015). Sustaining and scaling up the impact of professional development programmes. *ZDM – Mathematics Education, 47*, 117–128. http://dx.doi.org/10.1007/s11858-015-0671-x

CHAPTER 15

In the Pursuit of Impact

Design and Practice of Three Innovative Professional Development Programs for Mathematics Teachers

Jason Cooper and Boris Koichu

Abstract

Arguably, any professional development (PD) program aims to have an impact on the field. Yet there is likely to be significant variation in the nature of the impact that different programs aim to achieve, and in their ways of going about achieving it. We present three PD programs for in-service secondary-school mathematics teachers – one for middle-school heads of mathematics departments, one for experienced mathematics teachers who are interested in engaging in classroom educational research, and one for mathematics teachers who aspire to systematically incorporate high-level problem solving in their teaching. All of these programs are organized as professional learning communities. Through these three examples, we illustrate the impact we aim to have on the practices of teaching mathematics, recognizing that the effect of PD on teachers can be as varied as the kinds of practices in which they engage. We then reflect on the design and enactment of these programs, and discuss some tensions between various facets of the impact that we are striving for. In articulating some of the design principles of these programs, we attempt to make explicit the often implicit – or even tacit – theories of impact that guide our work.

Keywords

mathematics teachers – professional development – impact – implicit theories – fidelity-scaling tension – teacher-researcher partnerships – sustainability

1 Introduction

Impact is one of the holy grails of educational research. Arguably, the entire academic world of mathematics education aims to have an *impact* on the practices of teaching and learning mathematics.

 | DOI: 10.1163/9789004503625_015

The Mathematics Education Group of the Department of Science Teaching at the Weizmann Institute of Science is one of the recognized leaders of the pursuit of impact, as evidenced by its 50-year long history (Arcavi, this volume; Even, this volume; Friedlander, this volume). The group has gained institutional recognition for developing models of blending research and practice, establishing life-long support structures for teachers, creating and refining environments for research-based professional development (PD), and in so doing, becoming a "reference point" for practice, research and policy.

As current members of the Mathematics Education Group, we have the privilege of initiating and running novel programs and projects which, hopefully, bear the group's spirit and definitely bear signs of its established discourse, that is, the discourse of resolving problems of practice of mathematics education, including implementation, scalability and sustainability, or, more generally, of having an *impact* on mathematics education in schools by means of collaborating with in-service mathematics teachers.

In this chapter, we present three of our R&D projects that aim to create innovative opportunities for mathematics teachers' PD. Throughout the chapter, the projects' descriptions provide an empirical basis for exploring the following questions: What counts as the impact that we are pursuing as project designers and researchers? What characterizes our pursuit of impact? How can this pursuit be rewarding, given the well-known gap between research and practice?

We will attempt to make sense of the notion of "impact" by reflecting on our own practice. To create a conceptual framework for this attempt, we begin by considering one of the dictionary definitions of *impact:* "a strong effect on someone or something" (Oxford Online Dictionary, n.d.). We note that this definition leaves much unsaid: who and what are the "someone" or "something" that we wish to have an effect on? What kind of effect? In what sense should it be "strong"?

To demonstrate the complexity of impact, we draw inspiration from the well-developed research field of curriculum design, where the relationship between intended, enacted and experienced curricula has long been a topic of interest (e.g., Remillard & Heck, 2014). PD programs are designed with an *intended* impact on the educational field, their *enactment* takes on a life of its own through interactions with teachers, and their *experienced* impact on student learning is further influenced by the contextual realities of classrooms. When designing and enacting a PD program, we may hold theories of how the PD can hope to have an impact on the field. Conversely, when assessing the impact of PD, we may hold theories of how this impact is a causal result of what did or did not occur during the PD program. Accordingly, we ask what such theories of impact might look like.

The professional literature on the PD of mathematics and science teachers does not provide conclusive answers. We will demonstrate that the notion of impact is used in different ways by different researchers, often implicitly. Individual researchers attend to particular facets of impact and disregard others, rarely explicating their choices or articulating their rationale. Furthermore, the chain of causality, from PD design to effects on teaching and learning is, at best, tentative. Hence, we will argue that researchers and PD designers tend to have implicit – or even tacit – theories of impact, that is, unarticulated assumptions regarding the kind of impact they aim to have on educational practice, and the ways in which it may be achieved through PD (see Sternberg, 1985, for a compatible conceptualization of implicit theories in relation to other not-well-defined constructs). The main bulk of this chapter is then dedicated to articulating our own tacit theory of impact – the values, beliefs and norms that guide our activity, their implications on our conceptualization of impact, and the practical decisions and choices we make in designing PD programs in our quest to achieve this notion of impact. We elicit and demonstrate our understanding of impact through three PD programs that we are currently involved in.

2 Impact of PD in Academic Literature

For this section we conducted a search for research articles that match the keywords "professional development," "impact," and "mathematics education" or "science education" in Google Scholar. It is not our intention here to review the literature exhaustively (indeed, reviewing over 20,000 articles is beyond the scope and goals of this chapter), but rather to check how diversely the notion of impact is used.

Research typically addresses PD's impact on teachers' knowledge and practices and/or on students' achievements. In its PD Impact Study (Garet et al., 2011), the National Center for Educational Evaluation and Regional Assistance (NCEE) reports on "statistically significant impact on teacher knowledge… [and] average student achievement" (p. XXVIII). In a review of 44 studies on PD in science education, van Driel et al. (2012) found that most programs aim to enhance teacher cognition as well as classroom practice, and some programs also aim to improve student outcomes. We note that the notions of *teacher knowledge* and *student achievement* are value-laden and may not, in and of themselves, be well-defined.

Research addresses some additional facets of impact. Impact on teachers is sometimes referred to in terms of teachers' practices and beliefs (e.g. Swan, 2007), and teachers' individual and collective efficacies are also considered (e.g. Zambo & Zambo, 2008). Some research attends to particular practices and attitudes, such as teachers' assessment agendas (Pegg & Panizzon, 2007/2008). Impact on students, while usually considered in terms of measurable achievements, also reflects notions of efficacy (Ingvarson et al., 2005).

Faced with the diverse ways in which research looks at the impact of PD programs, some researchers have attempted to put forth frameworks of impact in PD and models of how PD activities influence teaching and learning. Clarke and Hollingsworth (2002) proposed a model of teacher professional growth that takes into consideration three purposes of PD: change in knowledge and beliefs, change in classroom practice, and change in student learning outcomes. Ingvarson et al. (2005) developed a theoretical model to investigate factors affecting impact. They considered four measures of impact: teacher knowledge and practice, and student learning and efficacy. Desimone (2009) made the case of a research consensus to support the use of a set of core features and a common conceptual framework in PD impact studies. The core features that she recognized were focused on content, active learning, coherence, duration and collective participation. These, she claimed, are the features of PD that influence increases in teachers' knowledge and skill, changes in their attitudes and beliefs, and as a consequence, changes in their instruction, which in turn can lead to improved student learning.

While these frameworks attempt to map out what and whom PD might aim to have an influence on, and propose some models of how this influence might come about, the question of what kind of change should qualify as *impact* is not directly addressed. Clearly, not all forms of change are valued equally by all researchers. To explore the characteristics of change that are implicitly valued in research, we looked at some adjectives and verbs that tend to precede references to impact. We found that some are concerned with *sustainable* impact (Zehetmeier, 2015; Zehetmeier & Krainer, 2011), sometimes in connection with upscaling (Goos et al., 2018). Fidelity of implementation is also considered by some to be an important facet of impact (e.g. Clements et al., 2015), i.e., how faithfully teachers are implementing what is proposed in the PD program. This notion of fidelity is sometimes contrasted with the notion of *adaptation* (Century & Cassata, 2016), whereby teachers' implementation must always adapt what is being proposed in the PD course to fit particular contexts, which include teachers' orientations and beliefs, students' needs (as perceived by the teachers), and institutional norms and constraints.

Taken together, it appears that there is some convergence in research on a list of factors that PD aims to influence. Individual researchers focus on some subset of these factors (e.g., teacher knowledge, student achievement), along with their own interpretation of these factors (e.g., what constitutes teacher knowledge or student learning, what kind of teacher knowledge – mathematical or pedagogical – is valued, or what kind of student learning – procedural, conceptual, etc. – is valued). There are many facets of change that qualify as *impactful* (e.g., sustainability, fidelity, scale), and here too, researchers tend to focus on no more than one such facet. This suggests that individual researchers hold implicit and idiosyncratic "theories" of impact that guide their work with teachers and their academic investigation of this work. We argue that making these theories explicit can be important. It is not difficult to imagine a PD program for which education researchers, teachers, students, parents, ministry officials and funding agencies would have very different ideas regarding the impact of that program on the field. A well-known example of such disagreement was reported by Cohen (1990): Mrs. Oublier participated in a reform-oriented workshop and subsequently "was delighted with her students' performance and with her own accomplishments" (p. 311), while Cohen, who conducted classroom observations, was much less enthusiastic about the impact that the workshop had actually had on Mrs. Oublier's teaching, which in his view remained by and large "traditional."

Clearly, different stakeholders may stress different facets of impact. Education researchers might focus on teachers' dialogical classroom practices, mathematicians who are sometimes involved in PD programs may emphasize teachers' advanced disciplinary knowledge, and ministry officials may be more concerned with students' grades in high-stakes tests. They may also promote very different ways of defining or measuring the impact of those programs in practice.

Our point is that explicating one's implicit or tacit theories of impact can be both important and rewarding. Important for transparently coordinating aims and goals across stakeholders, and rewarding in the sense that self-awareness of tacit theories, and of the underlying values that influence them, can advise and guide the design of programs that the designers will ultimately consider *impactful*. In this chapter, we demonstrate this point by reflecting on three PD programs that we are currently conducting, and on the nature of the impact that we aim to achieve (with each). The next three sections present these programs. Each section has the following structure:

- Rationale, context and the intended nature of the program's impact
- Enactment of the program, how the conception of impact is being pursued
- From implicit to explicit notions of impact

3 PD for Heads of Mathematics Departments (PD-HMD)

3.1 *The Program's Rationale and Intended Impact*

In Israel, the work of mathematics departments in schools is coordinated by one of the teachers who holds the position of Head of Mathematics Department (HMD).[1] It is perhaps surprising that, to date, there has been no systematic PD for HMDs in Israel. The professed goals of our program are to develop a model of PD for HMDs. The PD-HMD program[2] has been ongoing since the autumn of 2017.

3.1.1 Impact – Upon Whom and What?

As in most PD programs, the ultimate goal here is to have a positive influence on the teaching and learning of mathematics in schools. The rationale for a PD-HMD program is that HMD is a strategic position, and therefore effort invested in the professional growth of HMDs can potentially influence not only how mathematics is taught and learned in their own classrooms, but also how it is perceived school wide and how it is taught by all of their department's teachers. Such growth requires a significant change in the way the position of HMD is perceived and carried out. While we believe that these changes should eventually influence student learning and attitudes toward mathematics, it is unrealistic to expect that such changes will be evident in the short term, and it is methodologically challenging to include them in a pool of measurable outcomes of the program. Accordingly, we intended to focus on the professional growth of HMDs, on promoting a gradual change in their role in schools and in turn, on changing ways in which their mathematics departments operate.

In addition, as the PD-HMD program is conducted under the auspices of a research university, we believe that it should ultimately offer an opportunity to elaborate and develop theories of teaching and of professional growth of HMDs, hence having an impact on us as educators and as researchers, and, by means of some mediation and dissemination, on the larger communities of mathematics educators and researchers.

3.1.2 Impact – Facets of "Strength"

Fidelity. While we do hold some (tentative) visions of "best practices" for teaching mathematics, it was not our intention that teachers adopt them with any sense of fidelity. Recognizing the challenge of shaping the role of HMDs and reforming interactions among their mathematics staff, we consider it more important that HMDs plan and implement a change in the way mathematics is taught, while leaving the exact nature of this change essentially up to them. Two considerations underlie this attitude. First, once HMDs have the proven ability to lead a change in the way mathematics is taught, they will later be able to utilize this ability to introduce change in a more deliberate and pedagogically aware manner. Second, we do not believe that our academic background gives us the authority to decide on best practices for specific schools and teachers. Mathematics is taught in particular contexts that place constraints on what is practical and practicable, hence we tend to rely on teachers to exercise practical rationality (Herbst & Chazan, 2020) in making their own context-aware and content-specific pedagogical decisions. To this end, we see our role mostly in initiating and supporting a change-oriented discourse among HMDs, by showing a space of possibilities to choose from, and offering reflective tools for more informed decision-making. In this way, we aim to create an infrastructure for sharing pedagogical ideas, experiences and research-based insights, rather than pushing preconceived resources and practices.

Scale. Our goal was to engage 120 HMDs. This is not a large-scale project. However, the model of PD that we developed (described further on), along with the resources (sample activities and lesson plans, and principles by which they were designed) to be shared with the community of teacher educators, hold the promise of impact on a larger scale.

Sustainability. It is our wish that changes instilled and inspired by the program will be sustained beyond the 4-year funding period of the program.

3.2 *Enactment of PD-HMD – In Pursuit of Impact*

In many schools in Israel, the position of HMD is mainly administrative – monitoring teachers' progress through the curriculum, coordinating standardized assessment, dealing with issues of student placement, and conveying pedagogical goals of school principals and of the Ministry of Education to the staff. Our aim was to encourage HMDs to take responsibility for the way mathematics is taught in their school. Such a goal entails changes in the HMDs' professional identity – in the extent to which they see their role as one of leadership, and in the responsibility they take for the pedagogical practices of the teachers under their supervision. It also has implications for the way in which HMDs position themselves with respect to their staff, and how they organize the interactions with and among them. This led us to base the program on the model of professional learning communities (PLCs, see Stoll et al., 2006, for a review). This model of PD is particularly suitable for supporting and sustaining changes in professional identities, by setting up norms of communication that support discussions about practice in a safe and non-judgmental environment. Furthermore, changes in the role and practices of HMDs are bound to instigate objections, or at least tensions, in interactions with teachers and with school principals. Thus, a supportive community of peers is a crucial element in meeting the expected challenges, and for the HMDs' own well-being.

Our conception of who should be impacted (teachers? HMDs? the researchers and PD facilitators running the program? students? other schools that may take inspiration from the program?) suggested a "nested" configuration of PLCs. The first municipal-level community functioned as a PLC led by a researcher from the Department of Science Teaching and co-led by an experienced HMD; all HMDs from middle schools of that municipality participated in the PLC. At the school level, each mathematics department was expected to function as a PLC led by the HMD participant. As the program grew to encompass more municipalities, the leaders of the municipal communities also began to function as a PLC in its own right. This model supports a fundamental assumption regarding the importance of prototyping in PD. Every leader of a PLC is also a participating member of a PLC at the next nested level: the HMDs participate in a PLC at the municipal level and lead PLCs – comprising the staff of mathematics teachers – at the school level, and the leaders of municipal PLCs are themselves members of a leaders' PLC. Furthermore, teachers may take some aspects of their participation in the school-based PLC to classroom teaching and learning.

There are two parallel learning processes involved in any PLC: the learning of professional "content," which in the case of HMDs is the content knowledge pertinent to leading a mathematics department, and learning how to participate productively in a PLC. We have discussed these processes elsewhere (Cooper & Koichu, 2019), and have described some tensions that they created and ways they were attended to. In the case of HMD-PD, these two learning processes are strongly intertwined, because part of the professional content for the position of HMD is leading a school-based PLC. Hence, knowing how to participate productively in a PLC is doubly relevant for HMDs – first, each HMD must learn to participate productively as a member of the municipal community; later, this knowledge needs to be adapted for school-based PLCs.

This state of affairs, where the professional knowledge of mathematics teachers is a subset of the professional knowledge of HMDs (Borko et al., 2014), infuses each activity in the municipal PLC with a double role. Activities directly address some aspect of professional knowledge (mathematical, pedagogical, or interpersonal), while at the same time suggesting a parallel activity that the HMDs can carry out in their school-based PLC to help develop the professional knowledge of their staff. Accordingly, many of the PD activities had the following structure:

- Professional activity for HMDs (lecture, workshop, etc.)
- A short workshop in which HMDs design and plan derivative activities for their school staff, to be enacted in staff meetings following the PD session
- In the next PD session: HMDs report on these school-based activities as they were enacted in the staff meetings that they held.

Here is an example of one such cycle: a guest lecturer gave a workshop on managing dilemmas, i.e., questions (professional or personal) that call for a yes/no decision. The goal of the workshop was to open up a legitimate space for a third response – "it depends" – which encourages a deeper analysis of the dilemma by reflecting on what the answer might depend on (i.e., what additional information will warrant giving yes or no as an answer). The workshop was generic in the sense that the dilemmas discussed were universal, and not directly related to teaching mathematics. Following the workshop, the HMDs engaged in group work where they designed derivative activities for their respective staff members. Some planned to carry out exactly the same activity, some planned to conduct a similar activity around professional dilemmas of teaching mathematics which they phrased in advance, and others planned to conduct an activity that would elicit a collection of professional dilemmas from their staff, upon which they would then base the activity. Ideas were shared, activities were held in the schools, HMDs reported on these activities (in writing and verbally in the following PD session), and affordances were discussed. We note that in the context of mathematical activities, another level is added to the cycle, whereby the activity among teachers in the school-based PLC serves as a prototype for classroom enactment of derivative activities, which are subsequently discussed among the teachers.

3.3 *From Implicit to Explicit Notions of Impact*

Fidelity. The described PD model is not directly concerned with the fidelity aspect of impact. Our direct interaction was with HMDs, who then worked with their mathematics teachers in staff meetings. There was no direct interaction between the PLC leaders and the teachers in schools, nor was there any direct interaction between the HMDs and the individual classrooms (other than their own), hence no direct way to monitor if and how activities tried in the municipal PLCs were adapted by teachers and experienced by students. Information was propagated through reporting back: teachers reported to HMDs on classroom activity, HMDs reported on their work with teachers (including how they addressed the teachers' reports) in the municipal PLCs, and each PLC leader reported on the municipal activity in the leaders' PLC. While each level of activity was designed to serve as a model for activity at the next level, it was tacitly understood that there would be a "broken telephone" effect, whereby changes at the different levels might accumulate. Hence, it was accepted that the work of HMDs with their staff, and the pedagogy that was enacted in individual classrooms, might not be fully endorsed by the leaders of the program. However, along with this possible loss of fidelity, there is the promise of gaining relevance.

Scale. Besides bringing the notion of modeling to the fore, the nested-PLC design also attends to issues of scale: the model allows a small number of teacher educators to influence a large number of teachers "by proxy" – a project leader influencing a PLC of leaders, each of whom influences a community of HMDs, each of whom influences a community of school teachers, each of whom influences a classroom of students. Furthermore, it suggests a model for scaling up the project, whereby some of the participants in municipal PLCs are groomed to themselves lead a PLC of HMDs in a different municipality.

Sustainability. All too many PD programs have an effect that is limited to the period of intervention. In our conception of impact, programs should have a lasting effect. It is thus important to set up mechanisms that will be independently sustained after the program has terminated. This was enabled through our focus on changes in HMDs' professional identities – how they perceive their role as HMD – assuming that changes in identity have the potential to persist longer than mere changes in practice. Moreover, it was our intention that such changes in individual identities find their way into norms of the PLCs' discourse, so as to persist beyond the participation of particular individuals in the community.

However, for changes in identity and in practice to be sustained, we believe that the municipal PLC should continue to function after the Department of Science Teaching completes its facilitating role. This poses a dual challenge: HMDs should have both the motivation and the ability to sustain their PLC on their own. Accordingly, the final year of the program in each municipality was conducted with the goal of achieving independence, i.e., the motivation to sustain activity without the benefit of professional credit for participating in PD, and the ability to self-lead the PLC, which requires that some of the HMDs be able to take on the role of PLC leader.

Most important in the long run is the sustainment of school-based PLCs. We hope this will be achieved through the ongoing mutual support of HMDs who continue to function as a municipal PLC. In addition, we have created an online infrastructure for sustaining communities: an online collection of activities for municipal-level and school-level communities, and a forum for sharing experiences and collaborative working-out of emergent issues.

3.4 *Explicating Notions of Impact*

Reflecting on the implementation of PD-HMD to date, we can highlight the following aspects of our implicit theory of impact.

- Our notion of impact is based on the belief that HMD is a strategic position, which can be viewed not only as an administrative one but also include aspects of educational leadership and professional facilitation.

- The nested nature of the program aims for a relatively strong impact on the participating HMDs over a long period of time, yet we tacitly accept that the effect can be "diluted" while moving along the path from the community of PD-HMD leaders to the municipal PLCs, then to the school PLC and then to the classrooms.
- In a sense, the upscaling and fidelity aspects of impact are reciprocal in the program: the more teachers and classrooms are involved, the less likely it is that propagated activities will be implemented as intended. However,
- We believe that that the emerging need to be an active member of a vibrant community of peers, and long-term exposure to the change-oriented discourse and to the above-described mechanism of reporting back can sustain the program's impact.

4 Teacher–Researcher Alliance for Investigating Learning (TRAIL)

4.1 *The Program's Rationale and Intended Impact*

Wagner (1997) recognizes three forms of research-practice relationships: data-extraction agreements, clinical partnership, and co-learning agreements. In *data-extraction agreements,* the researchers have full agency over the research–practice cooperation. The teacher–researcher interactions in this kind of agreement revolve around questions about the nature of education and schooling that researchers suggest and investigate. Investigations conducted as *clinical partnerships* also focus on the nature of education and schooling. However, the formulation of research questions and methods in these agreements is oriented toward the joint work of researchers and teachers striving to improve, together, the understanding of mathematics teaching and learning in schools. *Co-learning agreements* share many features of the *clinical partnership,* but differ from it in a subtle yet essential way. Whereas in the clinical partnership the practitioner is invited into the world of the researcher to investigate the practitioner's world according to the researcher's rules of inquiry, in co-learning agreements, researchers and practitioners join forces to inquire together and aid one another in order to learn something new and worthwhile about their worlds and about themselves.

Many researchers lament the seemingly limited influence of research on the educational field (e.g., Cai et al., 2017), and are seeking new and more effective models of interaction between research and practice. Within this agenda, TRAIL offers an overarching approach to interactions between mathematics education researchers and mathematics teachers that provides an infrastructure for various forms of cooperation and collaboration to achieve various kinds of impact. The programs under the TRAIL banner all propose models for partnership and co-learning that essentially avoid the paradigm of data extraction (Koichu & Pinto, 2018).

4.1.1 Impact – Upon Whom and What?

Three kinds of TRAIL programs have been developed so far, and each has its own approach to impact.

TRAIL PLCs are a case of a co-learning agreement. A group of practicing mathematics teachers joins forces with education researcher(s) in a partnership to co-design and conduct research directly related to the teaching and learning that takes place in the teachers' classrooms. The TRAIL PLC program was first piloted in 2017, and has since been implemented in three additional communities (Koichu & Pinto, 2018, 2019; Koichu et al., 2020; Pinto & Koichu, 2021). As in action research, TRAIL PLCs aim to help teachers learn something about the teaching and learning that takes place in their classrooms, and to draw conclusions for improving practices and outcomes. In contrast to action research, TRAIL PLCs additionally aim to put forth generalizable research findings, thus impacting not only the participating teachers and their students, but also the researchers and the mathematics education community at large. What places these PLCs firmly in the realm of co-learning agreement (and not merely a clinical partnership) is their emphasis on symmetry between the communities of researchers and of practitioners, both having an explicit goal of learning something about their own practice (teaching/educational research) through the interaction. The teachers participate not only to learn something about their own teaching and their students' learning, but also to develop an inquiry-based and data-oriented approach to teaching and learning, where practices of data gathering and analysis are valued. The researchers participate not only to gather and publish research findings about classroom teaching, but also, through a continuous reflective process, to upgrade their research programs. The direct interaction between teachers and researchers provides opportunities to learn something new about conducting research in classrooms and schools, where teachers' practical rationality (Herbst & Chazan, 2020) can inform research in ways that are not directly accessible to researchers. This impact on ourselves as researchers can be extended to the academic milieu when our work is published.

TRAIL citizen science programs were conceived as extensions of TRAIL PLCs. The research questions and empirically validated research tools that are developed in the PLCs, along with findings from classrooms, can serve as a point of departure for more peripheral participation of new teachers at a later stage. For example, teachers may choose to join a virtual research community that forms around research that was previously conducted in a PLC. When teachers administer questionnaires in their classrooms and make the collected data available to the research community, this can be considered a form of data-extraction agreement. It becomes a clinical partnership when teachers not only gather data in their own instructional contexts, but also analyze it (based on methodologies put forth by the original PLC) to seek findings and draw conclusions about their own teaching and their students' learning.

TRAIL ad hoc initiatives, like citizen science programs, aim to engage teachers in research projects that transcend the paradigm of data extraction. An example of such a project was initiated a few weeks after the COVID-19 pandemic shut down face-to-face teaching in schools for the first time. Researchers involved in the TRAIL project designed a questionnaire and an interview protocol to collect data on the distance-learning practices that the teachers were engaging in, with an eye toward identifying affordances of these practices for "the day after." Data analysis was conducted by researchers in the department. The immediate value of the research findings for the community of teachers (as well as their academic value), along with the department's pledge to make these findings immediately and directly available to teachers (and not merely through academic publishing), position this initiative as a clinical partnership.

4.1.2 Impact – Facets of "Strength"

Fidelity. The notion of fidelity is quite foreign to our theoretical approach in TRAIL projects, where the alternate notion of adaptation (Century & Cassata, 2016) is more appropriate. In this program, teachers tailor the kind of data they will gather, the questions they hope to answer, and the implications of their findings, in ways that cannot be prescribed by researchers. Furthermore, researchers have little direct influence on the conclusions that teachers will eventually draw from the research they conduct, or on the implications that they choose to implement. In fact, teachers may eventually draw conclusions and implement changes that researchers would not necessarily endorse. This is consistent with our moral stance – that researchers cannot really know what is best for individual teachers and their students, which is necessarily guided by their own blend of professional obligations and particular institutional contexts in which they function. Thus, similar to the PD-HMD program, we see our role not in "dictating" best practices, but rather in helping teachers develop the ability to notice and make conscious and informed professional decisions on their own. In turn, as researchers, we learn how to capitalize on our own, as well as teachers' experiences to make some research practices feasible for the teachers, scaffolding them in their path toward gaining agency over these practices.

Scale. TRAIL PLCs are a “boutique” program – one or two communities per year comprising 10–20 teachers, who meet for professional credit (60 recognized academic hours for professional accreditation). Recruiting teachers at the stage when research questions and tools have already been established is much more scalable than PLC programs. While PLCs employ two community facilitators over a 60-hour program, citizen science programs do not require much (if any) synchronous facilitation or guidance, hence a single coordinator can support large numbers of participating teachers. Furthermore, the more peripheral participation may be attractive for many teachers who are not interested in a 60-hour PD commitment.

Sustainability. Practically speaking, teachers’ involvement in TRAIL PLCs is short term (typically 1 to 2 school years). However, we aim to have a sustained impact in two senses. First, teachers’ findings from the research may have long-reaching implications for their practice, especially since the research questions, which are developed and phrased by the participating teachers, are of intrinsic relevance to them. However, more significantly, we aim to have a sustained influence on participating teachers’ professional identity, bringing them to see themselves as reflective and inquiry-oriented teachers who continually gather evidence of learning, analyze it, and base their instructional practices on empirical data. This stance is sometimes called an inquiry stance to teaching (Jaworski, 2008).

4.2 *Enactment of TRAIL – In Pursuit of Impact*

In this section we discuss the enactment of the PLC program, which is currently the flagship of the TRAIL initiative. The nature of impact that was pursued was strongly influenced by our commitment to conducting the project as a co-learning agreement, whereby the conducted research should have an impact on both the teachers and the mathematics education researchers involved.

The TRAIL PLC program, first piloted in 2017, has since run its course in four communities (overall, about 60 teachers). The activity in the communities can be divided into the following stages: (1) phrasing research question(s); (2) designing the research and its tools; (3) data collection and analysis; (4) writing up findings and conclusions; (5) dissemination. We briefly describe each of these phases.

1. Deciding on research questions and phrasing them: A major challenge in this phase of the project was agreeing on research questions that were relevant to both the participating teachers and the research community at large. To elicit teacher-relevant questions, we asked the participating teachers a variety of guiding questions, such as: “if you had a ‘private mathematics education researcher’ who could answer your questions on

teaching and learning in your classes, what would you ask?," or, taking a less direct approach: "describe a classroom event that you found surprising or puzzling, and that you would like to understand more deeply." From the multitude of responses, we filtered out those that were non-researchable, too particular to be of general interest, or that already had satisfactory answers based on current academic knowledge, and those that could not be answered within the 60-hour framework of the PLC. Some questions – collaboratively decided upon in this way – that were eventually researched in the PLCs were:

a. In what ways can students' mathematical flexibility be nurtured? Mathematical flexibility was defined as the ability to move between solution strategies and/or representations of mathematical objects when solving a problem.
b. How is it possible to design and enact successful "pathways" of "talking tasks"? Talking task was defined as a mathematical task in an instructional situation that includes aspects of experiencing, discussing and reflection. Pathways are sequential collections of tasks that create learning opportunities for particular instructional goals. They are successful when their enactment generates empirical data showing that the goals were (partially) achieved.
c. What are students' preferences in choosing a representation when solving a mathematical problem? What do these preferences stem from?
d. What are the perceived benefits of having students fill in a personal reflection questionnaire on errors made in an exam?
e. What characterizes classroom situations in which the students ask meaningful mathematical questions, rather than merely answering questions posed by the teacher?

We note that the very process of generating research questions often necessitated and generated new concepts (e.g., "talking tasks") for identifying and naming phenomena germane to teaching and learning mathematics – an important co-learning outcome for both teachers and researchers.

2. Designing the research program and its tools: This was perhaps the most collaborative part of the project, with each of the communities bringing their distinct expertise. The researchers sought relevant literature, and translated and summarized it into language and terms that were accessible to teachers. The teachers, in turn, drew upon their familiarity with their students, and tailored the research tools to their context.

Mathematical problems, where relevant, were developed or adapted to fit the point in the curriculum at which they would be used, and questionnaires and interview questions were phrased in terms that students were familiar with. Research hypotheses were put forth based on what teachers already knew about their students.

3. Data analysis: This was a challenging phase for the teachers, who do not normally analyze the kind of data that were collected for the research. They encountered the need to anchor their reflections and conclusions on lesson episodes (both their own and those of other participants) in empirical evidence. Much scaffolding was required. In some communities, the teachers analyzed their own data and in others, teachers additionally cross-analyzed the data collected by their peers.
4. Findings and conclusions: This stage of the research had an impact for the participating teachers, in answering questions that were pertinent to their teaching practice – offering guidelines for selection or development of tasks, suggesting how to engage students with new approaches to solving problems, or validating a reflective tool that students can benefit from. For the researchers, the scope of the research, conducted in many classrooms on a scale that would normally be difficult to achieve, increased the diversity, trustworthiness and general validity of the findings.
5. Dissemination: Some teachers presented their findings in teacher conferences, potentially increasing the scope of the impact to additional teachers. We are undertaking academic dissemination, which will hopefully increase the scope of the impact even further.

4.3 *From Implicit to Explicit Notions of Impact*

Fidelity. Before we can address the question of the achieved fidelity, we must first clarify what it is that teachers are expected to achieve as a result of participating in the program. We list three candidates: implementing a developed research program, considering their teaching through the lens of their research findings, and in the longer term, developing an inquiry stance to teaching (Jaworski, 2008), whereby teachers adopt practices of critically investigating their teaching, collecting data and analyzing what is "working" and what is not, and adjusting their teaching accordingly. In the first sense, a high level of fidelity can be expected due to the intense involvement of researchers in the research process. In the second sense, the notion of fidelity is quite out of place; teachers are responsible for articulating the implications of their research findings and for deciding whether and how to adjust their teaching accordingly. The third sense of fidelity will be discussed in the context of sustainability.

Scale. TRAIL PLCs were conducted as a boutique program. It is difficult to see how this kind of researcher–practitioner partnership can be scaled up, due to its reliance on the intensive involvement of a mathematics education researcher in guiding and mediating the process. Citizen science projects are a natural way of scaling up the program, where more peripheral participation can rely on the research questions and methods developed in PLCs. Such projects have not yet been implemented, but we are working in this direction.

Sustainability. At this time, we are not particularly optimistic about the possibility of teachers' inquiry stance to teaching being sustained as a result of a 1-year TRAIL project. We believe that sustaining such a stance in practice would require ongoing support (such as the TRAIL PLC), where challenges of engaging in inquiry or research can be discussed and worked out among peers and with the researchers' assistance. However, analysis of teachers' reflections on their experience in two PLCs at the end of the yearly cycle of TRAIL (Koichu et al., 2020) suggests that some changes in the teachers' inquiry stance may be sustained. This is due to the memorability and novelty of the TRAIL experience, the well-appreciated opportunity to communicate with "interesting" participants, and the repeated engagement in thinking about implications of mathematics education research for teaching and learning. We conclude this section by presenting five characteristic assertions from participating teachers:

Teacher G.: This [TRAIL PLC] is completely different [from the other PD programs]; it changes your thinking style. This PD sets objectives that I don't know how to achieve… On the one hand, this is depressing, and on the other, attractive.

Teacher S.: Conducting research taught me a lot, mainly because of the community. I felt that I am among very intelligent people who are willing to contribute from their experience…

Teacher A.: I do use questions that require thinking flexibility in my classes. Now I see that I should use them intentionally, and not just in passing. I should use such questions not spontaneously but at the right moments and with the right emphasis… [Participation in the research on flexibility] gives me perspective on how I can enhance flexibility. That is, not only to assign a problem [that requires flexibility], but to create a situation with the problem that would have consequences.

Teacher P.: Data analysis turned out to be thrilling. I can compare it to looking at a white sheet of paper on which something is written in invisible ink, and then you pour a special substance on the sheet, and suddenly you see what is written. When I succeeded to extract relevant information from the data, information that could be "shared with others," I felt tremendous satisfaction. I can unequivocally say that I went through a learning process in this community and acquired tools that will serve me in the future.

Teacher N.: I am exposed to research occasionally. But here, every research paper that I read or am exposed to, it causes a switch in my teaching. That is, it influences me, my teaching, and it influences my students as well.

4.4 *Explicating Notions of Impact*

Reflecting on the TRAIL initiatives to date, we can highlight the following aspects of our implicit theory of impact. In fact, we view teaching as a case of problem solving (Lampert, 2001; Schoenfeld, 2011), whereby an inquiry approach to teaching is natural to us, thus we assume that this approach can be beneficial for others. As in mathematical problem solving, optimal strategies for solving the problem at hand are not readily available, and need to be tried, assessed and revised. In this context, the relevant expertise of mathematics education researchers is in the process of inquiry into practice. True to the conception of the program as a co-learning agreement, the outcome of the inquiry process cannot be known in advance. Furthermore, much of the process, and in particular stating and implementing implications of the inquiry, rely strongly on teachers' preferences, experience and tacit understanding of what is useful or practical.

In offering different kinds of TRAIL involvement, we hope to influence the teachers' inquiry stance and simultaneously scale up data collection and data analysis of "traditional" forms of mathematics education research. We can also now see the limitations of our implicit theory of impact in TRAIL projects, which creates opportunities to move forward in our future projects, as presented in the following section.

5 Raising the Bar in Mathematics Classrooms (RBMC)

5.1 *The Program's Rationale and Intended Impact*

The importance of mathematical problem solving as a central activity of mathematics instruction is widely acknowledged, both as a goal in its own right and as a means toward achieving curricular goals (Schroeder & Lester, 1989). However, systematically implementing this practice at scale remains a challenge.

The reasons for this are many. As a goal, teachers often do not have the time to digress from the already overloaded curriculum to attend to problem-solving skills, and as a means, there are arguably more efficient ways to help students attain the mathematical proficiency on which they are eventually tested, which rarely includes problem solving per se (Sweller et al., 2010). RBMC is a 4-year project that aims to encourage teachers to challenge their students with increasingly demanding problem-solving activity at an increasing frequency.[3] To this end, we are creating a collection of demanding problems, engaging teachers in PD around classroom enactment of problems from this collection, and developing a mechanism based on systematic reflection and sharing beyond PLCs, which is intended to support systematic incorporation of problem-solving practices in teaching mathematics in the long run.

5.1.1 Impact – Upon Whom and What?

Of the programs discussed in this chapter, RBMC is the most student-centered in the sense that its intended impact on students is well defined and theorized. Past research (see Koichu, 2014, and Lester & Cai, 2016, for overviews) has meticulously investigated students' mathematical problem solving, and has put forth criteria for successful implementation of a problem-solving curriculum, which is the intended impact on students in this project. Nevertheless, the practical focus of the project is on teacher practices, in providing tools and motivation to sustain a problem-solving agenda.

5.1.2 Impact – Facets of "Strength"

Fidelity. In contrast to the previously described projects, the notion of fidelity is central to this project, given that problem-solving activities can easily deteriorate to little more than practicing procedures if, for example, a teacher too readily reveals key aspects of a solution strategy (Kilpatrick, 1985). Hence, the activity should engage students in a productive mathematical struggle. That being said, we do not have a coherent preconception of what problem-solving activities should look like in each and every classroom. Rather, we envision that teachers participating in the RBMC communities will deliberately customize problems and their enactment to meet the goals and constraints of their classes. Inquiry into this process of customizing the activity is intended to have an impact on the researchers leading these communities, providing data and insight on the challenges of teaching problem solving, and promoting a theorized model of implementation.

Scale. The target is to reach at least 200 middle-school teachers throughout the duration of the project. Once the collection of problems has been developed and tried by a significant number of teachers, we intend to scale up activity by making the collection and insights on enactment accessible to teachers at large. Furthermore, we hope to influence teachers' intrinsic motivation to persevere in problem-solving activities by providing reflective tools to help teachers monitor their and their students' progress. Such tools, used for reporting on the activity, will also help us monitor and guide teachers when working on a scale that does not permit an intensive PLC program.

Sustainability. It is our intention that once teachers experience the benefits of a problem-solving-based curriculum, and develop the capacity and sensitivity to customize and monitor the activity for their students, intrinsic motivation to continue will sustain the impact of the program over time.

5.2 *Enactment of* RBMC *– In Pursuit of Impact*

The program is currently in its infancy; hence our description of its implementation is limited. In 2020, we piloted the activity with a "nuclear" community, comprising six practicing middle-school teachers, three experienced PD facilitators and the two authors of this chapter. Scaling up is planned to follow the "cascade" model, whereby some of the teachers participating in PLCs (including the pilot nuclear community) will be invited to facilitate teacher PLCs at a later stage. Tools for gathering classroom data (teacher and student questionnaires) will help us monitor fidelity of implementation, even if this notion of fidelity is inherently flexible. Figure 15.1 shows a sample problem (Arcavi & Cooper, 2014, p. 275, translated and abridged by the authors).

The problem was intended by the designers as a literacy problem, in the sense put forth by the Organisation for Economic Co-operation and Development (OECD, 2018). Students need to make sense of a complex yet realistic situation, propose a mathematical model that relies on assumptions that need to be explicated (e.g., question 1 requires students to make assumptions about walking or running speeds). Students need to enact problem-solving resources sequentially, sometimes through proportional thinking (e.g., question 4), and sometimes in ways that are not immediately obvious (e.g., question 5, where students need to set up an equation). Teachers who choose to offer this problem to their students will need to design a didactical context – when in the curriculum to pose the problem, whether and how to adapt the problem, in or outside of class, for a grade or not, how to arrange the students (individual work, pairs or group), etc. Options, advantages and disadvantages will be discussed within PLCs, and individual teachers will make their didactical decisions. Different students will experience different problem-solving opportunities, and the resultant data will be gathered, analyzed and discussed in the PLCs.

This is a sign from Miyajima Island near Hiroshima, Japan:

1. Try to estimate the distance from the sign to the ropeway station. Explain your estimate.
2. June walks to school every day. The distance is 1.5 km, and it takes her 25 minutes. How would she estimate the distance from the sign to the station?
3. Omar is on a track team. He knows that he jogs at 7.5 km/hour. How might he estimate the distance?

The sign was written by Koki, a Japanese student who timed the route from the sign to the station – 10 minutes walking and 7 minutes running.

4. If Koki runs 1 km in 8 minutes, what is his walking speed?
5. What part of the distance would Koki need to walk, and what part would he need to run, to complete the distance in exactly 8 minutes?

FIGURE 15.1 Sample problem used in RBMC project, 2020

6 Discussion – From Implicit to Explicit Theories of Impact

In this section, we articulate our "implicit theory" of impact, as it emerges from the reflection on three projects. This implicit theory includes facets of impact that we aim to achieve, and underlying beliefs and assumptions regarding how our work with teachers can hope to achieve them.

6.1 *Impact – Upon Whom and What?*

The work of the Department of Science Teaching aims to have an impact on the field of mathematics education, which includes teachers, students and also researchers and PD facilitators. When working with teachers in PD, it is easy to lose sight of the students, assuming that having an "impact" on teachers will indirectly impact students, yet clearly this may not always be the case. In our work, we make an effort to keep the impact on students in sight. In the PD-HMD, cycles of reporting include teachers reporting on students' work in school-based PLCs, which are aggregated and reported on by HMDs in municipal PLCs, and are eventually discussed in the leaders' PLC. In TRAIL, teachers collect more or less systematic data on their students' learning and also analyze data collected by other teachers. In RBMC, a similar mechanism is in place, where teachers and students report on classroom enactment of problem-solving activities. This approach can be summarized as follows: We aim to have impact on students' learning by means of our work with mathematics teachers and heads of mathematics departments; however, we do not take this chain of impact on faith, but rather plan and implement mechanisms for monitoring the impact on students, and instill these mechanisms in the teachers' PD activity, believing that some aspects of the inquiry practices of researchers can be beneficial for teachers. At the same time, we feel that designing, running and reflecting on the projects deeply influence us as mathematics teacher educators and researchers. Sometimes this feeling is so strong that we engage in academic dissemination of the lessons learned, and also in theorizing them.

6.2 *Impact – Facets of "Strength"*

Fidelity. Our basic stance is grounded in the theory of practical rationality (Herbst & Chazan, 2020). While educational research has contributed significantly to the understanding of teaching and learning, implementation of research findings, particularly in educational contexts, must be guided by teachers' rationality regarding what practices are practical, taking into consideration their individual weighting of professional obligations – to their students as individuals and as a social unit, to the discipline of mathematics, and to the institution in which the teaching and learning take place (Herbst & Chazan, 2020). Thus, in the dichotomy between fidelity and adaptation of implementation (Century & Cassata, 2016), we tend to lean heavily toward adaptation, while taking an open-minded stance regarding fidelity, which is broadly interpreted as preservation of the main chosen objectives of the projects that we are running. Yet our work with communities of teachers proposes a synthesis, which can be called adaptive fidelity. In this model, adaptation of implementation takes place in communities of inquiry (Jaworski, 2008) with the participation of the proponents of the implementation (researchers). This serves two mitigating functions. First, the proponents have some influence on the nature and extent of the adaptation through their participation in these communities. Second, and even more significantly, participation in these communities provides learning opportunities for researchers, whereby their vision of implementation can be revised through interaction with teachers. Thus, fidelity is not a seen as a static view of best practice, but rather as a dynamically developing view of what implementation might look like in different contexts. It is this stance to fidelity that places our work with teachers firmly in the domain of co-learning agreement (Wagner, 1997).

Scale. There is a basic tension between our wish to have an impact at scale, and the labor-intensive nature of our work with communities of teachers. Our programs, and the TRAIL PLCs in particular, require constant involvement on the part of mathematics education researchers that is not easily scalable. Accordingly, our projects aim to seek out novel models of scaling, including the citizen science model of TRAIL research, and technologically sophisticated means of supporting implementation and systemic preparation of community leaders in RBMC.

Sustainability. PD programs tend to have a life cycle with a "short tail": when the funding period ends, so does the researchers' involvement. It is not only the PD program that ends, but also the research on its impact, as it is difficult to research the sustained impact of PD after funding for the project has ended. The situation is particularly challenging when the model of PD is based on PLCs; to have a sustained effect, the community must take on a life of its own, independent of the PD proponents, which even B. Wenger-Trayner – a recognized expert on communities of practice – considers to be particularly challenging (personal communication, July 26, 2020). In our work, we are challenging the assumption that teacher communities that are set up in the context of PD must die out when the PD ends. To this end, the fourth and final year of the PD-HMD project is dedicated to weaning municipal communities of HMDs from their reliance on academic leadership, and setting up mechanisms of interaction that will keep them functioning in the years to come. The success of this initiative is far from obvious, and will be a topic for future research.

While individual programs may have a limited lifespan, sustainability may be attained by means of their "academic footprint," achieved through publication – both scholarly and practice-oriented – that may inform and inspire others. From this perspective, short-lived programs that serve the role of "proof of concept" may have an impact.

6.3 *In Conclusion*

In this chapter, we have attempted to explicate some implicit and tacit aspects of our approach to designing PD programs and its desirable impact on the field of mathematics education. Working at the Department of Science Teaching, with its long-standing tradition of engaging excellent teachers in PLCs, has allowed us to pursue a notion of impact that relies on a solid academic basis, while at the same time respecting and drawing substantially on teachers' professional expertise. The programs we have described do not aim to "educate" teachers, but rather to engage *with* them in activity that will support the professional growth of teachers and researchers alike, toward a better understanding of the challenges of mathematics education and of effective ways of addressing them. To us, the presented approach to PD is an endless source of inspiration and ideas for research, which we are eager to pursue in the coming decades.

Notes

1 The Hebrew term for this position translates literally as "coordinator of the discipline."
2 From its inception in 2017, the PD-HMD program has been funded by the Israeli Trump Foundation and by Israel's Ministry of Education.
3 The RBMC project is funded by the Trump Family Foundation for 2020–2024.

References

Arcavi, A., & Cooper, J. (2014). *Summary tasks for central topics in the junior-high school curriculum*. Mathematics Supervisor (mafmar). http://meyda.education.gov.il/files/Mazkirut_Pedagogit/matematika/osef_01.docx

Borko, H., Koellner, K., & Jacobs, J. (2014). Examining novice teacher leaders' facilitation of mathematics professional development. *The Journal of Mathematical Behavior, 33*, 149–167. http://dx.doi.org/10.1016/j.jmathb.2013.11.003

Cai, J., Morris, A., Hohensee, C., Hwang, S., Robison, V., & Hiebert, J. (2017). A future vision of mathematics education research: Blurring the boundaries of research and practice to address teachers' problems. *Journal for Research in Mathematics Education, 48*(5), 466–473. https://doi.org/10.5951/jresematheduc.48.5.0466

Century, J., & Cassata, A. (2016). Implementation research: Finding common ground on what, how, why, where, and who. *Review of Research in Education, 40*, 169–215. http://dx.doi.org/10.3102/0091732x16665332

Clarke, D., & Hollingsworth, H. (2002). Elaborating a model of teacher professional growth. *Teaching and Teacher Education, 18*, 947–967. http://dx.doi.org/10.1016/s0742-051x(02)00053-7

Clements, D. H., Sarama, J., Wolfe, C. B., & Spitler, M. E. (2015). Sustainability of a scale-up intervention in early mathematics: A longitudinal evaluation of implementation fidelity. *Early Education and Development, 26*, 427–449. http://dx.doi.org/10.1080/10409289.2015.968242

Cohen, D. K. (1990). A revolution in one classroom: The case of Mrs. Oublier. *Educational Evaluation and Policy Analysis, 12*, 311–329. http://dx.doi.org/10.3102/01623737012003311

Cooper, J., & Koichu, B. (2019). Reconciling tensions between lecturing and active learning in professional learning communities. In M. Graven, H. Venkat, A. A. Essien, & P. Vale (Eds.), *Proceedings of the 43rd Conference of the International Group for the Psychology of Mathematics Education: Research reports (A–K), Vol. 2* (pp. 169–176). Psychology of Mathematics Education.

Desimone, L. M. (2009). Improving impact studies of teachers' professional development: Toward better conceptualizations and measures. *Educational Researcher, 38*(3), 181–199. http://dx.doi.org/10.3102/0013189x08331140

Garet, M. S., Wayne, A. J., Stancavage, F., Taylor, J., Eaton, M., Walters, K., Song, M., Brown, S., Hurlburt, S., Zhu, P., Sepanik, S., & Doolittle, F. (2011). *Middle school mathematics professional development impact study: Findings after the second year of implementation. NCEE 2011-4024.* National Center for Education Evaluation and Regional Assistance. https://files.eric.ed.gov/fulltext/ED519922.pdf

Goos, M., Bennison, A., & Proffitt-White, R. (2018). Sustaining and scaling up research-informed professional development for mathematics teachers. *Mathematics Teacher Education and Development, 20*, 133–150.

Herbst, P., & Chazan, D. (2020). Mathematics teaching has its own imperatives: Mathematical practice and the work of mathematics instruction. *ZDM – Mathematics Education, 52*, 1149–1162. http://dx.doi.org/10.1007/s11858-020-01157-7

Ingvarson, L., Meiers, M., & Beavis, A. (2005). Factors affecting the impact of professional development programs on teachers' knowledge, practice, student outcomes and efficacy. *Education Policy Analysis Archives, 13*. https://doi.org/10.14507/epaa.v13n10.2005

Jaworski, B. (2008). Building and sustaining inquiry communities in mathematics teaching development: Teachers and didacticians in collaboration. In K. Krainer & T. Wood (Eds.), *International handbook of mathematics teacher education: Participants in mathematics teacher education: Individuals, teams, communities and networks, Vol. 3* (pp. 309–330). Sense Publishers. http://dx.doi.org/10.1163/9789087905491_015

Kilpatrick, J. (1985). A retrospective account of the past 25 years of research on teaching mathematical problem solving. In E. Silver (Ed.), *Teaching and learning mathematical problem solving: Multiple research perspectives* (pp. 1–16). Lawrence Erlbaum.

Koichu, B. (2014). Reflections on problem solving. In M. N. Fried & T. Dreyfus (Eds.), *Mathematics & mathematics education: Searching for common ground. Advances in mathematics education* (pp. 113–135). Springer. http://dx.doi.org/10.1007/978-94-007-7473-5_8

Koichu, B., & Pinto, A. (2018). Developing education research competencies in mathematics teachers through TRAIL: Teacher-Researcher Alliance for Investigating Learning. *Canadian Journal of Science, Mathematics and Technology Education, 18*, 68–85. http://dx.doi.org/10.1007/s42330-018-0006-3

Koichu, B., & Pinto, A. (2019). *Implementation through participation: Theoretical considerations and an illustrative case* [Paper presentation]. 11th Congress of the European Society for Research in Mathematics Education. https://hal.archives-ouvertes.fr/hal-02429776/document

Koichu, B., Zaks, R., & Farber, M. (2020). Teachers' voices from two communities of inquiry engaged in practices of mathematics education research. In H. Borko & D. Potari (Eds.), *Proceedings of ICMI Study 25 Conference "Teachers of mathematics working and learning in collaborative groups"* (pp. 364–371). National and Kapodistrian University of Athens.

Lampert, M. (2001). *Teaching problems and the problems of teaching*. Yale University Press.

Lester, F. K., & Cai, J. (2016). Can mathematical problem solving be taught? Preliminary answers from 30 years of research. In P. Felmer, E. Pehkonen, & J. Kilpatrick (Eds.), *Posing and solving mathematical problems. Advances and new perspectives* (pp. 117–136). Springer. http://dx.doi.org/10.1007/978-3-319-28023-3_8

OECD. (2018). *PISA 2021 mathematics framework (draft)*. https://pisa2021-maths.oecd.org/files/PISA%202021%20Mathematics%20Framework%20Draft.pdf

Oxford Online Dictionary. (n.d.). *Impact*. https://en.oxforddictionaries.com/definition/impact

Pegg, J., & Panizzon, D. (2007/2008). Addressing changing assessment agendas: Impact of professional development on secondary mathematics teachers in NSW. *Mathematics Teacher Education and Development, 9*, 66–79.

Pinto, A., & Koichu, B. (2021). Implementation of mathematics education research as crossing the boundary between disciplined inquiry and teacher inquiry. *ZDM Mathematics Education*. Advance online publication. https://doi.org/10.1007/s11858-021-01286-7

Remillard, J. T., & Heck, D. J. (2014). Conceptualizing the curriculum enactment process in mathematics education. *ZDM – Mathematics Education, 46*, 705–718. http://dx.doi.org/10.1007/s11858-014-0600-4

Schoenfeld, A. H. (2011). *How we think: A theory of goal-oriented decision making and its educational applications*. Routledge.

Schroeder, T., & Lester, F. (1989). Developing understanding in mathematics via problem solving. In P. Traffon & A. Shulte (Eds.), *New directions for elementary school mathematics: 1989 yearbook* (pp. 31–42). National Council of Teachers of Mathematics.

Sternberg, R. J. (1985). Implicit theories of intelligence, creativity, and wisdom. *Journal of Personality and Social Psychology, 49*, 607–627. http://dx.doi.org/10.1037/0022-3514.49.3.607

Stoll, L., Bolam, R., McMahon, A., Wallace, M., & Thomas, S. (2006). Professional learning communities: A review of the literature. *Journal of Educational Change, 7*, 221–258. http://dx.doi.org/10.1007/s10833-006-0001-8

Swan, M. (2007). The impact of task-based professional development on teachers' practices and beliefs: A design research study. *Journal of Mathematics Teacher Education, 10*, 217–237. http://dx.doi.org/10.1007/s10857-007-9038-8

Sweller, J., Clark, R., & Kirschner, P. (2010). Teaching general problem-solving skills is not a substitute for, or a viable addition to, teaching mathematics. *Notices of the American Mathematical Society, 57*, 1303–1304.

van Driel, J. H., Meirink, J. A., van Veen, K., & Zwart, R. C. (2012). Current trends and missing links in studies on teacher professional development in science education: A review of design features and quality of research. *Studies in Science Education, 48*, 129–160. http://dx.doi.org/10.1080/03057267.2012.738020

Wagner, J. (1997). The unavoidable intervention of educational research: A framework for reconsidering research-practitioner cooperation. *Educational Researcher, 26*(7), 13–22. http://dx.doi.org/10.3102/0013189x026007013

Zambo, R., & Zambo, D. (2008). The impact of professional development in mathematics on teachers' individual and collective efficacy: The stigma of underperforming. *Teacher Education Quarterly, 35*(1), 159–168.

Zehetmeier, S. (2015). Sustaining and scaling up the impact of professional development programmes. *ZDM – Mathematics Education, 47*, 117–128. http://dx.doi.org/10.1007/s11858-015-0671-x

Zehetmeier, S., & Krainer, K. (2011). Ways of promoting the sustainability of mathematics teachers' professional development. *ZDM – Mathematics Education, 43*, 875–887. http://dx.doi.org/10.1007/s11858-011-0358-x

CHAPTER 16

The Rothschild–Weizmann Program for Excellence in Mathematics and Science Teaching

A Story of a Partnership between Academy, Philanthropy and the Educational System

Bat-Sheva Eylon and Miriam Carmeli

Abstract

In 2008, the Weizmann Institute of Science and the Edmond de Rothschild Foundation started a 10-year program to promote science and math education in Israel. The program targeted motivated acting teachers of high-school biology, chemistry, mathematics and physics. It included two separate complementary components: a 2-year MSc degree track and a post-MSc track. The program exposed teachers to cutting-edge and core topics and approaches, and provided avenues to lead novel activities. Over its 10 years, 256 teachers graduated from the MSc track and about 100 teachers from the post-MSc track. Research and evaluation examined the outcomes and influence of the program in light of the "desired profile of the Rothschild–Weizmann graduate" developed in the first 5 years. Almost all graduates (97%) continued to teach in high school. Most of them reported having integrated new teaching strategies and topics in their practice and having adopted a reflective stance. About half of them assumed new positions after completing the program. Looking back on these 10 years is an opportunity to suggest insights on how to design and run research–practice partnerships in education. This chapter examines several challenges of the Rothschild–Weizmann program, and the strategies taken to address them.

Keywords

boundary-crossing – research–practice partnership (RPP) – scholarship of teaching – MSc for science and mathematics teachers

 DOI: 10.1163/9789004503625_016

1 Introduction

In 2007, realizing the deep crisis in the Israeli educational system, the Weizmann Institute of Science (WIS) was approached by the Edmond de Rothschild Foundation to work on a proposal for a 10-year program for promoting science and mathematics education in Israel. In light of international studies on the role of teachers in introducing changes into educational systems and studies on their professional development (e.g., McKinsey Report, 2007; Strauss, 2017), it was decided to focus on working with acting teachers in ways that would enable them to lead changes first and foremost in their own classes, and then in and outside of the school environment. The Department of Science Teaching, then headed by Prof. Avi Hofstein, designed a comprehensive Master's degree (MSc) program in science teaching, in collaboration with the scientific departments at the WIS. The farsightedness of the program enabled detailed planning, team development of science educators and scientists with long-term commitment, and design of resources. The MSc program was begun in 2008 at the Feinberg Graduate School of the WIS.

The goal of the program was to foster an elite corps of Israeli high-school science and mathematics teachers by providing them with unique opportunities to expand their knowledge and be involved in innovative professional activities that would impact students' learning. This was accomplished by exposing them to both cutting-edge and core science and science-teaching approaches, by engaging them in building a network of peer and academic connections, and by providing them with ample opportunities to initiate and lead novel activities of science learning. The program targeted highly motivated and capable biology, chemistry, mathematics, and physics teachers.

In addition to the MSc studies, the program included a separate, albeit complementary post-MSc track involving activities toward introducing innovations and initiatives to the science education field.

Three entities collaborated as a unit to carry out the Rothschild–Weizmann (RW) Program for Excellence in Science Teaching: the WIS, the Edmond de Rothschild Foundation, and the Israeli educational system. The research literature highlights important contributions of research–practice partnerships (RPPs) between academic institutions and the educational sphere as a means of enhancing education by joining the specialized knowledge and practices of both realms. These partnerships are often supported by funding agencies, as was the case in the RW program. Although there is evidence that RPPs can address persistent problems of practice (Bryk et al., 2015; Penuel et al., 2015), enable greater use of research in decision-making (Tseng, 2012), and improve educational outcomes (Donovan, 2013), many issues about running productive

RPPs are unresolved. In a review article, Coburn and Penuel (2016) claimed that

> Although studies in other fields provide evidence of the potential for RPPs, studies in education are few... We need targeted studies of specific strategies that partnerships use. Existing research tends to focus on the challenges, *providing little insight into how tools, strategies, and routines used by participants address these challenges.*

For convenience, herein we use the term strategy to refer to tools, strategies and routines.

One can conceive of the 10-year period of the RW program as a retrospective targeted study of a three-way cooperation between academy, the educational system and an actively involved foundation. This chapter is written with this conception in mind. Looking back on the first 10 years of the RW program (2008–2018) provides an opportunity to suggest some useful insights on how to design and run a complex educational partnership, and we discuss these insights in light of contemporary professional literature.

The chapter includes an additional five sections. The first describes the program. The second deals with challenges and strategies in promoting the two major interrelated short- and long-term goals of the program. The third focuses on the multitude of interactions among participants of the RW program. The fourth describes selected findings from research and evaluation on the program's outcomes along the years, and the last section summarizes the chapter, highlighting unique characteristics of the program.

2 The Program

The program included two tracks. The MSc track gathered active teachers from all sectors of Israeli society who studied together: women and men, Israeli-Arabs hailing from the center, northern, and southern regions of the country, and Jews from both the secular and religious school systems. About 40% came from the periphery and up to one-quarter of them taught in non-Hebrew-speaking schools. This integration of the various cultures that make up the colorful landscape of Israel served to enrich the educational experience and impact for its participants. Two-thirds of the participants were women. The post-MSc track provided further ongoing professional development for the MSc track graduates and other expert teachers. The two tracks are presented in detail below.

2.1 *MSc Degree Track*

Every year of the 10 years of the program, approximately 120 teachers in the four disciplines – chemistry, mathematics, physics, and biology – applied to the this track, and 30 were accepted. In total, 256 teachers graduated with a non-thesis MSc degree.

The design and operation of the program was headed by Prof. Bat-Sheva Eylon from the Department of Science Teaching and Prof. Shimon Levit from the Department of Condensed Matter Physics. Four disciplinary teams that included scientists, science educators and expert teachers were set up. In light of its goals, the design of the program involved the determination of an initial general structure for the courses in the MSc program. Then each of the disciplinary teams defined a unique set of goals and rationale, and an initial curriculum for the particular discipline (see Even et al., 2018; Mamlok-Naaman et al., 2010). Prospective lecturers designed and redesigned their courses through an ongoing process accompanied by formative evaluation and successive refinement. About 65 courses were developed especially for the program, with the involvement of about 50 scientists of the WIS.

The curriculum emphasized the building of a solid foundation in scientific content knowledge. Thus out of 44–48 semester credits, 24–28 credits were for science courses; 16–18 were for science education courses; and 2 were for the final project.

The projects were supervised by scientists from various disciplinary departments at WIS, and by science education experts from the Department of Science Teaching.

The program included a laboratory rotation in which the teachers worked in the laboratories of WIS scientists, many of whom are world leaders in their fields. The teachers benefited from collaborating with the laboratory staff and students. In addition, teachers participated in the monthly colloquium held in the Department of Science Teaching.

There were two categories of courses: (i) Science or math courses, most of which were especially developed for this program, with the goal of providing a wide perspective on the science disciplines. The courses focused on both the enhancement of knowledge relevant to the science content taught in schools, and familiarizing the participants with advanced and contemporary topics in their respective disciplines; (ii) science education courses, to expand teachers' knowledge and expose them to innovations in science education. Here, there were two course types: discipline-specific and especially designed for the program, and general courses in science education (e.g., educational technological tools, assessment and evaluation).

The studies in the program lasted 2 years and the students spent 2 full days weekly at the WIS. Most courses were offered once every 2 years. This structure led to useful interactions among students from different cohorts of the program.

The teachers had multiple options for support, including monthly scholarships which enabled them to reduce their teaching load, and they did not pay tuition (like other WIS students). The program also provided personal tutoring.

2.2 *The Post-MSc Track*

The post-MSc track served as a framework to run various activities for introducing innovations and initiatives to the science education field, reaching policymakers, teachers, and students. About 100 teachers took part in this track along the years (some participated for more than 1 year). This track included the following:

- Further learning of contemporary topics in science and science education (e.g., "summer schools" lasting 1–5 days).
- Participation in innovative "research, development and implementation" projects of the Department of Science Teaching. For example, in mathematics, graduates of the MSc program and other senior teachers were integrated in the development of assessment tasks for high-school students in a project aimed at improving student performance and reducing dropout rate (MesiMatica; see Chapter 9 in this book). In another example, the chemistry group with graduates of the program developed an initiative of annual regional day conferences for high-school students with the aim of motivating more students to choose chemistry as a subject for further study.
- Support for enhancing the graduates' impact on their students and peers. For example, in biology, two graduates, together with a scientist from the WIS, planned and implemented a school project for gifted 10th-grade students. In physics, many of the program's graduates served as leading teachers of regional communities of teachers around the country.
- A 2-year course for discipline-specific coordinators of assessment and evaluation offered to graduates from all disciplines. This program was carried out in collaboration with the National Authority for Measurement and Evaluation (RAMA) in accordance with a national initiative for introducing into schools coordinators for assessment and evaluation, to enhance assessment-driven professional development of teachers. Thirty-nine teachers graduated from this program in two cohorts, and about half of them were officially nominated to this role.

2.3 *The Steering Committee*

A steering committee, which was appointed by the Vice President and Dean of Educational Activities at the WIS, Prof. Israel Bar-Joseph, included one scientist and one science educator for each of the four disciplines – physics, math, biology and chemistry, the Dean of the Feinberg Graduate School and the Academic Secretary of the Feinberg Graduate School. Major decisions concerning the running of the program, changes in courses, new challenges or additions of various activities were discussed in the committee meetings. Representatives of the Edmond de Rothschild Foundation were invited and played a role as active partners in these meetings.

3 The Program in Action: Selected Strategies

This section deals with strategies chosen to promote the two major and interrelated short and long-term goals of the program: professional development of the participating teachers and genuine implementation of nontraditional teaching and learning initiatives. The strategies were based on extensive international experience in working with teachers (Loucks-Horsley et al., 2016) and specifically the Department of Science Teaching's experience.

The professional literature outlines several principles derived from the perspectives of 'scholarship of teaching' (e.g., Hutchings & Shulman, 1999; Shulman, 2011; Trigwell et al., 2000) and 'practitioner research' (Cochran-Smith & Lytle, 2001, 2009). These perspectives emphasize the nature of teaching as a profession, and the ways that scholarship develops within communities of teachers, teacher educators, and researchers. These principles influenced the strategies taken in the program.

Adult learning (andragogy) was an additional perspective that was instrumental in designing the strategies. For example, Knowles (1990) claimed that adults are "self-directed and expect to take responsibility for decisions" and that adult learning programs need to take this into consideration. Principles of instructional design relate to aspects such as adults' need to know the reasons for learning something and how it is related to their work; the importance of respecting their professional and personal experiences and using it as a resource for learning; recognizing the need to learn something and use it in practice. Knowles noted that growth of natural motivation may be blocked due to a negative self-conception as a student, lack of resources necessary for learning, or if the learning environment violates the andragogy principles listed above.

The literature highlights the complexity of bringing about changes in teachers' views and practices. For example, Guskey (2002) calls for an evidence-based approach as an important initial step in teachers' professional development that can lead to changes in views and practices. He claims that "significant change in teachers' attitudes and beliefs occurs primarily after they gain evidence of improvements in student learning. These improvements typically result from changes teachers have made in their classroom practices… they [the teachers] believe it works because they have seen it work." In the process of teacher change, "awareness" plays an important role. For example, Mason (2008) referred to the need to develop: teachers' awareness of the actions that they and their students carry out in the class (AIA); awareness of consideration in making disciplinary decisions (AID); and awareness of colleagues' needs with regard to developing AIA and AID. This is particularly important in cultivating leadership among teachers.

Finally, an ongoing concern of the program's designers was the relationship between two central goals of the program: the teachers' professional learning and their development as people and professionals. The acquisition of these goals is not always commensurate. For example, focusing teachers' learning on updated science without providing core knowledge may lead to superficiality and harm their professional development as independent learners and practitioners in the long run. Campbell et al. (2016) and Fullan and Hargreaves (2016) suggested that gauging activities in relation to the interplay between these goals is key to a program's success.

3.1 *Strategies*

- The program contextualized *activities in practice and actual experiences of teaching in classes* (Eylon & Bagno, 1997; Eylon et al., 2008; Timperley et al., 2008; Whitcomb et al., 2009). This strategy was accompanied by an *evidence-based approach* (Harrison et al., 2008) in which teachers discussed, collaboratively and systematically with peers, their practice and their students' learning using authentic materials from classes (e.g., students' works and lesson videos). This strategy was designed with two goals in mind: first, an immediate and long-term influence on teaching and learning (Borko et al., 2011; Darling-Hammond & Richardson, 2009; Little, 2012; van Driel et al., 2012); second, promoting the teachers' development as 'reflective practitioners,' a central feature of teachers' professionalism. The 'evidence' became 'community property' (Hutchings & Shulman, 1999) that could be critiqued, negotiated, and improved. The reflection that accompanied this process enabled the community of teachers to 'go meta,' and develop conceptual frameworks for understanding practice (Cochran-Smith & Lytle,

2001, 2009). The development of a reflective stance that is based on actual evidence has the potential for a long-term effect, as it can become a norm in the teachers' thinking on teaching and learning. Moreover, when teachers examine their students' learning systematically, their engagement, willingness to "listen" to their students, and to make important changes in practice evolves (Arcavi & Isoda, 2007; Feiman-Nemser, 2001). Realizing the strength of the collaborative reflection and learning from each other's experience can accompany teachers' behavior far beyond the participation in the MSc program. In evaluations of the program, we found that many of the teachers highlighted the development of a reflective stance as an important outcome of the RW program that made a genuine change in their views and behaviors (Schön, 1983).

- As mentioned above, the promotion of teachers as professionals is a basic tenet of the RW program and formed the basis for developing *two complementary tracks*, an MSc track and a track for graduates and other excellent teachers with MSc or PhD degrees. As already noted, the second track aimed to both expand teachers' professional development beyond their MSc (or PhD) studies and support the introduction of innovations to the system. Findings from research and evaluation confirmed the rationale of planning the two tracks and suggested their complementary roles. The MSc track expanded and enriched the participants' professional proficiencies and self-efficacy. Consequently, they were able to influence math and science education in the field through the second track. This latter track contributed to the teachers' life-long learning capabilities and to the development of their leadership skills. This strategy, together with the first strategy, are central in building teachers' capacity and capabilities for future life-long learning (Scherz et al., 2011).
- Both during and after completion of their studies, and as they became involved in projects of innovative activities in the educational field, participants received continuing guidance and support from WIS's science and science education researchers. As exemplified in the description of the second track of the program, the initiatives required expertise in design, resource development and implementation. The interaction between the partners followed the principles of cognitive apprenticeship involving modeling, scaffolding and fading (Lave & Wenger, 1991). The collaboration benefited both partners: the teachers benefited from the modeling of the WIS staff on how to carry out design, to prepare resources and to implement new materials and strategies. They also learned how to use feedback for successive refinements. The teachers contributed their knowledge as practitioners and as graduates of the MSc program which provided them with unique aspects

of knowledge in science and science education. These interactions also provided effective channels for the WIS's disciplinary and science education scientists to impact the field with high-quality research-based endeavors. Feedback from the participants showed that they highly appreciated this aspect in both tracks.

4 Building Fruitful Interactions in the Program

This section discusses the challenges and approaches in fostering fruitful interactions among the partners to enable the smooth running of the program, solve dilemmas, and promote the attainment of the program's goals. It describes how the "border crossing" perspective was used to deal with these challenges (Penuel et al., 2015).

One can discuss the interactions in this complex partnership via two contexts. One relates to the interactions between the three partners: academy (WIS), philanthropy (Edmond de Rothschild Foundation) and the educational system as a whole (Ministry of Education, schools). The other context deals with the interactions among the participants who designed and took part in the program (e.g., the scientists, the student teachers). In each of these contexts, the involved members had different backgrounds, views, interests and norms that required negotiation and mutual learning. The following are examples:

4.1 *Context 1*

Despite the wide agreement between the partners on the general goals of the program, each of them initially held different interpretations and expectations or definitions of the program's outcomes.

Members of the Department of Science Teaching expected to find innovations and changes in the nature of teaching content and practices (teaching–learning processes), the foundation's interests were to find an impact on the field expressed by school students' gains in matriculation exams, and WIS scientists and the Feinberg Graduate School highlighted criteria that emphasize the student teachers' academic achievements.

Negotiations between the partners and feedback from expert teachers led to an understanding of each other's points of view. For example, the foundation's representatives recognized the importance of various aspects that are essential in the professional development of teachers, such as the importance of deep disciplinary knowledge and teaching strategies. The participating scientists became more attentive to teachers' needs and the constraints of the system. The fruitful communication between the partners led to the design of a "desired profile" of a graduate of the program (see Appendix 1) which was used to evaluate the program's outcomes.

4.2 *Context 2*

The following example relates to the design process of courses in the MSc program. Early in the program, we sometimes observed differences between the science instructors' and course participants' perceptions of course goals, expectations of the content, and teaching approaches. We found evidence of changes in some of the instructors' points of view from cohort to cohort that resulted from becoming better acquainted with the course participants, accumulating experience from teaching, using feedback from formative evaluation, and through interactions between instructors. Changes also took place in the student teachers' views through opportunities to participate in authentic academic activities such as working in scientists' laboratories.

4.3 *The Boundary-Crossing Perspective*

The "boundary-crossing" perspective acknowledges the fact that when individuals or groups coming from different communities of practice meet, mutual learning is essential to realize and understand everyone's views and attitudes and to learn to work together (Wenger, 2010).

Akkerman and Bakker (2011) defined *four essential learning mechanisms*: learning to recognize others' points of view (identification); looking for ways to cooperate with others within the existing framework and constraints (coordination); taking the others' perspective into account in planning and acting (reflection); and transforming one's point of view (transformation). Although the enactment of these mechanisms may progress in different orders, reflection and eventually, transformation, usually stem from earlier identification and/or coordination processes. According to the theoretical perspective of Akkerman and Bruining (2016), in complex partnerships that take place in institutions (e.g., the WIS), the mutual learning needs to take place at the institutional, interpersonal, and intrapersonal levels. Table 16.1 characterizes the nature of learning in relation to these different learning mechanisms. Below we present examples from the RW program's work scheme that illustrate how multilevel boundary crossing has operated in the program and the resulting processes of learning and changes that we observed.

According to the boundary-crossing perspective, in the process of learning there is an important role for "brokers" who can act as a bridge between the communities and thus facilitate boundary crossing. In some of the disciplines, graduate students who tutored the student teachers acted as brokers. They interacted closely with both the instructors and the course participants and thus could serve as a bridge between them. A similar role of broker was fulfilled by staff members from the Department of Science Teaching who were assigned as mentors from each of the disciplinary strands of the RW program and closely accompanied the student teachers throughout their time in the program. We called these mentors "homeroom teachers" and indeed, their close interactions with the different partners of the program enabled them to facilitate the necessary border crossings.

According to Akkerman and Bruining (2016), boundary crossing is relevant to different contexts of RPPs: institutional, interpersonal, and intrapersonal. The following example relates to the institutional level (Table 16.1, column 2) through the steering committee's mode of operation. During the committee's meetings, ongoing issues concerning the conduct of the program were discussed, and participants provided important input to the program's ongoing development. Different views and opinions emerged at these meetings. Similar to the previous examples, the interaction between participants with different points of view resulted in mutual learning. The committee found ways to cooperate and to coherently lead the complex partnership. Representatives of the Edmond de Rothschild Foundation played an active role in the steering committee through the presentation of important foci and the foundation's directions, while concurrently demonstrating full trust in the professional expertise of the WIS team.

5 Research and Evaluation

Research and evaluation accompanied the program from its inception. The first 5 years involved ongoing formative evaluation and research design with the goal of adapting the program to the various participants (student teachers, scientists and science educators). Data were collected via feedback questionnaires on the courses and other activities (closed and open items), interviews and focus groups. Informal meetings and conversations with the different constituents provided additional rich qualitative data. The data gathered information on aspects such as perceived level of difficulty and interest in each of the courses and their relevance to the teachers' everyday work. Main findings were consistent along the years. Most of the scientific courses were rated as very interesting, some of them were also mentioned as very demanding and difficult to cope with (especially in physics and mathematics). However, most participants were very happy with these courses, claiming that they updated their knowledge and, in some cases, increased their understanding of certain school subjects. Most of the participants reported on introducing new topics

TABLE 16.1 Multilevel boundary-crossing framework (from Akkerman & Bruining, 2016)

Learning mechanism	**At the institutional level (action and interaction between organizations or organizational units)**	**At the interpersonal level (action and interaction between actors from different [institutionalized] practices)**	**At the intrapersonal level (participation of a person in two or more [institutionalized] practices)**
Identification 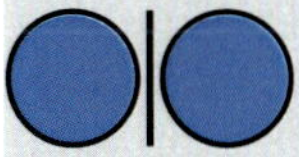	Organizations or units come to (re)define their different and complementary nature.	People come to (re) define their different and complementary roles and tasks.	A person comes to define his or her own simultaneous but distinctive participatory positions.
Coordination 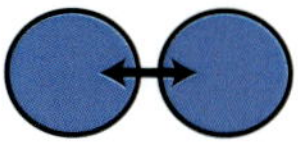	Organizations or units seek means or procedures for institutional exchange and cooperation.	People seek shared means or procedures for exchange and cooperative work.	A person seeks means or procedures to distribute or align his or her own participatory positions in multiple practices.
Reflection 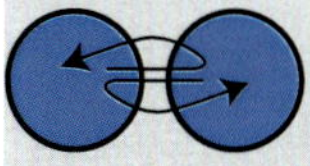	Organizations or units come to value and take up another's perspective to look at their own practice.	People come to value and take up another's perspective.	A person comes to look differently at his or her own participatory position because of the other participatory position.
Transformation 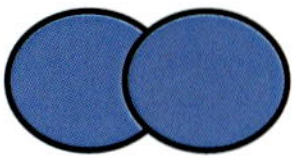	Units face a shared problem space and start collaborative work or merge institutionally.	People face a shared problem, start collaborative work, and may build group identity.	A person develops a hybridized position in which previously distinctive ways of thinking, doing, communicating, and feeling are integrated.

to their classes based on knowledge gained in the program. The use of new teaching strategies, assessment techniques or evaluation for understanding activities was mentioned as well.

When asked about their future aspirations, nearly half of the participants expressed their wish to acquire additional tools to promote significant learning among their students, reflecting a deep commitment to their professional identity. About a quarter expressed their wish to pursue central positions in the school system beyond the classroom, and some teachers reported their interest in participating in developing learning materials or seeking advanced degrees. The participants highly appreciated the ongoing support they got from the program's staff.

The findings were used to focus the program's goals and redesign the various courses and other activities. The findings also helped develop the "desired profile of the RW graduate" described in Appendix 1.

After these 5 years, the program was relatively stable. The focus of the research and evaluation changed from examining the program to investigating what happened to its graduates, through external research and evaluation. The various categories of the "desired profile of the RW graduate" were used as standards and criteria. Various research tools were used, such as questionnaires filled out by all participants, interviews with a sample of graduates and students, focus groups with lecturers of the various courses, documentation of group meetings, and program academic data (such as participants' grades). The following findings are organized according to the desired profile of the program's graduate.

5.1 *Knowledge in Science and Science Teaching*

The academic achievements showed that the student teachers coped successfully with the academic standards. Dropout rate was minimal. Several graduates along the years were found eligible to continue their studies toward a PhD at the WIS.

Responses of the graduates indicated that over 90% perceived having a deeper understanding of the core of their discipline. Moreover, the graduates reported that they gained scientific knowledge; were engaged with innovative research and theories; and learned how to navigate and read scientific literature.

Regarding science teaching, over 90% of the respondents claimed that they had gained a better understanding of their students' learning process; an awareness of difficulties in learning specific topics; and familiarity with diverse teaching methods (cf. Rozenszajn & Yarden, 2014).

5.2 *Meaningful Teaching Based on High Standards*

Graduates noted the integration of examples from concurrent research; the teaching of new topics; greater focus on the pupils' understanding. The teachers were also asked about their use of different teaching methods, and their replies related to nontraditional practices, such as: extensive use of classroom discussions, focus on the sources of students' alternative conceptions, and

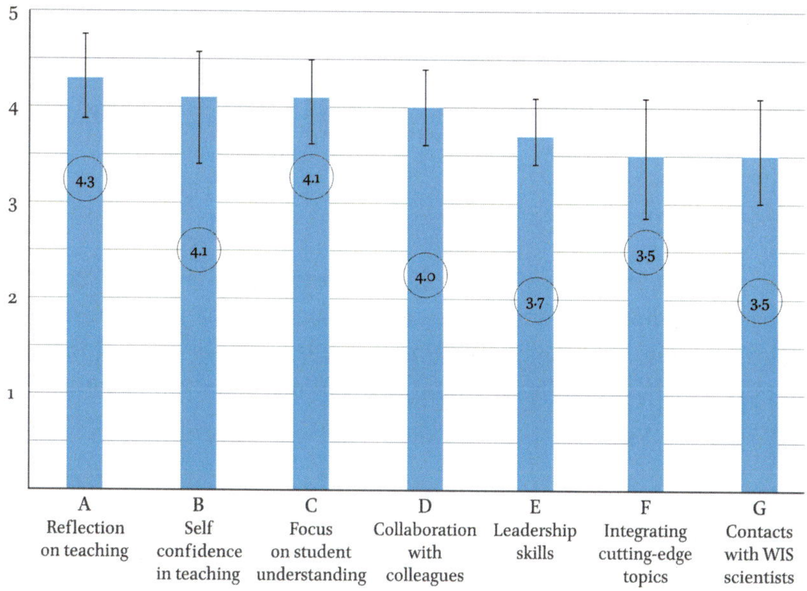

FIGURE 16.1 Graduate-perceived contribution of the program (N = 72)

students' active pursuit of explanations. The teachers reported on a reflective process of learning from the teaching experience.

Figure 16.1 presents means of the graduates' responses to the various contributions of the program on a Likert scale (1–5). The following are quotes exemplifying the findings:

> My knowledge is more profound; this enables me to go beyond the limits of ordinary learning. I received excellent teaching tools and I now feel that I have more confidence in communicating the lesson in the classroom, especially about the cell. The ability to delve deeper and provide more relevant examples is what engages and motivates students.

> I could see an entirely new dimension to science teaching – how it is based on very professional, methodical, and professional principles – not just a teacher's intuition.

> The most significant thing that has changed in my teaching is linking the lessons to 'real science,' including classroom demonstrations and contemporary examples.

> I use more teaching strategies; more student evaluation tools are now available to me; I have better access to scientific articles – and am no longer afraid of reading an article in English.

> The practical studies, during the lab rotations – working with scientists from Israel and abroad, opened a door to cutting-edge science and scientific methods. This bears directly on what we do with the children in class, as in chemistry, pupils are becoming more involved in research, and we provide excelling students with challenges that can engage them even further in the field.

> I put more emphasis on the theory; for example, I no longer teach the derivative without explaining the concept and provide enrichment in every class. My notebook from the program is always at my side. I can proudly say that teaching beautiful analytic mathematical thinking is truly my calling!

5.3 *Positions in the System and Continued Professional Development*

Almost all graduates (97%) continued to teach in high schools. This finding adheres with the program's vision to "keep" the teachers in close contact with their classes. Accordingly, they influenced a large number of pupils each year and were also able to contribute significantly to additional positions (see Figure 16.2) that they assumed in the system.

It seems that the program opened new opportunities to the graduates, as about half of them assumed new positions after completing the program. In these positions, they could use the knowledge that they had developed in their studies. Their affiliation with different professional communities created new contexts for further professional development as well as new avenues to impact the field. For example, about half of the RW graduates are leading teachers in physics professional learning communities (Levy et al., 2018). A few quotes exemplify this.

> Before participating in the program, I wasn't capable of taking on the role of national coordinator; only 6 months after finishing it did I feel that I have the confidence to take this challenge on – and agreed to do it.

> I feel a deep obligation now to serve as an ambassador for the program and to transmit what I received to other physics teachers in Israel, to improve the teaching of this subject.

An additional assessment of the program was carried out by the Israeli Council for Higher Education as part of a quality assessment activity on education and science education programs in Israel. In a report issued by the committee, they recommended that the WIS continue to carry out the program with its special features, and remarked:

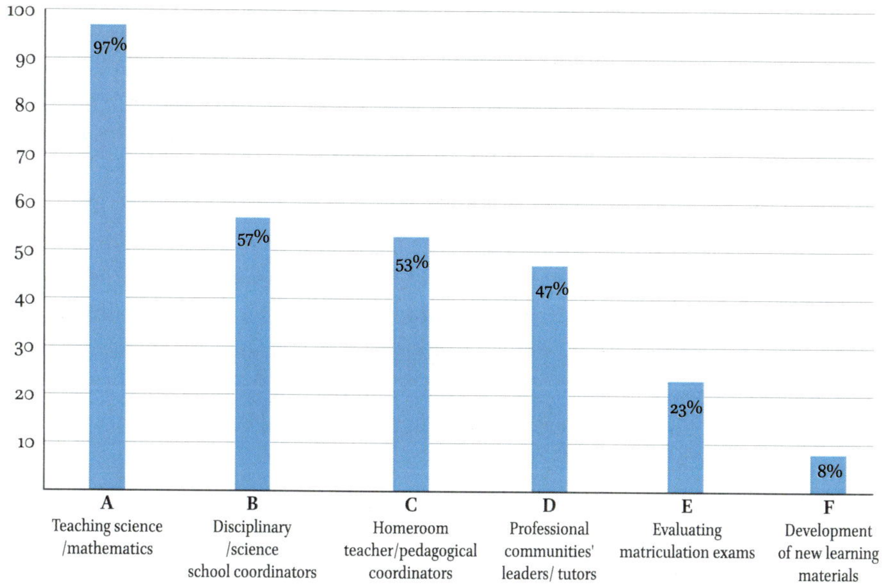

FIGURE 16.2 Positions held by program graduates in their school and in the educational system (n = 120)

> This synergy between research and practice at an elite institution, particularly a collective understanding that research must be used to improve teaching, is rare and commendable. This clarity of mission and sense of purpose seemed to be shared at all levels of the institution. The Department of Science Teaching attracts highly motivated students. The committee was particularly impressed by the caliber of students in the Rothschild–Weizmann Program and their potential to impact science teaching in Israel.

Appendix 2 presents two testimonies of RW graduates.

6 Closing Remarks

The RW program has been a major undertaking for the Department of Science Teaching, congruent with the department's raison d'être – to enhance the quality and effectiveness of mathematics and science education in Israel, to promote these fields as academic endeavors, and to develop future academics who are active in both academics and other leadership roles in the educational system. Obtainment of these goals was advanced through the following unique characteristics of the program.

6.1 *Educating for Impact*

From the outset, the RW program had a defined agenda of long-term impact. The program's designers challenged themselves to apply their resources and expertise to generate a real and lasting change in the field. The strategies aimed to equip teachers with new insights from the vanguard of science and science education research and show them how to become leaders in their own classrooms and beyond, among their peers and communities. According to the presented research and evaluation findings, the graduates claimed that the program provided them with a newfound confidence to explore, together with their students, novel areas; to cultivate inquisitiveness, and encourage questions and discussion in the classroom. Moreover, the impact of the program's graduates on the educational system goes beyond their own classrooms, especially as reflected by the central roles that many of the graduates have assumed.

6.2 *Connecting Theory, Research and Practice*

One of the prerequisites for enrollment in the program was that the applicant be an active science or mathematics teacher. Courses in the scientific disciplines and in science education took into account the teachers' classroom experience.

One of the unique features of the RW program in the scientific disciplines is the exposure of the teachers to the scientists' laboratories and concurrent laboratory experiments in real time. This feature was amplified in the final projects. These experiences had a strong effect on the teachers' notion of scientific work in a 21st century laboratory. They provided the teachers with an insider's view on the nature of science in terms of how science is conducted and the scientist's actual work. Quotes from the teachers highlighted the importance of this feature. The mathematics and science education courses also offered a variety of opportunities to promote the connection of theory, research and practice (cf. Furman Shaharabani & Yarden, 2019).

6.3 *Responding to Challenges in RPPs*

Reflecting on our 10 years' experience with the RW program, we describe here several activities that are relevant to RPPs and played an important role in the program (McKenney, 2016). Design of new courses considered both the goals of the program and aspects of content knowledge and pedagogical content knowledge that would facilitate the impact on practice (Shulman, 1998). The courses underwent successive refinement by responding to feedback from the relevant parties (e.g., student teachers, instructors, and the graduate school). The steering committee played an important role in this process. RPPs have the capacity to update the content and pedagogies that reflect current developments in science and science education. For instance, the current pandemic calls for action. The voice of the expert teachers taking part in the RPPs has an important role in such a mission.

- Fostering *long-term collaborations with the graduates*. Such collaborations can enrich all partners. For example, the program's graduates can enhance their professional development through participation in innovative projects, taking part in research, development and implementation. The research institute receives an effective venue to the educational field involving both research and implementation. To achieve this goal, special effort is needed to characterize what teachers conceive as relevant, interesting and contributing to their professional identity.
- Maintaining *long-term excitement and motivation* of the RPP participants is a central challenge. For instance, with time, leading teachers sought new challenges and avenues of influence and advancement. The responsibility for responding to this became more and more symmetrical (both top-down and bottom-up), suggesting new modes of cooperation. The Edmond de Rothschild Foundation responded to these challenges by agreeing to allocate resources. This was the case, for example in the program's initiative to develop discipline-specific coordinators for assessment and evaluation. In all of the above, modes of promoting fruitful interactions and "border crossing" were carried out.

The original RW program terminated after 10 years, as planned. In light of its contribution, the WIS decided to continue the program, adapting most of its characteristics and resources. The vision is that the educational system in Israel will continue to benefit from the models, materials and, most importantly, the human resources that have been developed in this program. An important challenge for the future is to find fruitful ways to use the leadership capacities of the graduates to continue to promote mathematics and science education in Israel.

Acknowledgment

We thank the Weizmann Institute of Science for the trust and partnership and for providing the professional home for the program during the 10 first years period: Professor Daniel Zajfman – the Institute's president, and Professor Israel Bar-Joseph – the vice president for resource development and dean of educational activities; the science and science education heads of the disciplinary tracks; the Institute's academic staff who developed and taught the courses; the deans of the Feinberg graduate school – Professor Lia Addadi, Professor Irit Sagi, and Dr. Ami Shalit, the Academic Secretary.

We thank "The Edmond de Rothschild Foundation" and its leadership for the foresight and long-term support and commitment to the Rothschild Weizmann Program. Specifically, we thank the Baroness Ariane de Rothschild for her deep interest, involvement and professional input; Eli Booch – director of philanthropy and Vardit Gilor – program academic excellence officer for kind and constructive interactions.

References

Akkerman, S. F., & Bakker, A. (2011). Boundary crossing and boundary objects. *Review of Educational Research, 81*(2), 132–169. http://dx.doi.org/10.3102/0034654311404435

Akkerman, S. F., & Bruining, T. (2016). Multi-level boundary crossing in a professional development school partnership. *Journal of the Learning Sciences, 25*(2), 240–284. http://dx.doi.org/10.1080/10508406.2016.1147448

Arcavi, A., & Isoda, M. (2007). Learning to listen: From historical sources to classroom practice. *Educational Studies in Mathematics, 66*, 111–129. http://dx.doi.org/10.1007/s10649-006-9075-8

Borko, H., Koellner, K., Jacobs, J., & Seago, N. (2011). Using video representations of teaching in practice-based professional development programs. *ZDM – Mathematics Education, 43*(1), 175–187. http://dx.doi.org/10.1007/s11858-010-0302-5

Bryk, A. S., Gomez, L. M., Grunow, A., & LeMahieu, P. (2015). *Learning to improve: How America's schools can get better at getting better.* Harvard University Press. http://dx.doi.org/10.5860/choice.191214

Campbell, C., Osmond-Johnson, P., Faubert, B., Zeichner, K., & Hobbs-Johnson, A. (with Brown, S., DaCosta, P., Hales, A., Kuehn, L., Sohn, J., & Steffensen, K.) (2016). *The state of educators' professional learning in Canada.* Learning Forward.

Coburn, C. E., & Penuel, W. R. (2016). Research–practice partnerships in education outcomes, dynamics, and open questions. *Educational Researcher, 45*(1), 48–54. https://doi.org/10.3102/0013189X16631750

Cochran-Smith, M., & Lytle, S. L. (2001). Beyond certainty: Taking an inquiry stance on practice. In A. Lieberman & L. Miller (Eds.), *Teachers caught in the action professional development that matters* (pp. 45–58). Teachers College Press.

Cochran-Smith, M., & Lytle, S. L. (2009). *Inquiry as stance: Practitioner research for the next generation.* Teachers College Press.

Darling-Hammond, L., & Richardson, N. (2009). Research review/teacher learning: What matters? *Educational Leadership, 66*(5), 46–53.

Donovan, M. S. (2013). Generating improvement through research and development in educational systems. *Science, 340*(6130), 317–319. http://dx.doi.org/10.1126/science.1236180

Even, R., Artstein, Z., & Elbaum-Cohen, A. (2018). The Rothschild–Weizmann Master's Program for practicing mathematics teachers. In N. Movshovitz-Hadar (Ed.), *K–12 mathematics education in Israel: Issues and challenges. Series on Mathematics Education, Vol. 13* (pp. 235–242). World Scientific Publication. http://dx.doi.org/10.1142/9789813231191_0025

Eylon, B. S., & Bagno, E. (1997). Professional development of physics teachers through long-term in-service programs: The Israeli experience. In *AIP Conference Proceedings, Vol. 399* (p. 299). http://dx.doi.org/10.1063/1.53115

Eylon, B. S., Berger, H., & Bagno, E. (2008). An evidence based continuous professional development program on knowledge integration in physics: A study of teachers' collective discourse. *International Journal of Science Education, 30*(5), 619–641. http://dx.doi.org/10.1080/09500690701854857

Feiman-Nemser, S. (2001). From preparation to practice: Designing a continuum to strengthen and sustain teaching. *The Teachers College Record, 103*, 1013–1055. http://dx.doi.org/10.1111/0161-4681.00141

Fullan, M., & Hargreaves, A. (2016). *Bringing the profession back in: Call to action.* Learning Forward. https://michaelfullan.ca/wp-content/uploads/2017/11/16_BringingProfessionFullanHargreaves2016.pdf

Furman Shaharabani, Y., & Yarden, A. (2019). Toward narrowing the theory–practice gap: Characterizing evidence from in-service biology teachers' questions asked during an academic course. *International Journal of STEM Education, 6.* https://doi.org/10.1186/s40594-019-0174-3

Guskey, T. R. (2002). Professional development and teacher change. *Teachers and Teaching: Theory and Practice, 8*, 381–391. http://dx.doi.org/10.1080/135406002100000512

Harrison, C., Hofstein, A., Eylon, B., & Simon, S. (2008). Evidence-based professional development of teachers in two countries. *International Journal of Research in Science Education, 30*(5), 577–591. http://dx.doi.org/10.1080/09500690701854832

Hutchings, P., & Shulman, L. S. (1999). The scholarship of teaching: New elaborations, new developments. *Change: The Magazine of Higher Learning, 31*(5), 10–15. http://dx.doi.org/10.1080/00091389909604218

Knowles, M. S. (1990). *The adult learner: A neglected species.* Gulf.

Lave, J., & Wenger, E. (1991). *Situated learning: Legitimate peripheral participation.* Cambridge University Press. http://dx.doi.org/10.1017/cbo9780511815355

Levy, S., Bagno, E., Berger, H., & Eylon, B. S. (2018). Physics teacher-leaders' learning in a national program of regional professional learning communities. In A. Traxler, Y. Cao, & S. Wolf (Eds.), *Physics Education Research Conference Proceedings*, Washington DC. https://doi.org/10.1119/perc.2018.pr.Levy

Little, J. W. (2012). Professional community and professional development in the learning-centered school. In M. Kooy & K. van Veen (Eds.), *Teacher learning that matters: International perspectives* (pp. 22–46). Routledge. http://dx.doi.org/10.4324/9780203805879

Loucks-Horsley, S., Love, N., Stiles, K. E., Mundy, S., & Hewson, P. E. (2016). *Designing professional development for teachers of science and mathematics* (3rd ed.). Corwin Press.

Mamlok-Naaman, R., Blonder, R., & Hofstein, A. (2010). Providing chemistry teachers with opportunities to enhance their knowledge in contemporary scientific areas: A three-stage model. *Chemistry Education Research and Practice, 11*, 241–252. http://dx.doi.org/10.1039/c0rp90005b

Mason, J. (2008). Being mathematical with and in front of learners: Attention, awareness, and attitude as sources of differences between teacher educators, teachers and learners. In B. Jaworski & T. Wood (Eds.), *The international handbook of mathematics teacher education: The mathematics teacher educator as a developing professional, Vol. 4* (pp. 31–56). Sense Publishers. http://dx.doi.org/10.1163/9789087905521_004

McKenney, S. (2016). Researcher–practitioner collaboration in educational design research: Processes, roles, values & expectations. In M. A. Evans, M. J. Packer, & R. K. Sawyer (Eds.), *Reflections on the learning sciences (current perspectives in social and behavioral sciences)* (pp. 155–188). Cambridge University Press. http://dx.doi.org/10.1017/cbo9781107707221.008

McKinsey Report (2007). *How the world's best-performing school systems come out on top*. http://alamin99.wordpress.com/2008/02/22/mckinsey-report

Penuel, W. R., Allen, A. R., Coburn, C. E., & Farrell, C. (2015). Conceptualizing research–practice partnerships as joint work at boundaries. *Journal of Education for Students Placed at Risk (JESPAR), 20*, 182–197. http://dx.doi.org/10.1080/10824669.2014.988334

Rozenszajn, R., & Yarden, A. (2014). Expansion of biology teachers' Pedagogical Content Knowledge (PCK) during a long-term professional development program. *Research in Science Education, 44*(1), 189–213. http://dx.doi.org/10.1007/s11165-013-9378-6

Scherz, Z., Bialer, L., & Eylon, B. S. (2011). Towards accomplished practice in Learning Skills for Science (LSS): The synergy between design and evaluation methodology in a reflective CPD programme. *Research in Science & Technological Education, 29*, 49–69. http://dx.doi.org/10.1080/02635143.2011.543799

Schön, D. A. (1983). *The reflective practitioner: How professionals think in action*. Basic Books. https://doi.org/10.2307/j.ctvpbnpjg.24

Shulman, L. S. (1998). Theory, practice, and the education of professionals. *The Elementary School Journal, 98*, 511–526. http://dx.doi.org/10.1086/461912

Shulman, L. S. (2011). Feature essays: The scholarship of teaching and learning: A personal account and reflection. *International Journal of the Scholarship of Teaching and Learning, 5*. https://doi.org/10.20429/ijsotl.2011.050130

Strauss, N. (2017). *Insights from past initiatives to promote science education in Israel – Learning from selected issues*, project report. The Initiative for Applied Education Research, Israel Academy of Sciences and Humanities.

Timperley, H., Wilson, A., Barrar, H., & Fung, I. (2008). *Teacher professional learning and development.* New Zealand Ministry of Education, Wellington, New Zealand.

Trigwell, K., Martin, E., Benjamin, J., & Prosser, M. (2000). Scholarship of teaching: A model. *Higher Education Research & Development, 19*, 155–168. http://dx.doi.org/10.1080/072943600445628

Tseng, V. (2012). *Partnerships: Shifting the dynamics between research and practice.* William T. Grant Foundation.

van Driel, J. H., Meirink, J. A., van Veen, K., & Zwart, R. C. (2012). Current trends and missing links in studies on teacher professional development in science education: A review of design features and quality of research. *Studies in Science Education, 48*, 129–160. http://dx.doi.org/10.1080/03057267.2012.738020

Wenger, E. (2010). Communities of practice and social learning systems: The career of a concept. In C. Blackmore (Ed.), *Social learning systems and communities of practice* (pp. 179–198). Springer Verlag and the Open University. http://dx.doi.org/10.1007/978-1-84996-133-2_11

Whitcomb, J., Borko, H., & Liston, D. (2009). Growing talent. *Journal of Teacher Education, 60*(3), 207–212. http://dx.doi.org/10.1177/0022487109337280

Appendix 1: Characteristics of the Rothschild–Weizmann Graduate

1. Knowledge in science and science teaching
   - Extensive updated knowledge in the discipline and in teaching
   - Understands the essence of the discipline and its development
   - Understands and critically analyzes innovations in the teaching of the discipline
2. Meaningful and high-standard teaching
   - Enacts innovations and current emphases in the teaching of the discipline (teaching methods, teaching strategies, alternative assessment methods) and teaches curriculum subjects thoroughly
   - Promotes meaningful learning and understanding of concepts and ideas
   - Committed to promoting heterogeneous classes (adaptive teaching)
   - In science disciplines, incorporates relevant scientific subjects and/or subjects that have not been taught before

3. Continued professional development: activities in the teacher community and holding key positions in the system
   - Leads innovations and modifications in the school system and school initiatives
   - Takes an active role in the activities of the teacher community (regional/national), such as conferences, symposia, presentations in conferences, publishing in teacher magazines
   - Holds key positions as a leading teacher – such as tutor/mentor for new teachers, discipline coordinator, instructor appointed by the supervisor, developer of learning materials/syllabi, leads a teacher community

Appendix 2: Testimonies of Two Graduates of the Rothschild–Weizmann Program

Graduate 1

I taught science for 7 years in middle school before joining the RW program. Through the program, I became acquainted with the research field of "science education" and was astonished to discover its richness and how much this wealth is hidden from many teachers. On the one hand, the program strengthened my belief that teaching is more than handling grades; on the other, I discovered that my teaching conceptions were somewhat behaviorist. I could see an entirely new dimension to science teaching – how it is based on methodical principles and not just a teacher's intuition.

Since I finished the program, my professional path has changed a lot. In a sense, I felt that after being exposed to the great wealth of the field of science and science teaching, it was hard for me to close my eyes and continue as usual within the educational system while ignoring much of what I learned in the program. I often compare the Rothschild–Weizmann program to Plato's cave. When Plato left the cave, he realized that what he experienced there was actually shadows of the real world. In a similar manner, I decided to make a genuine change. I decided to broaden my practical background, teach in high school and submit pupils to matriculation exams. This change enabled me to implement what I had learned and take a fresh view on my actions.

Over the last 3 years, I have participated in the development and implementation of teaching units for biology in cooperation with the National Center of Biology Teachers and Weizmann Institute experts. I am currently developing a teaching unit on cancer, running a pilot study with 10 expert teachers, and continuing my academic studies.

I was also appointed to be a leader of a new regional professional community of biology teachers. This involvement has led to strengthening my contact with the community of biology teachers. An anecdote: when I first arrived at one of the professional communities, the biology national inspector looked at me and asked, "How come I do not know you?" I hope she knows me today…

Graduate 2

I joined the Rothschild–Weizmann program as a teacher who thought of herself as being an excellent math and computer science teacher. I had over 20 years of teaching experience and had successfully submitted students at all levels to matriculation exams in math and in computer science. I was also a member of a committee that developed the matriculation exams in computer science. For over a decade, I served as a math coordinator at my high school and was responsible for the math studies of 7th through 12th graders, the placement of teachers into classrooms, and more.

And then… I started the program and discovered how much more I must learn! The first upgrade happened with my teaching in class. Even in my first year in the program I felt I was much more aware of the things I was doing in class and I tried to change and improve my practice. These processes intensified as my studies in the program continued, and even more so in the following years. The math courses I took greatly expanded my math knowledge and undoubtedly led to the upgrading of my instruction in class.

During this period, I first had to read articles dealing with mathematics education. Although I had great difficulty with reading English, I realized very quickly that there is a whole world of content here that is very relevant to what I have been dealing with all my life and I never knew it.

Aside from that, the program opened doors for me, and I found myself involved in various projects: it started with joining the development team of the MesiMatica project at the Weizmann Institute, where I was introduced to the field of task design and formative assessment. I was lucky to work with people from whom I learned a lot. While working on the project, I started to use various technological means (such as GeoGebra software), which soon became part of the routine toolkit in my teaching.

It became clear to me how small and intimate the community of leading math teachers in the country is. When you are known from one project – you get more and more offers to participate in additional ones. That is how I became one of the "Trump colleagues" who participated in the evaluation of various projects of the foundation around the country.

I continued to teach at school after graduating from the program. During these years, I was also busy with various activities related to mathematics education in Israel: I led sessions in in-service teacher professional development, and engaged in assessment as a "Trump Fellow." I also discovered that I had become a very reflective teacher. I often examined my teaching and my students' learning, and when I shared my experience with my new colleagues, I realized that I had interesting and special stories. Very quickly, I found myself deeply involved in the professional development of teachers. I was asked to lead seminars in different regional centers in the country. This situation, in which teachers sit in front of me with shining eyes, fully engaged in the activity and when the session ends – do not let me go, was rewarding. It made me realize that this is an area I am good at and can contribute to mathematics education. Earlier, I did not even think there was anything I know more than other teachers. During this period I also led a group of over 100 students from all over the country in distance learning for the 5-unit matriculation exams as part of the "Five Online" project.

Then... I realized that the hustle and bustle at the Weizmann Institute had infected me with the academic bug. Suddenly, I had a passion for research. This insight led me to enroll in another master's degree at the Weizmann Institute, this time with a thesis. During my research, I led, for the first time, a community of teachers (research partners) in Haifa. This experience was even more satisfying and fascinating for me. And who would believe that I am presently also involved in an educational-technological project. This started through the "Pie-Challenge" initiative and presently, I am a collaborator in the "Ali-chat" digital initiative promoting personalization in math education.

During the program I had the opportunity to learn from very impressive and interesting people from both the Department of Mathematics and the Department of Science Teaching. In retrospect, there is no doubt that these snowballing events were made possible because I was privileged to participate in the Rothschild–Weizmann program.

PART 3

Commentaries

CHAPTER 17

Reflections on 50 years of Research & Development in Science

Education: What Have We Learned? And Where Might We Be Going?

Alan Schoenfeld

Abstract

This chapter traces the evolution of the field's goals for science education, as exemplified by the Weizmann Institute's cutting-edge research over the past 50 years. It then problematizes the current state, asking: what next? Some of the issues that the field needs to address over the years to come include: the formation of student beliefs regarding science, their often counterproductive nature, and how to address them; issues of equity, and how to support the increasingly diverse student populations that enter our classrooms; and, reimagining science education to develop a much greater focus on having students become sense makers and problematizes themselves, so they can use what they have learned in the service of making informed decisions about issues of central importance. The chapter concludes with a description of essential goals for science education, and a discussion of the challenges we face in supporting teachers to achieve those goals.

Keywords

goals for science and mathematics education – student beliefs – equity – diversity – students as sense makers – supporting teachers

•••

Anniversaries are times to celebrate the past and to look toward the future. I what follows I will do both. There is much to celebrate: progress over the past half century has been nothing short of phenomenal. There is much to think about as well. My goal in reflecting on this progress is to problematize our current understandings as we move into the future.

In many ways this book is a book of a lifetime, not only of the Weizmann Institute's Department of Science Teaching, but more broadly of contemporary

 | DOI: 10.1163/9789004503625_017

science and mathematics education. (And more or less my entire career as a mathematics educator.) I want to congratulate the authors not only for distilling an extraordinary history of ideas, but for doing so in a stimulating and engaging manner. As is my habit, I took notes as I read through the book, focusing on things I find interesting, thought-provoking, worth of reflection. By the time I had finished reading, my notes were almost book-length!

At the dawn of the Department of Science Teaching sone 50 years ago, epistemological and methodological views were radically different than they are today. Back then, "knowledge" was generally taken to be straightforward and measurable. Tests determined how much you knew, period. This reductive view of knowledge was matched by a comparably reductive view of instructional interventions: Under the assumption that tests measure outcomes accurately, you can test the efficacy of any instructional intervention in the same way that you would test how well (for example) a new fertilizer works. Take two similar plots of land (or students), apply the fertilizer (new instructional idea) to one plot but not the other, and check the yield (test scores). If the yield is better for the innovative treatment, then it's superior.

I could go on at length describing the limits of this approach, but they're well known. I'll say simply that such was the state of the field when I entered: Instructional "treatments" were based on what investigators thought students needed, but studies rarely examined how students learned or how they interacted with learning materials. Happily, there were soon changes, in which faculty and staff at the Weizmann were full participants and often leaders. The cognitive revolution brought with it a massive body in inquiry into the nature of thinking, learning and teaching. Studies of inquiry in science, and problem solving in mathematics, flourished. Then, as the field began to focus on students as well as content, the field engaged in socio-cognitive studies, sociopolitical studies, questions regarding the relevance of curricula, the integration of emerging content, and more. This volume reflects such astounding growth, both in studies of thinking and learning (Part 1 of the volume) and professional development (Part 2).

1 Goals as Markers of Progress

One way of tracing the evolution of the Department is to examine the goals espoused by the Institute and by various projects over time. The "ultimate goals," as expressed in the preface to this volume, are as follows:

1. Advancing mathematics and science education as an academic discipline.

2. Enhancing the quality and effectiveness of mathematics and science education in schools.

I will suggest that these are institutional goals and that in fact they are grounded in even more encompassing societal goals – a key question being, what are the rationales for the existence of mathematics and science education in the first place? But before problematizing, let's look at the tacit or explicit aims of the various projects. I focus here on Part 1, because in a sense, Part 2 follows as a corollary: Once we have a deep understanding of the intended purpose(s) of schooling, the fundamental practical and theoretical question becomes, "How do we support teachers in helping students achieve these purposes?"

Hofstein and Mamlok-Naaman (Chapter 1) provide us with both a "traditional" base and a look forward. As they write,

> It is suggested that there is a call to rethink (and research) the goals for learning chemistry in the laboratory. This is especially true in an era when we are trying to promote the goal of teaching "chemistry for all students." For over 15 years, with our colleagues and students, we have researched the potential of an inquiry-type chemistry laboratory for the development of higher-order learning skills, namely, the skills required for future citizens.

The key phrases here are "inquiry" (but whose inquiry? – a theme to which I will return) and "higher order thinking skills," a leitmotif of late 20th and 21st century educational rhetoric. The authors note that traditional objectives for science (chemistry) labs include

- Understanding of scientific concepts
- Interest and motivation
- Attitude toward science
- Scientific practical skills and problem-solving abilities
- Scientific habits of mind
- Understanding the nature of science
- The opportunity to do science

Would that we had achieved these traditional goals! More modern goals, which are echoed in many of the chapters that follow, include:

> The science learning goals of laboratory experiences include enhancing mastery of science subject matter, developing scientific reasoning

> abilities, increasing understanding of the complexity and ambiguity of empirical work, developing practical skills, increasing understanding of the nature of science, cultivating interest in science and science learning, and improving teamwork abilities.

I have listed these at length because, although the formal content concerns chemistry laboratories, the issues are general.

Although Blonder (Chapter 2) does not use the language of goals, the "why's" of incorporating nanotechnology research into the curriculum are grounded in tacit goals:

> In 1902, John Dewey stated, "If we teach today's students as we taught yesterday's, we rob our children of tomorrow." Dewey's famous statement challenges science educators. One way to address this challenge is by adopting an approach that advocates science learning through contemporary research, offering students an opportunity to obtain up-to-date information on what science really is. In this way, students realize that the people involved in research are real, no different from them, and share the same concurrent norms. They also become acquainted with the open-ended nature of scientific issues that await research-based solutions (Blonder & Sakhnini, 2015). This approach obviously offers the students an opportunity to learn about developing research while it is still at the research laboratory stage. (Blonder & Sakhnini, 2016; Blonder et al., 2010; Bryan & Giordano, 2015)

The same is the case for Promoting Self-Regulated Learning (Eidelman & Shwartz, Chapter 3), and data literacy (Yarden & Levkovich, Chapter 4). Expanding outside the cognitive frame, one sees the evolution of the learning instinct theory in Orion's Chapter 5, with its explicit focus on holistic thinking and the notion of learning as an instinct. "Thus, the constructivist reform of the 1990s required that the science education establishment moves from the perspective of disciplinary-driven schooling, with the main goal of preparing a nation's new generation of scientists (reductionism) to that of integration and systems, with attention focused on educating students for lives of social responsibility within democratic societies (holism)."

In many ways, Scherz and Eylon, in Chapter 6 on Learning Skills for Science (LSS), sum up the goals for higher-order skills in their Figure 6.1.

I could continue – the computational habits of mind ("computational thinking") described in in Armoni's Chapter 7 echo what have been called disciplinary practices (see, e.g., the Common Core State Standards Initiative, 2010), "habits of mind" (Cuoco et al., 1996) or "productive patterns of mathematical thinking" (Schoenfeld, 2017) in mathematics. Similarly, Chapter 8 (Areas of Concern in the Design of a Mathematics Curriculum: The Case of Five Curriculum Projects, by Friedlander, Hadas, Hershkowitz and Tabach) highlights the following foci for curriculum development: emphasizing new and relevant content, promoting the use of context and multiple representations, and supporting student learning and reflection. Finally for Part 1, Even's chapter on the use of assessment to inform instructional decisions rounds out the picture of "what counts" in classroom environments.

A cynic might call into question a lot of the above, at least in implementation. One can, for example, point to myriad abuses of the terms "inquiry" and "problem solving" through the years. In both cases, what may have been intended as explorations of rich disciplinary content and practices have often become rote and formulaic. More often than not (in the U.S. at least, but in my experience world-wide, including in Israel) "problem solving" instruction has meant showing students a collection of tasks and the methods for addressing them, after which students are given practice tasks that resemble the ones they have been taught to solve and tested on variants of those. That is, students have (for the most part) been taught problem solving as content, rather than as a way of making sense of mathematical phenomena as they encounter them – or better, explore them. The same, in large measure, has been true of "inquiry." The question, to put it bluntly, is "whose inquiry?" If students follow a predetermined path to learn what you want them to learn, they may well have mastered some content – but have they really learned to be scientifically inquisitive? Indeed, a cynic could raise the issue of how much we have succeeded even at the traditional objectives for science education referenced in Chapter 1 of this volume. How much do citizens at large understand scientific concepts? How interested and motivated are they? What is their general attitude toward science? And what scientific understandings (knowledge, skills and problem-solving abilities, habits of mind, understanding of science, etc.) do our typical graduates actually possess? These are still vexing questions.

I am, of course, anything but a cynic. I am passionately proud of the field's advances over the past half century. But, stimulated by my reading of this volume and my reflections regarding my experiences of the past year, I feel the need to problematize them. I would like to reconsider the goals of science and mathematics education (fundamentally, Part 1 of this volume) and then, having done so, address issues of professional development (fundamentally, Part 2 of this volume).

2 Shifts of Frame, in Preparation for Problematizing Where We Are

Some shifts of frame are necessary to sum up the achievements of the past 50 years. The first is to consider, fully, just what it is that students learn in instruction. A large part of the relevant expansion is contained in Figure 17.1. In considering student learning, we consider far more than the scientific or mathematical content. We consider a range of higher order skills (what some would call 21st century skills, transcending mathematics and science education, but applying to the world of work as well): abilities to think logically, to collaborate, to inquire, and, centrally, to learn. Figure 17.1 delineates the cognitive goals and processes that matter in disciplinary learning. (I include in "inquiry skills" and "problem solving skills" the disciplinary practices and habits of mind that comprise the ability to go beyond what you've been shown. Moreover, problem solving skills include aspects of metacognition such as monitoring and self-regulation.)

Yet, there is more. I found it interesting (especially since I know the issues discussed below are of concern to my colleagues at the Weizmann) that certain terms were sparsely represented in this volume. That may simply be a matter of selection and emphasis; any distillation of 50 years of work by scores of scholars from multiple disciplines into a mere 400 pages must necessarily be selective. But it is worth highlighting some gaps as I frame possible areas of inquiry for the next 50 years.

Perhaps my greatest surprise is that hardly any space in the volume was devoted to the consideration of student (and then adult!) beliefs. It has long been known that student beliefs about the nature of disciplinary learning are major factors in students' disciplinary performance. In mathematics, for example, students whose mathematics experiences in school have consisted primarily of short practice exercises come to believe that problems that they are given to solve can either be solved within a few minutes using techniques they have recently been taught, or not at all. More generally, pernicious student beliefs (e.g., that learning consists primarily of memorizing, that what one learns in the classroom has little or no relevance to aspects of one's life outside the classroom, etc.) are developed from students' experiences in our classrooms. If such issues go unrecognized or unaddressed, the consequences are costly. (For example, Aikenhead (1988) found that "TV had far more influence on what students believed about science and its social, technological context than did numerous science courses." How much have things changed?) The 1988 publication date of Aikenhead's paper indicates the longevity of the issue; a recent piece by Mutjaba et al. (2018) indicates its ongoing relevance and import. They summarize as follows:

> Students' aspirations to study non-compulsory science in the future, and to study the particular subject of chemistry, were strongly associated with their extrinsic motivation towards science (their perceived utility of science, considered as a means to gain particular careers or skills), their intrinsic interest in science, and their engagement in extra-curricular activities. Additionally, their self-concept beliefs (their confidence in their own abilities in science), some teaching approaches, and encouragement from teachers and family alongside family science capital had smaller but still relevant associations.

In short, an individual's perception of what it means to engage in a discipline and the degree to which one sees one's future self as engaging in or with the discipline are highly consequential (and, of course, fundamentally shaped by the ways one engages with the discipline in formal instruction).

I am not sure if my final observation regarding goals reflects selection or cross-cultural differences. The conclusions in a recent report by the U.S. National Academies (2020) highlights the current pressures on the K-12 teaching force:

> There are more explicit demands placed upon K–12 teachers today. There continues to be an increase in the level of content and pedagogical knowledge expected of teachers to implement curriculum and instruction aligned to newer content standards and deeper learning goals. Teachers are called on to educate an increasingly diverse student body, to enact culturally responsive pedagogies, and to have a deeper understanding of their students' socioemotional growth. Integrating these various, layered expectations places substantially new demands on teachers. (National Academies of Sciences, Engineering, and Medicine, 2020, p. 187)

The focus on content and pedagogical knowledge, and on newer content standards, is clear – and shared. However, the second set of issues – the diversity of the student population, the need for culturally relevant pedagogies, and attention to socioemotional growth, does not have a significant presence in this volume. For example, I searched through the text for the words or phrases "equity," diversity," "culturally relevant," and "all students." Neither "equity" nor "culturally relevant" had any matches; nor did "socioemotional." "Diversity" was not invoked in the sense of meeting the needs of a diverse student population, and "Science (or a specific science) for all" was invoked as a broad contextual goal but not pursued in a meaningful manner. This is striking to me, because equity is *such* a major issue in the U.S., in addition to (the absence of) a general scientific literacy. From a distance, it seems that the same would be the case in Israeli culture as well.

As if to underscore these points, an email arrived this week from the National Academies' Board on Science Education inviting me to attend a June 1–2, 2021 workshop entitled "Teaching and the Teacher Workforce amid the Struggles of COVID-19 and for Racial Justice."[1] Two of the key goals of the workshop are to

- Explore the intersection of the pandemic, existing inequities, and the movement for racial justice with respect to the future of teaching, learning, schooling, and the teaching profession.
- Consider the potential for "re-imagining" or "re-inventing" education.

Those issues are timely and will be further addressed below. But first, I need to make the second shift in frame, to focus attention where I think it needs to be focused. Then I'll go on to problematize that framing, as I contemplate directions for the future.

In typical framings of curriculum development, the student is the *object* of instruction – what should the student know, what experiences should students have? When the focus shifts to the teacher the question is typically, what can or should the teacher do? To my mind, this is far too narrow. As the literature on beliefs makes clear, students abstract their understandings from their experiences – and those abstractions go far beyond the disciplinary content they are intended to learn. As discussed above, while the intentions behind assigning students short repetitive exercises were to have students develop content mastery, the lessons the students actually learned included "all problems can be solved in just a few minutes or not at all." Moreover, those are just cognitive outcomes. Other practices, such as "differentiated instruction," may send students messages regarding who is deemed mathematically able and who is not. Subtle instructional patterns may discriminate, e.g., *How schools shortchange girls* (American Association of University Women, 1992) documented the fact that in many classrooms, girls are called upon less frequently than boys and asked less difficult questions. Such patterns, over time, can establish and reinforce a range of societal stereotypes. (In the US, a talking Barbie doll said "math is hard"; there are as well broad stereotypes regarding the mathematical proficiency of various ethnic groups.) In conceptualizing the impact of instruction we need to place the student at the center of instruction, and to ask the fundamental questions, "what does instruction feel like, from the student's point of view? What opportunities do students have to learn not only content and productive disciplinary habits of mind, but to develop positive senses of themselves as thinkers and learners?" Note that this framing also de-centers the teacher. It emphasizes the learning environment.

This approach to conceptualizing what matters for student learning is encapsulated in the Teaching for Robust Understanding (TRU) framework (Schoenfeld, 2013, 2017, 2020). The central idea is that the degree to which students will emerge from a learning environment as knowledgeable and resourceful disciplinary thinkers depends on degree to which the learning environment offers affordances along five key dimensions: (1) the discipline (deep engagement with the content and practices of the discipline, and opportunities to develop disciplinary habits of mind); (2) cognitive demand (opportunities for "productive struggle"); (3) equitable access to core content for *all* students (a classroom in which only some students thrive is inequitable); (4) opportunities for all students to engage with the discipline in ways that support the development of productive disciplinary dispositions and positive disciplinary identities; and (5) formative assessment (making student thinking public so that instruction can be tailored, in the moment, to respond more productively to the current state of student understanding).

If I had written this reaction chapter pre-Covid, I would most likely have emphasized how the TRU Framework subsumes the goals discussed in the individual chapters discussed above and discussed its potential as a frame for taking the inquiries in those chapters further along. Indeed, I still believe that to be the case. But at this point I think the discipline-based approach underlying TRU (and all the chapters in this volume) needs to be problematized.

3 What Do We Need in Science and Mathematics Education?

I am about to argue that science and mathematics education, as typically siloed into discipline-based content and practices and as typically focused mostly on "learning" rather than "problematizing and sensemaking," provides inadequate preparation for the kinds of quantitatively based decision-making that contemporary citizenship increasingly demands. The following question motivates the discussion: what activities are "safe," in times of Covid-19? A key point is that making – or even understanding! – sensible decisions regarding the risks of Covid-19 transmission calls for thinking through issues related to biology (how is Covid-19 transmitted?), physics (how are infectious molecules dispersed?) and fundamental mathematics (e.g., risk is proportional to time spent in any closed environment; when do you add probabilities, when do you multiply them?) These are, literally, issues of life and death. Our goal must be to improve scientific literacy (in this broad sense) to the point where people can do sensemaking, and see through fallacious arguments. The alternative is to abandon the population at large to bewilderment at best and to readily available misinformation at worst. Indeed, it's not only malicious actors whose motives need to be questioned when it comes to issues of public health, as discussed below. To frame the issue in broadest terms: we live in a world in which people have multiple sources of information/misinformation at their fingertips, and they need to make consequential decisions.

Consider basic questions such as "What do I need to know about masks in order to use them wisely?" or "What do I need to know about the vaccines in order to make a sensible decision about being vaccinated?" Then, add to those questions – you'll see why in the following paragraphs – "who can we trust, and how much can we trust them?" As I was writing the previous paragraph, the news feed for the following article literally flashed across my computer screen:

3.1 *What Does the New Mask Guidance Really Mean?*

The C.D.C. now says it is safe for fully vaccinated people to take their masks off in most indoor settings. States, cities and businesses were sorting through what to do with the guidance.

1. More than a year after federal health officials told Americans to cover their faces when venturing out in public, the Centers for Disease Control and Prevention said on Thursday that fully vaccinated people could start taking off their masks indoors.
2. But the new federal guidance – announced amid a sharp decline in coronavirus cases and an expansion of vaccine eligibility to everyone 12 and older – came with caveats and confusion. And it sent state and local officials, as well as private companies, scrambling to decide whether and when to update their own rules. (New York Times, May 13, 2021)
3. Later in the article one reads the following.
4. The news stunned health experts, political leaders, business owners – and seemingly everyone else. Only two and a half weeks ago, the C.D.C. had given a far milder directive, saying that fully vaccinated people could remove their masks outdoors but not in crowded spaces.
5. "It feels like a huge shift, and I'm not going to follow it," said Dr. John Swartzberg, an infectious-disease specialist and clinical professor emeritus at the University of California, Berkeley's School of Public Health. "The most important point is that the C.D.C. is putting responsibility back on individuals. Each individual should look at what the C.D.C. is recommending and see if that fits for them."
6. To further complicate the picture, an article in the previous day's newspaper surveyed epidemiologists, indicating a wide range of preferences[2] – but also some consistency, generally in directions significantly more conservative than C.D.C. regulations. Whatever the scientific legitimacy

> of such a survey, the fact is that while 92% of those surveyed indicated that they had run errands in person, only 45% of the 723 epidemiologists surveyed said that they would or had "interacted outside within 6 feet without a mask" and 30% indicated they ate indoors in a restaurant. Just what is someone supposed to do?

I'll return to this issue in a short while, but I suggest you think about how you would address it before you read my commentary. In the meantime, I want to pose a more specific question. It's in the expository spirit of Pólya's problem solving heuristic, "in order to make progress on a large problem, explore an easier related problem."

It is now generally accepted that the main basis for Covid-19 transmission is inhalation of aerosol particles and that under most circumstances 6 feet of physical distancing is a safe distance to avoid infection. Let's take those as scientifically established for the sake of discussion. The other day as I was out for a walk (wearing a cloth mask) I was irritated by cigarette smoke produced by a smoker who was across the street, a good 30 feet away. If an aerosol irritant could bother me at a distance of 30 feet, why is 6 feet of physical distancing considered safe for Covid?

That question bothered me. Was there a contradiction between my experience and "established knowledge?" It's an engaging question – at least I thought so, as did a number of my scientist friends. Here's how I thought about it.

My first question was, "what matters in this situation?" We're comparing a person's reaction to "irritants" disseminated via aerosol: in one case cigarette smoke, in the other, particles laden with Covid-19. I thought of a few factors. First, there's the density of irritant. Might there be more particles of irritant in one case or the other? Second, there's particle size. If the particles of one irritant are significantly larger than the other, perhaps they don't linger in the air as long. (That was the rationale behind physical distancing.) Third, there's sensitivity. How much exposure does it take before the irritant "registers" (via nasal irritation in the case of cigarettes, or infection in the case of Covid)?

It turns out that all three factors "favor" the perception of cigarette smoke at a distance. First, cigarette smoke is quite dense – a lung full of smoke is primarily smoke, and when you exhale it, a huge number of smoke particles are expelled. It must be the case that there are many orders of magnitude more smoke particles per exhalation than Covid particles. Second, a little bit of research on the web reveals that smoke particles are much smaller than the particles that carry Covid. According to the Journal of Colloid Science, "tobacco smoke as it comes from a cigarette is an extremely concentrated aerosol with a relatively stable distribution of sizes ranging from 0.1 to 1.0 micron, peaked between 0.2 and

0.25 micron" (Keith & Derrick, 1960, p. 340). In contrast, according to a recent study, "The minimum size of a respiratory particle that can contain SARS-CoV-2 is calculated to be approximately 4.7 microns" (Lee, 2020, p. 6960). Thus the smallest respiratory particle that can contain SARS-CoV-2 is 20 to 25 times as large as the mean cigarette smoke particle. Not only are there tons more smoke particles, but they're much more "waftable."

Finally, there's the question of what it takes to notice an irritant like cigarette smoke, as opposed to how much of a pathogen like SARS-CoV-2 is actually required to cause infection. Cigarette smoke is highly detectable; you can be aware of it at very low concentrations. Of course you don't smell COVID particles. What is known, however (see, e.g., Robertson, 2021), is that the likelihood of infection is strongly affected by viral load. A brief exposure to a small amount of SARS-CoV-2 may well be below infection threshold. (That's why you're supposed to keep exposure short; it's cumulative exposure that's dangerous.)

Putting those three factors together: cigarette smoke is expelled in very high concentrations, it stays aloft and disperses very easily, and is highly detectable. In contrast, Covid exhalations are much less dense, probably don't stay aloft as long or as far, and may require greater concentrations ("viral load") to have an impact. So, there's no contradiction.

I hope you've enjoyed reasoning through this example – my scientist friends did. Now I'd like to "go meta," exploring the kinds of reasoning required to address it.

Where did my solution start? Not with the facts or the reasoning, but with a scientific disposition. I noticed a contradiction and thought, "this doesn't make sense – there should be a way to resolve this." I can't emphasize this enough. What makes us all scientists (and science educators) is our habits of observation, of problematizing, and of sensemaking. It's in the scientific folklore, of course: making observations and trying to understand what he saw is what made Galileo Galileo (and what got him into trouble!). There are mathematical examples as well. One of my favorite stories is about Henry Pollak, who, when visiting local supermarkets, noticed that one market's express lane allowed up to 15 items while another allowed only 6. "That can't be right," he said; "it's an optimization problem and the range can't be that large." (An applied mathematician, he went on to do the optimization.)

Indeed, some mathematics educators conduct research on "problem posing" – but the number is tiny, and the idea of problematizing has never made its way meaningfully into standards. Likewise, "inquiry" may be a holy word in the science education lexicon, but – apologies for my rudeness – it typically means "thou shalt inquire along the lines I want," not "Do you see anything interesting? How would you explore it?" The serious question is: where in our science or mathematics curricula do students learn to look at the world around them, ask interesting questions, and organize what they know so that they can make inroads on those questions?[3] Absent this experience, what students learn (and the reason I emphasize beliefs as outcomes) is that mathematics and science are done by experts, and that students must simply accept the results (or reject results and recommendations, as in the case of controversial public science!).

A minor point: I very much enjoyed the anecdote about Ira Remsen that began Chapter 1 – but I take a different moral from the story. I would argue that the fundamental driver of Remsen's career was his curiosity – he felt the need to know how and why nitric acid acted on copper, his fingers, and his trousers. Yes, the way to find out was in the laboratory. But if he wasn't curious in the first place, he'd never have made his way into the chemistry lab. So the question is, how do we support the development of curiosity and provide mechanisms for satisfying it? (Note that I did not say "how do we instill curiosity?" I believe children are naturally curious, and that we stultify most of that curiosity in schooling.)

In short, curiosity and a scientific disposition matter; we ignore them at our (literal) peril. But then what? For lack of a better term, sensemaking. In the situation above I was confronted with a problem and I asked, "what matters here?" Two things are important about this. First, doing so is fundamentally scientific. Second, what mattered in this case doesn't correspond to any one science course I've ever taken (or to my knowledge, any non-specialist course offered in the curriculum). Thinking about the problem involved aspects of physics (particle dispersion, density, etc.), aspects of advanced biology (the size of the smallest particles that can carry Covid), aspects of mathematics (proportional reasoning, orders of magnitude), and a non-trivial amount of heuristic reasoning. The thinking required to address my little dilemma falls outside all of our instructional silos – as does the thinking required to solve the big problems I started with, a theme I'll return to.

Finally, there's a meta-question. How much confidence should I have in my reasoning, and the specific data that. went into it? As noted above, suggestions from the C.D.C. can be shocking, and questioned by some very respectable scientists. How can I think about what I can trust?

In the case of my reasoning about cigarette smoke, some things are solid and some are not. The data on particle size was published in reputable journals. I think it can be trusted because it's basic science rather than public policy, which may be motivated by many factors (see below). The particle density argument seems solid (especially since the article on cigarette smoke referred to it as "an extremely concentrated aerosol") but the idea that Covid-infected particles, being much larger, won't spread as far, is somewhat conjectural – I don't know at what point particle size stops being relevant. Finally, there's clearly some handwaving involved in my argument about sensitivity to cigarette smoke versus viral load. I did find that 2 parts per million of CO in cigarette smoke cause significant irritation, but I didn't find analogous data for Covid transmission. Save for that weak link in the data chain, the arguments seemed plausible. (My scientist friends thought so too.)

To sum up the morals of this little thought experiment: (1) Inherent curiosity and a scientific disposition are fundamentally important. (2) Sensemaking calls for asking what really matters in a situation and for following through with (at minimum) heuristic models that cohere at some level. (3) The information required to approach real-world problems transcends disciplinary silos. (4) Finding relevant and useful information requires judgments of scientific reliability, as does a meta-level review of the reasoning processes involved.

And the big question, before I complexify things even more: How much of the above do students learn in school? You can guess my answer.

Let me briefly return to the larger issue of which activities are "safe" during Covid times – not to resolve them, but to complexify the story above. The C.D.C. announcement reversing its previous policy raises serious issues of trust, as a matter of public policy.[4] The C.D.C. is supposed to be scientific, and it appears here that they just "changed their minds." Not only that, but advice regarding how to avoid contracting Covid has changed radically since it was first identified. Early on, the focus was on disinfecting surfaces: counters were supposed to be wiped down with disinfectant and packages left to air-dry for days before being opened. Later, the focus was on large droplets and masks. Then aerosol transmission of Covid was taken to be central. Mandates regarding quarantining, masking, and other public activities varied from country to country (and it the U.S., often by locality). All this has taken place amidst massive misinformation – googling "covid vaccine conspiracies" just resulted in "about 35,700,000 hits."

For those of us who follow the science (and the politics), there are some plausible ways to sort through this morass. First, there is our general understanding of the scientific enterprise – namely, that our understandings grow and change over time. The transition from a focus on surface contamination to large exhaled particles to aerosols represents the normal progress of science. As new data come in, theories evolve. The challenge is that the decisions to accept these changes and change public health regulations have often been politically influenced. Acknowledging that one's ideas have been wrong can involve losing face, and some health bodies have been slow to publicly acknowledge what evolving data indicate. That, indeed, is a second point to examine. Basic science is basic science, but public health is simultaneously a scientific and political issue. Scientific literacy includes knowing the difference between the two and taking it into account. Indeed, one can attribute positive motives to public health officials and still take their directives with more than a grain of salt. The C.D.C. mask directives may be a case in point, although I hasten to say that the balance of this paragraph is purely speculative. Organizations like the C.D.C. deal with issues of public health writ large, the question being, "what is the most effective large-scale policy?" In the U.S. there is a great deal of "vaccine hesitancy," even among those who wear masks. If the "reward" for being vaccinated is that one no longer needs to be masked, would that reward tip the balance for some of the people who are vaccine hesitant? If enough people move in that direction, would that decrease infection rates, moving the population closer to herd immunity? From this perspective, the decrease in infections resulting from increased vaccination rates might be larger than the increase in infections caused by some vaccinated-but-unmasked people. That is, the C.D.C.'s suggestion might be reasonable in terms of the expected value of infection across the population – while for any particular vaccinated individual, remaining masked might still be a good personal decision. (I note that C.D.C. policies contain references to the underlying scientific studies, so those with a scientific disposition can find the science and decide for themselves. I'm in no hurry to unmask, both for my own sake and that of others.)

This last discussion adds two considerations to the four points highlighted above: the population at large needs a basic understanding of the evolving nature of the scientific enterprise, in order to (5) accept as natural the self-correcting nature of scientific understanding over time, and (6) to separate broad policy mandates from individual decision-making based on relevant information.

Here, then is my summary of *essential goals for science education.*

1. Nurture curiosity and support problematizing
2. Engage students with the core content and practices of individual disciplines,
3. Develop meta-knowledge regarding the ways science works
4. Foster the kind of sensemaking in which students learn to identify "what counts" in situations they are exploring, in ways that
5. Transcend disciplinary silos,
6. Assess the robustness of the information on which their arguments depend as well as the robustness of the arguments themselves.

All of this can be considered the expanded multidisciplinary version of Dimension 1 of the TRU Framework – the "what" that students need to learn.

To be maximally effective, classroom instruction will still need to be consistent with the four remaining dimensions of TRU: (Dimension 2) adjusting cognitive demand so that students have opportunities for deep learning through productive struggle; (Dimension 3) providing equitable access to core content for *all* students, in ways that (Dimension 4) support the development of productive disciplinary dispositions and positive disciplinary identities; and (Dimension 5) making use of formative assessment to tailor instruction to current student needs and understandings.

That said, let us turn briefly to issues of helping teachers grow.

4 Thoughts on Professional Development (Part 2 of the Volume)

I want to begin with some editorializing, perhaps more about the U.S. than Israel, but I suspect that what I am about to say applies to some degree in Israel as well. What I say here establishes the context for my comments below.

Teaching well is a challenge. Even if you consider the traditional goals for science and mathematics education – stimulating interest and motivation, helping students understand content and develop disciplinary habits of mind, developing inquiry and problem solving skills, etc. – you're talking about understandings and skills that take teachers years to develop under the best of circumstances. Moreover, as the literature makes clear, students are anything but passive receptacles of knowledge; coming to grips with what students understand and how to move them forward in terms of content knowledge alone is a significant challenge. That's why the notion of pedagogical content knowledge (Shulman, 1986, 1987) is so critical. And that's before you begin to consider things like the "whole child," students' disciplinary identities, etc. The development of expertise in any complex field requires many thousands of hours of practice and reflection.

Given this, the predominant model of teacher preparation in the U.S. (and with some variation in much of the world) is simply untenable. Typically pre-service teachers in the U.S. earn undergraduate degrees in disciplinary content areas if they plan to teach in secondary school, or in child development if they plan to teach elementary school. After a year of "teacher prep" including a comparatively small amount of practice teaching, they are given their own classrooms – and very little support for learning on the job. (In his classic volume Schoolteacher: A sociological study, Lortie (1975) referred to the "egg crate" model of teaching: in the vast majority of schools teachers do their work in separate compartments, isolated from others from whom they could learn.) Simply put, the kind of teacher "preparation" described here is a recipe for failure, in that it demands that teachers do much of their learning on their own. Although many teachers do figure out many things by themselves – that's how pedagogical content knowledge emerges – many teachers struggle. Such struggle, absent systemic support, is one of the main reasons for the consistently high drop-out rates among American teachers. About half of the people in the U.S. who embark on teaching careers make it through five years of teaching. If they are teaching in high poverty urban districts, about half have left the profession after three years or less of teaching.

The situation in the U.S. is extreme, but it establishes the context for thinking about the professional development efforts described in this volume. No matter how talented a beginning teacher may be, that teacher is still at the beginning of a very steep growth curve. If you think about the five dimensions of TRU, effective teachers for all students must understand disciplinary content and practices well enough to initiate students into them. They must be able to engage all students in ways that the students not only come to grips with key aspects of the discipline, but in ways that enable the students to develop positive disciplinary identities. Moreover, doing so requires making student thinking public and adjusting to it in ways that allow students to engage in productive struggle (formally, to work productively in their zones of proximal development). These competencies take time to develop. How and when is the issue of professional development.

5 What's Been Done, What Remains to Be Done?

In the interest of saving space, I am going to skip a historical discussion of professional development (see Arcavi's Chapter 10 for part of the history) and cut to the present. What I will note is that, not surprisingly, the evolution of professional development mirrors the evolution of theories of learning, starting with "tell the learners what they need to know" and moving to a current emphasis on the importance of communities of (professional) learners, or PLCs. Indeed, the parallels between what we know about classroom learning and what we know about professional represent more than an analogy. The TRU framework applies to all learning environments, including PLCs (See Schoenfeld, 2015). As such, any PLC should be focused on powerful professional growth (Dimension 1, the arena being focused on). It should offer challenges for that are meaningful but within reach (Dimension 2, productive struggle) for *all* participants (Dimension 3), in ways that build their agency and identities as professionals (Dimension 4). This, of course, entails active involvement! And dimensions 1 through 4 are facilitated by ongoing monitoring and adjustment (Dimension

5, formative assessment). Arcavi's Chapter 10 summary of desiderata for PLCs is, of course, consistent:

> Today, these PLCs are striving to move away from the classical course format (regardless of whether they focus on a particular curriculum or on learning about learning or teaching, or both). These PLCs should function like any other PLC, namely they have to engage their participants in an ongoing study of the profession, continuously rethinking its practice, and striving for ongoing improvement and implementation of innovations. A special characteristic of the PLC is to provide an environment that empowers teachers by fostering and valuing exchanges among peers, mutual cooperation and collaboration, emotional support, personal growth, and a sense of togetherness, in order to achieve what it is more difficult to accomplish alone.

Moreover, such PLCs are typically intended to be discipline-based, generative (i.e., not simply oriented toward the transmission of information), oriented toward understanding and responding to student thinking, and meant to be real communities with active engagement, meta-learning, mutual respect, and collective goals.

Each of the subsequent chapters has at least a partial PLC focus. Levy, Langley, and Yerushalmi (Chapter 11) compare the impacts of two different approaches to professional learning, one within the national network of PLCs for advanced-level high-school physics teachers. Mamlok-Naaman and Hofstein (Chapter 12) emphasize the need for teachers' life-long learning in "an environment of collegiality and collaboration among teachers who teach the same or related subjects, an environment that encourages reflection on their work in the classroom." They discuss action research, collaborative engagement with teachers in inquiry related to the classroom chemistry laboratory, and engaging science teachers as curriculum developers. Such approaches elevate teachers from the status of recipients of professional development to partners in the framing of their own professional growth, a key aspect of PLCs. As Scherz, Eylon, and Yarden note in Chapter 13, there is no consensus in the literature regarding the definition of PLCs. However, their distillation of the goals the established among their stakeholders:

- Relations of trust and norms of sharing;
- Regular meetings and mechanisms, structured processes;
- Focus on student learning, and the connections between teaching and learning;
- Decision-making based on data collection and evaluation;
- Reflective dialogues, inquiry, and reflection

is consistent with all of the points made above. Similarly, the "life trajectory" of VIDEO-LM as described by Karsenty and Arcavi in Chapter 14 rings true to me for many reasons, not the least of which is the extremely profitable (for me, at least) interactions between the VIDEO-LM and TRU-PD over their lifetimes. Although the two projects have taken on somewhat different shape due both to the contexts in which they were developed and the theoretical/practical orientations and styles of their principal investigators, they share much in common.

At a meta-level, Cooper and Koichu's Chapter 15 raises three fundamental challenges that one faces in building PLCs: issues of fidelity, scale, and sustainability. These are issues for every PLC, which I shall address in the next section of this paper. Finally, Eylon and Carmeli's (Chapter 16) retrospective discussion of the decade-long Rothschild-Weizmann Program for Excellence in Science and Mathematics Teaching highlights some of the key considerations that must be taken into account in fostering a PLC. A key component of their approach is a focus on boundary-crossing – the need to find common ground when, "despite the wide agreement between the partners on the general goals of the program, each of them initially held different interpretations and expectations or definitions of the program's outcomes."

6 What Are the Key Issues? And What Do We Do about Them?

Here I want to collect some of the issues that became apparent in reflecting on Chapters 10 through 16, and highlight some of the challenges we face. Some are obstacles, some are tensions inherent in respecting the wishes and understandings of various stakeholders. These are issues any project is likely to face. A challenge for the field is to address them in systematic and systemic ways. Before proceeding, I want to stress the obvious:

Solving the problem of professional development is hard – if it were an easy problem, it would have been solved by now. The challenge is that we're talking about developing teachers' expertise. The kinds of understandings we hope to help teachers build take thousands of hours of reflective practice, even when there is adequate conceptual and practical support for it. Such support may exist in a few places, but it certainly does not exist at scale.

6.1 *Tensions Regarding Goals*

As Eylon and Carmeli's paper indicates, different stakeholders may have very different goals for PLCs – even if they use the same language. In my experience working with PLCs, different stakeholders – in some case, "permission granters" – have the potential to undermine coherence to the point where it threatens a PLC's viability.

One example: meaningful change in teaching takes time. To take one example, moving from a teacher-centered "demonstrate and practice" approach to a student-centered "build on what the students understand" approach requires changes in belief systems, in routines, and in basic knowledge. If a PLC is working well, one can see progress in teachers' understandings over time as they try things, bring them back to the PLC for discussion, learn from their attempts, try something different, etc. It might take months before a teacher begins to "hear" what students might be saying and, instead of correcting errors, attempt to build on what the student says. It may take longer to build a classroom culture in which students feel free to demonstrate their partial understandings, and longer yet before a teacher's hard work translates into measurable student learning gains. That's the reality. But there are practical realities as well. We worked in a school district in which a top administrator said that, yes, he understood all this, and he also understood that tests were not necessarily informative – but he would consider our PLC a failure if student test scores didn't rise by a specified amount by the end of the first year. (His job included being responsible for student test outcomes.)

There are also more minor, but equally consequential issues regarding the maintenance of a PLC. In the U.S. many site-based decisions are at the discretion of school leaders. In one PD project I was engaged in, a school principal agreed to reserve two hours of afternoon time on the first Wednesday of each month for our PLC work. During that school year the principal called schoolwide faculty meetings on five of the ten days we had reserved for the PLC.

6.2 *Capacity Building and Sustainability*

A major challenge for many PD projects is that the community the project draws from does not have the human resources (e.g., knowledgeable coaches) to carry out, or even support, a project on its own. This raises at least two significant issues. First, participants in a real PLC must feel legitimately enfranchised – what the participants want to so, and how they want to spend their time, should matter! But… To be blunt, what do you do when the community wants to do something you think is ill-advised? This is a reality more often than one might like. The tensions of helping PLCs move in what research clearly indicates are profitable directions should not be underestimated.

Second, there is the question of sustainability: what happens when the funding for a PLC-related project ends, and there is no longer external leadership or funding to keep the project alive? (In the U.S., the vast majority of school-based projects simply die once the grant supporting the project ends.) A significant part of building a PLC is identifying and supporting nascent leadership within the PLC, so that there is site or PLC capacity to continue successfully once the initial project personnel have been "weaned" from the project. But even if that capacity exists, there's the issue of ongoing internal support. In the U.S. context I've found that requiring a school district to absorb an increasing percentage of costs over time makes it more likely that the district, having committed itself to a PD program, will continue to do so when external funding is gone.

Admittedly these are "practical" rather than academic problems – but they are very real.

6.3 *On Scaling*

My honest opinion is that there do not currently exist successful models for scaling PLCs or any other forms of interaction that depend heavily on their features as described in this volume (significant learning goals, intense social interactions, collective decision making, etc.). A number of the chapters in Part 2 of this book suggest a "cascade" or "train the trainers" model to achieve change at scale. I'm dubious. As Hugh Burkhardt pointed out some time ago: if each stage of a "train the trainers" model conveys 70% of the desired skills and understandings to its audience, the recipients at the second level are getting 49% of what the original leaders are trying to communicate. The mathematics here may be facetious, but the underlying issues are serious. If you consider the time required for meaningful professional growth, something other than a simple "train the trainers" model is called for – that kind of model is predicated on teaching simple transferrable skills. What we're talking about here has to do with more organic, continuous growth stimulated by and supported by a learning community.

6.4 *The Issue of Fidelity*

In my opinion the very idea of fidelity in professional development is problematic. The question is, *fidelity to what?* Think of the five best teachers you know. At a surface level, do their classrooms look alike? I doubt it. Part of their professionalism consists of doing things in their own particular ways; I'd bet most highly accomplished teachers would resist attempts to compel them to teach with fidelity to a particular approach. And, they should. There is no one "right way" to teach, in the sense that the best teachers orchestrate classroom events in ways that are consistent with their own styles and their understandings of their students.

Does that mean we should give up? Of course not: the question is, what is consistent in their teaching? I'd argue that what *is* consistent is that the teachers in question have managed to create powerful learning environments for their students – and that (my apologies for perseverating) those learning environments would score consistently well along the 5 dimensions of the TRU framework. That is, highly effective teachers demonstrate fidelity to the principles that underlie the creation of powerful learning environments, rather than to specific mechanics that one might prescribe to achieve them.

This raises a fundamental issue: How do we support teachers in learning to act in ways that are consistent with a set of underlying principles? Part of the answer is present in many of the chapters: it consists of understanding those principles and reflecting on one's practices in light of them.

Here again we encounter the problem of bootstrapping community capacity to act in particular ways. I will reference, briefly, my own success and failure. The TRU Framework offers a set of principles underlying powerful learning environments. In the right hands, it can be the basis for very interesting and valuable professional development. Since TRU began to mature I have deliberately resisted building a program of professional development that requires implementation with fidelity. Instead, partly because working in partnership with skilled colleagues results in significant improvement to my own ideas, the way I've moved forward has been to offer trusted colleagues free rein to "run with" TRU in their own PD, in whatever ways make the most sense to them. The result has been a small number of very successful – and very different – models of implementation (see Schoenfeld et al., 2019). I am confident that these implementations are of very high quality, avoiding the 70% "transmission" rate discussed in Section 6.3 – there is little question that in those implementations, there is very high fidelity to the underlying principles of TRU. The problem? Lack of scale. If only my friends and I can implement these ideas in rich ways, there's a serious problem.

6.5 *The Role of Materials*

I am not sanguine about the role of curricula in supporting major professional development, unless governments or other funders undertake the development of such materials at very significant cost. In the 1990s the U.S. National Science Foundation supported the development of curricula to support the implement of the then-new NCTM standards, at a cost of some $100M USD. The results were impressive: there is clear evidence that the NSF-funded, standards-based" curricula established a new floor for instruction. However, nothing on a comparable scale has been attempted since. Moreover, realistically speaking, such materials are inherently conservative. They were designed to be implemented, on publication, on a large scale.

There is, however, an intriguing possibility. Funded by a substantial grant from the Gates Foundation, the Mathematics Assessment Project (2021) produced 100 "Formative Assessment Lessons" – teaching materials intended to support teaching with formative assessment. There is evidence that the lessons themselves helped to improve instruction (see Herman et al. (2014; Research for Action, 2015). But that's not my point. I've had conversations with a number of colleagues who head PLCs, some related to lesson study, some focusing on teachers bringing in videos of their instruction for collective discussion. Those colleagues have reported consistently that the conversations in the PLCs were less rich than they would have liked, because the lessons the teachers were discussing just weren't that interesting. (Once again, that's the bootstrapping problem.) But, when the teachers in the PLCs tried teaching the Formative Assessment Lessons, the conversations in the PLCs got much richer. The lessons embody ambitious goals. As a result, attempts to implement them (or teachers' decisions to vary from them) led to deep conversations about both underlying issues and implementation.

The point: A PLC with established norms of inquiry can "up its game" substantially by taking advantage of ambitious curricular materials. The materials can serve as a catalyst for further growth. This may be a mechanism for addressing the scaling problem.

6.6 *Problems of Disciplinary Understanding, Teaching, and Learning*

Not that we need reminding, but the job of understanding what matters in individual disciplines is hardly complete. The fact that a significant proportion of what students learn is forgotten within a year (cf. the notorious "summer slump") suggests that there is still a lot missing in our conceptualization of what really matters in disciplinary learning. A key question is, what kinds of understandings would enable students to regenerate what they need to know, years after a course is over? There's no time to expound on this theme; I've addressed it partly in Schoenfeld (2020).

6.7 *Problems of Interdisciplinary Sensemaking, Teaching, and Learning*

Here I return to the main thesis in Part 1 of this review: the disciplinary efforts we have undertaken over the past 50 years are simply not enough to prepare our students for the coming decades. The main problems of scientific and mathematical literacy today fall outside disciplinary silos, and students need to develop reasoning and sensemaking skills to cope with them. These are, as I noted in Part 1, literally life-and-death issues. How can we make inroads on that major problem?

6.8 *A Path toward Progress?*

The challenges outlined in this chapter are daunting. Yet, I believe the seeds of progress are within reach. Over the past 50 years we have learned a great deal about disciplinary understanding and how to organize professional learning communities to support teachers in the mission of teaching for deep understanding. At present we face challenges with regard to issues of capacity building, fidelity, and going to scale, but there are ways to think about all of them – in particular, the idea of building rich stimulus materials that can serve as catalysts for progress in robust teacher learning communities. If materials can be designed that embody enough content understanding and grist for reflection to enable teachers to conduct and problematize rich instruction, then the burden of building capacity within PLCs may be lessened – as noted above, the task of maintaining community and running with rich ideas is much easier when the materials offer ideas to run with. At the same time, we need to face the set of issues discussed in the first part of this review. We need to prepare students to grapple with the kinds of issues that life will throw at them on a regular basis in the future – issues that call for scientific sensemaking that draw upon disciplinary knowledge but whose scope falls outside of our traditional disciplinary silos. What a wonderful challenge! We have a base for making progress, and much to do.

7 Coda

I first visited the Weizmann Institute in 1992 and have happily returned with some regularity, most recently for the 50th anniversary celebration. It has been an honor and a privilege to collaborate with my colleagues in the Department of Science teaching, from whom I have learned so much. This volume commemorates 50 years of superb progress. I can't wait to see what comes next.

Notes

1 See https://mailchi.mp/nas/teaching-and-covid?e=067a87390c
2 Epidemiologists were asked to identify which "activities they had done in the last 30 days, or would have done if necessary, assuming they would wear a mask or distance as needed."
3 I include the world of patterns and symbols, for mathematical inquiry.
4 I understand that this particular issue is most salient in the context of U.S. politics, but there are analogous issues with regard to W.H.O. credibility and policy decisions by government organizations in every nation.

References

Aikenhead, G. (1988). An analysis of four ways of assessing student beliefs about STS [Science-Technology-Society] topics. *Journal of Research in Science Teaching, 25*, 607–629.

American Association of University Women (AAUW). (1992). *How schools shortchange girls*. AAUW and National Education Association.

Common Core State Standards Initiative. (2010). *Common core state standards for mathematics*. http://www.corestandards.org/wp-content/uploads/Math_Standards.pdf

Cuoco, A., Goldenberg, E. P., & Mark, J. (1996). Habits of mind: An organizing principle for mathematics curricula. *Journal of Mathematical Behavior, 15*, 375–402.

Herman, J., Epstein, S., Leon, S., La Torre Matrundola, D., Reber, S., & Choi, K. (2014). *Implementation and effects of LDC and MDC in Kentucky districts (CRESST Policy Brief No. 13)*. University of California at Los Angeles, National Center for Research on Evaluation, Standards, and Student Testing (CRESST).

Keith, C. H., & Derrick, J. C. (1960). Measurement of the particle size distribution and concentration of cigarette smoke by the "conifuge." *Journal of Colloid Science, 15*, 340–356.

Lee, B. U. (2020). Minimum sizes of respiratory particles carrying SARS-CoV-2 and the possibility of aerosol generation. International Journal of Environmental Research and Public Health, *17*(19), 6960. https://doi.org/10.3390/ijerph17196960

Lortie, D. C. (1975). *Schoolteacher: A sociological study*. University of Chicago Press.

Mathematics Assessment Project. (2021). *Formative assessment lessons*. https://www.map.mathshell.org/lessons.php

Mujtaba, T., Sheldrake, R., Reiss, M., & Simon, S. (2018). Students' science attitudes, beliefs, and context: Associations with science and chemistry aspirations. International Journal of Science Education, *40*, 644–677.

National Academies of Sciences, Engineering, and Medicine. (2020). *Changing expectations for the K–12 teacher workforce: Policies, preservice education, professional development, and the workplace*. The National Academies Press.

New York Times. (2021, May 13). *What does the new mask guidance really mean?* https://www.nytimes.com/2021/05/13/us/cdc-mask-guidelines-vaccinated.html?smid=fb-nytimes&smtyp=cur&fbclid=IwAR1IoSGwyslO-_wSk6EJBb6NePhuJY8nC8SUgLKDRS5dHiZEcgQPuv4CCoQ

Research for Action. (2015). *MDC's influence on teaching and learning*. https://www.researchforaction.org/publications/mdcs-influence-on-teaching-and-learning/

Robertson, S. (2021) *Viral load the main driver of SARS-CoV-2 transmission*. https://www.news-medical.net/news/20210203/Viral-load-the-main-driver-of-SARS-CoV-2-transmission.aspx

Schoenfeld, A. H. (2013). Classroom observations in theory and practice. *ZDM – Mathematics Education, 45*, 607–621.

Schoenfeld, A. H. (2015). Thoughts on scale. *ZDM – Mathematics Education, 47*, 161–169.

Schoenfeld, A. H. (2017). Teaching for robust understanding of essential mathematics. In T. McDougal (Ed.), *Essential mathematics for the next generation: What and how students should learn* (pp. 104–129). Tokyo Gagukei University.

Schoenfeld, A. H. (2020). Reframing teacher knowledge: A research and development agenda. *ZDM – Mathematics Education, 52*, 359–376.

Schoenfeld, A. H., Baldinger, E., Disston, J., Donovan, S., Dosalmas, A., Driskill, M., Fink, H., Foster, D., Haumersen, R., Lewis, C., Louie, N., Mertens, A., Murray, E., Narasimhan, L., Ortega, C., Reed, M., Ruiz, S., Sayavedra, A., Sola, T., … Zarkh, A. (2019). Learning with and from TRU: Teacher educators and the teaching for robust understanding framework. In K. Beswick (Ed.), *International handbook of mathematics teacher education, Vol. 4, The mathematics teacher educator as a developing professional.* Sense Publishers.

Shulman, L. S. (1986). Those who understand: Knowledge growth in teaching. *Educational Researcher, 17*(1), 4–14.

Shulman, L. S. (1987). Knowledge and teaching: Foundations of the new reform. *Harvard Educational Review, 57*(1), 1–23.

CHAPTER 18

50 Years of Research on Science Teaching at the Weizmann Institute

50 Years of Inspiration for the International Academic Community and the Israeli Teaching Practice

Ilka Parchmann

Abstract

In this commentary, the author describes the activities and the rationale of the Department of Science Teaching at the Weizmann Institute of Science. This department was active over a long period of time. She writes that the holistic approach of connecting science disciplines to teaching and learning of the sciences in the educational system in Israel is commendable. This approach includes all the components that characterize science curricula: development, implementation to include intensive and comprehensive long term professional development of science and mathematics teachers, research and assessment. It has become a leading example of a multifaceted endeavor encompassing the creation of learning materials, preparation of teachers, and conduct of research on teaching and learning.

Keywords

science education – skills development – science teachers' professional development – holistic approach – science curricula development – research and development in science teaching and learning – holistic approach to curriculum development

•••

50 Years of Science Teaching and Science Education at the Weizmann Institute – this is not only a rich resource of individual narratives but also an outstanding example of how relevant science education research has become to global development. Challenges such as climate change, food and water supply and health threats are connected to high demand for a STEM-informed citizenry and workforce, while at the same time, there is a decline in students' interest in these subjects. This situation has led to international debates on how

 | DOI: 10.1163/9789004503625_018

to improve STEM education at school and beyond. The mission statement on the Weizmann's Science Teaching Department stated in their website: "A central goal of the department is to develop academic and practical leadership in mathematics and science education" is also a promise. Concomitant with the global task of linking science research and development to science education and teaching approaches, of building bridges between research and teaching practice, and of becoming involved in reform processes initiated by stakeholders in politics and society, the department has become a worldwide leader in science teaching and education. The holistic approach of connecting science to teaching and learning across school subjects and in non-formal education, of negotiating individual and societal values as well as measurable outcomes of knowledge and skills, and of developing models and research outcomes as well as products and support for teachers, are outstanding characteristics of the Weizmann STEM education group, making it a role model for other institutions worldwide. Without any doubt, this department has become a leading example of a multifaceted endeavor encompassing the creation of learning materials, preparation of teachers, and conductance of research on teaching and learning.

The Weizmann department's close relationship with international partners has not only formed strong research connections and opportunities for many early career scientists, it has also developed friendships and a better understanding of cultural diversity – which is hugely valuable in times of constant societal tensions and offers an anchor for better addressing different needs and opportunities in teaching and learning.

Teaching science does not mean bringing science content into the classroom and telling students how important it is to learn science. Successful science teaching stimulates and supports learning by creating learning environments that engage students emotionally and cognitively. It provides activities that offer insights into scientific phenomena and investigations, and that lead to developing explanations by transforming students' preconceptualized ideas into networks of science-based knowledge and understanding. What are the foundations of such learning environments and orchestrations? This book offers several journeys of research and development that provide its readers – whether scientists, teachers or interested citizens – rich opportunities for reflection and learning. The following reflections and quotes taken from the different chapters are my personal impressions, rather than a delineation of the most important points from an objective standpoint. This commentary is a caleidosope of perspectives, leading to a network of messages for fruitful teaching and learning as I see it. *Toda raba* to all of the authors for their enjoyable and stimulating narratives of research in science teaching and education!

1 The Laboratory – An Inspiration for Science Research and Learning, But Also Hard Work

Experimentation is perhaps the most inspiring activity for scientists, and children show the same enthusiasm for such activities. However, orchestrating a laboratory teaching sequence and designing a fruitful experimental learning environment require more: to connect students' hands-on with minds-on activities, and to develop inquiry-based learning that connects to the students' preconceptualized understanding as well as to the scientific explanations to be generated from the inquiry-type laboratory. The Weizmann Institute's research in this field has laid the groundwork globally, being cited in probably all papers on inquiry learning. The complexity that needs to be considered is well described by this quote from the first chapter of the book: "It is strongly argued that bringing argumentation into science classrooms requires the enactment of contexts that transform them into knowledge-producing communities, encouraging dialogic discourse and various forms of cognitive, social, and cultural interactions among learners. The ecology that fosters this practice is created through the social and physical environment – the laboratory tasks, and the organization principles used by the teacher." Hence, this first chapter lays the foundation not only for teaching in a laborotory, but also for using the laboratory to support and foster student learning – in science and beyond.

1.1 *Nanotechnology as an Example of Giant Steps in Research and Teaching*

"If we adults compare our children's science curriculum to what we studied three decades ago, we will usually find that the difference is small, even nonexistent." How do we incorporate new topics into an existing and already overloaded curriculum? This is impressively presented in the second chapter of the book, highlighting the research that is required to ensure quality and convincing arguments for new content areas in teaching. Not every innovation in science and technology is a suitable topic for learning. Science education researchers need to investigate and negotiate potentials for learning, considering different perspectives of science, society, teaching and learning. A lack of traditions on how to teach a topic poses a challenge, but also offers a chance for reflecting on established traditions, for developers, teachers and scientists. As a result, the smallest nuggets can lead to the greatest steps in learning!

1.2 *Science Teaching Research Goes beyond the Content*

Research on teaching and learning does not just investigate "*what to teach*" but also "*how to teach.*" Here again, traditions are often manifest but not always fruitful: "E-learning was once regarded by many as a negative form of learning, since both students and teachers believed that technology had a negative effect on their studies. Today, there seems to be a more positive attitude toward e-learning, and there is an understanding that this form of learning is beneficial in the long term." Today, it is hard to imagine a world without online learning tools; however, once again, the Weizmann Institute initiated this change long ago, showing how established approaches can be connected with the digital world in the Chemistry Online Blended Learning Environment (COBLE) – connecting experiences from home with virtual science experiments worldwide!

1.3 *Authenticity – Two Sides of the Coin*

"Learning solely scientific content knowledge is the actual common practice in the learning and teaching of science, which is often studied as a collection of facts. This commonly practiced mode of learning is in complete contrast to the way science is practiced by the academic community." Authenticity of science in science teaching is the thread that connects the first chapters of this book, and it is an ongoing issue in the international research field: how can we connect the authentic science practices of scientists with the authentic representation of science in the students' world? The Weizmann group has long focused on research and research simulations, producing impressive results, as well as learning environments that consider the complexity of authentic science for the design of science teaching: "The greater complexity of authentic scientific research requires continuous coordination between various stages of the scientific experiment, as well as between different knowledge elements."

1.4 *We Cannot Forget Emotions and Instinct*

"The emergence and development of the emotional axis indicated that learning is, first and foremost, an emotional process. Cognition joins the process only after the emotional need has been met."

No scientist would deny that science is highly emotional. Research endeavours are accompanied by negative emotions upon experimental failures as well as by great enthusiasm and joy upon developing new findings and breakthroughs in understanding. Similarly, science research is not just about connecting facts and information, it is also driven by instinct and every so often, by unexpected observations. Might school science too often neglect these facets of science, by focusing primarily on logic and linear developments? The Weizmann Institute's work points out the risk of following a reductionist paradigm in teaching and reminds science teaching researchers to bear this in mind as well: "Systems approach has great potential to stimulate students' learning instinct by helping them see the relevance of what they are learning to their own daily lives."

1.5 *Learning Skills for Science*

"Today, a learner in the knowledge era is expected to deal with knowledge-based episodes as a knowledge consumer or knowledge creator." Skill development is related to science but also to learning in general. Learners are both consumers of new information, inspiration and training, and creators of their own ongoing process of learning and development in citizenship and career aspirations. This connection between science learning and learning in general is another approach described in this book: "The program specifically aims to foster the development of skills considered necessary for enhancing science learning and to provide a good foundation on which science learning can take place."

1.6 *Computational Thinking – A New Field in Science Teaching and Learning*

"However, this position should be taken with a grain of salt." Reflection on the role of computational thinking is essentially reflection on a modern trend. It does not only communicate the message that we need to include this in school teaching. It also explores different meanings and learning opportunities in the tradition of the Weizmann department's approach of taking up and critically reflecting on new topics in education. It connects a new discipline to existing school subjects, and it focuses on problems as encouraging starting points for research and learning – like in the laboratory and in nature observations. "After all, problems lie at the heart of all disciplines… Activities that utilize computational thinking should be integrated into other school subjects, by means of cooperation between CS [computer science] teachers and those of other disciplines."

1.7 *Changing the World of Learning Mathematics*

There is (almost?) no science without mathematics. Still, mathematics in school is often regarded as an even larger challenge, being a preferred subject for some students and regarded as "not for me" by others. The world of maths has its own rules but is also related to the worlds of science, technology and society. Determining how to build better links to support student learning by strengthening teachers is another highly important goal of the department: "Changing the nature of mathematical content, promoting context-based activities, promoting multiple representations, supporting students' learning processes and reflecting intended teaching and learning processes."

1.8 *And Learning Is Also about Assessment*

Assessment drives curriculum and teaching developments. This is a challenge, as assessments are often not well connected to the goals of teaching or the research findings on learning. In the worst cases, a badly designed assessment even contradicts such research developments and values in education. However this is not a problem of assessment in general but of missing thoughtfulness in designing and assigning assessments. The Weizmann Institute's group also addresses this important area in education, "using assessment to inform instructional decisions." This chapter connects us to the second part of the book, bringing the teachers into play "Teachers interpret what students say or do 'through' various factors that act as semi-transparent screens." To support and encourage teachers to remain open-minded to alternative solutions is one important message, both in designing fruitful environments and in evaluating students' progress.

1.9 *So: Finally, It's All about the Teachers*

"From the very beginning, there was a clear understanding that the quality and outcome of education is highly contingent upon of the role of teachers and teaching, long before this was 'universally' sanctioned." It is all about the teachers, as pointed out again by the famous Hattie study. The Weizmann's science teaching research group would not be the Weizmann group without connecting science on the design and fruitfulness of learning environments to the design and investigation of teacher training and support in the different roles and duties a teacher has to, and chooses to fulfill: "TRAIL aims to actively involve teachers in the various stages of research, not to convert them into researchers, but rather to develop their abilities of inquiry, noticing, and reflection as an integral part of the daily teaching practice."

1.10 *Back to the Laboratory – In and for Teacher Education*

Learning in the laboratory was one of the first outstanding areas of research and development in the Weizmann department. It therefore comes as no surprise that it is also an important focal point in their professional learning programs for teachers. "The central challenge facing teachers is the change in classroom culture, i.e., the norms of the allocation of responsibility between the teacher and students." Teachers are learners as well, and need to develop their roles and competencies in the context of having and wishing to support student learning as the main outcome of their professional work.

1.11 *Educational Decisions: Involving the Teachers*

Decisions in curriculum and school-reform processes should be made based on research findings, as in other disciplines such as medicine or engineering. In the school context, however, they are often driven by political pressure as well. This not only carries the risk of negating research findings, it might also lead to teachers neglecting reforms. The Weizmann group has shown more successful approaches: "One way to attain these goals is to treat teachers as equal partners in decision-making. In other words, teachers have to play a greater role in providing key leadership at all levels of the educational system, by attending long-term continuous professional development workshops." Combining professional development with research, both by professionals and through action research, has proven fruitful and stimulating for many other groups internationally. Hence, leadership has more than one meaning in this regard: "Leadership in the context of science education should be regarded as a person's ability to bring about changes among teachers and teaching."

1.12 *Professional Learning Communities: Criteria for Success in a Popular Approach*

"Collaboration is considered a 21st century skill that relates to the potential for success in future professional careers." This quote, found in the next chapter of the book, applies to both students' and teachers' learning. Professional development in Professional Learning Communities is one of the most promising approaches. However, the skills to collaborate and the beliefs in the relevance of collaboration need to be equally addressed: "PLC characteristics were: shared setup and structured process; relations of trust and norms of collaboration; targeted focus on student learning; assessment-based learning and decision-making; and reflective dialogues and inquiry." In this regard, collaborating with the Weizmann team has been, and still is a very fruitful experience!

1.13 *The Life Trajectory of Professional Development*

"The role of frameworks in the design of PD [professional development] programs is under-researched." In designing education, researchers might also tend to be driven by their own experiences and enthusiasm (perhaps too much?), with the accompanying risk of underestimating the importance of clear and reflected frameworks to start programs, especially in professional development, with diverse groups of teachers according to their beliefs, skills and experience. The frameworks must not only provide fruitful learning environments for teachers, they must also provide support for a perhaps completely different working environment back in their schools:

> Despite various forms of communication and collaboration among teachers, teaching remains a lonely profession. Once they close the classroom door, teachers are on their own, and rarely get the chance to watch their peers in action. This is not merely a social deficit, but also a barrier to professional progress enabled by peer learning in situ.

1.14 *Design and Practice*

"In articulating some of the design principles of these programs, we attempt to make explicit the often implicit – or even tacit – theories of impact that guide our work." We all have implicit assumptions on what works and what makes outcomes of a teaching and learning program successful. The final reflection on impact and implementation from all participants' perspectives, including our own as researchers and designers, is thus crucial for success.

> According to the boundary-crossing perspective, in the process of learning there is an important role for 'brokers' who can act as a bridge between the communities and thus facilitate boundary crossing.

This is most certainly true for the Weizmann's Department of Science Teaching.[1]

Note

1 https://stwww1.weizmann.ac.il/

Index

Printed in the United States
by Baker & Taylor Publisher Services